Don't Take the Same Plane as Me

By Tricia Bennett

authorHOUSE®

AuthorHouse™
1663 Liberty Drive
Bloomington, IN 47403
www.authorhouse.com
Phone: 1-800-839-8640

Published by AuthorHouse 7/18/2012

ISBN: 978-1-4772-4141-7 (sc)
ISBN: 978-1-4772-4140-0 (hc)
ISBN: 978-1-4772-4139-4 (e)

Library of Congress Control Number: 2012912347

I dedicate this book to my husband John.

Table of Contents

A Message from the Author

I owe the concept behind this long awaited book to two very special people. One is a former girlfriend that I haven't seen or heard from for many long years, the other is John, my long suffering husband who at the time of this letter had rather unwittingly taken on the onerous task of being my boyfriend.

The girlfriend in question was out of town on a lengthy vacation when I decided to write her a long letter pouring out all the difficulties I had encountered when taking a short ferry ride over to a small island off the south coast of England in order to pay John a visit.

"This journey should have been so simple yet as usual it wound up being fraught with endless disasters," I wrote as I poured out this latest tragic tale of woe. Much to my surprise she wrote back immediately.

"Tricia, I haven't laughed so much in years. Trust me when I say that you have truly missed your vocation, for you my girl are a natural born writer." At the time I dismissed this supposedly kind appraisal mainly due to the fact that I had only taken her into my confidence in the sincere belief that her response would be one of great sympathy. I was therefore expecting her written letter of reply to contain considerable amounts of consolation, however after going over her letter innumerable times I was aghast to discover there was none whatsoever to be found!

"Girl I can't believe the amount of trouble you always appear to get yourself into," she had the absolute nerve to write, followed on by " I think it's fair to confirm that you are a living breathing Mrs. Magoo and Calamity Jane all rolled into one."

"How rude!" I muttered as I rather abruptly laid her letter to one side, strong in my determination to write back forthwith to inform her that if she wished for me to continue confiding any more potentially disastrous mishaps I would sincerely hope to find all future correspondence bearing much more compassionate words and consolatory phrases, than to date she had cared to supply. Truth be told I never got round to writing that letter as all the personal crisis surrounding my life seemed to be piling up faster than I could ever hope to deal with. Since the time of her letter I have continued on with my life of troubling mishaps and for a number of years I felt angry and frustrated, as I took it all very personally. Now if you think I'm being a tad paranoid, otherwise overly sensitive, I will furnish you with just one small example of many. On one particular trip to Florida our young boys were playing up so badly that my husband John, still suffering from jet lag, became extremely angry and suddenly he completely lost the plot "Boys, I've had enough of this, you're treating your mother like crap," he yelled.

No sooner had those words tumbled from his mouth, when for no particular reason I can think of, I turned and looked upwards. Without warning a bird flew directly overhead and at that precise moment he opened his bowels, and proceeded to drop his precision load directly into my right eye. It was an agonizingly painful tragedy but what I couldn't come to terms with was, how come out of everybody involved, I the only innocent party in involved in this upset became the 'Highly Chosen One' in receipt of this very unpleasant delivery. So I ask you, what are the chances of such a thing happening to anyone? The answer has to be one in nine hundred and sixty three billion trillion! I hereby rest my case.

I have spent a lifetime falling down workman's holes, under buses, between a train and the platform, and so on. Once, while wearing a pair of high heels on the dance floor of a heavily populated discothèque, I accidentally fell backwards to the ground and was nearly trampled to death by other clubbers. The catalogue of peculiar circumstances goes on forever!

Then came a day while bawling my eyes out over some latest catastrophe John turned and said something I consider to be most profound.

"Honey, the day you stop being the victim, is the day you recognize that you are being handed fresh and innovative material for your books. That day he went from 'middle of the road' husband to my guru extraordinaire! So trust me when I say that all the material in this book is painfully true and therefore needs very little poetic license, if any. (Please also note that many of the names have been changed in order to protect the innocent, oh as well as the downright guilty!)

CHAPTER ONE

Sad Bikini

I awoke from my sleep to discover I was still a fourteen year old unwanted 'kid in care' and, apart from being almost as blind as a bat, I still had far too many teeth missing for my liking. As for my hair, well having been given a cut styled around a pudding bowl, I still looked just as much like a straggly afghan dog as when I had fallen into bed the night before, and surprise… surprise, the ghastly old fashioned 'hand me downs' I was forced to wear on non school days did much to confirm my belief that I was indeed one of the ugliest people on planet earth. So, with all this in mind, my expectations that day were about the same as they were for each and every day of my storm tossed life as a kid in "care"… namely zilch!

However, if I survived this particular day without being given extra punishments from my Dickensian guardians, then maybe, just maybe, I would be able to slip out of the house unnoticed and spend a glorious summer's afternoon at the local outdoor swimming pool. That said, I wasn't holding my breath for, as Jeff Tracy from 'Thunderbirds' never failed to remind all children glued to the television "Anything can happen in the next half an hour," and as far as my young life was concerned, something invariably always did! However, whenever these unimaginable disasters threatened to overwhelm me there was never any sign of those tough talking marionettes from International Rescue, so just like everyone else they too joined the long list of those who let me down. It seemed that every time I left the building I felt a serious sense of foreboding as that dark unwelcome cloud saw it's personal duty to not only hang over my head, but to then daily commit itself to ruining my already seriously tumultuous life.

Now being a kid in care was in itself a considerably grim affair so I had little in my life I could be proud of. I also considered myself to be amongst the lowest in the unwritten pecking order back at the children's home. So the fact that I was a neat little swimmer and I could do some pretty awesome dives off the highest boards well that meant everything to me. So, that morning as I looked up at the glorious blue sky with it's brilliant ball of orange that continued to roast all persons below, I began to dream the dreams that a turbulent young fourteen year old might dare to dream, forever hoping that today would turn out a lot better than yesterday, not to mention the day before that, but as usual time alone would tell!

Any happiness and sense of wellbeing I experienced as a child was connected with the local outdoor swimming pool complex that opened its doors from mid May until the beginning of September. It had two large pools surrounded by beautiful well-manicured lawns large enough for families to congregate and have picnics. It was here that I felt momentarily freed from the constant remonstrations and punishments that were meted out to me back at the children's home, free from the jibes and bullying that came from many of the older children, and free from all prejudice that back then automatically came with being a 'kid in care'. Here at this pool I could just be me; now that to me was freedom.

It was at this special place when around ten years old that I met a very nice fifteen year old boy with sandy colored hair named Jeff. To keep up the interest I told him I was thirteen and a midget. I knew it was wrong to lie but he was the first person I had ever known who didn't just tolerate me but actually seemed to like me. That summer had seemed so wonderful as I experienced my first innocent, albeit fledgling romance that seemed to be blossoming very nicely without too much effort on my part, that is until someone very unkindly thought to go behind my back and tell him my real age. Once confronted on the issue I would never see Jeff again, and so I was left to mourn his sudden withdrawal from my desperately lonely little life.

Despite this major hiccup I still saw the swimming complex as my special place. It didn't matter too much if I was without the money required for an entry ticket, as all I had to do was offer to join in picking up all the litter that lay strewn across the lawns. If this task was already taken by others who got there before me, then I could just as easily offer my services in passing out changing baskets in exchange for entry.

On the day in question I had done my fair share of handing out the large wire baskets, so now I was finally free to swim at my leisure and to enjoy the rest of a hassle free afternoon. The melting sun was still brazen in its efforts to give all bathers a touch of sun burn, so I wasted no time getting changed into my latest acquisition of a bikini, a bikini that I hasten to add had seen much better days. Like most things in life I could only wish against all odds when it came to owning anything that others my age took for granted. So when I accidentally came across this bikini abandoned to the dustbin, I saw great reason to reach in and thus preserve it from its inevitable sentence, for as a self conscious fourteen year old girl caught in the first throws of awakening to the opposite sex, it now found me desperate to finally own such a highly desirable item.

It is true to say that sad bikini had seen much better days, but that was of very little importance for, at the end of the day, it was a real bikini, and such things mattered to a young girl such as I. The once zany pattern was now barely recognizable due to severe discoloration, and the threadbare bikini straps could best be described as holding on for dear life, worse still the under wire constantly forced its wily way through the material, so was in constant need of a firm finger to push it back into place. I was therefore reluctantly forced to accept that sad bikini's last minute reprieve was clearly down to me being the only girl on planet earth desperate enough to continue wearing it. Truth be known, having finally procured this most precious item I could hardly bear to think of what to do or where to turn for a replacement when sad bikini's natural life finally came to a permanent end. Still I had little idea on that most idyllic of summer days that its tragic end was indeed very nigh.

So it was with great joy and fervor that I secretly wrapped my precious find in a towel and hid it as far under the bed as possible, for I knew if my secret were to be discovered by any of the other children otherwise my mean guardians, I would never see sad bikini again. If I was wrong in my thinking I only had to look back at a previous disastrous incident concerning a 44 triple D bra that, for an extremely limited period, I not only laid claim to, but also had the dubious privilege of wearing to school, (albeit only for a few hours) before it and the realms of toilet tissue stuffing were to be permanently confiscated. So, as you must realize it was imperative that this new found possession remain under my sole jurisdiction leaving me to fantasize as to how I would hopefully look once I got the opportunity to wear it and then parade myself round the pool complex.

Once changed I found it almost impossible to find a spot on which to spread my towel for today this family orientated complex was over crowded as all in sundry took full advantage of a sudden and unexpected spurt of deliciously warm British weather. But as this glorious sun soaked day drew to a close, the pool began rapidly emptying, as thoroughly exhausted mothers attempted to haul their reluctant offspring out of the water, before heading towards the cubicles, to get changed.

Happily I had no one to give me such an order and, because I was never in any hurry to get back to the children's home, I continued to alternate basking in the sun with swimming back and forth the length of the pool, that is until my eyes suddenly caught sight of four very cute youthful lads sitting on a bench.

Why I had not noticed them up until now I had no idea. I quickly swam to one of the four corners of the pool where I could best continue on observing them from a distance, without the fear of being noticed. The young Adonis's were all in swim shorts, their admirably firm pectorals brazenly and unashamedly on view for all to see and admire, their expensive looking shades only adding to their charm and mystique. I could only sigh deeply as my eyes bulged from their sockets at their highly bronzed chests adorned like the gods with thick gold chains and medallions, that, when caught by the sun, glistened and flashed with their every movement, and it all made me want to give a very long and deep sigh.

"Are they a famous pop group in the making?" I mused at the same time imagining myself falling wildly and irrevocably in love with not just one of them, but maybe all four! "And why not?" I foolishly reasoned with myself.

I briefly removed my gaze from of them to hastily glance around the complex, and I was delighted to discover that, apart from the odd scrawny and toothless old pensioner peacefully snoring away on a deckchair, there was not a single glamorous bikini clad beauty to be found anywhere! Heaven was obviously finally taking note of my endless petitions and here was the first concrete evidence that my fortunes were about to do a ninety degree turn. Who knows maybe I was about to get my miracle! for I believed this to be the perfect opportunity to make my presence known.

I remained fixated by their perfect sparkling teeth, off set by their deeply glowing tans. The boys laughed out loud and continued to crack jokes and share stories, while remaining totally unaware that they were being watched. If I was going to make my move, I knew it had to be now, and so, without further adieu, I quickly swum across the pool heading towards the steps.

As I glided towards an area of the pool that was directly opposite the handsome bare-chested young hunks, my heart and head were racing, as I pondered as to what I might possibly do to get myself noticed. In no time at all I believed I had the answer. I would do my famous 'no hands dive' that had, in the past, caused quite a sensation, that is until a concerned couple thought to caution me that diving off a top board without the use of my hands to break the water could be considered very foolish, so for a while I stopped doing these dives off the high boards. But now this day I had a worthy cause.

I strutted around the pool until I was perfectly satisfied I had found the best position. I knew it wasn't going to be nearly sensational enough unless it was done from a great height, however if I wasn't going to use the diving boards then I would need come up with some other way to add that much required sense of style. I thought I had the answer and this was to move some distance from the pool's edge, this way I could break into a run and, in doing so, put some last minute extra spring as I dived into the pool. I was supremely confident that I was onto a winner. I stood up straight, took a deep breath and then, placing my hands behind my back, I began to gently run towards the edge of the pool, my steps gathering momentum as I neared the edge.

Suddenly, at the final and most crucial moment of the procedure, my right foot slipped on a wet patch, and, instead of springing into the air, I toppled forward, my right foot slipping down behind the steel hand rail that that ran the entire length of the pool. Oh I flew high into the air alright, but not nearly as sylph-like as I had imagined, for I hit the water hard and in a manner more befitting a heavily pregnant ten ton killer whale crashing through the surf.

I heard no ping as on impact the fragile strings on my bikini top snapped, forcing my top to flee my body like a caged bird flying to freedom. At the same time, and I guess due to gravity, my bikini bottoms very cruelly thrust themselves down my straddled legs heading for my ankles. It was only due to my trapped foot that they too did not also make a most desperate bid for complete freedom. With my bikini bottoms now flapping around my ankles, and my bare buttocks bobbing up and down frantic attempts to release my ailing trapped foot that was still ..edged behind the hand rail. In the few seconds that followed I could only try to ignore the lads shrieks of laughter that now emanated across the complex as I was more concerned by the excruciating pain from my trapped ankle, as well as the strong sensation of being stung by a million angry killer bees, as my stomach reacted with a terrible burning sensation, the consequence of my most terrible belly flop.

Oh the humiliation of being stuck face down in the water, my rear end exposed to the whole wide world as I continued to flounder like a beached whale. I was in dire need of help, a help that needless to say never came. Instead I could only hear a continuation of the loud raucous laughter coming from the direction of where those now horribly uncaring boys who remained seated and from what I could tell doubled up with laughter. My panic was such that I seemed unable to release my trapped foot and I began to believe I might well call it a day and just drown, but that was not about to happen for just when I thought things couldn't get much worse my despicable bikini top mockingly flaunted past me, as it made its merry way to the bottom of the pool.

The boys were now laughing like a bunch of uncontrollable hyenas as they reveled in my humiliating demise. With my need of air now dire, I began furiously flapping and wriggling until, thank God, my foot finally freed itself. The whole crisis could not have been more than twenty to thirty seconds but in terms of my humiliation it felt like a lifetime. Before I could even think to come up for fresh air I frantically reached down to hurriedly pull up my bikini bottoms.

Still all I could hear was the on-going unwelcome sounds of hysterical laughter coming from the incorrigible boys still sat on the bench. Needless to say I swam at record speed towards the nearest set of pool steps, then, breathing in hard, I mustered the courage required to climb the steps, with only one hand free to pull myself up, the other hand attempting to cover me what little dignity I had left! The walk to the changing rooms seemed both long and agonizing, as, clothed in deep humiliation and very little else, I hurriedly hobbled towards the nearest available cubicle. Even on dry land I was forced to avail myself to endless loud whistles and guffaws still coming from the mouths of those now thoroughly despicable young beasts who didn't know when enough was enough. Having found a cubicle, I hastily locked the door before sliding down onto the hard wooden bench to have a post mortem, as well as a good and hearty cry.

Minutes later I was forced to acknowledge that, due to being in such a fluster, I had unwittingly made the wrong choice, for in heading towards the nearest available cubicle, I now had no towel to wrap round myself and help me dry off, and worse still I had no clothes to get changed into! "How could this otherwise perfect day have gone so horribly wrong?" I miserably mused. All I could do was crouch on the bench my body shaking and quivering like limp jelly from both the cold as well as the deepest most painful humiliation, and I could only keep wishing that those most ungallant louts would quickly leave the facility; after all, the spectacular stage show was well and truly over!

As I went on to relive the whole disastrous event over and over in my tormented little mind, I could only be grateful that I had managed to retrieve my bikini bottoms, before they too had the chance to further shame me by joining my top at the bottom of the pool. It seemed an age before the sounds of much laughter receded to a point where I believed it might be safe to come out from hiding. Then, as I furtively ventured out from my hiding place, one arm still covering my unclothed assets, I went in search of the cubicle that hopefully still possessed my much needed clothes, towel included.

As I tentatively made my way down the long row of cubicles gently pushing open one door after another I finally got lucky. I was about to enter when I suddenly heard someone shout out from out behind me. It was the old wizened pool cleaner. I stood frozen to the spot, ignoring the urge to shut the cubicle door while pretending to be ignorant to his call, but I'd left it much too late.

He began his approach, his long swimming pool rod looking more like the lance of some chivalrous gladiator, as he neared to where I stood motionless and semi naked, my lips quivering from the cold.

I closed my eyes and swallowed hard, for impaled on the end of the steel hook of his swimming pole was bikini top.

"Excuse me love, but I was wondering if you might happen to know who the rightful owner of this here item of clothing might be?" He quizzed, his eyes playfully running up and down the entire length of my trembling body . I wanted to say I had absolutely no idea, but, as I looked at the roguish glint in his eye, I had no other choice than to admit full ownership.

"Uh.. yes, it's mine," I squirmed, my flushed cheeks having already given the game away.

"Well Miss, you'll never guess where I found it!" he said as he continued to hold the pole as far away as possible as though my dangling bikini top was some offensive morbidly decomposing skunk.

"Oh I think I can," I mumbled.

"Yes, and in all the weeks I've worked here, it's not the normal thing to find on the bottom of the pool," he said giving me a sly wink.

"Huh? Yes, well thank you," I anxiously sniffed as, with my one available hand, I reached over to grab hold of the offending item from the end of his pool rod.

"Thank you, but now I need to get changed," I muttered as I forcefully shut the door of the cubicle, before sliding down onto the floor to cry some more.

"Don't mention it love," he shouted through the door. "Oh, and by the way the pool complex closed ten minutes ago, so please be on your way A.S.A.P." he shouted before leaving to return to his pool cleaning duties.

With my head hung low in deep shame I sheepishly slunk out of the facility to make my weary way back to the children's home, with the full knowledge that this would not be the end of it. I was after all, very well acquainted with myself, so I knew that this incident would join the amassing list of ultra embarrassing moments that would cause me many a sleepless night as I mercilessly beat up my pillow while continuing to punish myself for being such a prize idiot. That emotionally storm tossed night saw me vowing that my 'no- handed dives' would from this day forth, be a thing of the past. Oh, if only the painful memories would be considerate enough to do likewise, become forever lost in history. That harrowing day also saw me part company with the remains of two disgracefully traitorous articles of clothing, that when twinned were known to me as sad bikini.

If this event had been a one off teenage disaster, then given time I would have eventually learnt to accept it as such, but sadly I would go on to leave a trail of carnage as over the next ten years I managed to outdo both Mr. Magoo as well as Calamity Jane in the "Most embarrassing moments" department.

Then one day, quite out of the blue, I met John, a very quiet and unassuming man who, after a long and exceedingly tumultuous courtship, threw all caution to the wind and married me. Looking back, I'm certain he was convinced he was the chosen gallant knight to rescue this pitiful damsel from every dragon and demon that sought to overwhelm her. However, if this wasn't the motive behind this marital alliance then I have absolutely no idea as to what he was possibly thinking! By the end of the fateful wedding ceremony he would have his suspicions, and, if the reception was anything to go by, those suspicions might well have become second thoughts! Add to this the endless tragedies that befell us on our Greek honeymoon and by now he should have been hearing the loud warning bells of the poet John Dunn in his ears. "Do not send to know for whom the bell tolls, it tolls for thee." Many years and an equal number of holidays and earth shattering events later would find him shaking his head in pure disbelief as my interesting if not unpredictable world had now collided with his and as marriage is a bit like super glue the poor man soon began to realize he was stuck with me and there really was no way out!

Over the coming years it would dawn on John that It simply wasn't safe to let me out the house alone because unimaginably strange things always seemed to happen! There even came a time when friends would try to cajole us into revealing our holiday plans, and I knew it wasn't because they wanted to join us, quite the contrary! They were eager to make sure that their whole family, household pets included, were heading off to an entirely different location, if not continent, as they had an overwhelming desire for the family ancestral line to remain intact.

So if I could leave you with one sound piece of wise counsel it would be this. If while reading this section of the book you are innocently seated on a plane waiting for take off I would urge you to check who is sitting next to you. Now, if you are sitting next to a lady who is behaving in a somewhat suspicious or agitated manner, it would be most wise for you to reach over and ask her name. Keep it friendly mind! Now, if it turns out to be me, then you have two choices set before you. One is to politely ask the dead cute flight attendant if you can be allocated a different seat preferably at the other end of the plane, however, the wiser choice would be to disembark immediately, and even consider changing your destination while you're at it. Do it now while you still have time! Oh and if perchance you happen to be a thoroughly decent citizen and by that I mean conscientious and concerned for others, well then you'll want to alert all remaining passengers of a possible impending tragedy long before the plane begins to roar down the runway, for by then it really will be much too late.

CHAPTER TWO

Two Funerals and a Wedding

So here I stand, some ten years later, having somehow survived my life "in care" with it's inherently high number of unspeakable catastrophes, and not only have I lived long enough to tell the tale, but guess what, today is the big day that I am about to get married to a terribly quiet unassuming English gentleman named John!

Needless to say the day of the wedding hadn't started too well. Personally I put this down to the fact that the week prior saw me attending not one but two funerals, one being John's mother, the other a good friend. So my last night as a single woman had found me unable to sleep a wink as I went through the whole panic bit that saw me beating the pillow to a pulp out of sheer frustration. Around seven am I dragged myself out from under the sheets feeling so ghastly I'm convinced I would've felt whole heap better if I'd spent my last night at some wild singles party.

I knew time was of the essence, for I had to get my hair done by 10.00 am by some gentleman of Greek persuasion whom I'd never actually met but who came highly recommended.

Having made it to the hairdresser's private residence I then sat in a sort of numbed silence, instantly feeling intimidated and unsure of both him as well as his quite bizarre hairdressing techniques.

"So darleeng, we must do something to resurrect this unhealthy head of hair," he snorted, giving an overly exaggerated grimace as he went on to systematically pick up clump after clump of my hair while making annoyingly loud sighs.

"When was the last time thees hair saw some deep treatment

he challenged, staring me directly in the eye like some High
dge about to send me down for many years.

m a student, I don't have the money for luxuries," I mumbled.

"Oh!" was his only comment as he hurriedly let go of my hair in a
manner that suggested I was suffering a serious case of lice infestation.

"Oh dear, is it really that bad?" I groaned.

He never asked me what specific style I was hoping for, and in my
stupidity I never once thought to stop him in his tracks to challenge his
so called "creation'. Yes I foolishly left it all up to Dimitri, believing that
this expert knew what he was doing. As he gracefully waltzed around
the chair waving his hands high in the air as though he were conducting
some large unseen symphony orchestra, I continued to feel somewhat
unnerved.

"So darleeng eet's your big day today so how are we feeling?
Hmm, a titsy witsy bit nervous I would think?" he gleefully cried as he
flamboyantly continued to skip around the chair, while playing with
imaginary stray wisps and winding my hair around large bristly curlers.
He then proceeded to embed long sharp pins mostly directly into my
scalp, as though he feared that a treacherously rebellious curler or two
might release itself and fall to the floor. I winced from the pain. Why I
didn't have the courage to at least question what he was up to I'll never
know, for all too soon with the giant curlers finally in situ, I looked
more like an old washer woman sitting in the local launderette, than
a radiant bride-to-be. All that appeared to be missing were the 'Ena
Sharples' hairnet to be cast over the rollers, and the all too familiar
cigarette hanging from my drooping bottom lip, and the picture would
be complete.

"Yes I'm a tad nervous," I quietly stuttered, as I continued to anxiously
wring my hands. "I was up late last night making my own desserts for
the wedding. It was too much and then I felt the urgent need to phone
my fiancé to help dictate his wedding speech," and now I am feeling
thoroughly exhausted," I quietly confessed.

"Oh darleeng, I'm so sorry to hear this," he sympathized.

"Here, let me stop what I am doing, and we can say a leettle prayer,"
he said. Not listening to my now very loud protestations he raced over to
an above the sink cupboard that, once opened, revealed a private shrine
and a large statue of Buddha. "Isn't it beautiful?" he cried as he stood back
to proudly admire the statue.

"Oh no no no" I stuttered. "Please, I'm fine as I am, honest."

"Sorry darleeng but you need elp, and you need it now!"

"No I'm fine really I am, and I certainly don't need any help from your Buddha!" I gasped in horror.

"Oh alright darleeng, but eef you change your mind we…"

"No never… nothing would ever make me change my mind on this one," I anxiously snapped back, a little too harshly for his liking. His response was to retreat into himself, like some wounded animal.

"Tut tut…. Do I see a leetle bit of a temper there," he sullenly challenged.

"Look I'm not trying to be offensive but Buddha isn't my cup of tea, really he isn't.

"By the way darleeng, I hope your reception is inside for, as we speak, the sky is filling up with very dark ominous looking clouds."

"Yes, as it happens, due to a lack of funds, the reception is outside and no before you ask I don't have a large marquee to fall back on," I gloomily confessed. "Worst still, it's been chucking down heavy rain all week long, so the lawns will be awfully muddy," I groaned.

"Then we DO need Buddha's help," he responded with a sense of triumph.

"No no …we really DON'T," I cried out in sheer exasperation.

"Oh dear darleeng, then let's hope the sun bursts through," he said, giving a deep sigh of resignation.

The wedding arrangements were being put together on a very tight almost non-existent budget, as I had no family that could give me any financial assistance. Friends had rallied to the cause in every manner possible. Some gave financially, another special friend offered to make my wedding dress as well as the bridesmaids dresses and another couple offered us the use of their huge palatial manor house with it's gorgeous English garden. I had rarely experienced such kindness, it was overwhelming. However pride got in the way when it came to organizing the buffet for I have to confess to having been very choosy over which friends got involved for there were many a dear friend who believed themselves master chefs, and, up, until this moment, I had never seen reason to tell them otherwise!

"Look Tricia, we've loads of volunteers eager and willing to make whatever dishes you fancy, so you just concentrate on enjoying being a bride eh," a kind friend suggested. I wasn't listening

"Now, this very morning, I was eating humble pie the price for my stupidity. I had been slaving away in the kitchen until way past midnight, then there was my belated call to John in which we argued about what he should or should not say in his wedding speech.

"John, I'm only trying to help, and by the way isn't that what wives are supposed to do?" I bellowed down the phone line.

"You're not my wife until tomorrow, besides, this may come as a bit of a surprise, but I'd actually like to write this speech all by myself."

"Well suit yourself darling, but please hear me out when I say please don't mention...and it would be great if you could say a word or two about....."

"For goodness sake Tricia, stop it now! allow me to say whatever I feel to say."

"Alright, I hear you," I groaned.

"Look it's almost one in the morning, so please let's say our goodnights and then hang up." It was around 1.30am when I climbed between the sheets hoping to just crash out. I should have known better for, despite applying every known trick in the book, insomnia had always been my closest companion so, with my mind in total overdrive, I found myself wide awake for the remainder of the night. Come morning and I felt wasted.

All too soon my artistic hairdresser had the hand held hairdryer far to close to my head and, apart from the distinctive smell that comes from singed hair, it quickly felt as though my head was about to burst into flames.

"Ouch, it's too hot," I yelled out in agony. He in turn overdramatically jumped back, as though my sudden protestation was totally offensive to his frail emotions.

"Oops, sorry darleeng," he sniffed, as his face transformed once more to that of a sullen six year old. While busying himself with the finishing touches to his latest masterpiece. I, in turn, began a few prayers upwards as I was fast losing confidence in this diva hairdresser. My uncertainty showed.

"Darleeng, try to have a leetle more faith in me, for I have worked in salons all over ze world." he jubilantly cried, as he momentarily abandoned his 'creation' to adjust his loud and over fussy silk cravat. I should have asked if that was way back in the sixties.

Once the sharp pins had been excavated from my scalp the pain did begin to quickly subside. But it still wasn't over for I had fifteen minutes of backcombing to then endure, combined with excessive amounts of hair spray from his mega giant canister. My eyes quickly began smarting. I was now convinced that my hair was well beyond entire ruination. I thought he'd finished, but sadly he hadn't. Once again, picking up his giant can of hairspray he then expended the remainder of its contents onto my already heavily backcombed hair.

"He's building a skyscraper," I miserably mused.

"There darleeng now eet weel remain in place," he ecstatically cried as he handed me a small hand mirror.

I had no doubt he was telling the absolute truth; for I too was equally convinced it was an immovable structure. Why even if I were to find myself hurled into the eye of a hurricane, otherwise smack bang in the path of a category five tornado, nothing would see his creation uprooted, for it would remain staunchly in place until finally I chose to do a spot of deep sea diving.

As I sat staring into the hand mirror in a small moment of madness I seriously considered shaving my entire head. I could also have cheerfully taken the silk cravat from my hairdresser's scrawny little neck and used it to choke the very life out of his little diva body. I paid up and, though I still can't believe it, I gave him a handsome tip.

Fifteen minutes later found me sitting in the back of the taxi cab in a state of unbelievable despair, as I fought hard to hold back the tears. Sadly I had wished for something resembling a modern hairstyle, a cut like Princess Di's perhaps, and yet here I sat sporting something resembling a grotesque 60's beehive. I also considered the possibility that as my reception was to be an outside affair the pungent smell emanating from the creation stacked high upon my head might well attract some rogue nest of bees to attack me for the express purpose of further pollination.

The young taxi driver, (bless his little cotton socks), looked extremely concerned as, through his mirror, he spied me desperately tugging away at my hair, like some half demented gorilla searching for extra fleas to nibble on.

"Are we alright Miss?" he ventured to ask.

"Yes, yes," was all I could mutter back, for I was well beyond any form of comfort, especially from a taxi driver who might think himself terribly gentlemanly if he were to hand me his oil ridden snot rag to wipe away my tears

My deluded hairdresser would have been devastated if he had borne witness to me frantically pulling and tugging at my hair until I managed to partially bring the high tower down. As I climbed out of the car, I couldn't help but notice that the dark somber looking clouds, moving fast across the sky, gave the appearance of wanting to even follow me into the house. As I reached the front door I felt the first drops of rain on my face.

"Oh please, spare me from a heavy downpour, after all, this is my wedding day," I murmured as I raced up the stairs to get ready.

Most weddings find the bride trying on the dress beforehand. They then go on to have a few practice runs with make-up, hairstyle etc as well as quick practice run at the church, in my defense I had none! So, if ever I had needed the help and guidance that can only come from a mother, it had to be then.

I spent less than two minutes on my make up and another five minutes trying to force my hair into some sort of acceptable style, then when I thought things couldn't get much worse, while brushing my teeth my small temporary partial inexplicably became loose. I immediately began having frantic visions of that bit in the service where the vicar proudly says 'you may kiss the bride' Oh heaven forbid that John in a moment of passion might get a little carried away causing my partial to accidentally transfer from my mouth to his, to then inadvertently get lodged in his throat. Knowing my luck it wouldn't stop there, Oh no, life would never be that simple where I was concerned! for with his air supply now cut off it would only be a matter of seconds before he dropped to the floor gagging, his face an agonizing blue, only to be saved by the quick thinking actions of the best man who in his endeavor to save the poor man's life saw it as his duty to give him a few brutal bear hugs from behind until the mystery blockage released itself to then fly past the startled congregation. Just think of the embarrassment I would be forced to suffer as falling to my knees I had little choice other than to grovel around on the floor until it was found. Worse case scenario yet equally plausible, what if my partial remained lodged in his passageway? Causing him to take his last gasp before expiring in front of a whole church load of our guests! It couldn't be ruled out. Well, I suppose if that were to happen at least he would die on holy ground. And to save time and money we could hurriedly swap the wedding service for that of a funeral. No it didn't bear thinking about!

I made a mental note to get myself an emergency dental appointment as soon as I returned from honeymoon, until then I would have to rely on endless chewing gum to keep it in place. I was indeed a deeply troubled bride.

There were further complications for I was about to discover that the dress did not properly fit. Years before I had fallen in love with a wedding dress on certain vogue pattern. I knew it was 'the one' as soon as my eyes beheld it so I bought the pattern and tucked it away, only bringing it out every once in while in order to sit and gaze down at it. Now was my one and only chance. The pattern demanded that the material be Ivory silk taffeta. Sadly no shop in my local town had ever heard of such material, so I was forced to take a trip to London. I felt so alone and defeated trudging around one London store after another as unhelpful shop assistants shook their heads. At one point I sat down on a bench desperately trying to hold back the tears as I longed not only for a mother's nurture but also her help and advice in this most important matter. Now if I'd required a camel, a young lion cub otherwise the rarest flower in the whole wide world then I need look no further than Harrods in Knightsbridge but as for a caring mother well this seems to be the one and only item that cannot be purchased in either Harrods or Fortnum and Masons so I was forced to soldier on all by myself. Finally at some belated hour of the day I happened upon a shop that sold this elusive material. I was then to be shocked by the price per yard. Some time later I left the London store having purchased only two thirds of the recommended amount of material, and as I was no clean out of money I had no hope of purchasing the hoop that the pattern clearly stated was necessary. My wonderful friend Susie, to whom this very hour I am exceedingly grateful truly did her absolute best with what she was given. So as I stared at myself in the mirror I only had myself to blame for my Vogue wedding dress didn't seem as vogue as I had hoped, for it had me resembling a close cousin of Miss Piggy!" It would only be a year later that our very own dear Princess Diana would walk down the aisle wearing her own Ivory Silk Taffeta dress, only she had realms and realms this expensive material, oh as well as the jolly hoop!

As I sat in the small poky sitting room of our first house a year later watching the whole grand ceremony on TV, I felt close to tears.

"I got there first," I jealously announced, as I blubbered into my handkerchief.

"Well Tricia, trust me the only similarity between your dress and hers is that you both chose Ivory Silk Taffeta," my husband very unhelpfully interjected.

"All the same I got there first," I sniffed in my best Orphan Annie voice.

"Well it all goes to show you do have very good taste," John rather belatedly tried to console.

Before I had time for a quick twirl, the doorbell rang, which was probably a good thing as I was now feeling more distraught than ever over my appearance. I took as deep breath all the while knowing I was not the least bit ready or able to cope with all that was to come. Sometime into the ride to the church I began to be aware that something was terribly wrong. Despite taking many deep breaths, I still felt sick to the pit of my stomach, and I also began experiencing weird sensations in both arms as well as my legs. I think they call it paralysis.

After swerving the taxi into the church drive, my attentive driver came round to open the side door to let me out. It was only then that I discovered that I was totally unable to move. He continued to politely stand to one side with the door open, before eventually realizing I apparently had no intention of disembarking. He then bent down and peered into the back.

"Madam, I do believe it's time to alight the car, and head into the church," he sniffed as formally as he could.

"Oh trust me, I would if I could, but to tell you the truth, I can't," I whispered back.

"What! Are you serious?"

"Oh, absolutely!" I gulped nervously.

"You say you cannot move at all?" he quizzed, poking his head further into the rear of the car, as if to question my very integrity.

"No, I promise you I cannot move, for even my bouquet appears welded to the palm of my hand. Here, see for yourself, I cannot even uncurl my fingers to let go of it," I wept out loud.

"Oh dear," he responded.

"What am I going I do?" I cried.

"Madam please restrain yourself. Just stay put, and I'll go and find us some help," he kindly advised.

All one hundred and fifty guests were seated, the organ was quietly playing, and John was standing, oblivious of any crisis, at the front of the church with the best man, patiently awaiting my arrival. Having dutifully passed the bad news onto the best man the taxi-driver, with head bowed low in reverence, hurriedly headed back outside to the car. The best man in turn promptly left his seat and followed after the chauffeur to see for himself the predicament in which I found myself.

"Goodness, we do have ourselves a sticky little situation," he remarked sucking in his lips, as if this little act might well help him come to a worthy solution.

"Well Tricia, I'm truly mystified, so I need to go back into the church and let the Vicar in on this most unfortunate turn of events. "But don't worry, for I'll be back in a jiffy," he stated reassuringly. I watched on as he disappeared back into the church. The Vicar listened intently, his furrowed brow rising and falling like the stock market on a tumultuous day, as he chewed over my unusual plight. "

"You'd best be the one to break the news to John," he hurriedly advised. "Meanwhile I will pray for a solution, and hopefully it will come."

"Right then, I'll go and tell him, although I so hate to be the bearer of bad news," the best man glumly replied taking in a deep breath as he attempted to summon up the necessary courage. He then quietly sidled up to John to break this latest most disconcerting piece of news.

"John, how are things, my man?"

"Thanks for asking, but I feel really great," John replied, but also sensing all was not well.

"Well now, I want you to hold yourself together. Yes, promise me that you will remain perfectly calm."

"Yes, yes, but tell me, is something wrong?"

"Well my good man, there is no easy way to say this, but we have ourselves a little sticky situation."

"Go on."

"Yes... well we may be forced to cancel the wedding," he said scratching his ear as he offloaded the troubling news.

"What...Why?" were the only few words that tumbled from the trembling lips of my maybe not so soon husband to be. "Tell me truthfully, she hasn't jilted me at the altar, has she? I mean I only spoke to her last night, and I know I refused her help with my wedding speech, but surely....."

"Oh goodness John it's nothing like that! No, the problem is...well I don't know how to say this, but apparently she's a trifle stuck."

"Stuck! what on earth do you mean?"

"Yes well she's sort of completely paralyzed in the back of the car."

"I don't believe it!" he gasped.

"No, I didn't think you would. Neither did I, until I was called outside by the driver to go see for myself. Apparently she is experiencing some form of temporary nervous paralysis. Hmm, it appears as though the stress of marrying you has finally got the better of her, but don't worry, for fortunately we are pleased to discover that we do have a doctor amongst your guests."

"Oh that's good news," John sighed.

"Yes, so just be patient my man and wait here."

The best man then went aisle to aisle until he found the doctor, who, upon realizing the urgency, left the pew to see what he could do to help.

"John, I've spoken with the doctor."

"That's great, so are things are looking up a bit?"

"Well not exactly, so let's not get our hopes too high. The doctor has informed me that there is not much he can do to help, other than wait until the paralysis naturally subsides."

"How many years of training does it take to come up with a diagnosis like that?" my normally calm man snapped back.

"John I understand your feeling fraught but try to remain calm, and um I hate to say this, but there is a further small complication."

"Oh?"

"Well, dare I say it, but the church is booked for another wedding that is to take place well, quite soon really."

"Good grief, it's getting worse by the minute!" John blurted out, while sinking faster and faster into the abyss.

"Yes, well try hard not to get yourself too worked up, for the good news is that the deacons of the church have just come up with a plan."

"Oh, goody gumdrops!"

"Do I detect an undercurrent of sarcasm?"

"Oh no forgive me it's just that it's all come as a bit of a shock."

"Well with a bit of help from above this newly conceived plan might just come off."

"Oh, and what might this plan be?" my now very concerned husband to be asked.

"Look, if I tell you, please don't be too quick to rule this one out."

"Yes…yes…go on."

"Well one of the deacons has just informed us that his son has a large skateboard," he confided in hushed tones.

"Skateboard?" John hissed back, even startling himself as his voice was now scaling tones normally reserved for professional sopranos.

"Yes hmm… a skateboard."

"What possible help could a skateboard be to us?" he squeaked, his throat visibly tightening from the shock.

"John, please just listen. Our man has just raced home to get it, and we are all unanimous in our thinking, that, if we can somehow get her out of the car, we can then hopefully pop her on the skateboard, and, with a few quick pushes from behind, hopefully whizz her straight down the aisle."

"Whizz her?" he gulped, shaking his head furiously in his endeavor to free himself of the very fascinating imagery now being conjured up in his imagination.

"So let's give it a go, eh, for it seems to be our only hope. After urgent talks with the Vicar he has suggested that we place two chairs down by the altar for the both of you to sit down on, and then we can only hope and pray she survives long enough for you both to say your vows, before passing out completely."

"Oh, right."

"Anyway, the Vicar says he will do his best to conduct the ceremony as quickly as he is able."

"Oh, great…"

"Don't mention it. Let's hope this works eh?" he said raising a brow in a show of sympathy.

"Yes, yes."

"So sit tight, and I'll keep you informed," he whispered, as he gave him a kind hearted pat on the back before turning to once more speak with the Vicar. They then both surreptitiously crept back down the aisle to continue on with this latest strategy, their movements now being surveyed by most of the congregation.

"It's all systems go!" the Vicar then whispered to his group of very concerned deacons. There was now nothing left to do except wait patiently alongside the young bridesmaids for some official word on the skateboard. The news was not good. Sadly the deacon's son had taken his skateboard with him, and gone off to visit friends in the neighborhood. On hearing this the deacons immediately regrouped, for they felt in urgent need of guidance on the matter. After much discussion they believed there was nothing else for it but to assign two of the strongest men to the dastardly task. They promptly dashed out to the car and, after opening both side doors, they pushed and pulled until they successfully prized me from the back seat, like an unyielding oyster out of its shell. This done, they then scooped me up off the ground, and, with a strong arm under each armpit, they dutifully half dragged and half carried me down the aisle, similar I guess to that of a re-arrested convict, my legs dangling a few inches off the ground, until they reached the altar. Finally I was gently placed down on a seat right beside John, in front of the altar.

"You look glowing," my gracious husband very charitably whispered as he gave me a big puppy dog smile. I very much wanted to argue the point and at the same time give him a blow by blow account of all that had befallen me since we last spoke, but I could only manage to give a distraught helpless look before plunging my head down between my knees, my immediate mission being to prevent myself from throwing up all down my Silk Taffeta wedding dress. I remained in that bent over position for most of the ceremony, only coming up intermittently for fresh air, otherwise to give John the odd weak and very tortured smile, oh and to eventually say "I do".

As I sat in the chair doubled over I sorely wished we'd settled for a quick registry office wedding, as these tend to be over in a matter of minutes, it left me wondering if this day would ever come to an end.

Finally, we got to the all important bit of the ceremony.

"John, do you take this wreck of a woman to be your awful wedded wife?" Actually the Vicar never said that, but, judging by the state I was in, I wouldn't have blamed him one little bit if he had. I was therefore extremely grateful to hear John formally respond with an "I do," albeit somewhat subdued.

"Tricia wilt thou take this man to be...."

"Yes, yes ...quick, get it over with, for can't you see that I'm about to throw up all over your shoes," I mentally screamed as I tried my very best to hold myself together.

"And keep thee only unto him as long as..."

Once again I found myself hyperventilating, for I urgently needed the dear man to gallop through my part of the vows, otherwise it was highly likely that his cassock would in less than a few moments find itself sprayed with a mixture of regurgitated breakfast cereal, coffee and wholegrain toast.

At one point I heard the thoroughly recognizable voice of one of my more vociferous Irish friends as she exclaimed, "Good God, the girl's about to be sick all down her dress, and wreck the entire occasion!" She might as well have been speaking into a microphone, for her booming voice echoed so loudly that you could hear the laughter ripple down the aisle as her words of heartfelt concern spread from pew to pew until they had been repeated systematically to the entire church load of guests.

"Go on Tricia, it's time for you to say I do," the Vicar anxiously coaxed.

"I.....I ...do," I gasped in a histrionic voice more reminiscent of a loud most unwelcome sneeze. This was followed up with a few seconds of acute silence as the guests checked with one and other as to whether they had actually borne witness to my consent or whether I was just getting the first signs of the Asian flu! As soon as this latest concern was officially settled, there was a rousing burst of applause from the delighted guests. I was feeling deeply relieved that it was all as good as over, when suddenly the Vicar loudly declared "You may now kiss the bride."

"What! Oh no.. no ...no... Go and kiss somebody else, anybody else but leave me well alone! Look we've exchanged rings, isn't that enough? Leave all that extra stuff until we are in private, for I still need space. It's my precious air and I don't want it sucked away. Oh alright if I have too, but just a quick peck on the my cheek will suffice, otherwise I'm going to puke all down my dress," I ranted loudly inside my hysterical head.

Luckily for me the kiss was short and sweet, leaving my loose partial safely in my mouth where it rightfully belonged.

Now all that was left for me to do was turn round, and walk back down the aisle.

"Have we found our legs yet, or are we still in need of a few strong men?" the Vicar anxiously whispered down at me as he closed his hymnal for the last time.

"Yes I think I can do this all by myself," I whispered back.

"Oh thank goodness," the deeply grateful man muttered as he then signaled to his deacons that, against all odds, their assistance was no longer required.

To other brides this must be the most joyful moment of the ceremony but, in my distressed state, it felt no different to walking the plank!

Taking a deep breath, I stood up and, grabbing hold of my new husband's free arm, I turned to face the throng of most concerned but well-wishing wedding guests.

"You can do this!" John whispered, as he gave my hand a strong supportive squeeze.

"You really think so?" I lamely replied back. I turned round and, faltering slightly, I began to take the first steps back down the aisle, my only goal being to get into the fresh air as soon as possible.

John, however appeared to be in no such hurry as, with his arm linked in mine, he walked at what seemed to me to be the pace of a semi comatose paraplegic slug scaling Mount Everest for the first time!

"John, please let's get out of here before I begin gagging again," I loudly whimpered under my breath as, still showing willing, I attempted to smile at my guests as I passed them by. The congregation all rose from their seats and, as a show of support began clapping and cheering loudly as I high tailed down the aisle and out of the church building, as fast as my pitifully weak and trembling legs would allow.

"Wow, we made it," I gasped as we stepped outside, delighted and relieved to be hit by glorious blue skies and brilliant sunshine.

"Only just," came his quick teasing reply. "Life in your lane certainly appears to be one long rollercoaster after another!"

I wanted to respond and say "Yes and, as we're now joined at the hip, you my darling are highly honored to become a part of it." Instead, for once in my life, I chose to remain silent, preferring to give him a weak all-knowing smile.

CHAPTER THREE

Meet the Relatives.

Having survived the church ordeal, without ruining my wedding dress otherwise the Vicar's cassock, I finally started to relax enough to begin enjoying what remained of my special day. The reception was taking place in the beautiful gardens of a delightful English manor house and, with the late September sun now unexpectedly fiercely blazing down from gloriously blue skies, I was beginning to believe I had come through the worst. However, due to many weeks of continually bad weather the lawns had become somewhat soggy and mushy so, when I was forced to stand for long amounts of time for the customary photographs and the receiving of gifts, the heels of my high heel shoes kept sinking deep into the muddy lawn, forcing me to almost topple over backwards. I would later appear to look quite inebriated in many of the photographs.

As I had been raised in children's homes I was sadly lacking in the family department, so the only relative on my side was my youngest brother, my eldest brother sadly residing at that time in the locked ward of a mental institution, and I had no idea where my other younger brother was, as I had not seen him for a number of years. John's side wasn't much better for, apart from his extremely aged parents, I had never met any of his relatives, except his older step brother. This very day however I would come face to face with John's very eccentric aunt Maud, and, having finally been introduced to her, well perhaps it was a good idea that the rest of his family remained his best kept secret.

The good friend who gave me away was the very best one could wish for, and our only sadness was that we had had to attend two funerals in very the week leading up to the wedding. One was a girl friend who died in very unfortunate circumstances, the other was John's mother who, without any warning, suffered a huge stroke and lived for only a few days before she too died. His father, then aged 95, a former Colonel in the British Army in India, was understandably still grieving and was anyway too frail physically to make the long journey, but he still managed to send us his love and best wishes.

Despite our tumultuous courtship that had weathered many ups and downs over the past three years, we decided that his mother would have wished for the wedding to go ahead, besides which, we would have been forced to cancel the honeymoon, something we could ill afford to do at this late hour. Sadly, some of his relations thought otherwise, so they stayed away, that is with the exception of his step brother, a distant cousin, oh and his famous Aunt Maud, who came straight from the pages of an Agatha Christie novel. She was even searching for a stiff gin or two, or was it three? long before the reception was even underway.

Aunt Maud arrived on the scene, not only requiring alcohol for medicinal purposes of course, but accompanying her was a thick fur that garnished her long turkey neck, a fur that one could not fail to notice still had the poor fox head attached and, if you cared to look closer, you could clearly see a number of its long sharp very brown teeth! I felt a strange empathy with very dead fox. I also noticed that, as she strode with great gusto and determination across the lawn to mingle with the other wedding guests, the head of the fox jumped up and down in complete rhythm with her every movement. Aunt Maud had cinnamon coloured hair and cheeks that glowed brighter than Rudolph's red nose, leaving me to ponder as to whether the colour was due to an excess of rose blusher, or some other dubious origin. Many weeks on I would hear from some of the other guests who, having met her that day, cared to share with me snippets of her lengthy and most intriguing conversations . Aunt Maud made it her firm business to put all guests straight as to where their side of the family stood regarding this particular very disconcerting wedding business so the conversation went something like this.

"I came here today to represent his side of the family," she confided to anyone who cared to listen

"They had no business continuing on with the wedding when there's just been a most saddening and sudden death in the family," she loudly stated as she popped a bite of finger food into her open mouth, before washing it down with a large slurp of Italian Chianti.

"Yes most distasteful, if I say so myself. That's why most of our family were rather regretfully left with no other choice but to decline the invitation to be here today."

"Really?"

"Yes, and I'm not sure if you're fully aware but, rather regretfully, the bride does not come from good stock, you know. Yes, not to put too fine a point on it, the girl does not come from any remotely decent heritage, so sadly there's not so much as a drop of blue blood coursing through her veins. No tut.. tut … none whatsoever! So, unlike our side of the family, there is absolutely nothing whatsoever to commend her. An orphan I'm told, and worst still, I hear she's deserted the Catholic faith to become one of these unconventional happy clappy people, judging by the service I've just endured.

"Oh really."

"Yes, though I feel that I must report that, over the years, even the groom has done nothing but trouble his dear parents, when, after becoming a hippy, he abandoned his senses to follow after some unknown Indian Guru, ending up living for a year in India of all places. I'm glad to report that he has, it appears, now come to his senses, though to what degree I cannot say for sure."

"Oh dear."

"Apparently and absurd as it must seem, a large number of these foolish and misguided youngsters went to India in search of so called enlightenment. Pure unadulterated escapism if you ask me, for I'd have thought a year in the military and a good thump on the head would have done much to sort most of them out, and bring them to their senses, and I hasten to add it would have proved considerably cheaper."

"Hmm…."

"Oh now, where was I? Ah yes, his poor, poor parents, they were indeed challenged to their very roots, for whenever he deigned to pay them a social visit, he blatantly refused to sit down to a Sunday roast saying he preferred to cook his own meal of plain brown rice and lentils, going on about his yin and his yang, or other such nonsense. Who in their right mind eats brown rice I ask you? Yes, he even abandoned his good family name in preference of some thoroughly weird Indian name. Apparently back then, it was the done thing for all peace loving hippies to give it a go. I blame the Beatles myself, yes, they sent a lot of young people astray, as they felt the need to stick two fingers in the air to everything both decent and law abiding, to then blindly head off to far-off places like India and Tibet. I can tell you straight, that there were many prayers uttered on his behalf, prayers that asked our dear Lord to knock some sense into his thick skull. And fortunately our prayers seem to have been answered. Mind you, it took nearly dying of some tropical disease to bring him round...."

"Really?"

"So I can't tell you how relieved his poor parents were when he finally dispensed with that ghastly orange robe, and once more sat down at the family table to tuck into the usual roast dinner. They were also thoroughly relieved that he also returned to using his proper name."

"Hmm...how amazing."

"Ah young man, do be a good boy and fill up my empty glass for me. Thank you so much. You know it's amazing how rebellious and insubordinate youngsters are these days, and therefore completely disrespectful of their families wishes. One can only hope that his new wife will allow any future off-spring to find their way back into the bosom of the only true church. And, by all accounts I hear the girl is in bad need of some peace in her otherwise troubled life. Oh, and by the way, I hope I'm not being too intrusive in asking, but are you good people practicing Catholics? No... Oh dear....Well you should look into it, for it's a truly marvelous faith that even has the Pope and Mother Theresa on our side.... Ah, young man, over here, over here, perhaps you would do the decent thing by leading the way to that thoroughly inviting dessert table."

Aunt Maud would only find relief and a soul mate when she finally met up with my youngest brother, who readily admitted to being of the same religious persuasion, even though somewhat lapsed.

"Young man, thank goodness we've found each other in what has otherwise been a most disturbing day," she deeply sighed. "Yes, and that said we simply must stick together, and don't say anything to the contrary, for that's an order. So, be a poppet and tell me everything you know about your sister, and I entreat you not to leave anything out, no nothing whatsoever!" she shrilly demanded, a crooked sly smile alighting her heavily wrinkled face. She then linked her arm through his, and excitedly marched him towards a quiet spot in the gardens, her mission to bear down on him hard until, like an almost empty tube of toothpaste, she had squeezed every last drop of spicy 'insider' gossip out of him.

We were in the process of having the traditional cutting of the cake when some unexpectedly bad news came through.

"Guys I've got terrible news for I've got the holiday rep on the line, and she says she's terribly sorry, but there has been a dreadful mix up with your honeymoon travel arrangements."

"Oh dear what's the problem?"

"Well I don't know how to say this but your flight to Greece is leaving Gatwick in less than three hours!"

"What, I don't believe it. We're not meant to be leaving for Greece until tomorrow!" I moaned.

"Yes, I'm sorry, but as it will take at least an hour and a half to get you to the airport, so we need to leave straight away. You'd better abandon the cake cutting and go quickly to get changed out of your wedding dress."

Moments later, and I was hurriedly flinging my suitcase into the boot of a car before flinging my bouquet into the crowd. We were then hastily bundled into the back seat of the best man's car, to then race at top speed towards Gatwick airport.

"Well, there goes our special honeymoon night at that lovely London hotel," I gloomily murmured.

"I'm afraid so,"

"John, I feel really upset for I deliberately chose not to eat much as I wanted to save space for our romantic champagne supper by candlelight."

"Me too."

"Now we've also lost out on the night in the special honeymoon suite, it all seems so unbelievably unfair."

"Look, never mind honey, on our return I'll write a letter to the hotel and explain exactly what has happened, and maybe they will still allow us to take advantage of their special honeymoon package at a belated date. I can't believe our travel agents have made such a horrendous boob."

"No neither can I," I confessed, as I tried to fend off further anxiety that foretold of even greater crises to come.

"John, I really need you to reassure me that from here on, everything is going to be alright."

"Sure thing honey," he responded, giving my hand a small squeeze. "Look, you've survived your wedding day and the reception, and I'm happy to report that you're still in one piece, although I might have to remove all your clothes to check on that one later," he said giving a mischievous wink.

"Behave yourself," I cried giving him a pretend slap on the wrist.

"So trust me Tricia when I say everything else should be smooth sailing."

"Oh right," I nervously responded, as I cuddled up close, breathing in his aftershave, while trying desperately to believe that my man now had everything in the universe under his firm control.

"Okay guys, we're here, but you've no time to hang around, for you need to race through the airport, as you're running extremely late," the best man announced as he dropped us off at the terminal. "Have a wonderful honeymoon in Greece, and we'll see you when you get back."

The initial shock came while standing in line as we waited our turn to board the plane bound for Athens, for this was first time I had ever set eyes on a real living breathing air stewardess, as up until this moment I'd only ever seen them on the television advertisements. I have to confess to having always been wowed by the sensational Pan Am and B.O.A.C. adverts that spoon fed us lower imperfect mortals, the vision of the most refined impeccable dressed young ladies with their Company color cravats graciously tied around their slender necks. I marveled at their crisp white gloves, only matched by the blinding white of their sparkling Hollywood teeth, as in stiletto heels they purposefully strutted across the concourse looking so darn irresistible and untouchable we all had to suppress the desire to simply fall down at their feet in total adoration. I also believed these magnificently pure and exceedingly remarkable specimens to be so full of angelic charity, that they oozed magnanimous amounts of love and tenderness from every pore of their sylph like bodies in a manner normally reserved for that of a mother with her precious newborn. They were after all the immortal Goddess's of the sky, ready and willing to give unimaginably courteous service to each and every individual passenger who cared to press that little red button on their armrest.

"You called Sir? Is there anything else I can get you?" readily tumbled from her frosted passion fruit lipstick lips, her sweet breath, and expensive sensuously heady perfume willingly drifting up your nostrils as she tentatively reached over to help adjust your seatbelt before take off.

However that night I would be terribly disappointed as my fantasy was to be forever annihilated, for on that particular evening flight I did not catch sight of even one such heavenly creature, for at the risk of causing great offence they all seemed very average and ordinary if not a little, dare I say it plump and middle aged with strong regional accents as oppose to the gentle melodic tones of the Queens English.

"Psst…. I thought the girls had to be both slim, as well as gorgeous looking, to be an air stewardess," I whispered in John's ear.

"Apparently not," was my husbands only comment as he began routing around in his carry-on luggage.

"Well, maybe all the gorgeous bodacious ones are reserved for the upper echelons of First and Business class, otherwise the transatlantic flights?"

"Maybe," my husband replied with a degree of irritation as he continued to rummage through his bag in pursuit of the latest book he was half way through reading.

"You're not listening, are you?"

"Yes I am."

"Well what did I say then?"

"Huh? something about wanting to fly first class."

"There… I knew you weren't listening."

One particular stewardess spent the entire flight with her overfilled purse slung over her shoulder. As a rule this would neither have bothered or intrigued me, except to say that, as the aisle appeared extremely narrow, she more than once unwittingly struck me around the face with her handbag as she determinedly strode past me to attend to some other demanding passenger further down the aisle who repeatedly pressed the button and so I presume required her full on attention.

"Ouch that hurt," I bleated. "Look John, her bag has already hit me on the side of my cheek, and now, would you believe it, she's just scratched my arm."

"Honey, why don't you tell her?" John helpfully suggested.

"No, I don't want to appear difficult."

"That's a first! Oh come on, just tell her; she probably has no idea."

"No, you tell her, that's your job now we're married."

"Oh right, well, if she does it again then I'll say something."

As I sat in my seat examining the features of the hostesses as they passed by, I thought it funny that I had always dreamed of being an air hostess, well otherwise a nun or fireman, but thankfully I had no illusion that I could ever fulfill such a dream as I was much too short and plain for the job. Oh and already I was finding myself both petrified and uncomfortably queasy and the wheels hadn't even left the tarmac. Little did I know it but things were also about to get much.. much worse. Back in 1980 there was no ban on smoking, and the large gentleman in the seat directly in front of me took full advantage as he lit one long Havana cigar after another. Unfortunately I alone seemed to be in the direct path of the plumes of exhaled smoke and so before long I found myself coughing and spluttering before my eyes began watering.

"I wish he'd take even a small break from smoking those awful strong cigars," I whispered in John's free ear.

"Likewise, so hopefully he'll have that break when the stewardess brings around the evening meal."

Dream on! Much to my dismay I was about to discover that there are a certain elite breed of humans living amongst us that are such clever multi -taskers; they can amaze us lesser mortals by eating, drinking and chain smoking, all at the same time! By now I had completely lost all appetite.

"John can't we ask to be moved?"

"We can't change seats for, as you already know, the plane is full to capacity, so we've no other choice than to endure it. But look would it help if you changed seats with me?" John very considerately volunteered.

"No no I must have the aisle seat incase I have a sudden unexpected panic attack," I whispered, my eyes smarting as large tears began to roll down my cheeks.

"Besides you know I urgently need to 'spend a penny' every fifteen minutes or so, due to my little problem, so I have little choice but to stay put," I simpered.

"Well I hate to say this, but your make up is now awfully smudged."

"John I really don't care," I declared closing my eyes as I struggled hard not too burst into tears.

Finally we entered Greek airspace and before long the chief pilot informed us that we would be landing in just over twenty minutes.

"Honey you need to use the bathroom."

"No I don't."

"Oh but you do."

"Honey trust me I'd know if I needed a pee."

"Tricia you need to give your face a good wash."

"I think I'll leave it until we're on the ground."

"Honey you really don't wish to be detained by customs officers, do you?"

"Why of course not."

"Well, don't take this too personally, but have you ever seen 'Bride of Frankenstein?"

"Uh?"

"Well, if I'm to be brutally honest...."

"Go on."

"If she had a sister...."

"Thanks a bunch," I moaned as I quickly released my seat belt and decided to go see for myself.

As I peered into the small mirror above the metal washbasin I required no further persuasion, for my so called waterproof mascara had run all down my face and with every wipe of my hand I had unwittingly helped to smudge it further until my entire face was now blackened. Precisely how long I'd looked this way he refused to reveal.

"What a day!" was all I could sigh as, with the help of some soapy water I attempted to scrub my face clean. As we disembarked the plane at nearly two in the morning, I had little idea that my special day was still nowhere near over!

CHAPTER FOUR

Our Greek Tragedy

Crazy as this may seem we did not arrive at our Athens hotel until about 4am in the morning, after the coach had stopped at a number of other hotels. Yes, ours was last, and yes, we were the only ones disembarking here! The good news was that there was a member of staff hiding away behind reception, albeit with his head resting on the desk as, lost to the world, he continued to snore away. We made loud coughing noises but he was so heavily out for the count that at first he failed to respond.

"Maybe he's drunk too much ouzo," I quietly suggested.

"Doubt it, I think he's just in a deep sleep."

It took John to falteringly gently tap him on the head for him to wake up and to then sit up straight. The overtired Greek receptionist failed to cover his mouth as he gave a loud yawn that exposed an almost full set of rotten teeth that would surely have sent most of us rushing off to the dentist to demand a rather large number of extractions. John politely said who we were and then handed over a number of documents. We were then left to patiently wait for a considerable length of time as the dozy man rummaged through various boxes of papers. We were beginning to get impatient with him for we were thoroughly exhausted and desperate to get to bed. A deep look of concern developed on the gentlemen's face.

"No sir, I am lookeeng in zee book and through all our records and you have … no reservation," he stammered in very broken English while appearing jolly annoyed that we had woken him from his slumber.

"Oh, but we do. Look for yourself, here, we have the documents that prove we are booked in at this hotel."

"Oh no sir, there must beee some beeg meestake for wee definitely are not expecting you. Maybee you are at zee wrong hotel?" he nonchalantly sniffed.

"Look, here are the papers, so please try again," my very concerned husband begged.

"Oh give me someone who can speak plain English," I anxiously cried.

The conversation would continue back and forth for the next fifteen minutes as he continued to deny the booking, and John in turn became increasingly adamant that we had one. Eventually he sighed and beckoned for us follow after him. As we reached the elevator he just handed us a key and mumbled some numbers in broken English, before abruptly turning around to head back to the desk in the reception area presumably for more shut eye.

"Thanks" we shouted after him. He did not look back, even to smile. When the elevator opened up on the ninth floor we were surprised to discover that there was no lighting in the corridor whatsoever.

"So now they expect us to play murder in the dark do they?" John moaned as we were left to blindly stagger down the long corridor dragging our heavy suitcases behind us. Back and forth we went as, with no light to guide us, we now were having great difficulty identifying the room numbers.

"Right, you can stop now, for I do believe this to be our room."

I waited with baited breath as John struggled with the key. Finally the door opened. John reached for the light switch and, as we walked into the room, I let go of my hand luggage letting out a loud anguished gasp. The ceiling light that was absent of any shade actually fizzled and spat while struggling in its grand mission to light up the horribly dingy room, and, as I looked upwards, my eyes were met by long thick strands of ghoulish looking slime hanging like motionless drapes right across the ceiling!

"John, WHAT on earth is that awful stuff?" I exploded, as I struggled to remain standing. "It looks horribly like the stuff from the trailer of that Alien movie."

"I've no idea for I've never seen anything like it in my whole life!" John muttered.

"John, don't breathe in, for if these mould particles begin to invade our lungs, we might well get a serious infection, or much worse die in our sleep" I cautioned.

36

I then turned my attention to the bathroom and was horrified to see that it was completely cordoned off and therefore inaccessible due to thick yellowing tape sealing the door. My eyes then moved over towards an old and rickety iron bed. The bed was clothed in just a worn out sheet and a couple of scrawny grayish wafer thin pillows that, prior to finding their way here, must surely have been binned by the local high security prison. I then noted that the bedside table was absent of any sort of reading lamp, but was home to a clock radio that was turned to face the wall revealing a mass of bare wires.

"Even the jolly clock is facing the wall in disgust," my husband limply cried as he continued his attempts to carry on joking. I couldn't even break into a faint smile as I slumped down on the bed to hopefully have a good cry.

"Oh John we can't sleep in this room, for who knows what we might catch," I hysterically cried.

"We don't have any choice in the matter."

"What if this slime slithers down from the ceiling and suffocates us both while we're asleep?" I blubbered. "I need Sigourney Weaver and I need her now!"

"Uh?"

"Well with all her knowledge of alien emissions she'd know what to do, wouldn't she?"

"Honey you're speaking absolute gobbledygook, so please try to remain calm?"

"Calm! Are you crazy? Do you really expect me to remain calm?" I bawled.

"Look I know it's terrible, but at least we're lucky enough to have a bed, for a few minutes ago it looked like we were going to have to camp out on the streets."

"John I can't believe you're being so darned accepting of this awful crisis."

"Tricia listen to me! I haven't any other choice, for not only does the guy downstairs not speak a word of English but he also couldn't give a monkeys. I therefore suggest that we try and get a few hours sleep and I promise we will sort it out first thing in the morning," he calmly suggested as he wrapped his arms around my waist to give me a little hope and comfort.

"I'm not sleeping with the light off. No way!" I cried as I began imagining the ghoulish slime stealthily slithering down the walls, then across the bed, their mission being to entirely enshroud our bodies with their festering bodily fluids before silently and avariciously feasting on our flesh. I knew we both needed to shed a few pounds but what a way to go! I could only shudder as I considered the possibility that by morning there would be nothing left save our skeletal remains, and they would only be discovered once the Greek chamber maids eventually came to clean the room.

"Look Tricia we'll be alright, after all this is a respectable hotel, so we're safe as houses." I was not the least convinced.

"Oh super duper, I'm really heartened by your words of comfort for that's what the poor darling in Psycho believed, and look what became of her," I loudly wailed.

"Honey you really need to reign in that over active imagination of yours. Come on babe, you're with me and trust me, nothing bad is going to happen."

"Alright, tell me straight at what particular stage of your life did you enroll for the part of Superman?"

"Enough! I'm going to turn out the light."

"We're a real Mr. and Mrs. Muggins, for I cannot believe we're going to spend the remainder of our honeymoon night in this run down highly toxic hotel room!" I bawled.

"Ssh… it's almost five in the morning, so let's try to get some sleep eh."

We had only just dozed off when we were woken by the most terrible noise that saw John jump up from the bed and race to open the curtains. The light was so blinding that he instantly fell backwards, dazed by its sheer brilliance. I left the bed to come over to join him by the window and, when our eyes had finally adjusted to the natural light, we were shocked to witness the most unbelievable traffic jam that saw scores of cars lining the streets, bumper to bumper, with their emotionally stunted and frenzied occupants excessively bashing their horns, and screaming out of open windows, as mopping the sweat from their heavily lined faces they gave vent to exorbitant amounts of uncontrollable rage. Until this moment in time we had no idea that our hotel was situated bang in the middle of downtown Athens and the traffic crisis was a daily occurrence that started around five am every day, with the exception of Sunday, when they honed in all excessive emotions and donning their hats they quietly made their way to their little orthodox churches, in order to repent of their week long rage.

The noise of the traffic was so deafening that I knew there was little hope of going back to sleep so I sat at the end of the bed, cupping my face in between my hands, as I continued to experience overwhelming exhaustion as well as unspeakable misery.

"John please go down to reception and speak to the manager," I begged.

"Tricia it's only six thirty in the morning, so it's much too early."

"But I need to take a pee."

"Honey I can't go stripping the tape from the bathroom door, for it's sealed up for a good reason. So you know that would be wrong." he sighed.

"Oh 'Mr.Goody two shoes,' will I ever get to witness you doing anything that veers even slightly on the bad side," I challenged. "Look honey, it's wrong that they've dumped us in such a terrible room in the first place." I wailed.

"Tricia try to have faith that things are going to get better."

"But I don't want to," I pathetically whimpered. "I just want to get out of this squalid slime infested room and get a plane back to England."

"Look tell you what, just stay here and I will go down to reception and see what I can do," he said as he then hurriedly began to get dressed.

"In the meantime put on a smile and try your best to remain positive."

Smile? I wanted to skin him alive and then boil his innards for that last trite comment. He was gone for quite a while.

"Tricia there's still nobody downstairs in reception who can help us."

"Oh so why the happy face?"

"Well, just hear me out. I took the lift up another floor and discovered a small rooftop swimming pool."

"Oh really?"

"Yes so why don't you slip into your bikini and we can go for a nice refreshing swim?"

"So are you granting me permission to pee in the pool?"

"Oh no.. of course not."

"Well what then?"

"There must be a public loo somewhere along this corridor so we'll find one on our way up to the pool."

"Oh and what about getting washed? Is it okay for me to wash my hair in the pool," I defiantly sniffed.

"No no…It's just if we go for a swim then you'll surely begin to feel better."

"Well then 'Mr. Let's Sweep Everything Under The Carpet And Bring Out The Party Poppers,' you really don't understand for nothing is going to make me feel better, I just want to get out of this awful hotel," I rebelliously yelled. "Now if you want to have yourself a little splish splash, feel free, but I'm going nowhere until things have been sorted," I announced folding my arms to emphasize the point. Oh I knew I was being hard on him, but I couldn't help myself. All my life I had dreamt about having a real holiday and now just like everything else this dream was already in tatters, so I wasn't quite ready to lay down and die, not just yet anyway! I have to say that if we had been experienced travelers we wouldn't have stayed more than twenty seconds in that disgusting potentially disease ridden room, but back then in 1980 we were oh so tragically young and innocent and therefore thoroughly unversed when it came to dabbling a toe in the school of legal rights and ethics.

My poor defeated ex hippie of a husband tried to remain upbeat but things were not looking good at all. So it was with great reluctance that he left me in the room to go for a lonely soul searching swim. I in turn closed the curtains on the blinding sun and climbed under the thin sheet, curling up into a tight ball to have another hearty grizzle as I tried and failed miserably to comfort myself. I must have dozed off for when I came to, John was lying beside me on the bed reading a chapter from 'The Meaning of Life' by Victor Frankel.

"Honey this book is truly amazing." he quietly commented.

"Excuse me," I muttered as I rubbed my eyes.

"I said this book is really incredible," he said as he flashed the front cover in front of my eyes.

"John, firstly I'm curious as to how a book about surviving the holocaust could possibly be considered wonderful? And secondly, why you would even think to bring such reading material on your honeymoon?" I queried as I rolled over to make stern eye contact.

"Oh Tricia, once you've read what these dear people were sadly forced to endure, then what's happening to us is …well it's nothing…yes there's no comparison."

"Nothing!" I screeched, my self sharpening talons igniting themselves as I hastily withdrew from the fetal position to sit bolt upright in the bed.

"You see this as nothing? John, are you barking mad?" I yelled as I gave the sheet a hard tug if only to restrain myself from scraping my nails down the entire length of his bare back.

"Well no… but compared to what these poor people were expected to endure surely we should consider ourselves very lucky." His voice trailed off as he quickly realized that every single word falling from his lips was getting him deeper into the mire.

"Lucky? Now I know you're loop the loop! John, forgive me but I need to ask what particular planet you're at present residing on? Because it's definitely one I'm not familiar with. For we, and I repeat WE, are not in some hellish concentration camp complaining about the unconscionably drab sleeping arrangements, we're on our one and only seven day very expensive honeymoon! And, to my way of thinking, it's perfectly reasonable to have a few high expectations."

"Okay honey, calm down. I was just trying to put things into perspective that's all."

"Perspective! John, as a rule of thumb, honeymoons are meant to be special. So help me out, if for some unimaginable reason I can't quite dismiss what has happened to us so far as being fortunate or lucky! For in spite of your insistence that the conditions here are considerably better than those of the German concentration camps, I feel ready to throw myself from the top balcony as I feel utterly besides myself with disappointment!" I raged.

He winced and looked slightly hurt as he quietly continued to endure my ranting, but being the gentle soul that he was, he somehow took no offense.

"Well promise me one thing, you'll read it when I'm done."

"I'll do no such thing. Anyway what's the time?" I glumly asked.

"Well it's just gone 9.30, so unfortunately we've missed any chance of breakfast."

"But it's only 9.30!"

"Yep but apparently this is a business hotel, so breakfast starts at 6.00am and finishes by nine."

"Oh great, so what will we do for food?" I asked.

"No idea?"

"Well have you spoken to the manager?"

"Not yet."

"Exactly what do you mean by 'not yet?"

"Um, I don't want to do it alone."

"Excuse me Captain Courageous but why ever not?"

"Well, if you could find it in your heart to rise and shine, we can go out of the hotel and search for a restaurant. Then, after breakfast, we'll go and find the manager. So come on, be a good girl and jump out of bed."

"Jump out of bed? Honey pie, I really don't like the use of that word, for jump implies I'm happy, I'm exhilarated, I've fresh air in my lungs and wind in my sails, Which if you cared to note, I have none!"

"Oh right."

"Also 'Mr. I hate to complain', I'm not going anywhere until I've used a proper shower and you my darling hubby have gone down to reception to speak with the hotel manager."

"Okay...okay.. I'll go now," he said giving a deflated sigh."

"Honey one more thing, please think to lay aside the gentle peace loving hippy half of your personality, and do try your best to appear just a tinsy bit upset, if only for my sake."

"I'll do my very best."

"I'm sure you will."

No sooner had he gone than I began to feel sorry that I had not accompanied him down to reception to stand dutifully by his side, especially as we were now joined at the hip, but in all honesty did he really want a weeping histrionic woman at his side as he diplomatically tried to reason with the manager? I didn't think so! So I could only hope that today he would muster the necessary courage from within while making a formal complaint. He was after all a kind and gentle soul who loved tall trees and week old fluffy kittens, as well as meaningful books that nourished the soul, oh and old Francoise Truffaut movies, so I knew with great assurance that taking on the management of some grimy back street Greek hotel was way, way beyond his scope of experience.

"Tricia, do you want the good news first or the bad news?"

"Try the good news."

"We are going to change rooms."

"And the bad news?"

"Well it won't be happening until later on today."

"What?"

"Well they don't have a room available until some of the guests have departed."

"I can't believe I am hearing this? Did you remember to complain about the unbelievably dire state of this room?"

"Well um…apparently according to the manager, this whole corridor has been cordoned off for a number of weeks because the rooftop swimming pool has been suffering a slow undetected leak, hence the stalactites," he said pointing upwards towards the ceiling."

"Right. So we are the only dumb guests they dared place on this out of service sealed off corridor AND when we're supposed to be our honeymoon."

"Call it special treatment if you will," he quipped flashing me an impish grin.

"Ho ho ho."

"Christmas arriving early this year is it dear?"

"Come on John, we paid a small fortune for this seven day honeymoon, so they should be falling over themselves to help us."

"I understand what you're saying, but what else can we do?" he sighed shrugging his shoulders.

"This is all so terrible," I moaned.

"Come on 'my kid from care,' please help me by coming up to the rooftop to have a swim and then we will go out and search for a restaurant. I don't know about you but I'm starving."

I finally gave in as I tried to remind myself it was his honeymoon too, and so this really was none of his fault so I forced myself to get out of the bed to put on my bikini. Then grabbing a towel I dutifully followed John into the lift. The rooftop pool was disappointingly small and was also completely devoid of any sun beds on which to lie. The pool deck consisted of some very strange imitation grass, not that I could see much of it, as virtually every inch was covered up by hotel guests lying face down on towels as they soaked up the mid morning sun, while trying to ignore the deafening noise of heavy traffic and horns coming from the streets below. Having established a small spot of grass that appeared free of a towel I found myself slowly inching my way between two semi naked bodies, all the while praying that nothing of my flesh would make unintentional contact with theirs and so disturb them. However I had little time to glory in this remarkable feat as it was at this point that my hot and bothered husband then rather unwittingly chose to do an over enthusiastic rather juvenile leap into the pool, a leap that instantly showered freezing cold water over all unsuspecting sunbathers, myself included!

Crazy as this may seem nobody flinched or moved a muscle to look round and see what bungling idiot had just drenched them and, even more amazing was nobody chose to hurl a few choice words in his direction. Instead they remained as silent as the grave as they continued to lie face down and motionless. I honestly wanted to reach over to quickly pinch their lily white flesh just incase they were really shop mannequins, but thankfully wisdom prevailed.

"John, are you crazy, for you've just soaked everybody?" I reprimanded.

"Oops sorry," he mouthed back, giving a little mischievous smile. I turned back on my stomach and closed my eyes as I wished for sweet oblivion. It was not to be for seconds later, I became aware of John's dripping wet body standing over me.

"Honey, can we talk?"

"What now?"

"Yes now. I... um have something that I urgently need your help with."

There was an undeniable sense of stress in his voice, that I really wanted to ignore.

"Oh what now?" I moaned as I resentfully turned over to face him.

He crouched down and began to speak quietly into my ear.

"Honey I don't know how to say this, but when I dived into the water my wedding ring accidentally slipped off my finger," he stuttered like a terrified child making a full confession to the formidable headmaster.

"Oh good grief! So where is it?"

"Um, it's on the bottom of the pool."

"Well go and get it then," I hissed.

"I can't."

"Oh come on John, you've got two arms and two legs so ....."

"No it's more complicated than that," he interjected.

"Oh really?"

"Well I don't know exactly how to say this, but at present the ring is balanced over the grate at the bottom of the pool, and I'm afraid that if I attempt to retrieve it then the likelihood is that it will be lost forever."

"Good grief!"

"Yes well, as you used to pick up coins from the deep end after swimming galas, then maybe you'd do a better job of retrieving it."

"Say no more."

I struggled to my feet and hurriedly made my way to the pool edge with my deeply repentant husband trailing behind me.

"Show me exactly where it is?"

"There, can you see it," he cried as he stood at the edge pointing downwards towards the grate. Sure enough, as I stared into the deep end I saw the ring precariously balanced on a small iron rung of the grate. I gave a deep moan as I considered that My personally owned dark cloud had now made it its business to maliciously stalk us all the way to Athens and that's why everything appeared to be conspiring against us.

"Okay, now I see it. John please do me a favor. Stand well away and Allow me to have a go as there needs to be as few ripples as humanly possible." I knew that if I failed in my mission the ring would be lost forever into the Greek sewer system. Seconds later I resurfaced with the ring.

"Brilliant! I knew you could do it," he cried as he held out his hand for me to pass it back to him.

"Sorry honey, but for the on going safety of my already seriously replete and emotionally balanced future, I think it best if I take it back down to the room for safekeeping. I'll come straight back, I promise."

I was gone less than ten minutes and, as I stepped out of the elevator back onto the rooftop, I was surprised to witness my husband of less than twenty four hours with another woman, taking a small home video with a camcorder up to his face. What made it more surprising was that we didn't own a camcorder neither had we hired one. I had been gone less than ten minutes, so what precisely was going on? Keeping my distance I continued to take in all that was happening. All too soon I had myself believing that we were little more than characters in some old quirky Fellini movie as John continued on with the filming, the subject matter being a dark haired, somewhat overweight, olive skinned lady of Greek origin.

At one point she lazily rested back on a chair before producing a large cluster of purple grapes which she dangled in front of her face, picking them off slowly before popping them one at a time between her cupid red lips to swallow whole. Minutes later she placed the grapes to one side and ordered John to continue filming her from this angle then another.

He appeared like a servile pussy cat as he obediently knelt down on one knee to then move this way and that as he faithfully attempted to catch her every subtle nuance and pose as though he were some brilliant but undiscovered moviemaker.

When I thought things were at an end she once more picked up her bunch of grapes and began to flirtatiously drift around the rooftop, her sun dress most deliberately revealing quite a hefty bare thigh, her aging face never leaving the camera, not even for a moment as she smiled, gestured and waved theatrically at the non existent crowd. Finally my new spouse handed back the camcorder and a few words and smiles were briefly exchanged before he turned to head back towards the pool.

"Oh John, what was all that about?"

"To be honest I've no idea," he said as he scratched his head as though that little motion would help convince me of his truthfulness.

"Hmm."

"What, don't you believe me?"

"Look John I leave you for just five minutes and come back to find you making a saucy home movie with some middle aged lady. So tell me now what am I supposed to think?"

"Nothing! Yes you're not meant to think anything."

"Well sorry but most guys leave it at least a week or two before they wander off with some bodacious Liz Taylor look a like."

"Tricia I've done nothing wrong. She just approached me and asked for my help and I gave it, simple as that. So before you mercilessly grill me like a ill tempered staff sergeant let's go back to the room to get changed, and then please can we go and find a restaurant as I'm starving hungry!"

I was extremely grateful that the ride down in the elevator was both short and sweet for I felt ridiculously uncomfortable as we both stood cramped and perilously enshrouded by half a dozen or more stern, businessmen impeccably dressed in expensive suit's, the air thick with the overwhelming smell of aftershave, their clean shaven faces peering down at me like I was some exceptionally rare fungus under a microscope. Feeling nervous I cleared my throat more times than I ought and kept my head hung low as I had no wish to make direct eye contact as, standing with my rat tail hair still wringing wet, my small towel draped around my half clothed body I pretended not to notice that I was dripping a thoroughly decent amount of chlorinated water onto their highly polished leather shoes. As soon as the elevator stopped at our number I brushed past as fast as I was able not even caring to look back to check if John was following on behind.

Before we went in search of food I insisted that we first go to the front desk to find out what was happening about our room change. The poe -faced manager was still unable to give us any positive news as to when another room would become available. The next few hours were spent trawling the streets desperately searching for a restaurant that would serve us recognizable food. Sad to say it was all Greek to us. We were paying a high price for our stupidity as, in the flurry of organizing a hurried wedding, we had given no thought to buying ourselves a Greek phrase book that might just help us communicate and perhaps translate a word or two of Greek. We were forced into trying a number of very suspect places as we yearned for a decent cup of coffee. Sadly all this took place way back in 1980 so Star Bucks had yet to rise to great heights to dominate the world with its wide range of aromatic coffee blends, we were therefore clean out of luck.

"John, forgive me but I can't even begin to drink this coffee, for it tastes like the thick sediment from the bottom of a coffee pot mixed with the contents of an old ashtray!" I announced as I immediately spat it back into the miniature cup. The owner winced at my undeniable indiscretion. "Please, do you have some Nescafe?" I begged in a pathetic voice hoping this might do the trick and cause him to produce some highly prized jar of granulated coffee otherwise a Macdonald's cup of coffee from out of nowhere!

"No understand," he replied in broken English while shaking his dark curly little head.

We pointed towards something that we hoped might taste similar to bread, but, as we struggled to swallow even one inedible mouthful we knew we were still at the mercy of the Greek gods who according to mythology seemed to favor misery over benevolence when it came to playing with the lives of ordinary human specimens such as the likes of us. The next café poured the same thick strong sludge into a larger mug, before filling it to the brim with ice cold goats milk. It tasted simply ghastly. I was indeed well on the way towards a full mental breakdown as I was suffering sleep deprivation, nervous exhaustion, hunger, and now severe coffee deprivation had added itself to my ever growing list of nervous complaints, but as insanity and madness were still some way off,

I was left to lick my wounds and whimper like a fragile broken animal. "Oh this is all so beastly. John please get me on the first plane home, for I can't take much more."

We arrived back at the hotel to news that they now had another available room for us to move to. Flashing a weak smile of gratitude we picked up the key and went in search of our new room. Things could only improve, or so we hoped. John fumbled around again with the key until finally the door opened. I stepped inside and yet again I was left speechless, for despite an absence of stalactites festooning the ceiling, this room smelt of stale sweat and Greek cigarettes, and, as I stood and surveyed the room, I noticed that the old wooden dressing table held a thick layer of dust and someone had very considerately taken the trouble to take their index finger and write some thought provoking message in the dust on the mirror, but as the message was in Greek we were both unable as well as unwilling to faithfully translate it.

"It probably says I was here in twenty B.C." my husband mournfully muttered.

"I don't agree, I think it says Gotcha, you stupid English idiots." I let go of my luggage and slumped onto the bed.

"This room hasn't been cleaned for months," I whined.

"Well, at least the bathroom's not cordoned off, although can you hear what I hear?"

"Yes, I think I can, and it's coming directly from that area." I wearily got up from the bed and went to investigate. "Goodness, it's the toilet, and it appears as though it won't stop flushing."

"Here let me take a look for I might be able to stop it," John called out as he came to join me in peering down the toilet. The next fifteen minutes were then spent with him tinkering about with the cistern, but sadly to no avail.

"I should've taken a plumbing course," he said gloomily.

"John, I'm sorry to say this but it's back down to the reception to pounce on the manager."

"Can't we leave it until later?"

"Sorry 'Mr. Let's Suffer in Silence' we're going downstairs to get this sorted once and for all."

Even with both of us tackling the management we were getting nowhere.

"John, we are clearly wasting our time. We urgently need to contact the tour operator and demand that they change our hotel, otherwise get us an early plane back to England for this is all truly intolerable."

"Honey I agree, but it's important to prioritize."

"What do you mean?"

"Well before we make that call I'm still literally famished so let's agree to go to the hotel restaurant for an early dinner, then afterwards we'll make that call."

As I looked into his pleading eyes I knew I had to bow to his wishes.

We stood at the restaurant door waiting to be seated but as my eyes nervously surveyed the room I was unable to see a single spare table.

"Bennett, come this way," the waiter said in broken English as he gruffly invited us to follow after him towards a table. A table that I might add, already had people sat down and half way through their dinner. I had hoped that as we were on honeymoon we would be given the privacy of our own small table, so we could whisper romantic sweet nothings into each others ear. Not that I felt the least in the mood for such things. We felt like intruders from the planet Zod as the waiter tapped his fingers on two vacant chairs to indicate that these were our allotted seats. The surly German couple were fuming at this sudden invasion of their space. In just a matter of seconds the gentleman abruptly reached over and like a petulant child with one clean sweep of his chubby oversized hand he pulled everything on the table, condiments included, over onto their side of the table.

"Right that's it! I'm not staying here a moment longer," I cried as I jumped up from my seat and stormed towards the exit door. John hurriedly followed after me.

"Tricia, I'm so hungry, and we've paid for all this, so I beg you, please stay."

"Sorry John, but I can't sit on the same table as that thoroughly rude and ungracious couple."

"But honey I'm desperate for just like you I spent most of the wedding reception talking to guests, I therefore hardly ate a bite of food, so I've got to eat for I'm starving and so are you."

"John, you're clearly not listening, I am not going back to a table where I am forced to eat alongside such arrogant people who believe they have the god given right to act with such unquestionably primitive behavior!"

"Okay… okay, but before you storm out of the restaurant, don't you think it might be a good idea to hand back their napkin?" he said wryly

"What?"

"Well honey, it's still hanging from your dress belt."

"Oh right here take it," I raged as I immediately swapped my anger for feelings of acute embarrassment at my latest blunder.

Tragically for John he would have to wait a bit longer to fill his belly, for my need to leave the restaurant and those dreadful people far outweighed my need to get something to eat. He tried to be understanding but he knew when he took me on that I was still struggling to find my way out of a painful past and in all fairness I had on numerous occasions been most faithful in warning him to 'think again' and in doing so find himself a more suitable easy going partner.

"If you're looking for normal, then go find someone else, for I really don't fit that category, and there's every chance I never will."

Clearly he had not given my challenging words enough thoughtful consideration! Truth is he left my life for a whole eighteen months while he mulled things over, so right now he was facing the full blown consequences of allowing romantic love to override rational clear thinking reason. He was in way over his head, and, much like Titanic on her maiden voyage, he too was seriously floundering and on the verge of sinking into a bottomless pit.

"Honey Pie, please can we go back and sit down for I am beginning to feel quite weak and faint," he gloomily begged as he slowly trailed behind me.

"John feel free to stay and eat for that's fine by me, but I'm leaving."

For a second he faltered like he was weighing up whether to take me at my word and head back to his seat if only to hurriedly stuff a plate of Greek samplers down his throat in record time, but the man was finally learning wisdom for having weighed up the consequences he decided it was in his best interests to ignore all griping stomach pains to simply follow after me.

It was now Monday evening, and our second day of our increasingly eventful honeymoon and still we had yet to eat. My gentle half starved husband was now struggling to shoulder the burden of this relentless Greek tragedy that seemed to be constantly unfolding itself further. After much pleading I agreed to leave the hotel to try once more to find ourselves a restaurant. Finally, after walking a considerable distance we came upon a small clean looking roadside café where, in a state of undeniable depression, we sat down to share a large crusty roll filled with unidentifiable meat, followed by a very sweet desert consisting of filo pastry, drizzled with honey and nuts. As we sat together, but inconsolably alone, we also drank more than our fair share of rough Greek ouzo, for with no translators to call on and no phrase book to flip through, we no longer considered ourselves the remotest bit capable of finding somewhere that sold either a recognizable brand of soda or a remotely drinkable cup of coffee. Now it is necessary to again establish that this all took place way back in 1980, when personal cell phones had either to be invented otherwise were in their infancy, so unless one wished to carry a portable one the size and weight of a large piece of masonry stone, you were at the mercy of the hotel, otherwise the Greek street vendors.

On our way back towards the hotel we tried a number of small roadside kiosks as we tried to make contact with our courier. Perhaps the number we'd been given was incorrect, but one thing for sure was the Greek phone system was not famed for its reliability, so, as we trailed from one outdoor kiosk to another we were having no luck getting through. Rogue vendors took our money even when they knew their phones were out of order, but we were too defeated to argue for our drachmas to be returned.

By the time we arrived back at the hotel I believed myself to have completely given up, when out of the blue I experienced a very unexpected surge of moment defining determination. Maybe it was the result of too much ouzo but, fuelled up I was, I handed the receptionist a piece of paper that held the number of our travel courier. Then, relying mainly on hand gestures, I stood at the desk in my best confrontational mode and demanded that she phone the number, the time for any further small talk being well and truly over! At first she played the 'I no understand' game but, as my mean glare burned into her ashen face, she quickly came to fully appreciate the seriousness of the situation. We needed help and we needed it now! A meeting with the rep was arranged for the very next day

"Is late afternoon alright with you guys?" Loretta our tour guide asked in a disgracefully cheery voice.

"No way! We've already endured two of our seven day honeymoon at Hotel del Disgusting! It's tomorrow morning or else!"

I carefully noted that the inhospitable manager who had always struggled to comprehend a single word of English now seemed to have his own personal epiphany that rather miraculously saw him masterfully translate my every utterance to the point where he promptly raised a disturbed eyebrow at my unkind but accurate reference regarding his hotel.

"Okay ..Okay... I hear you, there's no need to get your knickers in such a twist!" Loretta offensively shouted back down the phone. I swallowed the insult, despite wishing to wring her officious little neck. We had very little sleep that night and it had little to do with anxiety over our forthcoming meeting, and more to do with a constantly flushing toilet. The next morning found us anxiously sitting in the hotel foyer as we waited for Loretta our personal courier to turn up. Much as I suspected the meeting was not to be a pleasant affair, but we were determined to air our grievances! We demanded that she come and see our original room, however the management were now strangely unable to find the right key. Not to be deterred we insisted she accompany us back to our newly appointed room so she could see for herself that our complaints were seriously justified.

We walked our fingers through the dust and her only response was to heave a heavy sigh.

"Loretta I don't suppose you're up to translating the message on this mirror are you?" I cheekily asked. "No I didn't think so. Both of us are inclined to believe that it's Alexander the Great's last calling card, so what do you think?" She was not the least bit amused.

"Be honest Loretta, would you be happy sleeping in a room where the toilet in the bathroom en suite is continuously flushing?" John quietly asked.

"Well no, but the Greeks are well known for their poor plumbing. Yes it's a historical fact that...."

"Look Linda, Lulu, Lola or whatever your name is, may I remind you that we are on our honeymoon and, so far, it has been the honeymoon from hell. And, as much as we would love to take up the cause of the poor sewage systems of Greece, sadly we are only interested in being moved to another hotel," I interjected as, on the brink of losing all patience, I threw her a hostile glare.

"Oh alright, I'll get you moved to another room," she bristled.

"Excuse me, but we don't want another room. We've had two already

AND in less than two days, so if you do the math we only have five days left, and as we haven't the time nor the inclination for another round of musical chairs, we want to change hotels," John very solemnly and firmly spoke out.

"Oh I don't think I can do that," she sniffed her eyes shifting to the ground as she refused to make any further contact with us.

"We're not asking you, we're telling you. We want to change hotels, or fly us back to England right now."

How I wish we had taken pictures of the first room not only for the courier to reluctantly admire but perhaps also for an English Judge to muse over and fully appreciate on our return to England, but legal redress was the last thing on our minds at that point in time. About an hour later there was a hard knock on our hotel door. The news was music to our ears.

"Right I have arranged for you to be moved to another hotel, this time in Glyfada. However there is one small condition."

"Oh and what's that?"

"Well, if you accept the transfer, then you are expected to pick up the taxi cab bill." We readily agreed. We wasted no time packing up our belongings and we climbed into the back of the cab grateful in the knowledge that our nightmare was now reaching its finality. As we sat huddled in the back of the taxi we privately promised ourselves that even if it was the last hotel standing we would never ever return. However some promises are meant to be broken for unbeknown to me, I had packed in such a hurry, that I left the room leaving some important items behind in a drawer, items that once missed would force John to return all the way back to this dreadful hotel and less than a day later!

CHAPTER FIVE

Wish You Were Here

The drive over to the next hotel turned out much more expensive that we had first hoped it would be, that said, as the taxi neared our hotel we began to feel the first real sense of excitement as from the car window we observed the most stunning beautiful white sandy beach with its shimmering deep blue sea. Joy instantly began to rejuvenate my downcast heart as I realized this change of hotel was meant to be.

"Wow it looks absolutely fabulous," I gasped giving John a playful squeeze, as the taxi swerved round to the main entrance. I felt like John Voight in Midnight Cowboy when, following the death of his dear friend Rizzo, he arrives at a plush Miami resort Filled with beguilingly beautiful bikini clad babes. We both admitted to feeling exhilarated for compared to the where we'd been living for the past two days, we'd finally arrived in the perfect paradise for honeymooners. The hotel was smart and pristine clean and, as we walked into the lobby, we truly believed our troubles to be a thing of the past.

After signing the register, the handsome well groomed manager asked if he could have a private word with us. "Mr. and Mrs. Bennett I must let you know that our hotel chefs have just gone on strike and so sadly there will be no cooked food during the remainder of your stay. Please do not despair for we will be providing a continental style buffet for breakfast and evening dinner." We shook our heads and smiled. After all we'd been through we couldn't have cared less for, as long as we had the long beach with golden sand, as well as the large inviting pool to squander away the rest of our time, we needed little else to make us contentedly happy.

With our room key clutched tightly in our hands we made our way across the lobby just in time to catch sight of a gentleman being dragged towards the elevator by two impeccably dressed waiters. The unruly looking man looked up at us and, despite having a pained look on his face he managed to throw us a mischievous smile, while making some very loud and disgustingly rude burps. As all three staggered into the elevator he then chose that very moment to throw up all over the poor waiters. I felt so sorry for the young waiters but for some unearthly reason I couldn't help breaking into a smile.

"I think it best if we go in search of another elevator," John quickly suggested.

"Oh John while I'm at it, I'm sorry for having been so down and miserable, it's just that..."

"Enough! Let's just try to enjoy what time we have left of our honeymoon, shall we?"

I responded by giving his hand a firm squeeze. Having taken another elevator up to our floor we excitedly made our way towards our room dragging our heavy luggage behind us.

John fumbled around as usual as he struggled to open the door. We pushed the door open, then wait for it! We stopped dead in our tracks, overcome with amazement as we encountered a very Greek man in his paint splattered overalls continue most nonchalantly to dip his brush into his pot before applying more paint to the bedroom wall.

"Hi I'm Niklaus, thee hotel's feex-it man," he announced his bright eyes dancing, his bushy moustache twitching as he broke into a friendly smile.

"Pleased to meet you, Niklaus." my husband politely responded.

"He looks a lot like Tom Conti the actor," I giggled.

"Please forgeeve mee, I'm just putteen thee finisheeng touches, and then I weel bee out of here in less than ten mineets," he cheerfully chirped.

We shook our heads before bursting into fits of laughter which didn't stop even when our handsome Michael Angelo, climbed over the balcony and then asked John if he would be kind enough to pass over his paint pots so that he could apply the finishing touches to the exterior walls. Within moments our infectious laughter triggered our confused painter to join in, although he had not the slightest inkling as to why we were now laughing like a couple of unhinged hyenas.

After our maintenance man finished the touch up job, he bade us a cheery farewell and disappeared, and we were finally on our own. After hastily unpacking our swimming gear we headed down to the pool for an overdue swim. The remainder of the afternoon was taken up by us peacefully lazing on sun beds. You could hear the gentle drone of determined bees as they searched for pollen in the nearby flower beds that were filled with a blaze of every imaginable color and it felt beyond words to finally be lying under the gaze of the warm sun with not a single care in the world, and it did much to caress my formerly shattered nerves. Despite the strike the waiters still managed to provide a tantalizing Grand buffet which more than satisfied our needs. After dinner we went for a long stroll along the beach, stopping only to gaze up at the stars that sparkled intensely like expensive diamonds as they littered the hauntingly dark skies. It was official ; we were now exceedingly happy and content!

Later that same evening, things took a turn for the worse, when I discovered I was unable to pee without experiencing the most excruciating burning pain that in no time at all had me in a state of total delirium.

"I'm going to die well before the nights out otherwise throw myself off the balcony if you don't get me immediate help," I bawled through a sea of tears.

"Oh perish the thought," my poor baffled man replied, and as he had no particular desire to become a widow just days after becoming a husband, he began taking my threats seriously enough to hurriedly make his way to the reception desk to make that urgent call for a doctor.

He was a nice aging Greek doctor who did his very utmost to comfort me, for he had seen my type before. On his way out of the room he kindly thought to reassure my new spouse that, despite all appearances to the contrary, I was not about to die.

"It's a classic case of honeymoon cystitis."

"Right and you say she will once again become normal if I get her some antibiotics."

"Yes that's correct."

"Tell me doctor how long before she becomes normal?"

I wanted to shout over "Never in a month of Sundays!" but I was in too much pain to bother.

"Hmm…Within say twenty four hours. Until then I would best advise that you leave her well alone," he said giving him a knowing wink. The good doctor had no need to advise him as such, for as my sorely vexed husband observed me dramatically thrashing around the bed, there were no obvious romantic thoughts whatsoever to be found in his now deeply troubled mind. The doctor wasted no time in handing over the prescription as well as his exorbitant bill that saw my dear husband instantly balk. However he had no time to quibble the amount for he was still very unnerved and distracted by my on going persistent and loud hysterical screams.

The dear doctor was absolutely correct in his prediction for, by the morning I was once more back to feeling almost human, that is until having woken up around six thirty in the morning I suddenly discovered I had left my purse in a drawer back at 'Hotel Disgusting.'

"Oh no, this is all turning into a ghastly affair," I cried.

"Now what?"

"Oh this is bad! You've got to go back."

"Back to where?"

"Our former hotel."

"Oh no I can't go back, really I can't. You must surely realize that it's much too far to go. Besides they've probably let the room out by now, so it's almost one hundred percent likely that your purse is no longer there."

"Honey, it's perfectly evident that they hardly ever properly clean the rooms, so there's every chance that my purse will still be hidden away in the top drawer."

"Do I have to go?"

"Yes you do."

"Well I still say you're sending me on a wild goose chase."

"John, it's my purse filled with my belongiongs, so you've got to go."

"Sounds like I don't have much choice in the matter," he muttered in disgruntled tones. So, without any food in his belly, he trundled off down to reception and for the next few hours I heard no more as, forced against his will he took a long bus ride back to Hotel Disgusting! It would be well over two hours later before he returned...

"Honey, you were right. It was still tucked away in the drawer."

"Oh John, I really appreciate all you've done since we got here. You're turning out to be such a star, and you must be really famished." I said as I looked down at his watch.

"Yes I am."

"Well come on let's go and see if there's any breakfast left, shall we?" I said giving him a small peck on the cheek.

Having had our fill at the breakfast buffet we were heading back to the bedroom when we again caught sight of the intoxicated gentleman that, on our arrival, was being dragged into the elevator by the waiters. This occasion found him sitting fairly upright on a stool at the bar, his speech slurred as he loudly offered to buy a drink to any unfortunate guest who happened to pass by. There was an undeniable tension in the vicinity of the open plan bar, with most guests hurriedly passing by while choosing to ignore him, their taut faces displaying something of their utter disapproval.

We were going to do likewise, but something made us stop to talk with him. He offered to buy us a drink, we declined but still we made our way to the bar to join him. An hour later and we were still standing at his side talking with him. His name was Peter and he told us that he was a teacher at a well known English Private school. The more he talked about himself the more fascinated we became. This extremely intoxicated but highly educated man had traveled the world, spent many months in a Turkish jail and done just about everything in life he shouldn't have. Now this might seem strange but we really warmed to him. Finally a tiny slightly dumpy but very pleasant woman appeared on the scene and she wasted no time introducing herself.

"My name is Yanka and I'm his wife."

"Hi there," we replied as we both reached over to shake her tiny trembling hand.

"Look, I'm sorry if he is bothering you."

We were quick to reassure her that it was us bothering him.

"Oh Peter, you're so very drunk and it's only just gone ten thirty in the morning," she cried, her strangled voice betraying years of unresolved pain and conflict as well as an unfamiliar foreign accent.

"Yanka, don't embarrass me in front of my new friends. Go away, for I'm staying here and having another drink," he muttered, showing great annoyance before gesturing to the amused bar staff to pour him another double whisky.

"Come on guys, please join me," he urged, his speech more slurred than ever.

"Oh Peter, you're such a naughty boy. I beg you to come back to our room right now. You must not have another drink," she cried, her severely lined face further creasing as she determined against all odds to win this latest battle. Peter smiled down at her, and despite his loud protestations, it was easy to see that underneath all the drink he was a little pussycat.

"Peter, if you go with Yanka and have a short rest, perhaps we can meet up later and maybe go for a stroll along the beach. How about it?"

Yanka suddenly gripped my hand tightly and looked me directly in the eye.

"You are so kind, for let me say, most people mock him and, knowing he is blind drunk, they still allow him to buy them drink after drink, but you two I can see you are very different," she said, her eyes moist with tears as she broke into a tender childlike smile.

"Thanks for the compliment, but we really meant what we said. We would like to meet up again when Peter is sober."

"I will try my best to keep him away from the bar then maybe we can meet up later this afternoon."

She kept her word, as did we. Late afternoon found us all going for a long walk along the beach. We even discovered a small kiosk where we were able to purchase a couple of disposable cameras. From then on we were clicking the camera at every given opportunity. As we shared food we shared something of our honeymoon story, and not surprisingly, they found it all unbelievable.

The next day we waved goodbye to Peter in his usual place at the bar, and joined a tour bus that would take us down to the quayside to board a Greek owned boat as we then headed out to sea in search of a few Greek islands. It turned into a most wonderful and thoroughly memorable day. The sea was richly blue and calm and the sun shone gloriously above us. We moored at one small island after another, their landscapes filled with little white washed houses, goats and weather beaten fishermen with smiling crinkly eyes and white beards. That special day I fell in love with Greece. It's people are humble and kind, yet they have a hidden fire within their souls. Put a glass of ouzo in their hand and they will dance until they drop. Give them a second glass and they will talk about their life and loves and will not stop until you drop!

Back at the hotel we were pleased to discover that Peter was not yet unconscious. Apparently he was holding out for our return, and this little fact touched me. That evening was so warm and balmy that the staff decided not only to give us a spectacular buffet but tonight we would have waiter service. It was at this event that we came face to face with many of the other guests to whom up until now we had only muttered the briefest polite "Good morning" as we stood in the elevator. As we made our way to the poolside deck we discovered that many of the guests were from Northern England and the one thing about northerners, they know how to put a smile on your face. We were in for an evening of rapid fire entertainment, and they did not fail to deliver, though sadly much of it was at the expense of the shy servile waiters, many of whom were young in years.

"Oy waiter what do yer call this 'ere soup?"

"Sir it's called Bourou Bourou."

"Okay I understand you borrowed it, but tell me what the heck's in it?"

"Sir it's made from vegetables and pasta."

"Well then Spiros have you got a can of Heinz tomato soup tucked away up your jumper?"

"I'm sorry sir, I don't quite understand."

"Well, I don't know why coz I'm speaking plain English. Look Spiros, have you got any other soup you can offer me?"

"No sir, tonight we only have the Bourou Bourou."

"I'll send you packing to Bora Bora if you can't find me something else," he snorted. "Bourou ..Bourou.... Bora Bora...ha..ha...," they all howled together like a pack of restless hyenas as they broke into fits of uncontrollable laughter. It was one round of jokes after another. As I watched and listened on feeling a little ashamed of my fellow compatriots, I also considered how amazingly easy it is too laugh at anything or anybody after a few Retsinas and ouzos.

"Eh Zorba, where's me pud?" a rotumbular curly haired gentleman, dressed only in swim shorts and sporting an excessive, wildly overgrown forest of fuzz on his chest rudely shouted out to a passing waiter. "And Janice me missus is also needing something, go on Janice love, just tell im."

"Yeah Spiros, I've been waiting over an hour for me salad dressing," his equally cumbersome wife yelled as she reached over to grab the arm of another unsuspecting waiter.

"Tell me Janice, how do you know his name is Spiros?" I challenged.

"I don't, but it seems to me that wherever we go, at least half the waiters round here are called Spiros," she said throwing back her head to screech some more.

"Ere, come to think of it, where are you from? Coz you don't alf talk with a plum in yer mouth," she said giving me a quick frosty glare.

The gracious waiter interrupted the intense conversation with some delicious looking biscuits which he carefully placed down beside our temperamental gentleman.

"Sir, your dessert."

"Eh Zoltar, I asked for some pud, so what do yer call this 'er muck?" he snorted as he continued to mock and intimidate the poor confused waiter.

"I think they call it dessert," I loudly chipped in as I fervently wished to bring an abrupt halt and thus spare the poor demoralized waiter any further humiliation from Fuzzy Bear's very demeaning remarks.

"All the same to me squire," he retorted in his thick northern accent.

"Sir, they are known here as Koulourakia."

"Goodness, that sounds dreadfully painful, is it terminal? Er Sharon darlin' didn't you have a bit of Koulouraki when you had that awfully painful back pain."

"No yer daft idiot, that's called Racki." she howled with laughter.

"Same difference."

The patient waiter, who had graciously stood to one side while their juvenile banter continued, believed it might be helpful if he stepped back into the conversation, if only to explain the desert to the discontented guest.

"Well sir, as you ask, they are delightful cookies made from the finest olive oil, of this I assure you."

"I'll dip you're little Greek arse in olive oil, if you don't bring me a nice bowl of Jam Roly Poly or Spotted Dick with custard!" he tittered as Janice and his other friends continued on with their raucous laughter

"They're from up north, so they know nothing of proper manners," I quickly informed the dreadfully confused waiter. Lucky for me they were so worse for the wear that they took no offense.

"Now don't you southerners start thinking you're better or posher than us," Janice shrieked as she took a further slug from her fourth or was it her fifth glass of Retsina. If the waiters had endured enough so had we, so we hurriedly excused ourselves from the party and headed down to the beach in search of Peter and Yanka who, having finished their dinner well before us, told us to come and find them when we were ready.

That same night we had also learnt that many of the other guests had being upgraded from far cheaper more basic hotels. What caught our attention was none of them had been required to pay their own transfer costs. During our stay we managed to obtain a travel catalogue only to discover that our Athens hotel was hugely more expensive than the one we were now staying at, yet there had been no talk whatsoever of refunding us the balance, and that did not sit well with either of us.

Over the next few days Yanka plucked up the courage to tell us something of her desperate and abused life in Poland and how Peter had come to her rescue. In truth she had little need to give us the finer details for her severely pained face bore serious testimony to the relentless and tough challenges she had been forced to endure over many years.

Our last few days together were a pleasant whirlwind of walking along beaches, visiting tiny churches, Greek shrines, market stalls and tucked away café bars where Peter showed himself to be quite the knowledgeable expert when it came to tasting sumptuous Greek food that slid effortlessly down our throats. Sadly there were still a few occasions when he was a little worse for the wear, but we easily forgave him the odd indiscretion for we really found ourselves completely absorbed and mesmerized by many of his highly questionable but amusing stories, and therefore his friendship and company were much appreciated.

Much too quickly we arrived at our last night. I felt a deep sense of sadness for, not only did I loathe the inevitable parting of company, but I wished for us to stay and walk the endless silk sand shores barefoot, while staring up at the stars each warm and balmy night, as well as eat moussaka and stifado by the plateful while cherishing the hysterically colorful antics of Peter.

On this last night together Peter produced a poem he had written for us.

"Call it a belated wedding present," he declared.

As he read the poem out loud I could not stop laughing.

"Peter admit it! You certainly weren't sober when you wrote this," I challenged.

"I was!" he sniffed pretending to be hurt.

"Well it could have been written by a six year old… It's so childishly ridiculous that I'd hate to be one of your students. What's worse is you claim to have taught in a top private school!" I giggled.

"Tis true," he said giving an impish child like smile.

He was quick to forgive my unforgivable insolence. That last memorable night we walked for miles along the beach, dipping our sand encrusted toes into the warm frothy sea while talking our tongues off. It was way past bedtime before we bid them goodnight. "John, we'll see you first thing tomorrow and don't forget to write your address and telephone number down for us."

"Ditto."

We were both in a deep slumber when suddenly we were woken by loud and frantic banging on our door. "What on earth is going on?" John cried out as in the dark he reached out to pick up the alarm clock.

"My goodness, it's only two in the morning, so the hotel must be on fire," he muttered as he leapt from the bed and staggered across the room to answer the door.

Surprise… surprise! It was none other than Loretta our courier.

"You've got to get up and leave now," she brashly ordered.

"What now? But it's two o'clock in the morning!"

"Don't argue, just do as I say. The coach will be leaving in precisely ten minutes with or without you."

"Ten minutes?"

"Yes, and I repeat if you're not on board, I assure you it will leave without you."

The next few minutes were truly frantic as in an stupefied daze we stumbled around the room haphazardly stuffing our suitcases with all our belongings,

"I can't believe this. I didn't pack the suitcases before now because I thought we had until midday tomorrow," I wailed.

"Apparently not," John murmured.

"Oh and goodness we never even got to say our proper goodbye to our friends. We haven't even exchanged addresses," I moaned.

"Sorry honey, but there's nothing we can do about it, for we can't risk the coach leaving here without us."

Having made it down to the front lobby we were ordered to find ourselves a seat on a coach filled with other equally exhausted and disgruntled guests. As we made our way towards the first available seats John turned and whispered in my ear. "My goodness, the stench of vomit is truly unbearable."

"Yes you're right it's bad. But don't just tell me, tell Loretta, after all she's sitting over there," I said pointing down the coach to where she sat with her head hung low in defeat.

"Loretta, are you aware that this coach absolutely stinks of vomit?"

"To be honest Mr. Bennett, I don't care diddly squat about anything anymore for I feel sick to the back teeth," she cried.

John knew better than to stay and argue, so he hurriedly rushed back to his seat.

"I have no idea what's going on, but she appears to be in no fit state to be a courier or to shed any further light on this matter. So we've no other choice than to grin and bear it."

Once at the airport we were shocked to discover that we would have to spend the rest of the night sitting on the concrete floor of the airport for every seat was occupied and our plane was, believe it or not, not due to leave until two o'clock the next afternoon!

As the plane circled Gatwick Airport back in the UK, awaiting communication from the tower that we could begin our descent down, the very kind pilot felt strongly compelled to give us an up to date report on the weather conditions. I could not fail to detect more than a hint of mischievousness in his voice.

"Ladies and gentleman, this is your Captain speaking, if all goes well we hope to be landing in Gatwick in about ten minutes, but I regret to inform you, even though it is still only early October, it is snowing and well below freezing. Have yourselves a nice day! Oh, and if Rudolph the red nosed reindeer and his sleigh are not available at your pick up point, then it might be advisable for you to purchase some snow boots on your way out of the airport."

"That mean pilot really enjoyed giving us that piece of news," I sniffed as shivering in my thin short sleeved tee shirt and open toed shoes I leant over to glance out of the window.

"Oh my goodness, I can't believe it!" I cried, as leaving the airport, we were met by freezing snow, as well as harsh freezing gale force winds, that immediately bit into our flesh like a million sharp needles.

We arrived back in our small home town to discover that the house we believed we had just purchased had in fact fallen through while we were away. We were now officially homeless! Then, to cap it all, John arrived home from work the very next day with the news that, due to staff cuts, he had just been given two weeks notice at the furniture store where he had been working the past six months!

I shook my head in disbelief. "They only allowed you one week off for your honeymoon even though you requested two. So to do this on your first day back stinks," I cried.

With things as they stood, we had no choice other than to search for a new home, as well as new jobs for both of us, but that still did not prevent me from finding the time to write a very stiff letter to our tour company. Many weeks later we received a short letter of apology, along with a paltry fifty pound check! The travel firm in question only survived another year before going under, but still to this very hour, I regret not having taken things much further!

Once we were finally settled into our first home I immediately set about sticking the holiday snaps as well as Peter's special wedding poem into the back of our wedding album and while doing so I found myself rereading his poem. It made no sense to me that a man as highly intelligent and so jolly educated would write something so simple and absurd, but then one day I got it. For under his flimsy veneer of exceptional intelligence as well as too much wealth for his own good, lay a very misunderstood Peter Pan who reveled in the silliness of children's cartoons and living on the edge, in preference to living in moderation within the confines of an insanely ordered world. As I closed the book I felt a deep sadness that due to our hurried departure we had failed to exchange addresses so the likelihood of ever hearing from them again was indeed very remote. I was therefore amazed when many years later I answered the doorbell and the two of them were standing in front of me, large smiles on their faces.

Incidentally, on our return from Greece, I placed my wedding dress in a boutique that sold expensive second hand clothes, for sadly my house was too small to store the dress. A couple of months later when I hadn't heard anything I paid the shop a visit only to discover the building was empty. Yes it had gone into liquidation and the very considerate owners had left town leaving no forwarding address!

CHAPTER SIX

Don't Mention the War

I was sitting at my desk immersed in writing this book when John shouted for me to drop what I was doing and come into the sitting room. Moments later found me standing in front of the television, a smile of incredulous disbelief on my face, as with avid interest I listened to the story unfold. The date was Thursday 14th July 2011, and John had been watching ABC's Nightline. The subject under revue was the continued war between the Brits and the Krauts and as the news item reported it had nothing to do with Hitler and the Third Reicht and more to do with hotel sun beds!

"How come they are only now reporting on a feud that has existed for forty odd years or more?" I murmured.

I couldn't stop laughing when they showed unbelievable footage of hotel staff hurriedly unlocking the patio doors before standing to one side lest they were accidentally trampled underfoot by a stampede of Krauts and Brits as they raced and fought each other to be first to get that highly prized sun bed on the pool deck.

"It's a real bun race," I giggled as I watched the footage with a mixture of amusement and horror.

"Yes it's hard to believe that all these years later it's still going on," John replied.

The Nightline reporter would stun us further by saying that Thomas Cook our main tour operator in England was now selling the Germans' holidays that came with their own guaranteed sun bed. The cheek of it!

What about us Brits? Hadn't we suffered enough? Truth is my dear hubby and myself had much grievous experience on this touchy subject matter and it didn't stop at hotel sun beds! I had my first encounter with what I have come to term the 'Gerry crisis' when I was on honeymoon in Greece, and it would reach over into many other holidays that we took in the coming years.

This ongoing 'Clash of the Titans' was such a hot topic many years back, that in 1993 a British beer company cleverly cashed in by making a brilliantly amusing advertisement for primetime television. You can view it on 'You Tube' under Carling Black Label promotion 3. Better still if you view the Carlings 'Dambuster' advert first it will make it all the funnier.

Now I need to make it clear that despite the next few chapters being about our difficult encounters with our European brothers I hold no grudge or malice against them or their nation, I am just regaling stories as they happened. Also since opening my tearoom in Florida John and I have become firm friends with a number of delightful German couples who have hearts of gold. That said before I reveal anything of my own personal holiday frustrations with the Krauts, I would first like to tell you a little story concerning a very dear Irish friend of mine called Kate. Many years ago Kate was asked if she would be kind enough to play host to some foreign guests of Germanic persuasion who were coming to England for the weekend. All that was required of her was to provide Sunday lunch and then entertain them for the remainder of the afternoon.

Kate was easily the best cook and homemaker I'd ever known, what with her idyllic and quaint cottage that saw her country gardens brimming over with every imaginable flower that could easily adorn the glossy pages of 'Homes and Gardens' magazine. She was also known to be a first class entertainer hence the perfect host.

Kate immediately rose to the occasion by further cleaning her already spick and span cottage from head to toe. She spared no attention to detail as she sprung into action organizing and ensuring that her home be fit for a king. Her two boys were ordered to go off and collect bracken for the roaring log fire. Her gentle but slightly cumbersome husband was placed to one side in the sitting room along with the remote control of the television, while she in turn busied herself polishing the antique furniture until she could see her pretty small featured face smiling back. The white starch linen tablecloths were hurriedly brought down from the towering linen cupboard and were forbidden to grace the tables until they had been thoroughly inspected to ensure they were devoid of any small nuisance stains. The bathrooms were also given the same high level of attention with even the cherry wood loo seats being polished to such a shine you could well afford to eat your dinner from off them. Every room had an over abundance of large vases filled to capacity with bunches of the sweetest smelling woodland flowers, and she hadn't even got down to the baking!

Eventually, with the table laden with fine china and the smell of home baked bread wafting from the oven, she commandeered her husband and two sons, the youngest of which was around seven years old to follow her into the drawing room for a quick family tete-a-tete.

"Right boys, you've all done a grand job however before our distinguished guests arrive, I need to share something of great importance." They were all ears.

"I have been forewarned that our guests are very prickly when it comes to anything concerning World War 2, after all it is less than fifty years since that terrible war ended, and many people of German descent are still heavily burdened by it. Therefore I need a promise that none of you will make any reference to Hitler or the war."

"Why mummy?" her little wide eyed seven year old innocently asked.

"John darling, this is not open to debate. It just is. Everyone readily agreed there would be no careless talk, therefore not so much as a hint or inference with regards Hitler, the Gestapo or the Third Reich, no nothing whatsoever about that darned war."

Sunday came, and the highly esteemed guests arrived and were immediately given a spot of calming Jasmine tea to encourage them to further relax and unwind. The conversation was light but friendly and so it seemed everyone was enjoying themselves.

With the dining table laid with her finest silverware, Kate smiled and inwardly praised herself for all the food was as usual cooked to absolute perfection. The roast beef was a blushing pink, the Yorkshire puddings had risen to new mountainous heights, the crispy roast potatoes were a sumptuous golden brown and the delicious vegetables had a delightfully wholesome crunch. As for the gravy? Well that was lavishly thick and bursting at the seams with extravagant flavors. With all the food now garnishing the dining table she called for everyone to make haste and come to the table to be seated.

Having given the task of saying the grace to the German gentleman everyone closed their eyes, and bowed their heads as they waited on him to bless the meal. This he did in his best but broken English, his accent heavily betraying his Germanic roots. With the blessing at an end he then opened his eyes only to make a shockingly loud and dismayed gasp. For sitting across the table he beheld Kate's youngest son determinedly holding his dinner knife just above his top lip like a moustache, and before Kate could do anything to stop him, his other arm suddenly shot defiantly into the air and at the top of his lungs he shouted "Heil Hitler!"

Kate's jaw dropped lower than that of her highly esteemed guests. They in turn immediately began to cough and splutter, their stern faces redder than their iced raspberry tea. Kate then expended a exasperated gasp. Her guests followed suit. Not to be outdone her older son gave an embarrassed titter, and what of her husband? Well he nonchalantly continued on drinking his tea as he very much preferred to pretend that none of this was happening. Kate dropped the pan of hot roast potatoes she was holding and immediately raced around the long table until she arrived at the spot where her young son was still innocently sitting with an arm raised high in the air, the knife still balanced above his top lip. She very diplomatically struggled to remove the offending item from the clasped hand of her wickedly mischievous son. But deep in her heart she knew it had all come to late. The dastardly deed was irreversible, the damage irreparable, and, as she looked over at her guests twitching distorted faces, she knew there was nothing she could say or do to paper over this highly embarrassing incident that quickly had her thinking might easily bring about the start of World War 3

"Please excuse him for he's only seven, so he doesn't really understand these things," she mumbled, while praying for the floor to open up and swallow her whole. I creased up with laughter when, in her own inimitable Irish way, Kate first shared this funny but painful story. Since that time John and I have faced many a crisis with our European counterparts and, just like Kate, it took many years before we too could look back and laugh.

There came a day when walking along the high street that we briefly chose to stop outside our local travel agents. Posted in their window where plenty of last minute bargains.

"Wow, look John, Tunisia for a whole two weeks is only one hundred and ninety nine pounds!"

"Tricia, when you wind up staying in the toilet hut at the bottom of a Turks garden, with a long camel ride to the nearest shops, you might not think it such a bargain. It's important to get more facts before you consider something to be a bargain." I wasn't listening.

"Well look, there's Florida on a fly-drive for only three hundred and ninety nine pounds, what do you think?"

"Hmm."

"Oh please let's go in."

"Sorry honey but we've run out of time, otherwise I will be late for my afternoon appointments."

"Oh, it won't take more than ten minutes and you promised me that we would try for a second honeymoon as our first was such a catastrophic disaster. So please why don't you let me sort out a holiday, as I have much more time on my hands," I persuasively moaned

"Alright then, if you want to come back this afternoon and see what's available, but please don't book anything without first talking to me."

"It's a deal!"

I waited until he'd eaten supper before I once more broached the delicate subject.

"John, I'm sorry to say this but, by the time I got down there, all the bargains were already gone."

"They always are when you want one," he quipped.

"Yes well I did manage to find us another holiday in Greece, however this time, it's not on the mainland, but on the island of Crete."

"Sounds nice."

"Promise me now that you'll listen to everything I have to say before you rule it out."

"Hang on there, it's well out of our price range."

"Yes I know, but you did promise we would have a second honeymoon as the first one was such a doomed affair," I said as I masterfully played my trump card. "So please say yes…..please."

"Look honey, I don't wish to appear mean, but it's such a lot of money for just one week."

"Go on, please just say yes. I'll live on stale bread and water for the entire vacation if it means you'll say yes," I begged, giving him my best soppy puppy dog look.

There was a long moment of silence.

"Please.. please say yes," I quietly whispered, placing my arms around his neck as I prepared to give him a cuddle otherwise choke the living daylights out of him depending on his response.

"Oh alright then, but only on one condition."

"Anything! You name it."

"Well, when we arrive at the airport, either end, I don't want you asking anybody we meet what they forked out for their holiday."

"Of course not."

"Look Tricia I really do mean it. It seems that every holiday we go on, you meet someone who paid half what we paid, yet has an upgraded room with a colossal balcony, along with the perfect sea view, meanwhile our room is two feet short of a cramped airing cupboard, and if we're lucky enough to get a balcony it normally has a panoramic view of the staff car park or better still the community rubbish dump. It's so discouraging, really it is."

"My lips are sealed, and I promise hand on heart that I will ask nobody whatsoever," I announced giving him an exuberant hug as well as a friendly peck on the cheek.

At the time of giving my word I truly meant it, really I did, but having just landed at Heraklion Airport in Crete we were then ordered by the tour operator to go and stand at a special bay while they sorted everybody into separate groups to then board various coaches that would take us all to our different hotels. Well things just happened, so there's nothing more I can say in my defense.

"Bennett!" the tour guide loudly called out as we haplessly stood in a long line outside the airport terminal.

As our name had just been called we quickly grabbed our suitcases and walked forwards. We were surprised to see another couple do likewise.

"Right Bennett one and Bennett two, if you'll just go and stand over there, your coach will be pulling in shortly and it will take you to your hotel.

"Honey, can you believe these good people are also called Bennett!" I whispered as we dragged our luggage towards where we had been instructed to stand.

"Well it's quite a common name."

"Hi there, my name's Tricia and my husband here is John."

"Nice to meet you, I'm Sandra and this here is Steve," she stated in a 'no nonsense' northern accent that allowed me to believe we were now best friends, at least for the duration of this holiday.

We had only just exchanged names when quite innocently the unthinkable happened.

"Tell us Tricia, have you any idea what sort of hotel we are going to be staying at?"

"What do you mean?" I innocently asked as I clutched the rolled up details of the hotel in my hand.

"Well as of yet we've no idea where we're going. We got this special deal see, and all we know is we're booked in at the same hotel as you."

"Wow you're having me on, aren't you?" I quizzed, as I checked Sandra's face in my search for the truth.

"No I don't think so."

"You mean to tell me, that you booked this holiday without first checking to see where you were going?" I queried in a tone of pure disbelief.

"Well we couldn't turn it down, for it was an offer we simply couldn't refuse. It only cost us a hundred pounds AND it's for a whole two weeks, isn't that right Steve!"

I was now hyperventilating, for we had paid almost seven hundred pounds and our holiday was for just one week!

"Are you alright?"

"Yes I think so. Sorry but the intense heat is really beginning to affect to me," I lied as I continued rather deliriously to sway back and forth while fanning myself with the rolled up hotel details that I was still clutching in my hot sweaty hand.

"Yes the only downside to the deal, if you could call it a downside, was that it entitled the tour operators to place us in the hotel of their choice. Presumably this way they get to fill up the rooms in some of the lower grade emptier hotels, so it's a win-win situation for everybody concerned."

"My goodness I've never heard of such a thing."

"Hmm.. It was a bit pot luck wasn't it Sandra? Yes a bit of a risk as to whether we got something nice and comfy as opposed to some awful dump," her husband kindly interjected.

I was now frothing at the mouth and heading full throttle towards a full blown seizure.

"That's why we've still no idea where we're headed. Do you think it'll be alright?" Steve dared to ask.

"Yes… yes the hotel is four star. It's right on the beach and it's got everything you could wish for, here take a look," I said as I very graciously handed over the very scrunched up piece of paper that I still had tightly clutched in my sweaty hand. I was now feeling extremely hot and disorientated.

"Ooh, it looks right lovely, yes we've really hit the jackpot!" Steve interjected as he gently placed his arms around Sandra's sickeningly tiny waist to give her a little appreciative cuddle. Personally speaking I wanted to punch both of them.

"And we have full board. Yes breakfast, lunch and dinner!"

"Full board!" I hysterically cried as I grabbed hold of the rail in front of me, my eyes bulging from their sockets as I seriously considered collapsing to the ground to have my own very personal grand petit mal. John on the other hand chose to remain curiously silent.

"John, not only are they staying a week longer, but it's full board and yet we paid six times as much," I hissed through gritted teeth as we followed after the courier dragging our luggage behind us as we headed for the bus. I was now feeling emotionally bankrupt and we hadn't even left the airport!

"Psst.. John I cannot believe this is happening to us," I miserably whispered.

"Well, if you care to cast your mind back, you might just remember that we had ourselves a deal," he grunted.

"What deal?" I hissed back.

"Tricia, you absolutely promised not to ask anybody what they paid for their holiday."

"I didn't ask them, they offered up the jolly information," I informed him through clenched teeth. "And answer me this, what are the chances of arriving at the other end of the earth only to discover that the couple standing next to you not only share the same surname but are going to the same hotel, and on a ridiculously amazing deal?"

"You have a point."

"Quite! Yes well I know you're displeased with me but as they are the only other couple going to our hotel, it was only natural to start up some sort of conversation. I was just being polite and now forgive me but I jolly well hate them," I moaned.

"Well, let's just make the best of it, shall we?" he said as he placed a comforting arm around my waist to give me a squeeze.

"I'm sorry really I am," I sniffed as I continued to struggle with this latest harsh blow.

The hotel was coldly uninviting and so expansive that we felt like we'd never left the airport. Even our shoes click clacked across the cold flagstone floor as we dragged our luggage towards the nearest available elevator. Once we hit the right floor we were further surprised by the long corridor that seemed to go on for miles.

"I've never been in such a big hotel and it's not at all homely," I casually commented.

Making our way to our room, and later through the night, you could hear the constant loud bang of closing doors made worse by the total absence of carpeting on the floors and completely bare walls so there was nothing to absorb the harsh grating noise. It was at this point that I hoped with all my heart that I had remembered to pack my earplugs.

The room was unpretentiously modern and clean, and, as I peered into the bathroom, I was delighted to see that, though basic, it too was clean and happily it had that 'must have item,' yes a toilet roll. I'm also happy to report that the entire Greek sewage problem must have been sorted out since our honeymoon for we were not subjected to the sound of repeatedly flushing loos all night. That said we still struggled to sleep due to an excess of crashing doors and brash intoxicated guests whose noise echoed loudly down the sparsely furnished, uncarpeted corridor, so two in the morning found me frantically rummaging through my belongings as I went in search of my CD player which thankfully I remembered had its own set of earplugs. John, on the other hand, was left to commit suicide by any means he cared to choose. He opted for slow suffocation as in a deranged state of mind he piled pillow upon pillow over his head in a forlorn bid to block out the noise. When this didn't work he even had the nerve to try and requisition mine, but to no avail!

The next morning, with hazy heads and jangled nerves we ventured down to breakfast, and were immediately thrown off guard by the loud clashing noise of large canteen metal vats and cutlery, as well as an overwhelmingly large number of distinctively strong German accents.

We finally found an empty table and much later a waiter actually willing to temporarily abandon the Krauts to come over and serve us. However, as the breakfast menu was more to the liking of our German counterparts, we struggled to find something on the menu we could face eating. Eventually we decided to pay extra and have eggs and bacon with toast specially cooked for us. However, while we waited for the food to come, I suddenly began to feel most peculiar.

"John something feels very wrong," I muttered.

"Honey what is it?" he asked a display of great concern written all over his face.

"I don't know. I suddenly feel awfully queasy and the whole room has started to spin."

"Here drink this glass of water," he suggested as he placed a glass in my hand.

I did as I was told, but by now I was sweating profusely.

"Tricia take a few deep breaths," he urged. "Look, here comes our food, get some of that down you, and you'll soon be feeling a whole heap better."

The waiter placed the plate in front of me and I took in a sharp breath as I beheld a plate of piled high scrambled eggs intermittently dotted with chillingly large globular pieces of grayish fat. John quickly thought to consult with the waiter.

"We asked for eggs and bacon, so what is this?"

"It's eggs and bacon sir."

"So dare I ask, where precisely is the bacon?"

The waiter pointed to the large fatty lumps of white gristle on my plate.

"Oh dear I thought as much," John muttered under his breath

I had held on bravely for long enough, so without giving any warning I jumped to my feet.

"John, forget the bacon, I need to get out of here," I cried as I began gasping for air.

Seconds later I wilted to a small heap on the floor. I came around only to discover hot food being wiped from my hair and face.

"What happened?" I mumbled.

"You fainted."

"Fainted?"

"Yes and unfortunately you took your breakfast plate with you," John informed me as he used a spare serviette to wipe the food from my face.

"Oh good grief."

"Honey don't worry, though I have to say you do give new meaning to the expression 'egg on your face'."

"Ho ho ho."

"Hmm.. not a really good time for your Father Christmas impersonation! And we may have to pay something for the broken plate."

"Oh dear, this is all so acutely embarrassing," I muttered as, helped by a couple of concerned waiters, I was lifted off the floor and back into my seat, the scrambled egg still falling from my clothes and hair as a whole sea of touristy faces looked on.

"Get me out of here quickly," I hoarsely instructed.

John ignored my pleas as he seemed more concerned in pulling the lumps of grisly fat and scrambled egg that were still interwoven into my hair.

"Is she pregnant?" a concerned waiter cheerfully asked, as he began patting his stomach as though it was now his turn in a spontaneous game of charades.

"No I don't think so." John replied with a worried glance my way.

"Definitely not," I abruptly interrupted.

"Then, shall we call a doctor?"

"No, no, no…Please just leave me, for I will be alright," I muttered in hushed tones as I refused all further eye contact with the waiter. "Please just get me a glass of iced water,"

"Honey, at least allow me to take you outside for a breath fresh air."

As I sat outside on a patio chair a waiter sidled up to John and after asking after my health he handed the bill for a breakfast that neither of us had managed to eat one single morsel of.

"Sir do you wish to pay now, or shall I add it to your room," he politely asked.

John stood up and quickly glanced over the bill. "Well I guess I should be grateful for one thing."

"Oh and what's that?"

"At least it doesn't include the broken plate," he whispered as he produced some notes from his wallet which he then handed to the waiter. "Thank you and keep the change."

Apart from that rather dramatic and embarrassing breakfast episode there would have been little else of consequence to report that entire week, except that this hotel was utterly dominated by loud brash beer swilling German tourists. When some time later I found myself standing next to a fellow Brit and his pretty wife I was finally enlightened.

"The names Albert and me missus here is Darlene, and allow me to help you out for, since Freddy Laker went bust, not too many Brits are coming to this part of Greece. I'm afraid to say this but, just like the war, the Krauts have conquered the whole of Europe's best holiday destinations so we've got no choice than to grin and bear it."

And it was really true. They commanded the best rooms with the best views. In the huge dining room they bullied the staff into serving them before all other foreigners. Not satisfied with that, they also completely dominated the pool deck, forming a human chain of seriously overweight pasty white bodies sitting back to back on chairs, making it virtually impossible to get past them and into the pool. Most opted to wear apparel that one might be forgiven for assuming was best kept for the privacy of the bedroom, as their tiny leather thongs left nothing to the imagination and made them look like retired Sumi wrestlers, their grossly oversized bellies and sagging bottoms flopping all over the place.

"My goodness, John it's way beyond indecent! I cannot believe the hotel allows them to strip down this far," I whispered as feeling intimidated we gingerly attempted to get past a wall of near naked heavy set bodies in our attempt to get to the pool.

"Excuse me," I said loudly as I found myself blocked by the stocky legs of a couple of feisty bare breasted Frauleins who were inconsiderately blocking the walkway and not letting anyone pass. They were both reluctant to move to let us past.

"John, forgive me but I'm about to shout out Heil Hitler any minute now," I threatened.

"Don't you dare," he hissed back.

"Why ever not?"

"Don't even think of it," he glowered back at me.

"Try and stop me," I challenged.

"I will if I have too."

"Oh yeah, you and whose army?"

"Tricia, behave yourself for you don't want to start another war, do you?"

"Oh I think I do."

With our swim over, the search was now on to find an unclaimed sun bed but, alas there were none to be found, and this would be the case every day throughout our entire holiday. It didn't matter if we got up at the break of dawn we would still stand on the pool deck scratching our heads as our eyes surveyed the entire location with every single chair and bed coveted by a laid out towel and every parasol and table taken. What was more confusing was there was not a single sun starved body fat or thin lying down on even one of them! This would continue to puzzle us until once again we were tipped off by the ever so friendly and equally informative Albert and Darlene.

"Look guys these clever Krauts place their towels on the sun beds just as their heading off to bed."

"What the night before? Are you kidding?"

"Otherwise they sneak out at about 4.00 am in the morning and then head back to bed. If you're clever you'll notice that most sun beds remain completely unoccupied until around midday, that's because they sleep in late, otherwise they're nursing an almighty headache due to a hangover, for you should see the amount of beer they get through. It's no wonder they get all this unfair favor, for they really are the big spenders."

"Oh right.'

"Yes and don't start thinking that this special treatment is limited to just here, for it's going on all over Europe."

I believed all I was told that day, for as we forlornly made our way down the long corridor observing large collections of empty beer bottles outside many of the rooms.

Even if all this failed to offend, there was more on the way that guaranteed to dilate your pupils, give you hot flushes and send your heart into uncontrollable spasms. As we stood patiently in line at the poolside bar waiting our turn to order a hot lunchtime snack, many with a show of unbelievable arrogance pushed their way to the front in order to get served first. Their blatant disrespect for others who had waited patiently in line beggared all belief.

"How rude!" I loudly cried out on more than one occasion.

"Shh.. Honey! Keep your thoughts to yourself, for you don't want to pick a fight with a hundred or so sumo wrestlers, do you?"

"Oh yes I do," I lied.

"Well you're on your own, for I'm definitely not taking any of them on."

"Well quite frankly I've had just about enough of this fiasco for it happens day in, day out, and there's not so much as a pipsqueak out of anybody! So what's happened to us fearless Brits for standing in this long queue it appears we've become a nation of neutered wimps!"

"Have you seen the size of them?" John hissed through clenched teeth.

"Yes of course. What a stupid question."

"Tricia please keep your voice down," my poor husband begged.

"Whatever for?"

"Goodness, you can be so objectionable, I think it's time to press the mute button, or change channels, otherwise, put a sock in it."

"Excuse me for butting in on your conversation but…"

"No please do," I interjected as I turned round to make eye contact with a long haired gentleman who had the impertinence to join in this highly contentious debate. However, if he shared my views then he was very welcome to add his two penny's worth to this extremely volatile discussion.

"It's all down to the color of their money," the sandy haired boy readily informed us.

"What's wrong with our money?" I innocently asked.

"Nothing, except we haven't got enough and they've got too much!" came the informative reply.

"Oh great, so they still get to rule the world."

"So it would appear," the tanned man said giving a mischievous wink before turning round to finally give his order to the sweaty Greek chef standing behind the poolside bar.

"Two burger and chips, and while your at it, a cold beer would be much appreciated, as well as a club soda for me missus. Cheers mate."

As he turned to leave, his lunchtime snack precariously balanced on a lightweight tray, he gave us a wink and a smile. "They're here to stay, so We'd better just learn to grin and bear it."

"Yeah stiff upper lip and all that," I moaned

"Anyway guys, have a great day," he said as he then stuffed a couple of French fries into his mouth before turning to leave to go find his missus.

CHAPTER SEVEN

I Was Lost in France

I've heard it said innumerable times that we should place great importance on our words as they have some sort of cosmic influence, and therefore it's important to only speak what you wish to happen. We were about three years into wedded bliss of sorts when a girlfriend contacted me and asked if I would like to join some other girls on a trip to France.

"Honey, go, I think you'll really enjoy yourself," John did his best to persuade.

"I don't know John, there are still a thousand things that need doing since we moved to this house."

"Tricia, there's nothing that can't wait, besides you really love Christina and this opportunity might never arise again."

He was right. Christina had long since left town and I truly missed her, for she had been the best friend and flat-mate one could ever wish for.

"Alright, that's it, I need no further persuading, for I'm going."

As the time to leave approached I found myself feeling terribly excited about this girlie event, especially as since marrying I had rarely been anywhere without him. For, despite being twenty seven, I still hadn't learnt to drive a car or even open a bank account. I really left everything to John while I concentrated all my efforts on becoming or at least giving the appearance of being normal, which for me was like studying for a Masters Degree! People close to me would readily agree that I wavered on the 'scatty side,' and I have to admit it that every time I left the house something untoward always seemed to happen to me out of nowhere.

Why, only the week before, there had been trouble in the cinema and rather unwittingly I had been the root cause behind it all. It had been a hot summer's day and we had been walking along the promenade when we passed a large cinema complex.

"Oh, I've been longing to see that for that movie for some time," John casually commented.

"Well, we could make it to the six o'clock showing, if you like."

Heading back towards the cinema I realized I was still only half way through my can of soda, and as outside refreshments were not permitted inside the theatre I carefully wedged the can in the upright position in my shoulder bag.

After purchasing tickets we then brought ourselves the usual popcorn and a large soda to share.

"Here, you hold this," John said handing over the drink in order to show the tickets to the door man.

The cinema was packed and pitch dark, as they showed the trailers, and with my deficient eyesight I struggled to see where I was going.

"John help me for I can't see a bloomin' thing."

"Just stay close."

"In the good old days there would've been an usherette armed with a torch to help guide us. Haven't times changed, for nowadays we're left to play murder in the dark," I moaned.

"Ah… I see two empty seats over there," John whispered to me.

"Excuse me, can we just get through," John politely asked.

There were understandably a few huffs and puffs from annoyed moviegoers who, having settled down, now resented this untimely interruption. As I passed by one of the patrons, he had an extraordinary and unexpected outburst.

"What the dickens!" he exasperatedly cried, springing to his feet. The lady in the next seat then reacted in a similarly distressed manner, and so began a chain reaction as patron after upset patron began to leap to their feet with great gusto.

"What the blazes is going on?" one large lady shrilly demanded to know.

"I'm soaking wet," another hysterically announced.

I was still only halfway towards getting to my seat when I thought to turn around to see what the commotion was all about. As I peered down the line it seemed that everyone that had risen was now furiously wiping themselves down.

"Some darned idiot has just soaked the lot of us," a surly voice boomed out in my direction. I responded with a genuinely vacant look.

"Well, don't look at me! You're barking up the wrong tree for, as you can see, my drink is not only full but it also has a secure lid, and please note it's in my other hand, well out of harms way," I loudly exclaimed as I hurriedly held the large cup in full view of everyone.

Suddenly when I least expected, the penny dropped. "Oops!"

"Pst… John help me, for already I'm in trouble."

"So what's the problem?"

"I'll tell you once we're sitting down."

"Okay."

"Remember that half drunk can of soda I wedged in my shoulder bag. Well while I was trying to forge a pathway through a sea of legs the stupid can inadvertently upended."

"Oh no."

"Fact is half this row have been christened with a dash of diet soda."

"Oh dear."

"Yes and they're all terribly upset and angry so had we better leave now?"

"Don't be daft, with the lights out nobody is able to prove where and from whom the mystery shower came from. So just sit tight and act all innocent." he quietly suggested.

As this was just one more incident to become clocked up in what appeared to be a long list of curious events he would witness firsthand, so I was pleasantly surprised that he agreed to allow me to take any sort of outing without him, especially to a foreign country. Was he finally beginning to trust me? If this proved to be the case he was indeed a very foolish man.

"Tricia don't forget your passport, oh and your toothbrush as you'll be spending the night at Christina's before making the crossing," he cared to remind me.

The girls picked me up and we drove to the port of Newhaven. The Channel ferry crossing went smoothly and in less than four hours we arrived at Dieppe on the coast of Normandy in France. During the sailing I amused myself singing one of my favorite Bonnie Tyler songs entitled 'I was lost in France'. After disembarking the vessel Christina suggested that she be the one to take care of all our passports. I willingly agreed for I had a long history of losing vital documents, and this way I could relax, knowing my passport was in safe hands.

As we spent much of the afternoon wandering around Dieppe it became apparent that we all had very different interests when it came to shopping. Sue for instance had three children so she was desperate to buy some cute French children's clothes, Jackie's interest lay in purchasing some quality French wine, whereas Christina was longing to get her hands on some rather smelly French cheeses. As for me, I had no children at this point, and I wasn't that interested in wine or seriously pongy cheeses, but I had just started collecting pottery, so I was looking forward to delving into a few pottery shops in search of something different to add to my growing collection. I was about to give up on finding such a shop, when suddenly we walked past a window displaying some unique French pottery.

"Girls I'm just going to nip in here for a moment," I called out.

I assumed they'd heard me and would therefore follow me inside so I didn't wait for their reply as I turned and raced inside, anxious to view more of what they had on their shelves. It took less than a few minutes before I realized they had not followed me into the shop, so I abandoned everything to go back outside to find them. As I stood on the pavement looking to my left and right but there was no sign of them. At first I wasn't too concerned for I knew they couldn't be too far away, after all I had only been in the shop for a matter of a few minutes, but as time marched on there was still no sign of them, well then things quickly began to change.

"Okay girl, take a deep breath and whatever you do don't panic," I quietly ordered myself as I sought to calm down the first flutters of anxiety that were threatening to openly manifest. I decided that my best bet was to stay put, so I found myself a seat just yards away from the shop entrance, that way, when they discovered I was missing, they would retrace their steps back to the shop and hopefully to me.

I sat on that bench for what seemed an age, and still there was no sight of them. The agitation and panic welling up inside was getting stronger and louder as I began to fear the very worst. An hour later and still no sightings. I had no idea as to what to do next. I leapt to my feet and began racing from one shop to another as I searched out my good friends. I could hardly speak a word of the language so I was unable to ask for help and back then cellular phones were still in their infancy, so few people could afford to own one. I was alone in a foreign land and beginning to feel like a frightened child. I tried to hold myself together, after all I was now a fully grown adult, and as a rule adults don't usually break down into tears when they discover they are lost or do they? I was about to put that to the test.

I went back to bench and sat back down. As I closed my eyes I tried to empty my head of a mental picture that had inflicted itself and tormented me over many years. It was of a little girl sitting on a chair in a bleak and empty room. She's experiencing overwhelming abandonment and so she is stretching out both arms while crying out 'somebody help me, please will somebody help me.' I'd had this same picture since I was a little girl and I had no need of a therapist to help with the interpretation. So today she was again forced to make an appearance as this new crisis began to take a grip of me. It was now nigh impossible to hold back the tears as great fear began to overwhelm me. I had no idea what to do next and no inner resources to help me find the answer.

Eventually in a state of deep misery I decided to make my way down to the dockside, in the hope that I might get some help from staff that spoke English.

On arriving at the docks I was further shocked when told that, due to the threatening inclement weather conditions, all further sailings had been cancelled, making this the last boat out! Could things get much worse, I asked myself. Time alone would answer that one!

After finally finding a crew member who spoke English I tearfully told him my story.

"Don't worry pet, I'll have a word in the Captain's ear."

"Thank you so much," I whimpered.

When he came back, he had seemingly good news.

"Come this way love, for I have been ordered to take you up to the bridge," he said, placing a fatherly arm around my shoulder as he guided me onto the vessel. I began to believe my ordeal was almost over. After sitting me down the Captain asked me for the details of what had happened. Through a veil of tears I explained everything including why I no longer had my passport.

"All the way over on the crossing I was singing a Bonnie Tyler's song, and now it's come to pass," I sobbed. He handed me a tissue.

"Bonnie Tyler? Is she one of your friends, otherwise where does she fit into this tragic story?"

"She doesn't." I howled.

"Well, what then?"

"She's one of my favorite singers."

"Excuse me?"

"Yes she had the hit single I was lost in France."

"Am I missing something here young lady, for I'm at a complete loss as to the connection."

"Sorry, it's the song I've been singing all day, and then suddenly without any warning, I find myself actually lost in France, with no passport and I've lost my friends and I can't believe any of this is happening to me. I have no way of contacting any of them, and I'm at a complete loss as to what to do next," I wailed.

"Alright young lady calm down. We'll see what we can do to help," he said giving me a friendly pat on the back. I looked up into his face desperate for the sort of reassurance that only a beloved father could give his troubled child.

"Thank you so much," I whispered through a mist of tears.

He informed me that the ship would soon be on its way back to England.

"Captain, I cannot leave without my friends, as I have absolutely no way of getting back home when we get back to England. I live about 2 hours away from the port."

"Don't worry, I promise the ship won't leave dock until we have them safely on board."

"Promise?"

"Trust me, when your friends discover this is the last sailing until tomorrow they will certainly want to be on board. So do us all a favor, try to relax and you'll see."

I sank back into my seat temporarily reassured, however this would not last. Some ten minutes later and a man dressed in civilian clothing came into the room clutching a few heavy bags which once opened revealed a large number of bottles of whisky. He was obviously a friend of the Captain's.

"Captain, I've brought you some duty-free whisky as requested," he announced carefully placing the bags on the ground. "Right then, is this the young lady you mentioned?"

"Yes, apparently she became separated from her friends and one of them is still holding onto her passport for reasons of safety. Once we dock in Newhaven is there anyway you can help her get home?"

"Of course, don't mention it," he replied as he gave the captain a hearty slap on the back. "Now, show me where you keep your glasses and I'll pour myself a drink."

The tall pot marked gentlemen gulped his drink down in just a matter of seconds before pouring himself another, then another. Suddenly I heard the mighty rumble of the powerful engines starting up.

"Oh no you promised you'd contact the ground staff to see if my friends are on board," I bawled.

The captain believing he was out of earshot turned to confide his thoughts to the gentleman.

"This is turning into a nightmare, for with every second that passes she's turning more and more into a gibbering wreck."

"Hmm."

"Okay lady, please try and calm down for they are bound to be on board."

"But we don't know that," I gasped as I struggled to keep myself together.

"I'll put a message out over the speaker system, and I'm sure they are going to turn up, just you wait and see."

"Will a Christina, Jaqui or Sue please make contact with a member of our crew as we have a very distraught member of your party up on the bridge, thank you."

With the engines rumbling and the crew releasing the ropes that secured the ship to its mooring the vessel set out to sea. It was then that I realized that my problems were only just about to begin. Twenty minutes into the sailing and there had been no response to the Captain's message. I urged him to try again. Yet again no one responded. Feelings of anxiety now began to cascade over me.

Those in the room tried to comfort me even offering me a glass of whisky in order to calm me down.

"No thank you for I don't drink whisky," I mumbled as I fought back the tears.

"Come on love try some, it'll make you feel a whole lot better."

"Thanks but no thanks," I muttered as I wiped away the tears that were rolling uncontrollably down my face. Hours later the ship docked in Newhaven. The tall now worse for wear stranger grabbed hold of my arm and asked me to come along with him. I was reluctant but I had no other choice.

"Don't worry young lady, he'll see to it you get home safely," the Captain called out after me. I was not so confident. Minutes later I found myself boarding a coach filled with young over excited French students. The man walked me to a seat and then, after stowing his bags in the overhead locker, he fell into the seat beside me. With everyone on board the coach set off along the coast road.

Although it was early evening it was winter, so it was dark and very cold and I had no idea where the coach was headed. Even more troubling was the fact that, within seconds of the coach setting off, this seriously inebriated man began to show his true intentions and they were not good! Suddenly he was all over me. I thrust my head to one side as the stench of whisky on his breath immediately overwhelmed me.

"Please sir, behave yourself," I whimpered, for I was terrified that if I became too assertive he would order me off the coach and then I would be stranded in the middle of nowhere. He wasn't listening. Occasionally I became aware of the young faces of those French students seated nearby and, though they were from the Paris, the city of love, they seemed equally confused and concerned as they stared over in our direction.

"Please sir I've asked you nicely already, please leave me alone," I politely begged as I continued to spurn his unwelcome advances. I was feeling both anxious and scared as, ignoring my pitiful pleas, he continued to try to grope me.

"Come on love, I'm just being nice and friendly," he gushed.

"Then please keep things that way by keeping your hands to yourself for you promised the captain that you'd get me home safe and sound," I gently tried to remind him as once again I pushed his face from off my cheek. He still wasn't listening. I needed to get angry.

"Enough!" I cried as I forcefully pushed his body away from me.

"Suit yourself," he incoherently muttered. Thankfully, with the alcohol finally beginning to take it's toll, he gave up and began to doze off. Sometime later the coach pulled off the main road and, after making its way up a long drive, it came to a sudden halt outside what appeared to be a castle. The driver staggered up from his seat, and the young excitable students, having grabbed their personal possessions, also rushed to disembark the coach..

"Stay put, and I'll be back shortly," the unkempt man ordered. I wanted to argue and tell him I was getting off the coach, but yet again I found myself becoming obediently subservient and so I remained sitting alone on a cold darkened coach. The time ticked by and when nobody returned I finally summoned the courage to exit the coach to then go in search of everybody.

As I wandered down the long gravel drive heading towards the cluster of small lights I soon realized that this location was the rendezvous for the exchange students to be paired up with English families for their stay in England. I turned the corner just as the last family were driving away. I had a sinking feeling when I realized that I was now probably stuck on my own with this seriously inebriated man. I made my way back to the coach and I could only pray for help to come as by now I was crippled with fear.

Finally the coach driver and the man arrived back at the coach. After picking up his carrier bags of drink he now suggested that I follow him to head back in the direction of the castle. I heard the engine of the coach as it prepared to leave and I swallowed hard as I tentatively walked a few paces behind my supposed helper, my head in a fog as I wondered what to do next. As soon as we got to the other side of the building a massive door opened up and immediately I could see sparks flying from a pit as a number of mechanics in oil stained overalls and wearing goggles worked on the undercarriage of a large vehicle. This place was some sort of coachworks.

"Hi guys I've got your duty frees," scar face yelled as he strolled up to the men to generously hand out the bottles of liquor.

"Thanks mate, I'll settle up with you later," a bearded man in greasy overalls cried as he placed a large wrench to one side.

"Yeah Bob, let's find some glasses and have ourselves a little party." another lad announced removing his goggles and downing his blowtorch as he then went in search of some drinking receptacles.

"Oh goodness, where is this going to end?" I groaned in despair.

"Okay guys, before I head for home I need a volunteer to ensure this young lady gets home."

"But you promised the captain you'd personally see to it that I get home safely," I hurriedly interrupted.

"Don't worry you're little head my darling, for I'm just calling in a favor. So listen up, I'm leaving it with you lot to make sure she gets home, and I'll catch up with you later."

"Sure thing," they cried as they swigged from their heavily stained chipped mugs.

The tall man then abandoned me to a load of greasy mechanics, who to all intents and purposes saw me as little more than an untimely inconvenience, so had little motivation to set aside their impromptu party to help me out. I knew then I had to act fast.

"Hmm excuse me but is there a phone I can use?" I timidly asked.

"Yeah there's one over there on the wall," one of the guys called over before taking another swig from his mug. On the way over to the phone I began to deliberate over whether I should call home, the emergency services or the police, but as there had been no attempted murder as of yet to report I decided to call home.

"Come on John, pick up the phone," I exasperatedly mumbled. It all felt like I was in the middle of some thriller where the person on the other end fails to pick up until it's just too late.

Please John hurry up and pick up the phone," I begged, my anxiety rising with every moment that passed by. Why wasn't he picking up? Maybe he was in the bath, maybe the television was turned up too loud. I was only just holding myself together. I placed the phone down determined I would try again a few minutes later. As I looked over towards the pit it was plainly obvious that already none amongst them would be fit to drive me home. I picked up the phone again. This time he answered.

"John, this is Tricia," I said lowering my voice.

"Sorry, you need to speak up"

"John, can you here me now, it's Tricia."

"Oh, hi honey how's it all going?"

"Oh John, everything's gone terribly wrong," I grizzled.

"What? Are you with the other girls? Where are you?"

"I don't know."

"What do you mean you don't know?"

"Exactly that! I don't know."

"Tricia stop messing with me. Where are you?"

"John I'm not messing around, I'm stuck at the back of some stupid castle?"

"Castle?"

"Yes you heard right."

"Is it in England or France?"

"Does that matter?"

"Of course it does."

"Yes well it's in England."

"Well where is it, what's the name of the castle?"

"I've absolutely no clue," I sobbed

"Tricia calm down. Take a deep breath. Now you need to find out the name of the castle if I'm to have any hope of finding you, do you hear me?"

"Look John, I have no way of finding that out, for I'm in a garage with a load of drunk men," I whispered down the phone, as I looked over to where the mechanics were still plying themselves with alcohol.

"Drunk men?"

"Yes, there are about six of them, and they are getting drunker by the minute"

"Tricia, what on earth is going on? I thought you said you were in a castle?"

"I am."

"Well castle, garage, which is it to be?"

"Don't ask anymore questions, I just need your help."

"Okay then, give me the number on the….."

"John, I can't hear you anymore…"

Suddenly the phone crackled then went silent. I gulped and tried the number again. Nothing! The phone was dead. I was now convinced my time was up, for who else do you know that in the dead of night accidentally lands up in some strange castle in the middle of nowhere with a load of worse for the wear men, then the phone goes dead? I mean, who walks away from that particular scenario alive and in one piece? Not in any movie I'd ever seen. It simply doesn't happen! I was shaking from head to foot as I stumbled back to where the men were still partying. Then a new determination began to rise up from within, a courage that banished the 'little lost girl syndrome', albeit temporary, as I found myself forcefully demanding that one of them drive me home, and now!

"I've just spoken to my husband and he's very happy to reimburse for your time and petrol, but I need to leave now."

"Okay lads, one of us has gotta get her home." the bearded one very begrudgingly announced.

"Oh alright then," they unenthusiastically groaned like a load of adolescent schoolboys ordered by teacher to take a shower.

"So who's volunteering?" Dead silence.

"Well we promised him, so someone's got to do it." You could have heard a pin drop.

"Okay then if nobody's going to volunteer we'd better pull straws."

Straws! are you kidding me! Before I could even think to vent my thoughts on this one, the skinniest lad leapt up and walked over to an office space. After placing his hands on some miscellaneous paper he tore it into six pieces of varying lengths before heading back to the pit where he instructed his workmates to take their pick from his enclosed hand.

"Whichever of us gets the short straw, well he's the unlucky one whose gotta drive her home," he gruffly announced.

I watched on with baited breath as each one reluctantly reached over to pick a straw from his tightly clasped hand. "Dear God let it not be the really gross fat one," I mentally prayed.

"Oh great, well it seems like it's all down to me," the really fat gross one announced.

"Sorry mate, you'd better get going but don't worry, we'll look after what's left of your booze for you, and who knows, you might get lucky!"

The cumbersome man snorted his disapproval at their bantering as he struggled to get to his feet, before staggering towards a mate to grab hold of the remains of a bottle for one final swig.

"See you guys tomorrow then."

I stood there in a stupefied trance not sure whether to follow after him, take my chances and stay back with the rest of them, or run screaming into the surrounding forest. None of the choices seemed too brilliant.

As I trailed behind him towards his car all that was running through my head was the thought 'Have you lost your mind? You've been warned all your life never to accept a lift from a perfect stranger and now here you are doing it.'

He brusquely threw open the passenger door of his old rusty car and gruffly ordered me to get in, before going round to open his side. I watched as he struggled to fit through the door and then as he fell down into the driver's seat it registered a loud depressing creak as his hefty torso pressurized the seat into descending nearer the floor of the vehicle.

As we drove along in the darkness I had the distinct feeling that all was not well. This thought was further heightened as I sat mesmerized by the black bat dangling from his front mirror, an insipid rubber thing whose wings flapped up and down with the movement of the car. As we began to drive down a better lit road I turned around and my eyes caught attention of something glistening on the back seat. I turned once more to take another look and I could just make out a large tool box on the back seat then, wait for it, I thought I saw the outline of an axe! Who did I know who chose to have a bat hanging from their windscreen mirror, and an axe amongst their possessions on the backseat, answer, absolutely no one, at least not in my circles! And in my mind bats equals vampires which equals Count Dracula! Collectively it surely meant the end of my life as I knew it. So having just done the sums, I discreetly moved my hand over towards the passenger door handle, just incase I was forced to make a quick escape.

We drove in total silence for many miles and I fervently searched for a landmark, some familiar place that I might recognize. When that didn't happen I decided that if anything untoward was going to take place then it was less likely to happen if we had become firm friends. I needed to find some common ground. As I glanced over at this overweight hairy and wild-looking man with his heavily stained armpits, two day stubble and oily ripped overalls, I found myself at a complete loss at to how to make that necessary connection, but I knew with great certainty I had to try.

"Um I cannot thank you enough for helping me out like this."

"Whatever," he angrily growled.

"Well, all the same I'm extremely grateful." Total silence. Minutes later and I felt confident that now might be the best time to launch into my hurriedly rehearsed mission of getting home in one piece.

"Tell me, do have a wife and kids at home?" I casually asked, hoping this might be the very connection I was looking for. Without warning he flew into a fearful frenzy as he informed me that the stupid ignorant excuse for a woman had left him a few years back and taken the brats with her. Actually he called her a number of very uncharitably mean names that would cause great offense to many if put into print.

"Oh dear, I'm sorry to hear that," was all I could think to mumble as he continued to rant and rail. Finally when he'd expressed as much hatred as he felt able he began to calm down. It time for the next question.

"Well, what about other family, I mean you must have a mum and dad…"

I wasn't even given the time to finish my sentence before he once more fell into an foaming rage that had me instantly realizing that yet again I had got it terribly wrong. It would appear that his parents had disowned him long ago so he hated them with a vengeance, almost as much as his ex wife. I was not doing very well at all. It seemed an age before he eventually calmed down.

"How much further is it until we reach my town?" I shakily asked.

"Oh about twenty five minutes or so," he evasively mumbled. Minutes later I took another deep breath and launched into my final question, a question I truly hoped would hit the nail on the head in making that vital connection. How I could get it so wrong I will never know.

"Um tell me, do you believe in God?" In a matter of seconds he flew into the worst demonical rage ever as he thrust his whole body forward and began to shout and hit the dashboard with his clenched fist. I sat back trembling from head to foot, for it appeared that I had just asked the worst question I could ever care to ask. While venting his fury I quickly learnt that he had been raised by Jesuits who he claimed had badly abused him. As I observed this deeply troubled beast I believed there was nothing more I could say or do to persuade him to calm down, so any hope of getting out of this perilous situation in one piece was fast fading. Just when I thought he was thinking to turn off the main road I hurriedly pleaded with him to take me straight home.

"Look, I'm truly sorry for all your pain and I really feel for you, but my life has been no picnic either. My heartache didn't come from Jesuits but I was raised in children's homes and from the age of five I was regularly sexually abused by a member of staff besides other stuff to terrible to mention. I have even attempted suicide in the past, so if you have any honor and decency left inside you, please don't think to hurt me." He remained silent to my appeal as though he were weighing up my words, and even his lack of response troubled me. Not one further word was spoken by either of us for the remainder of that journey. However in the space of a few minutes I began to recognize familiar roads and street signs and so I began to breathe. When we finally reached the bottom of the road where I lived, he skidded to a halt and suddenly reached over and pushed open the door.

"Okay get out," he gruffly ordered. Before I had time to turn around and thank him he put the car into first gear and then sped down the road literally like a bat out of hell. It was now around two in the morning.

John was still anxiously waiting up for me when I knocked on the living room window.

"Goodness, you're shaking like a leaf and you look a right mess."

"Thanks a bunch."

"Look sit down while I make you a cup of tea," he insisted. He then quietly listened as my story unfolded.

"My goodness, so where are the other girls?"

"How would I know?" I wept. That night I took medication to help me relax but still sleep refused to come as I mulled over all that had taken place and the stark fact that the outcome might well have been totally different. John allowed me to sleep in until lunchtime when he brought me up a cup of tea.

"Tricia, I've just heard from the girls and they're all back safe and sound."

"Oh thank goodness."

"It appears they went down to the port and asked around but none of the crew seemed to know anything. They even told the girls that you couldn't possibly be on board for without a current passport there is no way you would ever have been allowed to board the vessel. The girls made the decision not to get on the boat for they felt they could not leave the country knowing you were lost in France without a passport."

"John that was really decent of them, but it all makes me feel so awful that it ever happened."

"Yes, it's one tragic mistake after another."

"Did you think to tell them what really happened?"

"Well only the bare bones. I thought I'd leave the blow by blow account for you to explain at your leisure, but one things for sure."

"Oh, and what's that?"

"No more girlie trips to France for you, at least not for the foreseeable future. Oh and if I were you I'd also put that Bonnie Tyler tape away, or better still bin it!"

"What! No way! for I love her almost as much as I love you."

CHAPTER 8

A Shortage of Shekels

A few years passed by before we once again bumped into our surly fellow Europeans this time on the shores of beautiful Eilat in Southern Israel. I think it was the beginning of 1987. By this time we had the first of three children, a most precious little girl whom we'd named Antonia. She was just eighteen months old when we decided to head off to Israel. At the time Israel was not the most popular holiday destination due to the ongoing troubles, but that was not going to stop us, besides we'd heard rumors that Sylvester Stallone liked to snorkel of the coast in Eilat, so if I got really lucky I might just bump into him at the Meduza diving centre, otherwise at Coral World. Why we were going for a whole three weeks I have no idea, as we just about scraped through each month when at home. This holiday would see us surviving for three weeks on boiled rice alternated with vegetable soup. Due to Israel's on-going crisis, their economy was in pretty bad shape and so I was shocked at the price of just about everything. I could hardly afford a pack of nappies for my little girl. However I must not complain for I had always wanted to visit Israel and now I was going to realize this dream.

It was just after Christmas and not only were we held up in bad traffic causing us to arrive belatedly at the airport, but I began to have panic attacks about getting on the plane. I have to confess that I spent much of my childhood dreaming of becoming an air stewardess, oh as well as a nun, and a fireman, only to discover that, if I wanted to be a nun I would have to learn to stay quiet for more than three seconds and to be a fireman I would need to develop some serious muscle tone and as for becoming a stewardess I would have to drop a few sizes, be stretched on a rack, oh and have I forgotten to mention it? conquer my fear of flying.

Before my honeymoon I had never been to an airport, let alone stepped on a plane and, since that time, I have found plenty of opportunities to break into a sweat as filled with overwhelming panic I would find myself pleading with John to turn around and go home. For any number of weeks before a planned trip I would endure endless torturous nightmares in which I was the only passenger aware that we were flying with both wings missing and the tail section completely sheared off. There was an embarrassing occasion when, as a result of my anxiety, I was taken on board early along with unsupervised children, the physically challenged, and those with chronic medical conditions. (I think the last one was the category they bracketed me under.) On a few occasions I was invited by the stewardess to join others in visiting the captain in the cockpit as, for some inexplicable reason, they believed this might well alleviate my panic attacks. Of course I always politely refused for I could not even begin to imagine how standing in some tiny cockpit looking down on a hundred or more switches would in anyway lessen my anxiety, even if the thoroughly handsome square jawed captain were to reach out to sympathetically squeeze my seriously trembling hand.

As if all this was not enough I also had problems with the whole lifejacket thing for I could never remember the exact order I was meant to do things. One question that consistently bothered me was, would the jacket fit properly? I mean it was a complete mystery to me as to how they were able to work out my personal body size before I even boarded the plane. You think that's crazy talk? Well, what if I got a jacket that was meant for a child otherwise an extremely large person? I mean, would you ever go and buy a jacket from a department store without first trying it on, and yet the airline expected the lifejacket under the seat to be a perfect fit. (Johns efforts to reassure me that they all have adjustable straps did nothing whatsoever to remove my anxiety).

The next worrying question was, am I meant to blow it up straight away, or leave it until after we'd crashed into the ocean? Also, what sort of knot was I supposed to use when tying the jacket around my waist? I had studied knots and got my Girls Guides badge to prove it, so I knew that some knots work better than others according to the need. Worst still, what if my whistle didn't work? I mean, I'd bought many whistles in my time and the whistles on those life jackets looked pretty similar to the tinny ones usually found in Christmas crackers, and trust me, they rarely ever functioned properly! So it would surely be much too late to find out your whistle wasn't working, as the high Atlantic waves crashed around you in the middle of the freezing ocean. I mean, it's not as if you'd be able to swap your whistle with any of the other survivors I don't suppose. Yet that stupid little whistle could mean life or death if an ocean vessel sailed right past, because it failed to see or hear you due to the dysfunctional whistle that only made a tiny peep, peep noise similar to that of a day old duckling. It's true to say I was utterly exhausted by these agonizing concerns that mercilessly sought to invade my mind as every planned vacation neared, but still they kept coming.

After my children came into the world, the theme of my ongoing nightmare altered slightly, for now with the no-winged plane losing altitude I would spend half the nightmare desperate for a baby cot that, if you care to ask the darling flight attendant, will be more than happy to provide. Oh help me out, for that's perfectly crazy to someone such as myself! I had often waited a good fifteen to twenty minutes for the blanket or pillow I'd requested, otherwise the coffee top-up, so with the damaged plane now perilously hurtling at full speed in the direction of the ocean, are you really expected to have the presence of mind to not only press the button but then presumably wait an age for the stewardess to crawl on her hands and knees along the aisle of the plane to answer your call. If you're lucky and the plane has not already hit the ocean, you might just get your request for a cot.

"I'm awfully sorry madam but did you by some chance press the bell?"

"Yes stewardess, I have to confess that on this occasion it was indeed my good self. I'm awfully sorry to trouble you at such a difficult and inappropriate moment as this, but I would be eternally indebted to you if you could see your way to finding me a baby cot, as I love this precious young infant with all my heart and soul, and so would you if you knew her."

"Yes madam, please remain seated with your head down while I search out a cot for your little sprog."

"Thank you and, if perchance you've got any spare time left on your hands, I'd so love a decent cup of coffee to help swallow down my travel sickness pills, as well as all these prescription anxiety sedatives." Nope, somehow I couldn't see it.

So as we raced to catch our plane to Israel, the anxiety attack got so bad that my face suddenly sprouted a large number of horrid looking welts. I collapsed on the nearest available seat and tried to catch my breath.

"Tricia get up. We're late enough as it is."

"No take Antonia and go without me," I wailed.

"Don't be stupid, you know I can't do that."

"Please just go."

"Look honey you've got to calm right down, otherwise they'll never let you on the plane looking like this."

"Looking like what?"

"Well…"

"Go on just say it."

"Well you don't look anything like your normal self. In fact at present you look as though you have some highly contagious disease."

"John, do you think I don't know that?" I gasped and wheezed.

"Please Tricia, just tell yourself you can do it."

"But I can't," I cried as I attempted to wipe away large beads of perspiration that were now rolling down my face.

"Here, hold onto Antonia while I run and get you a cold flannel, and then we've got to make a mad dash to get through Customs, do you hear me?" Somehow we made it onto the plane, but only just.

El Al is one of the most stringent airlines when it comes to safety, which is good news if you're a normal reasonable minded passenger but bad news if you're a severely emotionally retarded woman whose not only hyperventilating but sweating so profusely that it is thoroughly plausible she has contracted either Scarlet fever, Typhoid, or some other highly contagious and deadly disease! The interrogation seemed to go on for an eternity, as the officials naturally treated us with the greatest suspicion, and our luggage? Well that was screened and screened then screened again for good luck! I desperately wanted to intervene to assure the El Al staff that not only did I love the entire Jewish nation with a passion but I had cried my way through every Holocaust movie, so if they would care to throw me a few trivia questions they would see for themselves that I would pass with flying colors!

Finally they allowed us through to board the plane. Having found our seats the plane was finally given clearance to take off and, as soon as those seat belt signs went off, I leapt from my seat and headed for the toilet cubicle. I felt so ill I remained behind locked doors for a good portion of the journey, that is, until a stewardess was accosted by other irate passengers wishing to use the bathroom.

"Look, whoever is behind those doors has been in there for a ridiculously long time," I heard the voices of many concerned passengers inform the stewardess as she made a pathway through the people to then knock on the door.

"Is everything alright in there?" she called out.

"Look, if nobody appears in the next few minutes I will inform the captain and then we will see what we can do."

"Perhaps they've fainted, or maybe they're on drugs." I heard one lady suggest.

"Yes and Stewardess what if there is more than one of them and their doing 'you know what?" another helpful old dear chipped in.

"Well, let's not jump to any hasty conclusions," the flight attendant advised as she tried hard to invoke a sense of calm.

"Well, don't leave it too long for there's only a few toilets down this end and we've all been waiting here for ages," one man grumpily added.

Finally, as I had no desire for the plane to turn and head back to London in order for the local SWAT team to charge the door, I had little choice but to venture out and face the music. Their wrath never came for, as soon as their eyes beheld this pitiful wreck of a human being with a face so swollen and blotchy, they were all instantly filled to overflowing with the milk of human kindness.

"I'm awfully sorry. I feel so dreadfully unwell, and I promise I'm neither drunk or on drugs, or doing any other unconscionable act! it's just I have a real fear of flying. So please forgive me," I mournfully mumbled.

"We understand pet." a sympathetic red headed lady sighed, gently patting my shoulder.

"Ooh Agnes, she does look right awful, doesn't she?"

"Yes Doris, I couldn't agree more."

"Such a crying shame love, hope this doesn't spoil your holiday. Would you like someone to help you back to your seat, pet?"

"No I'll be fine," I lied as I shakily staggered back down the aisle holding onto every chair and shoulder for support as I went in search of my seat.

"Where on earth have you been all this time?" John anxiously asked.

"Where do you think?"

"No tell me"

"In the jolly loo," I muttered as I collapsed down onto the seat and began gasping for air.

"What, all this time?"

"Okay Inspector Clueso, where else would I have gone? You know there aren't too many places of interest on a plane, unless you suspect I've been rummaging through the hold in search of Belgian chocolate, otherwise sitting on the Captain's lap while he shows me his navigational instruments!"

"Oh dear, I would've come looking for you but I thought it best to stay put with Antonia."

"John I feel terribly ill. Sorry but can we carry on this conversation some other time, for I need to head back to the loo," I whimpered as I shakily stood up to head back down the aisle. Once more it was quite a while before I returned to my seat.

When the meal was placed under my nose I could only turn my head to one side and beg John to quickly remove it. Pretty soon word got round the plane that there was a sickly passenger on board and before long I had a long line of very concerned passengers handing me a variety of colorful pills that they swore would do the trick, and if not pills, well then they wished to pass on some weird home grown remedy that had been handed down from generation to generation. It felt like the movie 'Airplane' as they patiently took their turn to hand out their kind advice. It was just a matter of time before someone in the line produced a hammer to knock me unconscious and so put me out of my misery.

Happily the El Al plane landed with both wings and nose intact so, after picking up our luggage from baggage reclaim, we headed off towards the taxi rank.

"Tricia see all those beautiful ladies carrying flowers. I've never seen anything so kind and special at an airport, have you? It's like San Francisco in the 60's!"

"No, can't say I have."

"I've always believed these people to be peace loving."

"You're absolutely right but much as I'm loathe to bring you down to earth I urgently need the little girls room again."

"What so soon? You've only just used one."

One glare from me, and that was enough.

"Okay okay," he muttered as he remained firmly fixated on the young women waltzing around the airport accompanied by big bunches of flowers.

"No I mean it. I don't think you're listening to me."

"Oh look, one of them is heading over. Now what's the word for peace. Oh yes, Shalom."

"John, much as I truly love and appreciate moving experiences, I'll have one right here on the floor, if I don't get me to a bathroom and soon."

I was right, he wasn't listening to me. The very attractive delightful lady sidled right up to John who was holding Antonia in one arm and a suitcase in another. His jaw dropped just about the same time as his luggage hit the floor. He then held out his hand to accept the rose being offered to him.

"Ah yes, the rose of Sharon," he sighed bringing the flower up to his nose. "Here Antonia you hold the flower for daddy. Shalom," he said turning to give the pretty lady his best smile. "Oh and before you go, I must say that handing out flowers to total strangers is such a wonderfully inspiring way of sharing love and peace with all those arriving on Israeli soil. So tell me what possessed you girls to think of doing such a touching thing?"

"Well sir, we are a local Car Hire company and quite simply we want your business."

"Uh?"

"Yes, we wish for you to choose our rental cars over the others."

I immediately creased up laughing.

"Oh!" my husband muttered again, a hint of disappointment now emanating from his very deflated tone of voice.

"Shalom sir."

"Honey right now I'm feeling more than a tad stupid, for back in my day handing out flowers to passers by meant something else entirely," he admitted handing me the rose as he needed both hands to carry our luggage over to the taxi rank.

"Sure Man you mean peace and love in San Francisco? I mischievously grinned as I made the ever familiar peace sign. "Well don't worry for I'll make jolly sure you never live this one down," I teased as we climbed into the taxi cab.

"So here honey, don't forget your precious shalom filled rose."

We arrived at the resort and were shown to our villa apartment. I was surprised that the apartment was so basic for there was no sign of even a television. The fridge was so ancient you couldn't ignore the noise as it chugged away desperate to survive another season or two before heading off to the dump. There were two rings on an old oven to cook on, and the sofa in the living area was threadbare and lumpy. However the pool was large and beautiful and popular music was played all day. We must have heard Dire Straits 'Brothers in Arms' at least twenty times a day until I couldn't get it out of my head. For three whole weeks we lived off a very basic diet of rice and vegetables, occasionally treating ourselves to sharing a poolside snack of burger and chips between all three of us. Everything was unbelievably expensive. The nearest we came to finding Sylvester Stallone was when passing by a café one evening we were surprised to see many families huddled around tables, their infants in pushchairs, their men at the bar drinking, as they watched a dated Stallone movie on an old black and white television. Naturally we took it upon ourselves to pull up a chair and join them, even though it was dubbed into the Israeli language. "I could watch darling Sylvester all day and night," I sighed.

Our young daughter, who always woke early, had us heading down to the pool at some unearthly hour every single morning. However, much to our astonishment we were to discover there was not a single available sun bed, even around the toddler pool. Needless to say my dismay turned to disgust when around midday unshaved nomads began to stagger out of nowhere with bottle in hand as they arrived to claim their pre booked sun bed. Worse still, the most favored sun spot appeared to be the area around the toddler pool and yet not one of these hotel guests had a baby or toddler in tow. I was one of many frustrated parents unable to keep a watchful eye on their young children as they paddled around in the shallow end. Before too long there were many furious and disenchanted parents who wanted something done about this unacceptable practice and so I turned my attention on the hotel manager, making an appointment to speak with him in private. John thought I was wasting my time.

Surprisingly the manager wholeheartedly agreed that this insane practice was neither fair nor right. He also admitted that in the past he had tried hard to put an end to it, but sadly to no avail. However I wasn't buying it!

"Look, I'm aware that they are the big spenders, but it is preposterous that parents of young ones are unable to get a sun bed anywhere near the toddler pool when these selfish tourists don't even appear until midday, only to have a sun bed waiting for them as they came down the night before to drape their towel over the sun bed of their choice. It's outrageous! "

"I couldn't agree more."

"They then spend the afternoon getting pickled before leaving their countless empty beer bottles for others to pick up and bin in order to avoid their children getting injured on the broken glass."

"Look Mrs. Bennett, I will do my best to get things changed. I will order my secretary to print off some fliers stating that no towels can be left on the pool deck overnight. Hopefully this will bring this situation to a speedy halt". It didn't. Our European friends took absolutely no notice of the fliers, preferring to turn them into paper airplanes to chuck at one and other. So the next day found me back in the managers office. This time he agreed to add a warning to the bottom of the flier. It said that all towels left on sun beds overnight will be rounded up by a member of staff and taken to lost property.

The manager kept his word and late that same evening he sent members of his staff to scour the pool deck and clear all sun beds of towels. The next day saw many confused and unhappy guests arriving around midday who could find neither their missing towel or a sun bed on which to rest their heavily intoxicated bodies. Finally some progress, or so I thought. The next evening was once again a challenge with many of the sun beds covered with large variety of towels but unbelievably no member of staff followed through by collecting them up. I went back to the front office to speak to the manager.

"This is insane," I cried.

"Tell me what more can we do?" he said shrugging his shoulders as though he were some helpless week old kitten.

"Well you could try being the manager."

"Excuse me?"

"Forgive me for being so brutal but if as the manager you feel powerless to make the necessary changes then surely you should resign and let someone with more backbone take over your position."

"Hmm," he muttered giving a weak insipid smile.

"Until then you could try sticking to your word and have a member of your staff collect up all the towels until they finally get the message."

Sadly he just shrugged his shoulders as if to suggest complete surrender, something I found most annoying.

Perhaps this confession will shock the socks off you and maybe it will get me banned from landing in certain European airports, otherwise ever placing a foot on their soil, but I have such a keen sense of justice that I felt I was left with no other choice. I had done everything by the book to get action and the management had failed me as well as every other desperate parent so for the first time ever I joined the likes of Charles Bronson, Bruce Willis and Sylvester Stallone by becoming a vigilante! There it's out! I watched from a distance as bands of them claimed their sun beds before heading out to the bars. I waited until it grew dark when I believed it was safe to come out. Then, like a super sleuth I furtively headed to the area around the children's pool and stripped every bed of its towel. But I wasn't finished. Oh no! I threw some of my spoil into the main pool, and the rest I threw into the large waste bin that by the end of each day was filled to overflowing with beer bottles, cigarette ends as well as half eaten burgers fried onions and German sausage. Beat me up and throw my bones to the dogs if you will, but I felt fantastic! The next morning found us, as well as countless other parents with deliriously happy dispositions as we all enjoyed a well earned laze on a sun bed directly opposite the toddler pool. It was such a momentously triumphant moment that to this very hour I remain disgracefully unrepentant.

Midday arrived and with it came the usual stampede of bloated bleary eyed men and women wandering up and down the pool deck searching out their personal sun bed. I sat up, my sunglasses perched on the end of my nose, my heart hammering away as I took in countless confused Krauts scratching their heads as they could neither recognize their towel or sun bed. Some looked awfully perplexed when they were directed to a large heap of sodden towels that some thoughtful person had kindly fished from the water. If after inspecting the heap of waterlogged towels, theirs was still missing, well the next clue might come from another large pile of heavily soiled towels that the hotel staff had salvaged from the dumpster filled to overflowing with cigarette ends, fried onions and tomato ketchup, so had an army of flies and other unsavory bugs circling overhead.

If the manager suspected me as being the culprit behind this radical event he chose to keep it entirely to himself. As for me? Well I kept going with the towel stripping until I believed they got the message. I thought it best to keep this secret from everyone my husband included, for I reasoned that if I was to be caught in the act I would try claiming diminished responsibility, and if that didn't work, then it would be me alone heading for the firing squad and judging by our European cousins ferociousness this didn't seem beyond the realm of possibilities!

During our stay the Israeli military had a large number of young soldiers on site. Every day they sat cross legged in a circle on the lawn area and, despite the intense heat, they were always dressed in full military combat gear, their large loaded weapons by their sides as they laughed and shared jokes whilst playing endless rounds of cards. Antonia, though still an infant preferred their company to ours, so decided to jostle her way in and became part of their inner circle. We could not help but giggle as this little blue eyed very white-skinned blonde girl sat bang in the middle of their circle, copying the soldiers by sitting cross legged in their midst. To this day I regret not having had the wherewithal or wisdom to take some photographs of this most splendid affair! Had a photo been taken I think I would have named it 'Innocence in a seemingly mad world.'

Three weeks later and all shalom was long gone, for we arrived back home to be faced by the biggest tax bill we had ever received in the post. We also determined to one day find ourselves a corner of the globe that remained unconquered by our good European neighbors. I knew this assignment would prove most challenging for we would bump into them in Portugal, Spain, in fact wherever we cared to venture. There came a day when I began to believe there was no little piece of Paradise they hadn't yet laid claim too.

CHAPTER NINE

She Was Oh So Beautiful

There came a brief moment in history when our powerful European friends seemed to almost disappear from the holiday resorts. To many this was indeed mystifying. I personally put it down to the dismantling of the Berlin Wall in November 1989. You think I'm joking? No I'm deadly serious. Everybody was pleased as punch when that infamous wall first came down, the parties and merriment went on for many weeks as brother hugged brother and talked of a new world. But in all the celebrations no one had taken time to consider the true cost of this new alliance. Suddenly things began to change as the poor East Germans put their hand out for their share of the prosperity pie. With the balloons and party poppers long gone, reality finally set in and pretty soon things turned sour as the West Germans were finally forced into job sharing with their former East German comrades.

Until the destruction of the wall changed everything, the hard working German nation had for many years been so prosperous that it was usual for employees to expect two if not three paid annual holidays, add to this a week or two at some expensive health spa courtesy of their company, so life seemed pretty good. With the wall gone it meant they had to put some of their hard earned money into helping their East German brothers and that meant cutting back on former luxuries including those highly desirable holidays. Suddenly European holiday resorts that had always relied heavily on the Deutschmark began to see a decline of their most appreciated customers. For the first time in many years reports began flooding in of sparkling empty pools, as well as many sightings of vacant tables and chairs with closed up parasols that yearned to once more be flapping about in the cool breeze and then, wait for it, there was a wealth of unoccupied lonely sun beds screaming out for a towel to be lain down if ever again they were to feel loved and wanted. Gone were the alarming sounds of the stampede for the pool side restaurant, and the distinctive smell of German sausage no longer wafted across the pool deck. Better still, you could now chose the location of where you wanted your sun bed to rest, in the shade or in the sun. It should have made headline news.

This sense of new found freedom was greatly appreciated by us, until many years later John and myself were invited to join some friends and neighbors on a trip to South Africa. The flight on South African Airways was the best experience ever. The food was sumptuous, the stewardesses truly helpful and gracious, oh as well as stunning to look at, (my husband told me to add that bit) and, as we flew into Cape Town with its captivating Table Mountain, I felt sure we were about to experience a little bit of heaven on earth. And we did! The weather was fabulous, the dazzling clear blue sea not only sparkled like a million diamonds but was peppered with dolphins and whales and other large sea mammals that found time to both laze and effortlessly frolic in the surf. The shops were spanking clean and filled with expensive looking clothes and, as my good friend commented, the houses over here are to die for. One of the most touching events of this holiday turned out to be a private viewing of Nelson Mandela's Government House and his more humble home next door. This was made possible because our South African friend had a previously infamous relative who had been imprisoned with Mandela on charges of terrorism, but was now part of the new government.

Our good friend who is South African had done her homework and so for the first few days we stayed in a beautiful hotel on the spectacular shores of Cape town. The morning after we arrived I looked out of a window towards the inviting pool and was dismayed to note that every sun bed already had a towel. I stormed into the reception like John Wayne with all guns blazing.

"Please, I would like to see the manager."

"Certainly madam, I will get him for you." The manager was in a side room, so in plain earshot, immediately came out of the room to address my problem.

"Madam, how can I help?"

"I'm sorry to have to say this, but I am troubled by the fact that every sun bed on your pool deck is already taken and it's only 9.30 in the morning! Now I know our German friends spend a great deal more money than us Brits but ...."

"Madam please, may I stop you."

"Yes...what?"

"Well may I assure you that nobody has laid claim to those sun beds."

"Uh? Well then please do me the courtesy of explaining why all the sun beds already have towels placed on them?"

"They belong to the hotel madam."

"What, all of them?"

"Yes madam, all of them."

"Oh!"

"Yes madam, each morning our staff specifically place a rolled towel on each bed unless of course its raining. It's for your personal convenience, so you as a guest do not have to search out a towel."

"Oh right...I'm so sorry, I truly misunderstood," I murmured, my eyes dropping to the floor before make a hasty retreat from the reception desk.

"You certainly do step in where angels fear to tread," John whispered in my ear as we slunk out of the reception.

"Well how was I supposed to know," I sulked.

"Quite!" was his last comment as stretching out on his sun bed he opened his latest Hermann Hesse book at the marked page, all the while yearning for a bit of peace and quiet. He needn't have worried for, after this latest faux pas, I determined to remain not only as good as gold, oh as well as quiet as a lamb for the remainder of our stay. But all too soon that little promise went bye the bye!

A few nights later, after eating at a restaurant near the fabulous Victoria and Alfred waterfront, we were making our way to the bus stop to get the last bus back to the hotel. We had been warned by hotel management to get there in plenty of time, for if we missed the last bus, it would be dark and possibly very dangerous. I had no trouble believing them, for over the period of our holiday we met many people who, due to the violence, had lost a friend or two in this beautiful but deeply troubled land.

It was very dark when we arrived and took our place at the end of the long line. As time went on others joined us, some with young children who were clearly overtired and in urgent need of their bed. Some ten or fifteen minutes later a large group of our European cousins arrived at the stop. They immediately walked to the front of the line and this caused many of those already standing in the line to become clearly agitated, myself included.

"Psst…John, go and tell them that there is a line, and some people have been here for over half an hour, for perhaps they have not realized."

"No Tricia, I think it best if we just leave it." I wasn't the least persuaded.

"Leave it? Are you kidding me?"

"When will you stop being the kid from care who regularly feels the need for a scuffle?"

"John, what on earth are you talking about, for this isn't some childish backyard squabble, this is about doing what's right and just," I exclaimed, as I now felt incensed by his off the cuff remarks. Still, I believed this latest situation needed some form of gentle intervention by my good self.

"See yah," I said as I hurriedly left my place to go and speak with them. I was polite but insistent that they should head to the back of the line. Their annoyance showed, but I dug my heels in and remained extremely persistent. Finally they turned round and reluctantly and slowly headed towards the back of the line.

Suddenly the bus appeared, and then, without warning, they quickly turned on their heels and raced to the front of the bus line, forcing everybody in the line to stand back otherwise get trampled underfoot. I watched on, feeling a mixture of disgust, as well as horror as, after boarding, they raced to the rear of the bus and due to their ample proportions they took up more than their fair share of seats. Some young couples with tearful children were turned away as the bus was now overcrowded. We were among the last to be allowed on and, with all seats now occupied, we were forced to stand for the entire homeward journey. I was so enraged, especially for those left behind, so, as I glared down the bus in their direction, I intentionally began to loudly express my utter contempt towards their outrageous behavior.

"Bloomin disgraceful,' I boomed. "You'd think that at their age they'd know better. Look at the poor children still standing at the bus stop. I don't know how you creeps sleep at night."

"I'm not with you," John hissed in my ear.

Back at the hotel I continued to vent my frustration.

"Tricia, you really need to ask yourself a very honest question."

"Oh, and what might that be?"

"Have you become prejudiced against the German nation?"

"What ! I can't believe you're even asking such a thing. You know full well I hate any kind of prejudice with a passion, black, white, Jew, gentile."

"I only ask because, whenever you cross swords with our European cousins, you're almost ready to have a full blown seizure."

"Well I'm so sorry 'Mr. Incredibly Perfect,' for I think it has less to do with prejudice, and more to do with bad manners and injustice."

"Look I happen to think that deep down most of us have some mild form of prejudice."

"Why thank you for your thoughtful insights, Doctor Herr Bennett. I now know who to call when I next need a mental check up of my conscience!" I immediately retorted.

"Anyway, I suggest you just think about it." he replied, while choosing to ignore my latest disparaging remarks.

Our South African holiday felt far too short, therefore we felt sad when it came to say goodbye to our kind hosts. After dropping us off outside the airport we struggled through the very crowded terminal as we went in search of the South African Airways check in. That done, we then made our weary way to the large eating area for not only were we hungry but we had plenty of time to kill. The cafeteria was ridiculously overcrowded so there was not a spare seat or table to be found. However, with time on our hands, we decided to stay put and wait for a table to become free. It was well over thirty minutes before we were able to lay claim to a very small café sized table. We then waited a while in the hope that the food station line would become shorter.

"Tricia, stay put and I'll go and get us something to eat," John announced getting up from the table.

No sooner had he left his seat to go buy refreshments than a group of burly Germans that had been standing nearby raced directly towards our tiny bistro sized table. I politely told them that the table was taken, but that did not prevent one of the group from taking John's seat. The rest of his group then quickly encircled me and the table before dumping their overloaded plates of food down on the tiny table. I was momentarily speechless! Then, as if all this was not enough to bear, they reached down to grab the food from the plates, their jaws wide open, their necks extended backwards as with minimal decorum they proceeded to stuff handfuls of food into their open mouths. Words continued to fail me, as looking up into a sea of faces, they continued jabbering away while the food that unintentionally missed their mouths rained down on me and the table. They only stopped eating to give the odd belch and burp as, with no conscience, they continued to ignore my presence at the table. I could only hope that John would quickly return. They were still standing and eating when he arrived with a tray of food. "Excuse me ladies and gentlemen but this is OUR table," my husband quietly insisted.

"You'll need to do much better than that," I called out.

"Excuse me, but we waited over half an hour to get this table, and I would like to sit down and enjoy lunch with my wife." Still there was no response as they deliberately chose to ignore him.

"Try clicking your shoes together while shooting a hand into the air," I hissed.

"Tricia, your utterly incorrigible."

"Oh really, you think so?"

It was another five to ten minutes before, having finished their feeding frenzy, they gruffly picked up their hand luggage and simply walked away, leaving us to clear away their entire mess before he could place the tray he was carrying down on the table.

"Oy! Excuse me but this is your bloomin' mess," I shouted after them. They chose to ignore my exasperated cry as they carried on walking towards the exit door.

"Tricia, stop it!"

"What, you're just going to allow them to walk off and not say anything?"

"Well, shouting across the room isn't going to help things, besides it's degrading."

"So is cleaning up their mess."

"Well I thought I married a polite caring girl?"

"Yes well I never promised you a rose garden and, unless that whole party suffers from severe congenital mega esophagus, what we've just witnessed defies all belief."

"Hmm quite ..quite ...unbelievable!" John wearily muttered. He then went in search of a waste bin to offload their disposable plates and other litter as well as find a washcloth to wipe their mess from the surface of the table, so that we could begin eating our meal in peace.

The plane was ready for take off and as usual I had an aisle seat for reasons of my frequent trips to the bathroom, leaving John to take the middle seat next to me, and to date the window seat still remained vacant.

"Hey Tricia, wouldn't it be great if it remains untaken, for then we can spread out and make ourselves more comfortable."

"Yes that would be nice but, knowing our luck, it will soon become occupied by some enormous obstreperous sausage reeking gentleman of European persuasion."

"Say that any louder and you could find yourself in trouble," he warned.

"Quite honestly, I don't care a fig."

"Come on honey, be more charitable, for if you get what you say, then you're asking for trouble."

"Preach it to me brother."

"Tricia, just button your lip and listen for one minute will you? For it's best not to have a problem with any other nation. Why, even us Brits have a terrible reputation abroad, especially in Europe."

"As if I need reminding! But John, that's only a small minority, mainly lager louts and soccer hooligans, for most of us are very civilized and respectful."

"Yes, but not everybody knows that, and may I dare remind that there is good and bad to be found in every nation."

"John, why are you always so predisposed to sainthood," I dismissively retorted before closing my eyes, my way of indicating our conversation was officially over.

The cabin crew began to prepare for take off, firstly by walking down the aisle politely checking that everyone's seatbelt was buckled up.

"Looks like we may have an extra seat after all," John leant over to whisper in my ear before giving me a quick peck on the cheek. "I think I'll use this opportunity to kick off my shoes and give my feet a little breather."

"Oh no please keep them on," I begged. He chose to ignore my pleas.

The plane was about to venture towards the runway when the pilot made an announcement that we were still waiting for one stray passenger to board and then we would be on our way.

"Oh, that's just what we need."

"Well remember, we've almost missed the plane before, so I guess we should try hard to be patient," John muttered.

"Oh, sorry Mr. Goody two shoes," I mumbled as once more I closed my eyes to begin mentally preparing for the possibility of a long delay.

I was soon interrupted by the sound of footsteps heading down the aisle. They stopped right at our row.

"Hi there, can I just slip past you to get to my seat," came the soft purring voice of a young female. Recognizing the accent as being German I immediately opened my eyes and in that small moment I knew why the plane had remained on the concourse desperately awaiting her arrival! Well either that or the plane had crashed and I was now having some sort of outer body experience! The request had come from the lips of the most stunningly tall and gorgeously curvaceous girl of man's most highest dreams. This angelic creature had deep blue eyes, a perfectly shaped nose, flawless peaches and cream skin, seriously kissable lips and straight sparkling teeth, oh as well as more stunning blonde hair than she should ever be legally allowed to grow. As she made her way past us to her seat I could only drink in the heady sensuous smell of expensive perfume that would in just a matter of seconds bring most men to their knees in utter adoration and, if that was just my private opinion, heaven only knows what every testosterone filled male on that plane might well be thinking!

"Pst…. John she looks just like Farrah Fawcett." I whispered in his available ear. Could she really be of Germanic persuasion I asked myself, when she spoke in such soft melodic tones that gently soothed instead of grated? I could clearly see that John was both mesmerized and smitten as he sat boggle eyed, and in a stupor, his jaw extended as she came to sit down right beside him. If he was correct in this thinking then this was going to be a trip of a lifetime, yes a flight made in heaven, and so he was extremely happy and grateful to be on a long haul flight. With just one graceful movement she swiveled her bodacious body his way to make yet another friendly exchange in his direction, carefully crossing her golden tanned legs that seemed to have no end, before smoothing down the imaginary ruffles from her smart and chic dress. She then began flouncing her hair before reaching for her seatbelt. I could see that John was now on the edge of his seat hoping and praying that she might ask his assistance as she struggled to snap the seatbelt, and he was more than ready to offer his services if it meant adjusting her belt so that it was securely fitted round her perfect non existent waistline. Sadly for him she managed this small action all by herself. As I continued reading John's face I knew he could hardly believe his good fortune to have such a vision of beauty sitting right beside him, their retractable food trays just inches apart, his thoroughly un-deodorized swollen feet inclining themselves towards her delicately painted pink toes as they both Filled their nostrils and lungs with the same stale air only made sweet by lingering perfume.

Seconds later saw him come out of what looked like a drug induced state as he hastily stuffed the paperback he had been reading down the side of the chair, like he were some naughty boy who had just laid his hands on some girlie magazine. I have to add that this was not his normal reading material, so understandably he would hate for her to think otherwise. The book was called. 'How to attract money!' and he had just purchased it second-hand at a large flea market in the centre of Cape Town. Truth be known he had been forced against his will to accompany us on a last minute shopping expedition that included trawling round Cape Town's open market. Not unlike most men he absolutely loathed shopping, so this day had been no exception, that is until he espied a large second hand bookstall owned by an almost financially ruined fellow ex hippie. Just looking at the rows upon rows of books it was clear that Christmas had arrived early for him, and so he immediately perked up.

"Tricia, if you don't need me, I think I'll stay here and browse through these books."

"Are you sure? I queried. "After all, didn't you say you wanted to look for a new leather belt and…." He quickly cut me off.

"Oh no… no… I'd much rather stay here, if that's alright with all of you."

"Is this wise when it's not considered safe for a tourist to be downtown on their own?"

"Look, feel free to buy anything you like, only please leave me here," he pleaded.

"Oh alright, but I did hear you correct when you said I could purchase anything I liked."

"Well, within reason," he murmured.

Sometime later we made our way back to the book stall just in time to witness John purchasing a second hand paperback. "Well, from one ex hippie to another, I hope you have more luck with this book than I did," the long haired stall owner wryly sniffed as he placed the book in a plain brown paper bag.

"What's the title?" I asked mainly out of curiosity.

"Um well, it's not the sort of book I usually read, but as you asked it's called How to attract money."

"Oh right. Well that's great, for if it only half works I'll be a very happy lady," I giggled.

Having been married for many years I could so easily read his mind so, as he purposely stuffed the paperback down the side of his seat, I knew he believed this particular girl to be much too pure and angelic to ever allow herself to be tainted by nasty material things such as the sordid quest to make money, hence the book would unquestionably meet with her disapproval and it's reader likewise!

Even I had dared question him buying such a book when most of his literature had more to do with the plight of the last Congo tribe, or some meaningful self help book designed to make him a better, more reasonable person to live with. I had always approved such literature, especially when I was to be the sole beneficiary of all his efforts to become the perfect husband. Why, there had even been a flight home from Spain when, after reading a best seller called "The Ten Second Kiss", he had spent most of the homeward bound flight annoyingly trying to catch up for lost time, giving me one sloppy kiss after another. Of course I was not amused and so I did my very best to fend him off, alas to no avail, for he seemed strangely persistent.

"Look honey, according to this book, if we want to stay happily married, then daily kissing sessions are a must, but don't worry for, according to this book they needn't be lengthy, just ten seconds per kiss per day is supposedly enough.'

"Oh, don't honey me," I retorted as I immediately rejected his playful kisses that involved puckering his lips and making that awful infantile sucking noise that most men choose to leave behind at their mothers breast. However, as he was in such a playful mood, he wouldn't take no for an answer, giving me one kiss after another. I was now beginning to feel acutely embarrassed.

"Oh go snog someone else," I more than once cried out as I playfully did my best to fend him off.. I was therefore deeply indebted to the concerned flight attendant, for my deliverance only came when the darling lady finally arrived at our seats with the food trolley.

"Excuse me sir, if you would kindly care to extricate yourself from your wife's lips to pull down your tray, I will then attempt to serve you both your hot meal." she said in a loud and most determined voice. It did the trick! John immediately blushed a little as he released me from his grip and then began to profusely apologize to the amused stewardess.

So, having concealed his how to attract money book, he then began to chat away to this personification of perfection. I in turn shut my eyes and pretended to doze off, but really I was paying close attention to their conversation as every soft word that cared to tumble of her sweet smelling tongue began to soothe his jangled nerves like some masterful masseuse working deep into his sinews and muscle tissue. It came as no big surprise to learn that her job was that of a flight attendant, for, with her stunning looks, she had to be that, otherwise a movie star, why else would the plane sit so for long on the tarmac as it waited so longingly for her to board!

By eavesdropping I would learn that her parents were divorced and she was in South Africa visiting 'daddy' who just happened to own a large number of wine vineyards. I opened my eyes only when the food trolley drew near and I caught sight of them both still deep in conversation, my husband's face glowing almost as much as hers, despite the absence of cheek bronzer. When the disposable food carton was placed in front of her I could not fail to note that, most predictably, she had opted for the healthy choice, yes a boring little low in carbohydrates salad that would hardly satisfy a hapless chipmunk and I took note that the salad was accompanied not by a harmful soda or wine, but a bottle of pure mineral water. If all this was not enough she then graciously offered up her pre packaged slice of fruit cake to John, who readily accepted it, if only to make the briefest amount of physical contact with a couple of this immortal goddesses manicured fingernails.

"Psst…Don't even think about consuming her slice of cake, you're already more than a few pounds over after this holiday," I whispered loudly in his free ear as I then whisked it from under his nose before he had anytime to complain. "John don't even go there. I'm helping you here, really I am."

I could only sigh deeply as I considered the affect all this sudden remembrance of healthy living might well have on my besotted husband, who, prior to marrying me, had been a committed health freak. To this very hour I have no idea why he foolishly believed he could even begin to influence and change a stubborn woman who was slavishly addicted to every imaginable unhealthy food product. Why he had wasted many long years trying and failing horribly to force me into drinking more water, eating whole wheat pasta, brown rice, cruciferous vegetables, nuts and pulses and just about every other nutritionally wholesome food that I struggled to even place on my tongue, all of which I knew with equal clarity my mind and stomach would readily reject. I was, after all, extremely happy with my regime of triple layer chocolate cake, continuous cups of strong coffee, interspersed by endless cans of diet soda, and so I wasn't about to change, thank you very much!

"Tricia, for goodness sake, I'm trying my best to help you, for can't you see that, if you continue eating all this junk and highly processed food, you'll probably die really early, and well before me," he would regularly cry. Privately I could not understand why he would even want to sustain my life and in doing so prolong his personal suffering for a minute longer than he had to? But, like everything else in life, I had an immediate answer.

"Oh John, I doubt very much that I'll be the first to enter the grave, for I'm proud to say that my body holds more preservatives than the local funeral home embalmer pumps into the veins of dead corpses in his busiest months!" Naturally he was at a loss for words.

With the meal at an end they continued to connect, then, with no coercion whatsoever, she chose to reveal how ashamed she had been on the flight over from Germany as she had witnessed first hand the disgracefully bad manners of some of her fellow compatriots. As she was being so openly candid John chose to share a few of our stories, including the latest airport incident. She shook her head knowingly before apologizing on their behalf, and later, as their conversation drew to its natural close, she as good as apologized for the last world war! Now I knew this girl was not really who she said she was, for she was surely some angelic being on assignment sent to comfort and strengthen my dear long suffering husband after our latest torturous holiday drama. This conclusion would be further strengthened when, later that night, on returning from a quick visit to the bathroom, I was not the slightest bit amused to discover that, rather inexplicably, the armrest that would normally act as a divider, was resting in the upright position, and John's head and shoulders were slumped across her ample chest.

"Pst, John, for goodness sake wake up," I hissed as I tried to rouse him from his deep slumber by giving him a couple of extremely sharp prods.

"What …what's wrong?" he innocently asked as he opened his eyes and gave a large yawn.

"You're almost in her lap, that's what's wrong. It's disgraceful. Lucky for you she's fast asleep. So sit up straight and behave yourself," I sternly reprimanded.

Around 3.00 am I would once again remove my sleep mask to pay yet another visit to the bathroom, only to discover that once more he had fallen still further down into her lap. I could only sigh as I placed my mask over my eyes leaving him to carry on sleeping like some blissfully contented young infant steeped in peaceful slumber as in his dreams he was transported well beyond the very gates of heaven.

Of course all good things must come to an end, so, when she awoke at around 5.00 am she had no other choice than to gently try and prize him off her lap as she now had urgent need of the little girls room. John was, of course, most contrite and began profusely apologizing for this unforeseen yet highly embarrassing incident. Amazingly she just looked him directly in the eye and, with a smile so sweetly innocent and yet beguiling, she kindly reassured him that, despite her thighs now feeling horribly numb, no offence had been taken.

As I stepped off the plane I knew there was a lesson in there for me, if only I cared to find it. That said, I do occasionally ask myself the question, was my husband really asleep as he claims to have been? When recently challenged about this unfortunate episode, he gave a boyish grin and pleaded the fifth amendment, otherwise known as the right to remain silent!

CHAPTER TEN

It Will Save Your Marriage

There came a day, when switching on the television, I found myself glued to the spot as some unfamiliar speaker announced to his audience that he intended to reveal the secret behind couples staying together and a happy marriage. He had my full attention. For the next ten minutes he kept us all waiting on the edge of our seats before he suddenly came out with it. There were immediate gasps of disbelief from his audience. My response to this sudden revelation was a little more melodramatic to say the least.

"Camping! He thinks camping saves marriages, the man's right off his rocker! for now I've heard it all," I shrieked.

As I gave further thought to his profound and startling revelation I began having my own personal epiphany. You see, for all those amongst us who've been camping, most come back home with amazing stories of horrendous hardship, such as endless days of sheet rain that find us permanently looking like drowned rats as our tents then get washed away in a river of mud and rain. Then there are the positively horrific stories of cows and sheep trampling over the tents, wild animals stealing our provisions, dangerous snakes hiding away in our sleeping bags and so on. So it seems that, for those foolhardy souls amongst us who dare to give camping a try out, we immediately become part of some global brat camp that instinctively demands that we learn a lesson or two in the brutal art of endurance. We unintentionally lose our lethargy and become so bound together in our seemingly terminal suffering that we are eventually forced to work as a team with everyone pitching in, and, with no television to distract or otherwise amuse, we finally begin to interact and communicate with those around us. As we continue to let our guard down we discover we actually like each other, so much so, that we are willing to spend most evenings sitting around a camp fire, chattering away about nothing in particular while playing silly games such as charades and 'Name That Tune.' Worse still, some bright spark never fails to produce a guitar out of nowhere and then we are all forced into a rousing round of "Ten Green Bottles, or better still 'Sweet Caroline, and Hi Ho Silver Lining' and it matters not a jot if we all sound like a load of freshly neutered cats doing the moonlight sonata.

Such an esoteric epiphany rarely takes place if you're vacationing at some luxury resort where your every whim is met by highly trained staff, whose sole reason for existing is to ensure that your holiday runs smoothly and is thoroughly memorable. Suffice to say the reason behind this 'Nothing is too much trouble' pampering to is to ensure that the minute we arrive home we'll waste no time in booking the next year with them, if not the following year just for good measure.

As for the camping vacation it doesn't end there either, for in the years to follow we gather our beloved ones around us as we then produce photographic evidence as visible proof of our terrible ordeal. What is also true is that, as we relive and revitalize those frightful camping tribulations, they ultimately bring us closer together as, for the first time ever, we roll about laughing at events that back then took us to the very brink of a well earned breakdown. I now knew that the speaker on television wasn't as balmy as I originally believed him to be, for actually it all made perfect sense.

My first camping experience took place way back when, as a child, I lived out my troubled existence in a small number of children's homes. One day, just like in a fairy tale, I was invited by a friend to go on a Girl Guides camp. I felt quite excited, however, like everything else in my torturous little life at that time, it very quickly went awry. I was placed in one of four teams, which in my case was the Robins Team. Why I became the 'chosen one' entrusted to stay behind and prepare my teams supper over a small camp fire I will never understand, for I can't actually remember volunteering. With no real outdoor cooking expertise under my belt, I was in way over my head. The team leader thought to hand me a few packs of sausages, tomatoes and some instant potato, and then her group bade me farewell to on an all afternoon flower searching expedition. At first I wasn't too bothered at being left behind to make supper but that soon changed. Things went drastically wrong after the loaded pan of sizzling sausages overturned into the open fire. Within seconds the fat encouraged the flames to rage higher making loud very unpleasant spitting noises that severely hampered my attempts to salvage the sausages before they became totally unrecognizable. I mean you try rescuing twenty or more pork sausages from the midst of a highly volatile mini volcano when they are in the final throes of spontaneous combustion, and I might add with only a three pronged dinner fork at your jolly disposal!

Having managed to salvage what I could my next predicament lay in the fact they were completely covered in black ash and leaves. There was no getting away from it, they looked and tasted like shriveled doggie turds! Put bluntly, I was up the creek without a paddle! The girls from my team arrived back at camp tired and ravenously hungry so, needless to say, they were shocked to be handed a plate of what now resembled the unearthed remains of a number of extinct Raphus Cucullatus, served up on a bed of sauted flora and fauna! They may have been middle class girl guides but they were completely lacking in 'Kumbaya,' as they threw some very uncharitable words in my direction before heading off to beg food from the other teams. Like everything else in my life my time in the Girl Guides would turn out to be exceedingly short lived.

Keeping all this in mind it would be a number of years later before I was invited to attend a church youth camp, this time as a helper. I had just launched into my twenties and my only current ambition in life remained the same and that was to feel and appear normal. Trust me, it wasn't easy. I arrived at the camp at a very late hour, with a one man tent that someone had kindly lent me. With no idea how to pitch the tent I walked towards a small hill and tried to put up the tent as best as I could.

During the night the wind picked up but happily my tent prevailed, although I did find it almost impossible to get any sleep. The next morning the first sensation I experienced was being prodded. I opened my eyes only to discover that during the night my sleeping bag, with me still inside, had slipped right out of the tent, and so from my neck downwards I lay outside on the grass at a ninety degree angle. As I weaved further out of the tent I became immediately aware of a number of curious children gathered round and looking down at me, their faces betraying a sense of bemusement at my unfortunate demise.

"Looks like you'll be needing help pitching your tent elsewhere," a very wise and serious dark haired boy mused, his arms folded as he glared directly into my eyes.

"Thanks, I'd appreciate a little help," I mumbled as, still cocooned in my sleeping bag, I attempted to sit up straight and act normal.

"And you've missed breakfast," a young freckle faced boy casually informed me.

"Oh right."

"Yeah, and you've only got five minutes before we're due to choose teams, so you'd better get a move on," some snotty pig tailed tom boy kindly reminded me. I headed down to the shower block and hurriedly got dressed, giving myself a quick spray under the arms as I had no time for anything else.

Back at base I stood in line with all the children and helpers as two young boys were ordered to handpick their teams. Now you would think that being many years older than all other participants, they would be clamoring to have me on their team. Not so! For by the end of the selection everybody had been picked for either the red team or the blue, with the exception of me. Both teams now had even numbers.

"Aw, you can 'ave her," Captain Magnanimous of the blue team very kindly offered the young captain of the red.

"Nah, she's all yours," he generously sniffed back.

"No go on, you take her," Captain Magnanimous gruffly insisted.

"We don't want her, so you can 'ave her," came the speedy reply from the young captain of the blue team. Still there were no takers. It was then taken out of their hands. Needless to say I felt extremely awkward and discouraged.

This little touching dialogue took place every morning without fail, and there was nothing I could do or say to change their minds, for sadly they had very legitimate reasons for not wanting me on their team. I think they saw me as something of a liability. In my defense my extremely poor vision was indeed part of the dilemma, as well as my little problem with dispraxia, which in layman's terms means I struggle to catch the ball, hit the ball, or even see the ball, and if you ask me to turn right, I will to this day instinctively turn left and visa versa. (In years to come this made my multiple attempts at the driving test all the more interesting). In the shooting contest not one arrow made it anywhere near its intended target as, without fail, each and every arrow came to gently rest at my feet. Day two saw me come in last on every race. In the ping pong tournament I spent more time under the table attempting to retrieve the balls, and I knew I was losing my last strains of credibility when on day three I rather unfortunately rolled over my team's canoe. I couldn't even win a single point in the "name that flower' competition, because, with the exception of the very identifiable dandelion, I had never stayed awake in biology class for long enough to appreciate or learn the names of any woodland flowers.

Thankfully my then fiancé John turned up at the camp on the last night and so he was able to comfort my bruised feelings.

"I feel so humiliated," I cried.

"Well, most sane adults wouldn't dream of going on a kid's camp in the first place," he consoled as I messed up his crisp white shirt with black mascara. That children's camp brought a welcome end to all camping trips for many long years. Then 1980 saw me get married and, weeks after our fateful honeymoon while innocently strolling past a local camping shop, we noticed a selection of tents for sale in the window. Now back then both of us would go weak at the knees when it came to a bargain, though over the years he had tempered the urge to spend, and thus resist all temptation, however the same could not be said where I was concerned. I don't care if the item in question is torn, cracked, chipped, singed, scorched, marked, missing half the product, whatever, for, if it has a bright red or orange reduced sticker, then I am utterly seduced as the urge to buy and take lawful possession completely takes over. Having wandered into the store to simply browse we left some ten minutes later having purchased ourselves a tent, a tent that for many years to come would not see the light of day, and so would safely remain in its original box hidden away in the attic, that is until a certain day when John had another of his amazingly brilliant ideas.

"Honey, it's vacation time, but with money being tight, I think it's time we tried our hand at a bit of camping."

"Uh!"

"Camping honey, yes and I think you're going to love it."

"Forget it, there's no way I am going to suffer two weeks of torrential rain and misery under canvas in some dung infested field surrounded by cows and a few testosterone filled bulls desperate to go on the rampage."

"No and guess what?

"What then?"

"I'm not expecting you to. Tricia, please just take a look at this advertisement. This campsite is near St. Tropez on the French Riviera in the South of France. As you know in my early twenties I lived and worked in the South of France, and I'm convinced that just like me, you'll just love it there."

"Yes, but that was way back when you were a hapless hippy."

"I was never hapless, whatever that means, but tell me what has that got to do with now?"

"John, if I rightly remember, didn't you tell me that you lived in a chicken shed while you worked on a French building site in Marseilles?"

"That's correct, but the chickens lived on the other half of the shed, although you wouldn't have known it when they started clucking around 4.00am in the morning."

"4.00 am! Bet that ruffled your feathers. And tell me straight what prevented them from coming over to your side?"

"Well, as it happens, there was a lot miscellaneous junk that separated us."

"John, I cannot even begin to imagine what possessed you to go and live in a chicken shed?"

"It wasn't my first choice. After my Morris Traveler caught fire, I had nowhere to live and the chicken hut belonged to my boss. He did however take me and the men out for dinner every lunchtime during the work day, and for a drink at various cafes on the way home."

"How kind and thoughtful of him."

"Well it was, although, saying that, the evening never ended until we were all well and truly sozzled."

"Perhaps being utterly inebriated made sleeping in a chicken shed more bearable, although forgive me saying this, but I think it would have been kinder still to offer you a proper bed as opposed to a pillow and blanket in a chicken shed, for I'll have you know chicken poop can cause serious illness and disease."

"This conversation is beginning to get a bit heavy so can we direct our thoughts back to our original conversation? Yes, let's get back to this holiday, shall we?"

"Well, was that the same time you met that strange hippie family who were going in search of paradise and so were looking for an island where they could live happily ever after?"

"No, that was another time."

"Did they ever find the island they were all searching for?"

"Tricia, I have no idea! However I want to discuss the here and now, so I need you to take a look at this French site that's right on the French Riviera."

"Hmm I don't know, it seems like hard work to me."

"Look, I promise you don't even have to do a thing. The tent is already on site with a cooker and everything else you might need, so we can leave our tent in the attic. All we have to do is turn up. Think of it as a second honeymoon."

"I thought we'd already tried the second honeymoon phase." The holiday was now booked.

CHAPTER 11

It's Time to Give It a Go

And so it was that we traveled to Victoria train station in London to then board an overnight coach bound for the South of France. The journey went without incident, despite the driver illegally fiddling the tacograph so he could drive the whole distance without taking a break. The next day we arrived at the site to be met by what looked like a large crowd of ghoulish ancestors from the Adams family clan, for, not only were they all drenched to the skin, but they all appeared morbidly depressed. As they stood in the mud looking like drowned rats, their personal luggage on the ground beside them, the rain heartlessly continued to beat down hard on them and, in that moment, I experienced my first deep sense of unease.

As we waited for the driver to pass out the luggage from the hold, some of those going home chose to move over towards us to tell us their tales of woe. I felt saddened to hear they had endured two whole weeks of non stop rain that saw all their tents waterlogged with water, within and without. For many their clothes and personal belongings had been ruined. There was worse to come. The brochure told us that the campsite was a mere three miles from St. Tropez, but what it failed to mention was it was actually three miles as the crow flies, so, unless we were going to sprout wings any time soon, we were stuck half way up a mountain a solid twelve miles from anywhere!

Later that afternoon, when we entered the campsite shop to buy essential provisions, we and others were to be further shocked as everything they sold was exorbitantly over priced, even down to the very basics. A burly unkempt man who went by the name Ron stood by the door offering his services as a taxi cab driver. He was one of the campsite workers who had the hindsight to make the journey in his large taxi. Over the years he had made a tidy killing from those desperate enough to use his unconscionably expensive services. Many families who'd brought children with them were immediately catapulted into great despair, a gloom that essentially overshadowed the holiday for everyone on site.

If the last campers had endured two full weeks of continual downpour we were in for two weeks of scorching heat and the small tent they provided did little to protect us from the blazing sun, for there was not a tree in sight. We didn't even have a mini fridge or cooler box to cool our bottled water let alone keep any food chilled and fresh. The site was overrun by swarms of giant ants who, despite the absence of an invite, had the liberty to think they could feed on our sweating flesh throughout the entire night and, in a matter of a few days, we were both covered in insect bites that quickly became infected.

John struggled to cook breakfast on a small portable gas stove for by eight in the morning the heat from the sun was already unbearable as it beat down hard on him. If only we could get to a supermarket then we could buy ourselves a decent sized cooler, insect repellant to douse our bodies and poison strong enough to send a goodbye message to those flesh eating termites.

A meeting was called so that we could all express our concerns to the main organizer, a seriously overweight and tardy woman who sported a moustache and answered to the name Jill. I never thought to ask her outright but I presumed her last job was surely a prison warden, for none of us were on an equal footing as she growled and bellowed insult after insult at any unruly and unworthy camper that dared even think to open their mouths and complain. Even the tears of distressed children failed to pierce her cold calculating heart. We tried to reason with her. We even offered to club together and pay the coach driver to take us to a French hypermarket to shop, but she was having none of it.

"Sorry, it's against company rules."

"How about we stop at a supermarket instead of a café on the next coach outing?"

"Sorry, it's against company policy."

"Well, show us now what your Company rules state."

"Sorry, I don't have the documents at my immediate disposal."

"Can't you bend the rules just a little and allow the coach driver as a token gesture to take us to a supermarket, so we can at least stock up on basic items."

"Sorry, but rules are meant to be adhered to."

"So you have been instructed by senior management to make sure we can only buy provisions at this campsite shop. Is that true?"

"Sorry, I refuse to answer that specific question."

"My god, it's like talking to a legally qualified parrot," one of the campers shouted over my head. We all left the makeshift office feeling very unhappy and annoyed. Outside, despite our frustration we still managed to exchange a number of friendly greetings.

"Tricia, this is Dave and Maggie, they're from up Manchester, and you must also say hello to Mick and Sharon, they're from Ipswich."

The next day many of us signed up for an organized sight seeing coach tour, secretly still hoping that, if en route we saw a supermarket of any size or description, we would try to make a run for it. We felt like a bunch of jailbirds on a days outing with the prison warden not only breathing down our necks but ready to whip us into shape should we even think to breach one of her many rules! Still against all odds we hoped to outsmart her. This trip would take us just across the border into Italy to a small seaside town named Ventimiglia. The coach stopped on the way to allow us to get some fresh air and to use some public toilets. In no time at all many other passengers congregated around us as we discussed our urgent need to buy reasonably priced food.

"Pst… that place over there looks like it might sell food," I furtively whispered in John's ear.

"Why are you whispering?"

"Because I don't want Jill to get wind of what we're about to do."

"Well that's daft because, if you look behind, you'll see that she's still back in the coach."

"Oh. Anyway John, as you speak fluent French, it's up to you to make a quick run for it, and I'll cover for you if she dares ask where you've disappeared to."

"Okay, but don't let the coach go without me" he anxiously begged. He arrived back completely out of breath.

"Sorry everyone, but it only sold sweets and magazines."

"Oh dear. Well, the Gestapo have twice called out for everyone to re-board, so there's not a lot more we can do. By the way, my name's Richard and my girlfriend here is Sally"

The trip turned out to be a futile waste of money, for back then Ventimiglia appeared to be a very poor Italian town and, if this was not to be the case, we certainly never made it past the poor district, even the beach was littered with used needles. As we sat on a bench to share a small sandwich it was official, we were depressed and terribly homesick.

On the way home the coach broke down so Jill left the coach to watch over the coach driver as he took a look inside the engine. With her out of earshot the moans of many grew louder and louder. It felt sad to hear all these big men groaning and complaining, so I hit on a plan.

"John, pass me a sheet of paper and a pen."

"What are you up to now?"

"Never mind you'll soon see." I moved further down the coach then in a loud voice I asked for everyone's attention.

"Look, before things get even worse I think we should contact a newspaper in London, and maybe they'll want to do a story. So if you interested in getting some action, please sign this piece of paper. The more signatures the better, for we then have a much better chance of getting some positive action."

"We'll completely run out of money before we get to the end of the first week," one very depressed young mother cared to share.

"I'm in the same boat," another young mum chirped up. "We all feel so helpless and fed up."

"Yes well, just get everybody to sign and then leave the rest to me."

The piece of paper made its way around the entire coach before coming back to me. I was immediately taken by surprise as I noted that hardly a soul had written down their name.

"I can't believe this, what a bunch of wimps! For all their whining and moaning they are too scared to act."

"Tricia, when will it dawn on you that, when you think you have a wealth of support urging you on, it's still wise to check behind before you go charging onto the battlefield all guns blazing."

"You don't say!"

"Yep, for it's normally at that point you discover you're entirely on your own."

"Okay then, we will go it alone. and first thing tomorrow we'll get ourselves moved to another site." We arrived outside Herr Commandant's office early the following day. There was no sign of her. Finally we caught up with another member of her team.

"Hi there, we were hoping to speak with Jill."

"Sorry, it's her day off.'

"Then whose in charge until she returns?"

"No one."

"So nobody is in any position to help us?"

"Afraid not. You could come back tomorrow."

"Come on Tricia, let's leave it, for we're clearly wasting out time," John mumbled as he grabbed hold of my hand and tried to get me to leave with him.

"Alright, but we're definitely coming back, that I promise," I shouted back. After returning to our tent we got ourselves organized and then headed down to the beach. The sun was beating down hard on our backs as we walked the two or more miles that saw us scaling a huge hill covered in large ants.

"John, I can't even begin to comprehend how families with toddlers or any of the old age pensioners could possibly make it onto the beach for I feel as though I've just successfully completed an SAS military exercise," I gasped as I wiped my dripping forehead. After placing our towels down John momentarily remained standing, a hand shading his eyes as he surveyed the horizon.

"Tricia, I can't be certain but I'm pretty sure that's Jill over there.

"Really, well that's good news, for can I make a small suggestion?"

"Hmm.. Your 'small suggestions usually take on the form of a court order, but carry on."

"Well, as we've found her hiding place, I think that now would be a good time for you to go and talk to her."

"What now?"

"Well, now's as good a time as any."

"Yes but remember, we were told that this is her day off."

"Oh gosh, so we were. Well, I'd hate to disturb her on her day off," I retorted very tongue in cheek.

"Well then, let's leave her be."

"Look here 'Mr. Non Confrontational' for, sad as it must seem to interrupt her personal space as I truly care about big Bertha's abiding happiness, but I would have thought it equally imperative that we get our situation resolved as soon as possible."

He knew right there and then there would be no rest whatsoever until he had done his duty for queen and country, well for his personal drama queen anyway.

"Oh, do I have to?" he moaned. I didn't care to answer. I just gave him the evil eye.

I watched on as John reluctantly meandered over towards her, and I have to say that the communication between them seemed a little too short for my liking. He arrived back and slumped down onto the towel.

"Well then how did it go?"

"Um right… it wasn't easy," was his extremely timid response.

"Quite what do you mean?"

"Just that."

"Come on John, spit it out! What's the problem?"

"Well she's wearing almost nothing, just a tiny extremely ill fitting thong."

"Just a thong! You've got to be kidding me."

"Yes well this is French Riviera, so it's considered the norm to be topless. Anyway forgive me, but my natural instinct was to just stare, I mean turn away."

"So you failed to discuss anything connected with getting us moved to another site, did you?"

"Oh come on! Don't be furious with me, for how could I have any sort of reasonably intelligent conversation when every time I looked down I was confronted by a pair of gynormous bazookas. Trust me, when I say it was downright impossible talking to them, I mean her."

"Oh alright," I groaned loudly as I lay back down on my towel.

"Answer me this, big Bertha must be at least be a whopping 44 D."

"Add another D or two to that! Now please can we change the subject."

CHAPTER TWELVE

Hey That's No Way to Say Goodbye

That same evening there was an organized coach trip to a restaurant in a beautiful town of Port Grimaud which is like a mini Venice built on man made waterways. It sounded very much like our cup of tea. We paid up in full and were glad to hear that our new friends Richard and Sally as well as Dave and Maggie were coming along. The coach quickly filled up and before long we were heading along the winding French roads heading for Port Grimaud

The restaurant was situated on a canal and as soon as we entered I wondered, how they were going to seat us all? That nagging question was soon answered when the restaurant staff took us outside to their pretty garden. The waiter then attempted to squeeze us onto some small wooden tables and benches that were positioned alongside the canal, however they were far too small to accommodate us all, and I found myself at the end of the table, right next to the canal, hanging on for dear life.

"John, this really isn't going to work, for if I let go of this table for even a second, I'm a goner!"

"Okay, just give the others a minute or two to settle down then I will get us moved to a safer spot." I waited patiently for quite some time.

"Honey, I don't think you fully understand the urgency, for I really can't hold on much longer," I hissed in his ear.

"Okay okay, let's order our food then I will get us moved to another table, I promise."

When the waiter finally approached our table to take our order he informed us all that drinks of any description were to be paid for separately.

"What, even water?" I queried.

"Yes madam, we only serve bottled water that comes straight from the Alps," he informed our table in the most appealing sexy French romantic sounding voice.

"John, you speak fluent French, so why don't you speak to me like that," I challenged.

"But you wouldn't understand a word I'd be saying!"

"Oh, believe me I would."

Having been told by Jill that everything was included, most of us had stupidly left our purses and wallets back at the campsite for we had foolishly believed everything to mean just that, everything! Suddenly Richard abruptly stood to his feet.

"Right that's it, I've had about as much as I can take, so we're out of here," he announced looking down at his girlfriend. "John, Tricia are you coming? And what about you Dave, are you guys going to join us?"

"I think Mag's and I had best stay put," Dave sheepishly answered.

"Okay, see you guys later. So John and Tricia have you made up your minds? Are you coming or staying?"

"Yes we're coming, but if we leave what are we to do about our pre-paid dinner?" John queried.

"Well I've got a few franks on me, so we'll find somewhere else to eat, but first we need to let Jill know our decision," Richard bravely suggested. I was most grateful for this sudden change of plan as my main concern had nothing to do with paying extra for liquid refreshments and more to do with surviving the evening without falling headlong into the canal, and in all fairness if I was to look back at my long personal history, the odds were heavily stacked against me.

As was to be expected Jill went berserk, however, unless she was going to chain us to the benches she had little choice but to let us go.

"You'll not be getting all your money back," she angrily shouted after us.

"Fine by me," Richard very nonchalantly replied.

Before leaving we very wisely thought to check with her regarding what time the coach would be leaving to return to the campsite. "Eleven o'clock, and not a minute later," was our furious Herr Commandant sharp response.

"We'll be back in plenty of time," Richard stated staring her directly in the eye. We soon found ourselves a delightful restaurant but with little to money on us we were forced into sharing a small portion of chicken and chips accompanied by a couple of bread rolls. The waiters stood to one side and watched on with amusement. It took more time to fairly divide the humble bird than it took to consume it we were that ravenous. We all agreed we could easily devour another chicken ten times over and still have room for dessert. After much light hearted conversation things took on a more serious note.

Richard was the first to speak.

"I don't know about you guys but this whole camping holiday is a flippin' joke."

"We think so too. Saying that Tricia has been studying contract law at our local college and she thinks there is a clear case of misrepresentation."

"So Tricia, what do you intend to do?"

"Well I'm not going to leave it. Everybody at the site is moaning and groaning away yet they'll all go home and do nothing. It's all so jolly British, yes chin up and all that, but it's wrong, because they will continue deceiving innocent holidaymakers until they're stopped."

"You're right."

"There is a famous legal case, Jarvis versus Swan Tours which went to court in 1973."

"Go on, we're all ears."

"Well for some inexplicable reason the case was presided over by the most prestigious judge in England, Lord Denning, Master of the Rolls. Anyway the plaintiff, a lonely English attorney, craving a bit of fun and companionship, booked himself a two week Christmas holiday in Switzerland. The tour operators promised two weeks of sizzling entertainment starting with a welcome party on arrival. There would also be a daily sumptuous afternoon tea where chocolate cake would be served up. Add to this a candlelight dinner, a yodeling evening and a whole host of other things, and he believed he would have himself a holiday to remember. On arrival he was slightly concerned that the manager didn't speak a word of English, also there were only thirteen guests in the hotel, so the arrival party was sadly lacking in atmosphere. If that was bad enough, in the second week the hotel was empty of all guests except our non English speaking manager, making it jolly difficult for him to even begin to get into the party mood. Worst still the plaintiff was forced to eat the candlelit dinner all on his own. Now how romantic is that? The final straw came on the yodeling evening when the Yodeler, a local village man, turned up halfway through dinner looking hot and disheveled in his grubby work clothes, and after yodeling his way through a couple of songs, like he were some highly strung athlete running a ten minute marathon, he then left to go home for supper and a shower. And if you hadn't already guessed there was no ….'

"No chocolate cake for tea?" Richard hurriedly interjected.

"You're absolutely correct, no jolly chocolate cake! Come on guys stop laughing for this really was a real legal case."

"Okay… okay."

"Well Lord Denning ruled in favor of the plaintiff, stating it was a clear case of breach of contract, so our lawyer friend was awarded damages albeit limited for distress and disappointment."

"Wow that's such a funny story."

"Yep and it's all true. You know something, I really regret not taking legal action over our Greek honeymoon but, when we returned home, we were so shocked to discover our house purchase had fallen through and then John lost his job, so we had more than enough on our plate. However this camping trip was supposed to make up for our disastrous honeymoon and although it doesn't even begin to compare in terms of the distress I still feel so fuelled up that I fully intend to do something as soon as we get back to England, even if its just to contact the Department of Fair Trade."

"Hmm… well good luck," Richard said as he suddenly looked down at his wristwatch. "Look I know it's only 9.30, but my gut instinct is to head back to the other restaurant for our seething Herr Commandant would surely love to drive the coach home herself, if it means leaving without us!"

Our concerns were not groundless for, when we arrived back an hour early than agreed time, we were flabbergasted to see the coach driver revving up the engine with everyone on board, and it was clear they were just about to head back to the campsite without us!

"Thank goodness we were one step ahead of her," John muttered as we quickly boarded the bus. Jill's face was as viciously tight and distorted as that of a raging pit bull.

The next morning we paid our seriously hostile commandant a visit, and refused to leave her office until she had agreed to move us to another of their many campsites. Her hatred was visible.

"I'll see what I can do," she angrily spat.

"Thank you we would be most grateful," John politely replied. A short phone call later and we were informed by Jill that it was all sorted so finally we were going to be moved to another site.

Needless to say, but we were elated!

"Good riddance to the both of you," she snorted as we hastily left her office.

"How rude!" I loudly announced.

"Tricia, stop it! Sometimes to win is to lose, so let her believe she's won."

After hurriedly packing up our belongings our taxi arrived to take us to another site.

"Oh wow this looks great," I exclaimed as the taxi came to a halt at a camp which was set just off the beach in a beautiful woodland area. After where we'd just come from it was indeed, Utopia!

Jill made it her top priority to warn the staff of this next camp that we would be nothing but trouble, but we didn't care for, having finally been released from a prison camp we were in seventh heaven! The remainder of our holiday was one of utter bliss, although we never got used to bumping into half clothed holiday makers as we made our way down the small pathway that took us directly onto the beach. I couldn't help notice that John would immediately drop his head down like some schoolboy in the headmasters office, his eyes examining his feet whenever topless young ladies passing us by on the pathway, innocently chose to stop for a friendly chat.

"Why is it whenever we meet partially dressed young ladies on the pathway you feel the need to have some hearty elongated conversation?" he would moan.

"Oh come on, I love teenagers for they're so interesting, so I'm just being friendly. Besides, you know full well I'm a people's person."

"Yes well, I love people too."

"Hmm… but more from a distance."

"Oh right."

"Yeah right. Well it's hard to stand around chatting in the sweltering heat while the back of your neck is being scorched, This is possibly why the French give it the name soleil de plomb, which means a sun like red hot iron."

"Go on, admit it, you're really embarrassed aren't you?" I playfully challenged.

"I don't know what you mean."

"Oh I think you do," I teased.

"Yes well, we have to remember that this is the South of France and the French are much more comfortable in their skins than the rest of us Europeans put together," he sighed.

"Well I think the German's top the list for sunning in the raw."

"Anyway Tricia it would be much appreciated if you could consider keeping all future pathway conversations down to a bare minimum."

"I like the bare bit."

"You're not taking me seriously."

There came a day when we decided to head along the sandy beach that stretched for miles. About an hour into the walk I began to feel the first signs of sunstroke.

"John, if it's okay with you I'd like to head back for I'm burning up and feeling faint from thirst."

"Okay, but you'll have to hang on for that drink, for we're clean out of water

"John, I really do need a drink," I gasped.

"Look I think I can see a shop over there," he stated as shielding his eyes he pointed into the distance.

"Right let's make our way over and see for ourselves." As we approached I was delighted to discover that for once he was right and it was a supermarket. Getting a sudden spurt of energy I raced ahead of him.

"Oh my goodness!"

"What Tricia?" John gasped as he came to stand at my side.

"John look those men are completely...... starkers! Oh my goodness I can see all their didgeridoos!" I screeched, my eyes out on stalks as I pointed down the aisle towards a cluster of extremely elderly gentlemen.

"Tricia stop shouting and pointing!" John hurriedly ordered.

"I'm not shouting," I insisted.

"Oh yes you are."

"Well sorry but not only are they as naked as the day they were born but they're standing right by some open freezers."

"Oh dear we must have accidentally strayed onto a nudist beach," John deeply sighed.

Suddenly the men were joined by some elderly equally naked heavy bosomed women carrying weaved baskets who, after exchanging a few brief words, began leaning over the freezer as they rummaged around for the meat of their choice.

"John I've heard of frozen chicken breasts but these women are taking it to new found heights!"

"Sh.. Do be quiet."

"Well, if they lean over any further their nipples and other bits will surely freeze over."

"Hush… you're so unbelievably loud and offensive at times."

"I never knew such supermarkets existed. We need to get out of here and fast," I cried.

"What about the water?"

"Forget the water, let's just get out of here."

"No honey, you can go and stand outside while I get us some water."

"Alright but I'm going to hide round the corner well out of sight, so be quick."

Clutching a chilled bottle of water we raced as fast as our legs could take us back in the direction we had come, back to the world we knew.

"John I can't imagine why anyone especially old people would even want to go naked," I remarked, breathing a sigh of relief that we were finally back on the normal beach.

"Nope, neither do I," he replied as a couple of stunning topless girls passed us by giggling as they made their leisurely way down to the waters edge.

"By the way can we come back next year?" he quipped.

"Absolutely not," was my swift response.

A few days, before leaving for home, we chose to do one final excursion that included an evening meal at some up-market restaurant that had it's own disco.

"John, help me out, the lighting is so poor in here, I can hardly see in front of me," I whispered as we tentatively entered the restaurant. Suddenly and much to our joy we accidentally bumped into our friends that we had left behind at the other campsite.

"John, Tricia!"

"Hey Richard, Sally."

"Come and join us," they urged pointing to some spare seats.

After drawing up a chair we began excitedly exchanging our gossip, beginning with 'Camp Gestapo.' The news was not good, but it did make for hilarious dinner time conversation that saw us all almost falling off our seats.

"Jill now hates us almost as much as she hated you two."

"I very much doubt it," I hastily retorted. "Anyway what are you eating?"

"Oh we chose the salmon but we must warn you, this restaurant is ever so pricey, so take great care when ordering off the menu."

As our friends were already half way through their dinner it was left to us or rather me to do most of the talking. I rose to the occasion as I regaled one story after another in my normal inimitable fashion which included the use of both hands, when suddenly all laughter stopped and their faces now appeared very pinched and strained.

"Oh my goodness, what have I said to offend them so badly?" I thought, suddenly feeling quite panicked. Even though it was very dark inside the restaurant I couldn't fail to see that Richard's face was now furiously twitching. Still I carried on talking, as the silence was agonizingly uncomfortable, and I still had no idea what was wrong. Seconds later he leapt to his feet and began frantically shaking the front of his trousers and it finally dawned that, as a result of my gesticulations, I had accidentally knocked over the whole of their bottle of their very expensive Merlot!

"Look please forgive me, for I had absolutely no idea. I'm so sorry," I repeated over and over as I hurriedly began wiping the table with my serviette. Sadly there was to be no forgiveness that night, even though I offered to buy them another bottle of wine and pay his dry cleaning bill. Moments later he called over to the waiter to announce that they wished to settle up, then, with their bill paid they got up from their seats, threw down their serviettes and, without so much as a passing glance, they marched out of the restaurant, and out of our lives.

We remained at the table with no words passing between us, our despondent hearts heavy as we tried to make light of what had just taken place. I would never know if the meal placed before us that night was wonderful or inedible, for hardly a morsel passed our lips, for not only had our new friends abandoned us, but our appetites also. We weren't up for any dancing either.

"Tricia, how come you never noticed you'd knocked over their bottle of wine?"

"John you know full well I'm as blind as a bat, and besides you didn't notice either! Trust me, I couldn't feel more terrible if I tried, and it only goes to show just how fragile friendships can be," I ruefully stated as I reflected on just how much we'd enjoyed their company.

"Yep, well try to keep your hands to yourself, for this is not the first time you've accidentally knocked over peoples drinks and I doubt if it will be the last either."

"I know. But telling me to keep my hands to myself is like ordering me to stop breathing. So I think I'm ready for that lobotomy," I miserably mused

"That's a bit drastic isn't it?'

"Not really, for living out the remainder of my life in a vegetable state seems quite the safest option to me."

"Honey, it's a vegetative state."

"Same difference

"Come on Mrs. Magoo we'd better make a move, otherwise we'll miss the coach home, and only heaven knows what would happen then!"

Even though we hadn't seen Jill since leaving Camp Gestapo, not wishing to be outdone she had one final little surprise up her sleeve. She had kindly arranged for us to travel back to England on an entirely different coach, and it also meant losing a day off our two week holiday. The morning of the pick up we were amazed to discover she had very thoughtfully organized for us to travel back with a coach filled with physically and mentally challenged kids and their helpers. I imagine Jill had a good chuckle thinking she had got her full sweet revenge. Yes it's true the journey home was quite an unusual experience and yes we had little to no sleep due to the constant noise, but if Jill thought she had the last laugh, she was wrong. I did, as I had promised and wrote a short letter of complaint to the Department of Fair Trading. Some weeks later I was paid a surprise visit by one of their inspectors who sat down and, over a cup of tea, we went through all the details with a fine tooth comb. Some months later I received a letter from their department informing me that as a result of a visit to the campsite by one of their inspectors, they had made the decision to prosecute the company. The company were also ordered to rewrite their brochures more accurately. Sometime later I heard that they'd ceased trading.

CHAPTER THIRTEEN

La Voiture Ancienne

Within months of meeting John I came to understand that he had a deep abiding love affair with France that started when he was a schoolboy going on exchange visits, so, despite my endless protestations he would once again persuade me to revisit the French Riviera for our summer holiday, again this was before we had children. To get me on board he agreed to abandon all thoughts of camping, opting instead for some cheap and cheerful accommodation. This way we could keep all potential crises to a bare minimum. I readily agreed as on our previous trip we had passed by a lovely looking guest house, so surely if we stayed there, well away from tents, nothing could or would go pear shaped. Wrong again!

In my desire to enrich and empower myself I decided to attend a French evening class so that I could communicate better with our French neighbors. I hated it when John met up with someone of French origin for I always found myself left out in the cold, and jabbing him hard in the ribs to translate didn't work either, as he just kept blabbering on.

"What did he just say?" I would ask.

"Oh nothing really."

"Look John, it's so unfair, all you ever give me are the bare bones, yet I need more, so that I too can feel involved," I whined

"Sorry no can do, besides you always expect everything down to the tiniest detail."

"It's a girl thing."

"The answer is still a resounding no."

"Then, you're downright mean."

"Well for goodness sake if you don't like it, learn the language or get your own translator."

"Oh trust me I will."

The French evening class was a blast, and when a year later I found myself in the final session, I was touched when our extremely nice tutor handed me a bouquet of flowers and chocolates. I must add this was not the usual thing handed out to students, the rest of the class were awarded certificates for passing the exam.

"These are from us all to say thank you for all the Evening soirees you've thrown for us. I think I speak for everyone present when I say this has been the best and friendliest evening class I've ever taught."

"Here here."

At the time I was thrilled by this kind accolade, but I was also somewhat ashamed that, after a whole year taking these classes, I still could only string a few French words together, although I have to say those few meaningful words were to me priceless! For example top of the list was: "Est ce que cette hotel a une piscine?" Which translated means "Does this hotel have a swimming pool? Of course this was top of on my list along with "Can you direct me to the nearest loo?" Despite being secretly impressed that I could mutter anything remotely translatable in some foreign language John saw things very differently.

"What's the point in wasting all that time and money when you've only managed to learn a few sentences, whereas all your class colleagues now have a certificate."

"Yes, but certificates are inedible."

"True."

"John, let me remind you that I was the only one who got flowers and chocolates."

"Oh right, what more can I say?"

"Well, it's an extremely difficult field, but don't worry I'll do better next year."

"Yes, who knows what further few words you might add to your growing French vocabulary," he said in a manner I concluded was not meant to be the least bit complimentary. Anyway back to the holiday. Our car not only felt a lot older than both our combined ages, but in my mind it was only one step up from Fred Flintstones stone age wagon. I therefore felt a trifle anxious when John proposed that we abandon all thought of taking a plane and take the old rust bucket to save money. We were up at 3.00am, and off by 4.00, and on the ferry to France by 7.00. Up until this point I had not been the least bit snobby about our old beat up banger, that is until, having crossed the English channel, we headed down the Autoroute on our way back down to the French Riviera. Well then things changed dramatically.

"John, seeing all the cars slow down so that they can stare at our car is making me squirm."

"Honey, trust me, it's only because it's almost a collector's item." he enthused.

"But look at them gawping at us. Anyone would think we were a couple of chimpanzees that have just escaped the zoo."

"Take no notice."

"No notice? John we're about to cause a serious motorway pile up as every car that passes slows right down to get a good look. Why some are even making funny faces at us. It's becoming really embarrassing."

"Look honey, they are just being friendly, so why don't you just close your eyes and try to ignore it."

"I can't. I'm too upset. I'm never doing this again."

It was now dark and late into the evening (John having decided to do the whole trip in one day to save on hotel bills), and we turned into a small car park for we needed the restrooms, as well as refreshments. Twenty or so minutes later we climbed back into the car to go on our way. John placed the key in the ignition, nothing! He tried over and over but not even a measly whirring sound to give us the tiniest bit of hope.

"There I knew it! We should never have made this trip in this old rust bucket!" I cried.

"Okay honey please just calm down."

"Calm down? We're stuck in France in a old banger that's only fit for the Demolition Derby, and you expect me to calm down," I bawled.

"Oh honey, you're speaking utter twaddle for there's hardly any rust on it all!"

"Oh rubbish!"

"Look, we may well have to push it to the nearest garage."

"No get that right, YOU will, for there's no way I'm going to push this old heffalump anywhere."

"Oh come on Tricia, now is not the time to give up. I need your co operation for I can't do this on my own."

"Read my lips, for when does no become yes?"

"Please, let's just give it a try."

"Sorry honey, but I'm not going to push this ancient jalopy along the motorway while half of France decides to take snapshots of us for their local television channel otherwise the family album. It's simply not happening!"

"Look, I know you're feeling a trifle upset but…"

"You really think I'm just a trifle upset?" I gasped. "No John, allow me to put you in the picture, I'm hopping mad!"

"Okay, then wait here while I go and find us some help," he ordered.

I watched him until he disappeared out of sight and I tried my very best to remain 'adult' about this latest crisis, really I did, but inside extreme fear was already beginning to well up. What if he arrives back without help? Oh, and what if we were about to be ripped off by a local garage? Worse case scenario, what if our old jalopy was pronounced to be unsalvageable? Oh, what a great time to be finding that out! If my worst fears were confirmed, and the car was certified as being ready for the scrapheap, would we then find ourselves having to head back home on foot? If that was the case, would John be capable of carrying all our heavy luggage? These and many other questions needed a serious answer for, if we did manage to get a lift, how could we be make certain we had not been picked up by France's latest serial killer? After all, these things do happen, don't they? Oh why oh why did everything we planned go so hopelessly wrong?

"Feel the fear and do it anyway" had yet to be penned but, if it had been in print, I would have ordered myself at least a dozen copies, for, after a harrowing childhood I trusted no one, not even myself! I was therefore a slave to every imaginable fear. So here this day stranded and alone in some run down French car park, I found myself yet again at the mercy of every crippling thought that my runaway mind could cruelly care to conjure up, and before too long I had even succumbed to the idea that I might not live to see another day. With that thought now settled I busied myself organizing my impending funeral by composing both the order of service as well as the numerous comforting hymns that would make it a funeral service to remember. As I went on to write John's public address I began feeling stirred to the seat of my emotions.

"Finally, having said almost everything I can think to say concerning my dearly departed wife who sadly died alone in some run down French car park, I want to leave you with a few thoughts, for despite all the madness and mayhem that so unfairly surrounded her, she was actually an extremely compassionate person. Why, she even confided that when only a child she had shed many tears over the assassination of President Kennedy that one might be forgiven for thinking she was a close member of their tightly knit family. Oh, and on more than one occasion she asked me if we could organize a remembrance service for all those who went down on Titanic, as the movie 'A night to remember,' had affected her so deeply. Finally Tricia would most likely have liked to use this occasion to make amends for the many untimely deaths that may well have occurred during her extremely brief career as a trainee nurse and so to alleviate her conscience she proposed at some point to cash in her three million cigarette coupons in exchange for kitchen equipment which will be sent to the wing of the hospital that counsels the bereaved. Having just read her last will and testament I have also given in to her wishes that on her gravestone, instead of a simple word or two, it will now read 'Here lies the body of 'Miss Eversomisunderstood'.

Now, if we could all kindly rise to our feet and join in singing the last song which you will find on the back of your 'Order of Service' sheet and is aptly entitled 'It's a heartache' by Bonnie Tyler. Those close to us will be aware that we claimed this song as 'ours' during our long and exceedingly tumultuous relationship. So thank you all so kindly for attending here today. God bless you and please drive home safely."

The gravediggers were in the process of lowering my flower strewn coffin into the ground when John suddenly arrived back at the car park with a little Frenchman in tow. The man looked swarthy and unkempt with thick stubble and tatty blue paint splattered overalls.

"John where on earth have you been?"

"Searching for help of course."

"You've been gone so long I was really worried."

"Well I'm back now."

"John, listen to me the man's not only fat and scruffy but I can smell the garlic from here and, if you hadn't noticed there's at least a days stubble sprouting from his chin, so surely he can't be a decent garage mechanic."

"I never said he was."

"Well why couldn't you find us a proper mechanic?"

"Well, beggars cannot be choosers, and this little guy assured me he could help us."

"Honey I'm perplexed for he's anything but little, in fact he's positively on the large side!"

"Hang on honey, what entitles you to assume mechanics have no right to be overweight, grow stubble or have garlic oozing from their pores?" Of course I ignored his latest downright ridiculous question.

"John, he won't know what he's doing!"

"Oh Tricia, change the channel, and give the poor man a chance." I was left to watch on in stupefied horror from the car window as, after lifting up the hood of the car, he suddenly produced a large hammer from some secretive compartment of his overalls to then systematically bash down hard on various parts of the temperamental engine.

"Oh good grief! He's probably used up our last hope of ever getting this car fixed and back on the road," I loudly exclaimed.

The grubby little Frenchman came out from under the hood and, after wiping his greasy little hands down on the front of his dungarees, he took John to one side and, with a furrowed brow, he began to talk in a manner that suggested that bad news was imminent.

"Sacre Bleu!"

"Now what does that mean?" I asked leaning further out of window.

"It means sacred blue."

"Well then he's making no sense whatsoever!"

"Oh Tricia, it's a sort of old fashioned acceptable French cuss word."

"Oh right."

"Quelle voiture ancienne! Elle est si belle!" he then cried

"Is that grubby little man still cussing?"

"No."

"Well then what's Tubby saying?"

"He's says our car is very ancient."

"How unbelievably observant this dear man is."

"Oh and beautiful."

"Is he blind as well as stupid?" I snorted in pure disgust.

"Yes well, I pointed out that it does have exceedingly low mileage on the clock, so he is now suggesting that the mileage is unrealistically low, and may well have been altered by some dodgy previous owner."

"Yes well he's probably onto something there."

"He's now saying it looks more like a gangster car, and you are my moll?"

"Tell Frenchie, this is not America!"

Our effervescent and very talkative Frenchman gave an almighty grin as he dutifully wiped away the large beads of sweat running down his forehead.

"Good god where are the poor man's teeth?" I cried out the window.

"Oh don't worry, he has them safely tucked away in his top pocket."

Our endearing garlic scented Frenchman continued to rant on in his native language and John now in a very uncooperative mood refused to interpret anything further.

"John I feel left out in the cold."

"Honey, may I remind you that you wouldn't need an interpreter if, instead of repeatedly inviting the whole class back to our place for impromptu evening soirees, you'd chosen instead to pay more attention and actually done some the homework given you," he stated in what I perceived to be a most disparaging manner.

"Oh right, 'Mr. Life and soul' of the party."

"I think it's high time for the mute button, don't you?"

Suddenly our excitable little Frenchman popped up from under the hood and surprised us both by speaking out, albeit in very broken English.

"Your leetle wife, shee eez not at all happee," he cried, more as a statement of fact.

"That's an understatement," I moaned loudly.

"Well actually, believe it or not, this is her at her absolute happiest." John quickly retorted. "Yes as you can see she's overflowing with irrepressible joy."

The Frenchman shrugged his shoulders to express that he did not fully understand.

"Ho.. Ho.. Ho."

"Honey remember it's not Christmas."

"Right."

Eventually Frenchie ordered John to get back into the driver's seat and turn the key. Still nothing.

"John, just give him the money for a couple of rounds of Pernod and a pack of Gauloise cigarettes, then let him go, for he's clearly not up to the task," I piped up

"Just give him a few more minutes. will you?"

"I'm trying, really I am, but this is altogether crazy."

Every time I poked my head out of the window the little fat Frenchman seemed to look up and give me a quirky little toothless grin. I tried hard to smile back, but it wasn't easy. A few minutes later he once again shouted for John to give the key another try. Suddenly, against all odds, the car sprang to life. Oh the sound of the car shaking and vibrating suddenly seemed so intensely wonderful. Leaving the engine to continue turning over John hurriedly stepped out of the car and, after opening his wallet he walked towards our liberator to offer money and to express our thanks, but now, like a fly on food, he was impossible to catch hold of as he began to leap and dance around the car park as if he had just won the jackpot on the fruit machine of the local village bar, such was his sudden outburst of joie de vivre. When he finally came to his senses he was completely out of breath.

"I wonder, does he do this often?" I shouted out the window as John took a hold of his hand to give him a small wad of francs as a thank you for his help.

"John I hope it's enough," I cried out. However it wasn't anywhere near enough, and I'm not talking money! Oh no, for this ebullient man appeared to crave physical affection over filthy rotten lucre. With the francs safely deposited in his pocket alongside his teeth, he stretched out his arms and began to embrace my stiff as a board husband. The dear man then refused to let go of him until he had almost crushed his ribcage to a pulp while expending numerous sloppy kisses to both sides of his cheeks.

Then having finally finished showering John with more passionate kisses then he'd surely ever had from me, he then worryingly turned his full attention in my direction! As he began his advance towards the car I had an overwhelming urge to rapidly wind up the window, for, despite being filled with immense gratitude I still felt quite incapable of expending even the very minimum of my new found joy on a lengthy kissing session with a sweaty fat Frenchman who oozed garlic from every pore of his podgy little being. Taking quick action I shot my hand out of the side window to say "merci' over and over while giving his grubby little outstretched hand a formidably hearty shake while noting his other arm remained high in the air as he continued swinging his hammer high above his head.

"Quick put your foot on the pedal and lets hightail out of here before he knocks himself out, for then we'll be forced to stay and call for an ambulance," I shouted out to John who was now getting back in the driving seat, ready to set off.

"Au Revoir……Merci beaucoup…" we yelled out the window while waving at our French savior until he was less than a polka dot on the horizon. At last we were on our way, although, having broken down once I was feeling anxious that it could well happen again, and if it did, would we be able to find ourselves another irrepressibly jubilant toothless Frenchman with a large hammer tucked away in his paint splattered work overalls? I very much doubted it.

CHAPTER FOURTEEN

Eggs, Eggs and More Jolly Eggs

Finally it grew dark, and we were still some way from our intended destination, so we came off the motorway to go in search of an inexpensive hotel for the night. We thought we had found one, but, having peered through a window, we despaired to see it filled to capacity with a large number of heavy set Frenchmen sitting hunched together over a jug of rough rouge wine, while engulfed in a thick swirling haze of smoke. Sadly it was a little too rough and ready for our liking, so we agreed to drive on. That little stop nearly cost us our lives for, as soon as John began driving down the dark lane, he went into automatic pilot, and in doing so he moved over to the left hand side of the road. Five minutes later a car was coming very fast at us in our lane, and we only just averted a major head on collision through a dramatic last minute swerve. The people in the other car were naturally shaken and therefore extremely upset so began to hurl abuse in French

I knew this could have happened to anybody driving in another country where they insist on driving on the wrong side of the road! All the same I now felt very nervous, so I decided there and then that the next time we poked our heads inside a small hotel I had already decided the outcome beforehand. Yes, even if the unshaven greasy haired manager suffered from a most disturbing case of psoriasis, while the hotel chef used his index finger to excavate his left nostril before moving on to remove all embedded wax from his ears whilst serving up our continental breakfast, and if after a close inspection of the bed sheets a large number of suspicious looking curly hairs were to be discovered, and if the place was overflowing with obese, garlic loving, chain smoking truck drivers with pants so low the crack in their derriere was on view to all, and if they stayed up half the night noisily challenging each other as to who amongst them could down the most cognac before passing out on the floor, it didn't really matter, we were still staying!

The next day found us booking into the lovely little guesthouse we had promised ourselves we would stay at the next time we came down to this part of France. The room was basic but clean and every evening found us savoring the unbelievably divine smell of wonderful French cooking that wafted up the stairs to then pervade our room from the kitchen of the gourmet restaurant. Sadly none of this sumptuous French cuisine would ever get past our noses and into our hungry stomachs so would only serve to tantalize our keen palates, for sadly their mouthwatering menu was well beyond our purse strings.

"Can't we just eat out at the hypermarket?" I asked.

"Not really, for if we do that too often we will soon be out of money."

Not to be defeated we brought ourselves a cheap little kettle and for the next ten days or so, when not boiling water for the purpose of tea, we used it to boil ourselves eggs, and plenty of them. In fact eggs were on the menu every single mealtime. John would cross the road to the nearest Carrefour to buy long sticks of French bread, green salad, yoghurt and fresh fruit. All too soon I was in trouble.

"John my gut has clearly gone into attention seeking mode."

"What do you mean?"

"I've got the most intense stomach spasms," I cried.

"Well you probably need the bathroom."

"I know that, but it's been over three days."

"Three days since what?"

"Well you know… um I'm constipated."

"You don't say?"

"Oh don't make out it's just me breaking wind all day and night, for you've been doing your fair share too."

Having thought to finally share this deeply profound revelation with him, it would be only a matter of a few hours before I began rolling round the floor hugging my belly as I curled up in excruciating pain.

"John I'm in agony so you need to urgently get me some laxatives," I moaned.

"Okay I'll go and find a chemist." An hour passed.

"Honey I'm back," he cried as he let himself into room. "Sorry I've been so long, but I've got the laxatives. The chemist also suggested you try a little fig syrup as that's the more natural way."

"Fig syrup! Oh please!"

"Look you either want help or you don't, the choice is yours." He was right. I was now so jolly desperate I found myself swallowing at least double the recommended dosage of laxatives before downing the entire bottle of fig syrup.

"Actually John it doesn't taste that bad," I casually commented as I drained the dregs from the bottle.

"Honey you weren't meant to drink the lot". Later that same evening when nothing positive seemed to be happening I went to the bathroom to secretly take a further four capsules. Then, just before bedtime, while cleaning my teeth, I took another two, just for good measure. As I lay in bed I began experiencing severe and lengthy bouts of flatulence but nothing else.

"John nothings happening," I cried.

"Well forgive me if I beg to differ," he cried pinching his nose. "For I bet if I dared to light a match this whole hotel might explode."

"Ho ho jolly ho."

"Tricia beware for you could easily be imprisoned for impersonating Father Christmas. Calm down and let nature take it's course, until then try to get some sleep."

Now the trouble with diarrhea is that it's always violent and there appears to be absolutely no jolly warning! No none whatsoever! The brutal happening took place around 4.00 am and found me racing towards bathroom as my troubled gut went into some pretty violent and extremely unpleasant spasms.

"Psst…Honey you need to keep the noise down or I swear I'll behead you."

"Don't just threaten, do it! for nothing could be worse than this excruciating pain," I howled

"Tricia, we'll be thrown out on our ear if you don't try to lower your voice, for your noise will wake up the other guests."

"I can't, for I promise you that at this moment I feel as though I'm being disemboweled."

"Goodness, you can be such a drama queen."

"Drama queen! I'll have you know that I've probably flushed away at least half my shredded intestines," I wailed as I remained doubled over in the bathroom for the remainder of the night. That harrowing night was surely a sign that it was time to moderate our diet, so the next morning I suggested that we eliminate eggs from at least one of our daily meals and substitute them with some nice juicy steak.

"Tell me honey, we're in a sparsely decorated ill equipped hotel room, so how do you propose to cook the meat?" my curious spouse challenged.

"Simple! We drive around until the car engine is hot, we then place our steaks on some silver foil and pop them on top of the hot engine, then voila, the heat of the engine will perfectly cook the steak. Now do you like yours well done, medium or rare?"

"What?"

"Medium or rare it's a simple question, for if you like your steak well done then we need to take a much longer car ride than if you prefer it rare."

"Tricia, at times you can be very worrying."

"So I've been told many times before. Anyway you haven't answered my question."

"Oh great, so if the French police choose to randomly stop us and then if they open up the bonnet and see blood dripping all over the engine, what then?"

"Oh, don't be so silly."

"Well, knowing the French they will dismiss all efforts to explain ourselves, the car will be impounded and sent off for forensic testing, meanwhile having been arrested on suspicion of murder most foul, we get to rot away in a French jail and all because you fancy a nice bit of flash fry steak!"

"Okay, what if we swap the steak for a small succulent ham instead, then we only need cook it on the engine until it's been seared long enough to hold in the juices."

"Go on."

"We then wrap it overnight in one of the blankets from our bed and I promise it will be cooked by the next day."

"Are you serious?"

"Absolutely! Look I've seen it done before, so trust me it works."

"Well, having kept the hotel guests awake all night, you now want to mess up the hotel blankets."

"We'd only be borrowing one small blanket from the bed."

"Okay as usual you win, let's go and eat in the hypermarket cafeteria."

And so it was that for a real treat we emptied our pockets to share a steak hashe and frites which for the uninitiated is a very nice top of the range burger accompanied by French fries.

"John, listen to me, we need to do this more often if I'm going to remain with all my biorhythms running smoothly and efficiently." It was a done deal for he had no wish for another night of pure unrestrained hell.

They say only mad dogs and Englishman lie out in the midday sun, and not only is this splendidly accurate but I believe it has much to do with our awful and very erratic climate, so, without realizing it, we have become a nation of sun idolaters. Many holidays abroad saw me stepping off the plane in London with my face peeling so badly that I looked like I had fallen foul to a most horrendous case of Pemphigus Vulgarus, otherwise Impetigo, but I didn't care a hoot for at least it proved I'd been abroad for my vacation, so as I lay outstretched on my towel I remained as committed as ever to getting that highly desirable even tan. It was here on the beach that I would faithfully observe that his face was always the picture of pure contentment, as treasuring every precious and much deserved moment of peace he dedicated his allotted time to savoring the writings of some latest meaningful author that he had so come to love.

As for my good self, I concluded that I was indeed a creature of entirely different habits so I was therefore both indisposed as well as thoroughly unaccustomed to such dedicated work that being a contemplative reader affords. I much preferred to plaster myself in frivolous amounts of tanning cream in order to enjoy yet another lackadaisical day basking under the warm Mediterranean sun, intermittently cooling myself down in the sea before passing out to rejoin my very own private world that demanded nothing more of me than to dream of great things to come.

If I needed anything deeper, help was at hand for I could always flit through my hefty selection of women's magazines that came bulging with useful articles such as how to successfully potty train your child otherwise lose a staggering thirty pounds in just seven days. I always cared to note that the following page of such an article consistently held not only a mouthwatering recipe but a full page photograph of a thoroughly decadent twenty thousand calorie chocolate fudge cake. I rest my case.

Towards the end of our stay I was desperate for something more substantial and palatable than boiled eggs. Happily I believed the solution to be on the horizon for we would be spending our last two days with Olivier, a childhood friend of John's who had a fairly high up government position as a Sous Prefecteur in the French town of Aurillac. I was already anticipating a number of gastronomic meals such as Filet mignon, chicken chasseur, Beef Wellington and so on. Until then I believed it was just a matter of holding on. The day before we left for Olivier's John decided it was time to show me a real bit of France.

"Honey, it's the authentic France, the bit the tourists rarely get to see," he excitedly exclaimed. Naturally I was very suspicious. Had he finished reading all his books? If so, was this the reason behind this unexpected desire to break with convention and head off into the hills. Why else would we be heading out into the middle of nowhere? Although thinking about it, this would surely be a good time and place for a murder. I mean with all those eggs I had been regularly devouring I had been suffering from considerable amounts of flatulence, but was that really my fault alone? I wondered as I continued to speculate that this might be the perfect way for him to dispose of my seriously constipated gas filled carcass. He could then go back to living a quiet introspective life with his endless supply of books that stimulate the mind and nourish the soul, and I daresay nobody would even think to ask the pertinent question of 'where is that lovely wife of yours?" It was all very troubling.

"Look John, I don't think we dare risk it, for if the car breaks down in the middle of nowhere, well then what?"

"Tricia, don't worry. I've organized for a small motorbike to be delivered here."

"Motorbike! John, are you barking mad? Tell me truthfully, have you ever ridden a motorbike before?"

"Well no, but don't worry, I'll master it in minutes." I

Truthfully? I was not the least bit convinced! The spotty young adolescent delivered the bike to the front entrance of the hotel, and I watched on with a somewhat bemused look as John tried and failed miserably to master the beast. The young boy made it look as easy as ABC and John, well he made it look like something that would surely take years of committed practice to conquer. He wobbled and wavered and almost fell off too many times to mention, but he always heroically got back on, such was his determination. Apparently it was the gear changes that he was struggling with most.

"Hey Night Rider, will we be leaving anytime soon?" I called out.

"Honey perhaps it's time to take that long awaited vow of silence," he gently scolded. I could easily read the young man's mind, simply by observing his facial expressions and so I knew he was having serious doubts as to whether his beloved machine would be returned in the same mint condition. Likewise I too had genuine concerns for the bike's safety as well as my own.

Finally with John precariously balanced on the bike the young boy chose to depart leaving his prized possession with my novice husband. Now it was all systems go!

"Tricia, quickly just hop on the back," he yelled over as he tried to keep the engine revving. I was reluctant, but I felt I had little choice than to obey. No sooner had I made myself comfortable than the engine cut out, then the bike began to seriously wobble to one side. Disaster felt imminent so I chose to quickly get off the bike before it plunged sideways to the ground. It was a bad decision, as decisions go.

Unfamiliar as I was with bikes, my leg unwittingly made full contact with the scorching hot exhaust pipe. Yelling loudly I threw myself to the ground to begin thrashing around like a young heifer who had just been branded. I clutched the lower portion of my leg as I was now experiencing excruciating pain. When I finally peered down I was shocked to discover I was brandishing a massive burn that ran the entire length of my calf.

"Tricia I'm so sorry," John cried abandoning the bike to rushed to my aid.

"Get away from me," I yelped curling into a tight ball while still tightly clutching my burned calf.

"Here, please let me help."

"No go away. I hate you," I howled. John ignored my hostility as he came to crouch down by me. "Oh my goodness, it does look bad."

The pain felt intense as I struggled to my feet but I was feeling so angry towards him that I only had one thought on my mind and this was to get as far away from him as possible.

"Leave me alone," I yelled as I began hobbling away. He wasted no time following after me. This made me more determined than ever to pick up speed. At one point I found myself running across a large mound of sand only to fall and then roll to the bottom of a sandpit. Picking myself up from the ground I crouched down low so he would not be able to see me. I could hear him calling out my name but right this minute I did not wish to be found. It took him quite a while to find me. When I'd calmed down he once again asked to see my leg.

"John, the lower portion of my leg has gone completely numb," I whimpered.

"Oh goodness, it looks worse than ever. We need to get to a chemist and quick."

The pharmacist shook his balding head and twitched his bushy eyebrows while suggesting a doctor might be more appropriate, but once we told him that we could ill afford one, he recommended a specific antibiotic cream and a bandage. He also suggested that I keep a steady supply of painkillers with me for the remainder of the holiday. With my leg now heavily bandaged John insisted that we get back on the bike and try again. I wasn't sure if I was up to it but he finally persuaded me to give it a try. I agreed as long as we kept to the main road and forgot about touring the hills.

He drove as fast as the bike would allow while I sat scrunched up behind him, my arms so tight around his belly they were surely cutting off the blood supply to his lower regions as I nervously clung on for my life. If he had intended for this outing to be memorable he had succeeded, for I would have great difficulty trying to forget the persistent pulsating pain in my leg, plus the wide deep scar would remain as a constant reminder for a number of years to come.

By the time we arrived back at the hotel I had downed so many painkillers it was a miracle that I hadn't passed out and fallen off the back of the bike. Not that John would have noticed he was far too busy reveling in the spirit of the moment as he rode along the coastal road imagining himself to be Dennis Hopper in Easy Rider. It was early evening when the boy returned to pick up his bike and he seemed pleased if not relieved to see that his bike was still in same pristine condition.

The next morning, after settling our bill, we loaded our suitcases into the trunk of the car and headed off to Olivier's. There were no satellite systems back then so John chose to rely on his map and our combined common sense, but just like money we appeared to have little of that in the bank either.

"Look Tricia, trust me, I've checked the map, and not only will we be at Olivier's around lunchtime, but I could do this trip with my eyes shut." What a sucker I was becoming! We agreed to do the journey in one hit as we were both nervous about breaking down. This meant no coffee breaks or bathroom stops unless absolutely necessary. Lunchtime came and went, and then teatime with its egg sandwiches passed us by, and still we were nowhere near our destination.

"If you rightly remember you said we'd be there by lunchtime or just after. I've been holding on for a bathroom so long, maybe it would have been wiser of me to settle for a catheter bag!"

"Sorry but I thought we'd be there by now."

"Well thoughts and you are a dangerous combination!" I snorted.

"Look I've heard it said that the only man who never makes a mistake is the man who never makes anything. At least give me some credit for trying."

"Well, even with maps and years of experience you still always manage to get us lost. Anyway, you're going to have to stop soon for I need the little girls room for I can't hold on much longer. Besides I hate to tell you but I have the beginnings of a splitting headache."

In hindsight we should have made sure we kept ourselves fully hydrated as the weather was hot and humid and the car had no air conditioning, yet we drove an incredible distance without ingesting even a few sips of water, coffee or soda. Without knowing it we were heading for trouble, and we or rather I got it! Before long my headache managed to turn itself into a migraine. I had rarely experienced a headache let alone a full blown migraine so I had no clue what to do to help myself except clutch the sides of my head as I began to thrash about in the passenger seat desperate for the pain to subside. I reached in my purse for the bottle of painkillers, it was empty! It wasn't too long before I became indisputably certifiable as I moaned, mumbled, blubbered and babbled on like some bi polar demonical woman under the influence.

"Tricia be reasonable, I can't carry on driving with you carrying on like this."

"Be reasonable! Are you joking?"

"Now you don't have to act so hostile."

"Oh, trust me, hostile doesn't even begin to express how I feel at this very moment for Someone is pounding my head with a humungous claw hammer and if I let go of my head I'm positive it is going to split into two."

"Goodness Tricia, you're so jolly highly strung!"

"No I'm telling you it's like having your head squeezed between an enormous garlic crusher."

We arrived at our destination around seven that evening and, as we pulled up the drive, I could see a number of French Flags flying from the turrets of his mighty fine French chateau, then, as we drove nearer I noticed Olivier and his young wife standing in the spectacular courtyard accompanied by the maids and servants of his household as they stood in a perfect line waiting to greet us on arrival.

"Oh this is very.. very.. bad," I moaned, shaking my head as I gave serious consideration to the fact that there would be no easy way to explain any of my proposed forthcoming and quite troubling conduct.

"Listen Tricia, you've got to calm right down."

"I can't, I'm in a terrible state, for not only is my head strongly pulsating but my legs are cramping, and the pain from the deep burn is also getting much worse."

"Take a few long deep breaths."

"That's not going to help me at all," I bleated. "Can't I just stay in the car?"

"No you can't."

"But I need to. You just go ahead and leave me out here." I screeched.

"No I cannot do that. He's standing alongside his staff so I'm not leaving this car without you."

With both hands unavailable as they were still forcibly holding my head together I struggled out of the car only to begin swaying to and fro. I then staggered forwards to greet my gracious unsuspecting hosts, aware that all eyes were on me. John quickly came around to my side of the car and sidled right up to whisper something in my ear.

"Honey please try and behave yourself," he hissed through gritted teeth.

"Behave myself?" I echoed.

"Well you're acting kind of crazy, like your drunk as a skunk on a pirate ship."

"Excuse me, but my head is about to explode."

"Well, at least try to stand up straight and for goodness sake give them both a friendly smile," he ordered as he reached over to place a hand around my waist for support.

"Okay clever clogs, you try smiling when your head feels like its just been smashed underfoot by a heavily pregnant fifty ton rhinoceros," I bitterly complained.

"Look, just do it," he demanded in a most exasperated tone of voice.

"John if I don't find a bed and soon, I swear I'll throw up all over his Pierre Cardin suit, otherwise his Louis Vuitton shoes Oh this couldn't be any worse."

"Look all you've got to do is smile and shake his hand, that's not asking to much is it?"

"You're really mad at me, aren't you?" I whimpered.

"No I'm not."

"Oh yes you are," I simpered as having reached the line of household staff I waited to shake Olivier's outstretched hand.

"Bonjour John, my good friend, it has been such a long time," Olivier cried as he grabbed hold of John's shoulders and proceeded rather dramatically to kiss both sides of his cheek.

"And this must be your lovely wife." he announced as he suddenly found himself grabbing hold of me to prevent me from falling sideways to the ground.

"Thank you," I muttered as I continued to reel to and fro.

John for his part expelled a loud horrified gasp as did Olivier's equally shocked staff before they hurriedly moved forward to give me some assistance. I cannot even begin to express how embarrassed and demoralized I felt. Cringing with deep shame I had little choice other than to allow Olivier's staff to help me up the stairs and towards the guest bedroom. Minutes later found me throwing up all over the bathroom floor. Having attempted to clean up the mess I then threw myself under the bedcovers as I couldn't bear any light. Despite my exhaustion, sleep refused to come and so I spent the next few hours trying to get tomorrow's apology absolutely right, sadly no words seemed to even begin to satisfy that need.

When John finally climbed in beside me I was still writhing around in agony and punching the pillows as though I was in some primal therapy session.

"I'm so sorry," I whimpered. "As usual I've ruined everything."

"You did make a rather stunning entry."

"Oh go on then, make me feel worse than I already feel," I moaned.

"Well I don't suppose they'll be in any particular hurry to invite us back again."

"Oh how I hate myself."

"Tricia, calm down, for everything's fine. I explained that you are suffering a severe migraine. They are just concerned for you, that's all."

"Oh, I feel as bad as that dreadful day when you introduced me to your other close friend, Terry, at his London apartment. That incident was just as unavoidable, for how could I have foreseen I would accidentally smash two bottles of milk over his expensive cream sofa?"

"Quite!"

"He's never forgiven me, that's for sure."

"Well perhaps he'll come round once the lingering odor finally disappears."

"Disappears? It's been well over two years now!"

"Yes well, soured milk tends to inflict a lasting memory. Anyway honey, if you remain this upset your headache will…."

"Migraine," I interrupted.

"Yes, well migraine."

"Oh I'm such a Calamity Jane and Mrs. Magoo all rolled into one!"

"Oh boy is that an understatement!"

"Why oh why do these things happen to me?"

"I haven't the faintest idea honey, but mess up you do, and I might add normally with great panache."

"I'll ignore that unkind critique but while we're on the subject, do you remember that time Monique's family invited us to stay at their house in Montpelier?"

"Why would you want to further punish yourself by recalling that particularly embarrassing disaster?"

"Because I'll never understand why they chose to serve us from a tea set that was a family heirloom, that's why, AND it was one they had never previously used. I mean, how crazy is that?"

"Obviously not crazy enough!"

"I still don't understand how the incident happened."

"No neither did any of their family."

"The cup and saucer just slipped out of my hand as I moved forward to top up my tea."

"Yes I know that, but I don't think they fully appreciated your unique skill in turning a normal everyday event into a full blown crisis."

"Oh dear, there really is no hope for me."

"I think they took the accident very well all things considered, but before we left they took me aside to tell me that this priceless tea set had been handed down through many generations, even surviving two World Wars, that is until you walked through their front door."

"Enough! I can't take any more. Anyway, how was tonight's dinner?"

"Do you really want to know?"

"Yes do your worst and tell me."

"Well everything was simply delicious ..for starters there was….."

"No please don't tell me anymore," I groaned.

"You did ask.'

"I know it's just that I never got to taste any of it," I wept bitterly.

"Yes such bad luck, but try to get some sleep and hopefully you'll feel much better by the morning."

"I very much doubt it," I sobbed.

Shh……. give yourself a well earned break by just going to sleep."

As the staff served up our breakfast they informed us that Olivier and his wife had had already eaten and had left the house, but they gave us directions as to where to find them. When we arrived at the centre of the market town we were surprised to see Olivier and his wife hosting an event from a makeshift platform that had been set up in the centre of the town square. The champagne was flowing freely along with silver dishes of petit fours as well as small cheeses and French pates.

"John, I urgently need to go over and apologize to Olivier."

"Not now, for can't you see he has a large number of dignitaries at this special event."

"Yes but my heart will continue feeling heavy until I have apologized for my seemingly erratic behavior."

"Well I suggest you wait until lunchtime."

"Well judging by the amount of champagne being consumed up on that platform there may not be a lunchtime."

As we were chatting Olivier caught sight of us and beckoned for us to join him and his guests on the platform.

"Ahh Treecia I 'ope you are feeleeng veree much better," he said in broken English giving me a wide irregular smile.

"Yes thank you, but I'm feeling so terrible that, if you wished to take me out into some nearby woods to shoot me, well that would be more than okay by me."

"I don't theenk that weel bee necessary," he laughed as he took hold of my hand to give it a friendly squeeze. "Well, pleese stay and make friends weeth these good French people, and wee weel talk more later. Oh and John my friend, eef I can organize eet with thee locals, how about a game of cricket?"

"Oh absolutely."

"I've told all my friends and acquaintances that eet was you who taught me this veree Engleesh game, that it was you that brought thees game to France!"

The rest of our short stay was calm and peaceful and happily very uneventful. There was much discussion, mainly politics, with Gaullism versus socialism becoming the hot topics. Soon it was time to go. We thanked our kind and gracious hosts and invited them to come and stay with us in England.

"John do you think they will ever consider paying us a short visit?"

"Do you want the honest truth?"

"Yes of course."

"Okay, then I very much doubt it."

"I'm sorry I've really ruined things, haven't I."

"Well yes you have, but don't worry honey, for Olivier and I have been friends since our schooldays, so I'm sure given time everything will be fine."

"Yes, but you said that about Terry, and two years later and I'm still waiting for a truce."

Before long we found ourselves back on the auto route heading for home. There came a point when anxious to break the silence John decided to start a conversation.

"Penny for your thoughts," he said quite out of the blue.

"At present I don't appear to have any," I casually replied.

"Don't be daft, you must be thinking something?"

"No not really, it's as though I'm adrift at sea!"

"Come on honey, nobody's mind is simply a blank."

"Well I assure you mine is."

"Look, you're not a Buddhist monk."

"Hang on there, for I'm allowed to have an empty mind, aren't I?"

"Look Tricia, it's supposed to take a Buddhist a lifetime to achieve this heightened state."

"Well I must be a highly enlightened then, for it's taken me less than five minutes to empty my mind."

"Tricia, it's a known fact that everybody has around 70.000 individual thoughts each day, so are you saying you have nothing going on in there?"

"No but I'll have you know that the brain does eventually stop growing, mine probably stopped around twelve."

"So yours is the size of a pea is it?"

"No darling, that's my bladder. By the way, did you know that the amount of blood that courses through the brain every single minute of your life would fill three twelve ounce soda cans?" John was temporarily lost for words.

"Look here oh 'Star Spangled Master of the Universe', I know you think I'm being flippant but we don't all happen to be deep thinkers like you, so there really is nothing going on up here at present. No thought, no word, good or bad and certainly no deed. I'll try to keep you informed if anything changes." We were now having a minor tiff that in a matter of seconds would inexplicably turn into a major.

"Okay Tricia, if your mind needs some sort of battery recharge, then tell me how do you see our future?"

"How would I know? We just are, aren't we?"

"You tell me."

"Duh! How would I know what the future holds? That's why it's called the future, coz it hasn't happened yet!" Not surprisingly he wasn't the least bit happy with my answer so it wasn't too long before our little tiff escalated to higher ground.

"I'm still waiting to hear an answer from you."

"Listen up oh 'Wise One from the East', I'm not one of your former encounter group members, so stop baiting me."

"I gave those groups up many years ago, but right this moment I'd love to get you into one."

"Think again, for it's never going to happen."

"Well, you could surely benefit from a little Gestap therapy."

"Oh so now you've become the latest R.D. Lang prodigy, have you?"

"Come on, just answer the question,"

"Look, just because you were once a trainee mental nurse doesn't mean you know everything."

"No but there are things you've never fully faced. Go on admit it."

"So… everybody has issues."

"Some more than others."

"John trust me I've lived with enough families to know that the only thing that can be guaranteed normal is the dial on the bloomin' washing machine, so underneath we're all pretty dysfunctional. Anyway maybe you're just as much in need of a bit of therapy."

"True, but it doesn't hurt to take a good hard look at ourselves every now and then."

"Right that's it! I had no idea when I married you that I was marrying some oddball psychologist! So please just stop all this ridiculously crazy conversation," I implored.

"I'm still waiting for an answer."

"I'll let you know as soon as I've checked in with my 'Tardis."

"Tricia, it's not some trick question, I'm simply asking you to give some thought to what your dreams and aspirations are, and I'm not leaving it until you tell me."

"Then you've got a long wait."

Suddenly he pulled over and stopped the car.

"Right get out," he demanded with a very raised voice.

"What here?…why?…what have I done?"

"Just get out of the car."

"No I refuse too. John, this is crazy. We are on the autoroute in the middle of France and not only is it very dangerous but the only French words I know are Good day, Good evening, Where's the nearest loo? Oh as well as, does this hotel have a swimming pool?"

"I said get out of the car."

"Come on John, I beg you please don't do this to me!"

"Well if you cannot even manage to share with me how you see the future then sadly I have to ask you, do we have any future?"

"Alright Darth Vader I'll give it some thought. Just don't leave me out here in the middle of nowhere, please."

He didn't answer, he just sat and stared into space. Finally and much to my relief, he turned the key in the ignition, the engine actually started, and we quickly rejoined the traffic on the auto route.

As we drove along in total silence I began to wonder if this trip had triggered the onset of a seeming mid life crisis. If so, it was indeed much too premature for my liking for according to my calculations he still had years to go before the onset of such a crisis, as he had only just turned thirty two. I mean, all the books suggested that this sort of emotional meltdown was meant to be saved up until we'd reared at least three or four bi polar kids and then only after they'd left home, so what on earth was going on?

In that desperate and most puzzling moment I found myself having an unexpected epiphany. Yes, that was it. I needed to find him a specialist counselor! And not just any counselor, oh no. I needed someone with specific qualifications. It was preferable that it be a woman, and she be something of a man hater, as this might prove very beneficial, especially when it came down to taking sides! After all, if I was the responsible partner in this relationship, yes the one taking the initiative by commissioning her marital expertise, then I fully expected her loyalty to be wholeheartedly inclined towards my side of any prospective disagreement. I now believed I could have him sorted out in no time at all.

CHAPTER FIFTEEN

Help Me Make It Thru the Night

And so it was that all further trips to the South of France were put on hold, that is until John had a bright idea that we should take our young brood on their first camping trip! I was very quick to remind him of the youth camp we'd attended as well as our harrowing trips to the French Riviera, then, when all this didn't appear to deter him I just blatantly refused to entertain the thought a minute longer. However he was not about to give up.

"Alright then, we'll start by just having a few overnighters and weekend trips in England, and then when we've gained the necessary confidence, we'll head off to Europe.

"Sorry John, still not interested."

"Well what if it was just one night's stay at an organized campsite?"

"Nope."

"How about we go camping with our good friends Steve and Judy, would you then reconsider? They always go camping, and they're experts!"

"John read my lips for when no decides it really means yes, well then I'll be the first to inform you!"

"Oh please change your mind," he pathetically begged. "The kids will treasure the memories for the rest of their lives, so come on, don't hold out on me."

"I'm not holding out on you, it's just that all past experience screams at me to leave camping well alone."

"Look, we can do this," he reassured me in a soft manner taking hold of my hands, his blue eyes penetrating mine in the hope that I would finally cave in. However I was not in retreat mode.

"John, I am going to be perfectly candid, for after reflecting on all former camping crises, it has all led me to believe that I was born for much higher things, namely five star Marriott hotels as opposed to moth ridden, mould stinking tents in the middle of some dung filled cabbage patch in the heart of the countryside. You might find the smell of manure and damp grass thoroughly engaging but I don't. So forget it! It was bad enough camping with just the two of us, so I promise you now it's never going to happen."

"Well honey, may I be just as refreshingly honest and somewhat blunt with you, for until our bank manager stops all threatening letters, replacing them with bank statements on rose scented paper underscored with endless kisses, I cannot see any Marriott hotel breaks on the immediate horizon, can you?"

And so it was that I stupidly threw all caution to the wind by allowing John to organize our first ever family camping trip.

"You promise me now that it's just for one night."

"Promise."

As I packed the food into the back of the car, John went in search of the tent we had so optimistically purchased just weeks after we'd got married, some ten or more years previously. My dear husband was most emphatic that he could put his hand on the tent that was buried under a pile of junk somewhere in our crawl space.

"I've found it honey, and it's still in its original box, so let me pass it down to you," he excitedly cried from the opening in the attic. An hour or so later, with everything packed tightly into our car, our three children and one extra child, a deliriously happy John placed the key in the ignition and we were finally on our merry way. We had our maps, a weekends supply of groceries, our sing- a- long tapes, oh and not forgetting our expert camper friends who had agreed to be at the other end, so what more could we wish for? I looked over at my husband singing along with the Donut man and he seemed so ripe, so energized, so abounding with fresh hope and vigor as he prepared for this new experience with open arms. Our friends had given John the instructions of where to find them, but that meant absolutely zilch when it came to my husband and maps.

"John, you definitely assured me that the journey would be less than two hours, and yet we've been on the road for almost four," I despairingly cried.

"I'm sorry, I thought we would be there by now."

"Typical! There we go again, that nasty little word you love to use called thought," I sighed, giving him a reproving glare.

"What do you mean?"

"Honey trust me, you couldn't find your way out of a paper bag." I very cheekily moaned.

"Well it can't be too far now," he beamed. I responded with a skeptical shake of my head. Despite the two hour journey taking nearly six hours, we finally arrived at the site and in one piece, now that was a positive sign, was it not?

Even though the site was large and expansive we managed to find our friends without any trouble. I felt greatly reassured as I saw John's friend Steve stoke up the barbecue and an unnatural calmness washed over me as I studied their teenage girls sorting out other equipment with an ease that surely only comes from much hands on experience. I was so relieved and comforted to think that we would not be doing this alone. Steve finally handed the cooking over to Judy his wife as my dear spouse expressed the need for help in setting up the tent.

Having emptied the contents of the box onto the ground, John then sifted through until he found the instructions leaflet, which he hurriedly handed over to Steve our expert. Yet again I felt relieved to have a connoisseur of camping on hand, as John had always struggled with complicated instructions that seemed to come inside every box he cared to open. Even simple instructions with basic drawings seemed to stress and confuse him.

"I'm more left brained than right, or is it the other way round?" he would question as he realized he'd just super glued otherwise nailed the wrong pieces of something together. Steve looked impressively serious as he squatted down to examine the contents of the box that John had rather helpfully scattered over a small area of grass that had been allotted for us to pitch the tent. However I noticed straight away that our good friend seemed unnaturally quiet, and this made me nervous. I also noticed his brow was now raised to give him that most distinctive look of deep concern. As he continued to browse through the instructions his mouth began to pucker and I waited with baited breathe for his words of great wisdom.

"Uh guys I hope you realize this is only a two man tent?"

"What!" I screeched.

"Yes I'm afraid so," he sighed shaking his head.

"But there's six of us! Oh no I can't believe it. John how could this happen?"

To answer this most pertinent question John did what he always did when he didn't know what to do or say, and this was to shrug his shoulders and throw a helpless look. It never worked on me.

"Well it seemed massive when we saw it in the shop window all those years ago."

"Yes, but back then there was only two of us, so tell me, what are we going to do?"

Steve very diplomatically chose to stay out of it preferring to scratch the back of his head.

"Well we'll just have to accept that it's going to be a bit of a tight squash," he said while enthusiastically rubbing his hands together.

"John that's a bit of an understatement, if ever!"

Then, as if this surprise revelation was not enough, Steve came over to show us that, despite having never taken the tent out of its box, all rubber support bits had still managed to completely perish.

"Oh great, and there's no "Camping World" out here."

That night saw us all try our best to get comfortable in the small two man tent. It was nigh impossible! The night air was humid and, due to lack of space, we were virtually lying on top of one and other. Despite lying in a scrunched up ball every time I tried to turn over I had someone's foot or elbow in my face. With hours to go until morning, I was already needing to stretch my legs as I was now getting cramping pains and my right arm had gone numb as I had someone's limb resting heavily on top of it. "Never again," I thought.

I was at the stage of feeling nothing could get worse when the unthinkable happened. One of the children who just happened to be lying almost on top of me suddenly suffered a gastric explosion down below and it was of such epic proportions that the contents shot out of both ends of his shorts. At first I thought some terrible humongous bug had spilled its entrails all over my face but that thought quickly faded as the familiar smell of poop hit my nostrils! Clambering over the pile of sweaty sleeping bodies I wriggled him and myself out of the tent and raced in the darkness down to the toilet block anxious to shower us both down. Back at the tent I then spent ages struggling around in the dark as I attempted to find us both some clean clothes. The whole procedure took almost an hour but finally I crawled back into the tent clambering once more over the sticky bodies as I searched for a small space to stretch out. Sleep never came for me as the stench in the tent was undeniably strong, however I was relieved that everyone else remained fast asleep and unaware of the disaster. As for me I just closed my eyes and prayed for the morning to come quickly, but the night was not yet over.

About twenty minutes later our foster child woke up and started to whimper saying that she too was feeling awful. I shifted my body around until I was beside her ready to give whatever comfort was necessary. Suddenly without warning she threw up all over me. I was now in a state of complete shock. It was back down to the shower block, and after washing us both down we clutched towels around our bodies and headed back to the tent, to once again fumble around in the darkness, as yet again I searched for fresh clothes.

Bt this point I had a strange desire to finish the rest of the night sleeping outside the tent, but common sense prevailed, as the dawn would bring a large amount of dew and the last thing I needed was to freeze otherwise catch a cold. The tent now stunk to high heavens, and my legs were still suffering from cramps due to many hours huddled in the foetal position, when John finally woke, he took one sniff and almost passed out.

"Goodness this tent reeks high of vomit!"

"Oh you think so?"

"Tricia, what's going on, for it stinks to high heavens."

"Really darling, I hadn't noticed? Actually one of the children suffered a terrible bout of 'Delhi Belly', then another just happened to throw up everywhere, so listen John we all need to head down to the shower block A.S.A.P."

"Can't it wait until after breakfast, because I'm starving."

"There's no breakfast until everybody's cleaned up," I announced giving him an officious glare.

After breakfast I did my very best to wash the soiled ground sheet as well as wipe down the inside of the tent that in some areas had become splattered with unmentionable bodily fluids. After the tent came down we rolled it up a tightly and covered it in plastic bin liners before placing it in the trunk of the car. We said our goodbyes to our camping friends who apparently had slept like logs, thanking them profusely for all they had done. They were surprised we were leaving so soon.

As we made our way down the motorway I was puzzled by the

fact that after such a troubled night there were no further signs of any illness whatsoever! Drained of all energy I closed my eyes thankful that I had only committed myself to one night. However, back home, before I flopped into bed, I determined that I had one final duty and this was to secretly sneak out of the house to place the tent in the bin!

It seemed only a matter of months before John was once again pleading with me to go on yet another camping expedition.

"Look at the brochure Tricia for this place is not out in the sticks and it's really civilized."

"John have you got a memory like a sieve? Don't you remember all that happened last time?" I wailed.

"No, so it would be helpful if you could remind me."

"Oh what a dope I am, for how could you possibly remember? After all you were out for the count while I was hosing down the children in that freezing cold shower block in the middle of the night."

"Well, it will give us all some wonderful memories to look back on and perhaps cherish."

"You're quite unbelievable."

"That may be true but I still need you to back down and say yes."

"Okay John, go and find the tent!"

"Well, come to think of it, I haven't seen it since we came back last time."

"Right well, if you want my consent then guess what, it's time to start looking."

"Okay. Where do you think I should start?"

"You could try the attic!"

"Okay then and thanks for changing your mind."

"Happy hunting, honey pie."

CHAPTER SIXTEEN

Help, I Need Somebody!

John spent quite some time scouring the attic in search of our tent, sadly to no avail. But if I thought I had won I could think again, for he was not about to give up.

"Tricia, come to think of it, even if I manage to put my hands on it, it would be no use to us now for, having taken on more foster children, we've grown in both size and numbers, so I'm thinking it's time to upgrade from a tent to a second hand trailer tent, so how about it?"

"You think so?"

"Yes honey, you deserve better than a tent." he very thoughtfully announced

"Well if you really believed that, you'd happily deposit me in a five star Marriott or Hilton."

"Right, well we've already been over that one," he said flashing me a look of thorough disapproval.

"I'm serious. I'm getting too old in the tooth for all this milarky!"

He wasn't listening. And so it was that, using many words of persuasion, the dastardly deed was finally done and we found ourselves the proud owners of a grossly shabby, exceedingly miserable looking second hand trailer tent.

"Oh honey, it looks such a horrible poopy color."

"Tricia, it's called brown, and it's just a bit faded in places."

"Seriously you really paid that much for it?"

"Tricia, try to show some enthusiasm will you?"

"Uh you must surely know by now that brown is my least favorite color, especially when it comes to camping!" I sighed, strategically crossing my arms as I attempted to share something of my exasperation towards him.

Days later an overexcited John took me on a shopping expedition to buy all other necessary equipment. I imagine it was very similar to his first day at school as, clutching a large scrap of paper on which he had compiled his shopping list, he nervously made his way around the camping section of the store venting deep sighs as he deliberated over what to buy or what not to buy.

"Tricia, come over here and look at this large double burner gas stove, it's definitely a bargain."

I unenthusiastically wandered over and then what did I do? I rather stupidly smiled. He needed no further encouragement.

"Right, that's it then, we'll take it. You know something Tricia, it won't be too long before we find ourselves becoming experts at this," he mused as he packed the boxed cooker into the boot of the car.

A date was set and before I could say Bob's your uncle, we were once more heading down the highway, this time on our own and worse still for a whole nerve wracking weekend.

"Kids you'll just love where we're going, it's a place called Sandy Balls, not exactly sure why it's called that, but it comes highly recommended. I hope you've all packed your swimming stuff, for they have lovely indoor pool on site, and a river as well."

I glanced back at the children and without exception they were all beaming from ear to ear, their tender hearts bursting with excitement and premature anticipation. Amazingly we made it to the site while it was still light and, with our history, I considered this to be quite an achievement. John was right, Sandy Balls despite it's ominous name, was an exceptionally lovely site with a large swimming pool and children's play area, and a long winding river. Who knows, maybe things were finally looking up? With the car emptied of all our gear I now looked to my man to set up the trailer tent.

As I watched him spread out the canvas on the grass I tried to hide the onset of disappointment that came from rediscovering that this patchy brown second hand trailer tent was not only considerably threadbare in places but had me instantly reviving memories of that last painfully demoralizing camping trip.

"John, remind me how much did we pay for this?"

"A little over three hundred pounds."

"I can't believe it, they must have seen you coming, for take a long hard look at it. Can't you see it's dreadfully old and moth eaten and there's so much sand stuck to the canvass that it's surely a cast off from some long lost Bedouin Tribe!"

"I'm so sorry honey, but before you go off on one, I have to tell you now there's worse to come."

"Oh no this cannot be!" I despairingly gasped.

"Well, when they sold it to me they assured me that it came with instructions, but I've searched right through everything and there are no instructions whatsoever! So I've no idea where to even begin."

We had only just started our camping adventure, it was getting dark, and already I was on the verge of moving into a deeply deranged psychopathic breakdown.

Our hot sweaty children had been very patient up until now, however, on hearing this latest news they began to show signs of frustration, and before too long the unmentionable subject of Dick our handyman neighbor was once again brought into the equation.

"Oh daddy's so useless," they pathetically cried. "We wish Dick had come with us, for he'd sort it out in no time," they bawled.

"Now then children, that's not kind. Remember Dick builds houses for a living and as for daddy, well let's just say daddy's skills lie in an entirely different arena, admittedly yet to be discovered." They simply weren't listening.

"We want Dick…we want Dick," they chanted in unison.

"Children stop that now."

"No. We want Dick or else we want to go home," they cried.

"Oh, and how do you propose to make your way home?" I challenged.

"We'll find a way," they threatened.

"You know full well I don't negotiate with terrorists, even if they're miniature sized." John quickly intervened. "Look kids try your best to be patient, and Tricia, please get them all a cool drink while I go off and try to find help."

He was gone a long while leaving me to comfort a bunch of very hot and bored children. When he finally returned he appeared dreadfully downcast.

"Tricia I don't know what to do for I haven't been able to find anyone who can help us."

"John, this is all so crazy, the kids are hot and miserable and it's already nearly completely dark!"

"I'm so sorry."

"Tell you what John, you take the kids for a swim and I'll stay here and ask around, for there is always a camping expert lurking around a campsite, who will take great pride in showing us how useless we really are. Oh, and by the way, do we have a torch with us?"

"Oh dear, I don't think so."

"Right, well if things don't turn round and pretty soon, we'll have to consider abandoning this campsite to go and book into a nearby hotel."

"Wait a minute, that will prove incredibly expensive and disappointing."

"Darling, allow me the privilege of saying that it will be no more expensive or disappointing than what will take place if I'm forced to spend the night with the children out in the cold, otherwise cramped inside the car, so the choice is all yours!"

It was not too long before I finally came face to face with the expert camper that I had been dreaming of. As the scrawny bearded gentleman stood in front of me, hand on hips and chest puffed out, he looked as though he'd just walked off the plains of Africa. I noted that he was all skin and bone and he was wearing a Aussie silly hat complete with dangling corks, that made him look like some sort of emotionally stunted Boy Scout leader. Anyway, as I wasn't about to conceive his love child, looks where the last thing on my mind. Seconds later and I was delighted to discover that tucked away inside his keenly zealous mind was the full A to Z Campers Handbook.

"Ma'am, word has quickly got round that you are in urgent need of some practical help."

"You heard right, for you have no idea how grateful I would be if someone could help with the setting up this stupid trailer tent," I said jumping to my feet to shake his hand and address him eyeball to eyeball. "You are a true godsend and gentleman for I'm here with four small children and a husband who at present is showing himself to be a little 'non compus mentus' as far as putting up this trailer tent is concerned."

"Hmm, sad to say but, in this day and age, there are still a few of those sort around," he casually commented.

"Well he never became a boy scout, so he's a real novice when it comes to anything remotely practical."

This man had my total approval for I observed him disapprovingly shaking his head in a manner not too dissimilar to my good self as I continued to discuss my seriously floundering husband.

"Well, back in my day all the boys in our town joined the local Cub Scouts. Yes, Baden Powell not only taught us how to live under the stars but how to be real men," he said giving me one of his all knowing looks that immediately made me want to roar like a lion.

"Well, his mother certainly has a lot to answer for, but what more can I say?" I announced throwing my hands into the air to show my sense of despair.

"Say no more, for in no time at all I'll have this situation under my full control." he said using both hands to pull up his makeshift shorts that were threatening to drop to the ground if he failed to temporarily wedge them into the crack of his buttocks as well as over his frail bony hips.

Control…. Oh how could such a tiny seemingly insignificant word that normally I was so adverse to hearing, somehow this day or rather night, sound so wonderfully comforting. Yes right here, right now, I urgently needed this partially anorexic but most delightful control freak to use his full expertise in putting up our tent before I got round to hammering a stave through my dear husband's ever so contrite heart.

Moments later and John returned with the children. The look of relief on his face was clearly visible.

"Does the gentleman need some assistance from me?" John ever so thoughtfully cared to ask. I simply shrugged my shoulders.

"No thank you sir for as I have already told your lovely wife I have everything fully under control."

"Yes under control," I repeated as with arms folded I threw John a mean stare.

I couldn't thank this kind hearted man enough for, without his intervention, our weekend would most certainly have plunged to an all-time new low. He refused all financial remuneration choosing rather to bask in the on going and continuous praise coming forth from my lips that served to stroke his pride.

"Just glad to have been of service," he muttered as with his chest puffed out, and his camping knife secured in his thick belt he boldly strode off into the darkness, no doubt fully intent on killing some dangerous wild beast, otherwise to make his good old missus her bedtime cup of cocoa.

"Well, thank goodness he turned up and I hope he's here for the whole weekend," my man commented.

"Why? Do you see a close friendship blossoming? Perhaps if you ask nicely, he'll take you out to do a spot of hunting in the woods," I retorted tongue in cheek.

"Stop it, but if I'm honest it's for purely selfish reasons,"

"You don't say?"

"Yes, I was just hoping he'd still be around long enough to help me when it comes to dismantling and packing up this massive tent."

"Darling, when we get back home I think you need to find some sort of outdoor course for absolute beginners, otherwise this our last camping trip ever, and consider that official! At least we now have somewhere to sleep, so let's abandon everything and go find ourselves somewhere to eat."

"Oh, but aren't you going to cook us all some supper?"

"Excuse me?"

"Well honey, we've just bought a brand new double burner?" he said his voice tapering off as he noticed the hard nosed look on my face.

"Honey get real, it's nearly nine o'clock at night, and it's almost pitch black! So we're eating out, understood?"

"Right."

Later that night as I climbed into the camp bed I was hit by an overwhelmingly strong and unpleasant smell of dank musty mould.

"This tent hasn't been used since the Anglo/Zulu war reached its climax," I loudly commented.

"I'm sorry, I should have thought to air it. Never mind, next time I'll know."

"Next time?"

"Oh trust me, Tricia there will be a next time, especially now we've bought this trailer tent and the double burner. I am determined to get full use out of it."

"Great, then you can be the one to get up early to cook breakfast for everybody."

"You're on. Anyway goodnight, and don't let the bed bugs bite."

"Now why did you have to say that, when you know full well how paranoid I am concerning bugs."

"Tricia stop wriggling about, you're keeping me from sleeping."

"I can't help myself, for just the mere mention of bugs and my skin starts crawling."

"Oh dear."

"Do we have a torch, for I need to quickly check inside my sleeping bag."

"Oh now, I've really started something," he loudly groaned.

"You two, please be quiet for we're all trying to sleep," one of the kids despairingly cried out.

"Please John, I need your help."

"Nope just go to sleep. There are no bugs in the bed."

"Then lend me a torch."

"We don't have one, remember?"

"Do you guys always talk all night?" Antonia cheekily chirped up.

"Tricia, you do realize that you are solely responsible for putting the fun into dysfunctional?"

"Why thank you."

"It's not meant as a compliment," he snorted as he furiously rolled over onto his side. "Any more silly talk and I'm definitely sending you back to the kids home."

"Yeah right, you and whose army of well wishers."

"Now what are you doing?"

"I'm taking my sleeping bag down to the shower block to give it a hearty shake."

"See you in the morning," he grumbled giving a deep very displeasing sigh as he punched his pillow hard before rolling over to go to sleep.

The next day saw John cook us all a mighty fine breakfast.

"Well done darling, you've mastered another skill, so to put you on notice, you're down to cook breakfast tomorrow as well."

Things were going well, all the children were so happy and content so I was temporarily on cloud nine, however unbeknown to me at that time all that was about to change. It was later the same morning when the call came through.

"Tricia, would you believe it, David and Ruth are in the area so they are asking if they can pop by with their kids."

"Wow, I thought they were still living in America."

"Yes, well it seems they're back."

"Well, what are you waiting for? Ring them back and say we'd love to see them."

We had a great afternoon with our good friends whom we had truly missed. Our children were also thoroughly delighted to have four slightly older children to play with and so they disappeared off for most of the afternoon giving us time to catch up on all their news. The time raced by much too quickly and so we invited them to stay for supper.

"Alright guys, you've twisted our arm, since we've only just arrived back we're pretty broke, so we'll stay for supper and then we must dash off as we still have more friends to see."

It was sad seeing them off for we really loved this couple who seemed to live like nomads and who, just like a pop up book, would surprise us with a visit when we least expected to see them. The children in particular were very disappointed and did all within their power to beg our friends to stay longer, but to no avail. As we stood in an unofficial line to wave them off, David wound down the window to wave back at us and then, without warning and much to our utter dismay, he suddenly reversed the car. The noise of twisted metal was extremely loud, at least from where we were standing, but he continued on regardless. I could only let out a loud gasp, my eyes almost popping out of their sockets as, feeling horrified, I watched him then put the gear stick into forward to then re -run his car over our brand new double burner cooker! There was now no hope of salvaging our prized possession, as it lay out on the grass like a flattened pancake. He then drove off at top speed still oblivious to all that had just taken place, his kids hanging out of the side windows as they cheerfully waved us goodbye.

"He has absolutely no clue as to what he has just done, has he?" John miserably muttered

"Nope, I think you're right on that one, and, as they are always stony broke, so there's no chance whatsoever of getting them to contribute towards another."

"Oh, I can't believe it," I wailed as I forlornly knelt down by the deformed remains of our spanking new gas burner that now lay on the grass squashed to the thickness of a thin crust Domino's pizza!

"Oh John, trust me, it's had it," I cried as I tried to prize open the compacted lid that was well and truly welded to the bottom section.

"Well I guess I won't be cooking tomorrow's breakfast after all?" he ruefully stated as we both stood dazed and mourning the very untimely loss of our new beloved stove. Now, in terms of loss adjusters language, it may well have been considered a write off, but all the same I still carefully packed it in the boot of the car to take home with us.

"Tricia, help me out here. Why are we taking it home when it's crushed to a pulp so it's clearly beyond repair?"

"Because we are."

"Tricia, for goodness sake, can't we just throw it away in one of the campsite trash bins."

"Don't even go there! for you might be able to discard everything willy nilly, but I can't, at least not at the moment, so it's coming home with us."

"Oh, you're such an unbelievable hoarder. You never throw anything out."

As usual he was right, I did need a therapist for I had always held onto things, even when the item was way beyond repair, and I found it just as impossible to bin the damaged item even once it had been replaced. It's just how it was. John called it 'the kid out of care syndrome.'

Back then there was no recognizable treatment for hoarders so, out of sheer desperation, he chose to do his own intervention that was not at all well received. He waited until I had organized an outing with a friend before he rather sneakily decided to have a spontaneous clear out. Now this worked beautifully on the first few occasions until I decided to join a girlfriend and spend the day traipsing around the many charity shops (thrift stores) in our home town. I was immediately taken by surprise to see a number of jackets and dresses that were exact replicas of ones I already owned and were unbelievably the same size. Why, they even had the same odd bit of loose stitching on the hem or minute stain on the cuff or shoulder. "How could this be?" I pondered as I took them up to the cash register, thrilled to be purchasing these identical items at a fraction of the original cost. The exact same scenario would take place in the next thrift store, only this time there were shoes, room ornaments and books, as well as a number of other precious keepsakes that were identical to ones I already owned.

It was probably while visiting the third or fourth thrift store that it finally dawned on me that these identical possessions I so miraculously kept finding and purchasing might actually have been mine all along! I was now on the warpath! No sooner was I through the front door than I wasted no time challenging him, and the moment I saw that totally identifiable look of boyish sheepishness pass over his face I knew I was onto something. For the first time in history, I was almost speechless. I say almost, because in just a matter of seconds many suitable words of chastisement began to rise up from the back of my throat to then spew forth like a brimming witches cauldron from between my trembling lips.

"Darling, would you care to humor me by telling me precisely what you've been up to behind my back?" I asked shooting a frosty glare.

"What are you talking about?"

"These!" I snorted as I began holding various shopping bags up to his face.

"Well, they look like shopping bags to me."

"Yes I know that. But what's in them?'

"As I'm not psychic, and I don't hold séances, neither do I profess to be anything of a magician I actually have no idea!"

"Then allow me the pleasure of showing you," I snorted, dangling a pair of shoes in front of his eyes."

"Oh those. Well um…. allow me to explain."

"I'm waiting. And I've got all day, so continue on at your own pace."

"Actually, if I'm honest I don't know what to say," he rather stupidly dared to confess.

"Ha ha, now you're caught out!"

"So it would appear. So tell me now do I need a lawyer?"

"John, how could you do such a mean thing?" I scornfully yelled.

"Well I just wanted to help you out, that's all, anyway try to think of it as a timely intervention."

"Intervention! I cannot believe I'm hearing this! How would you feel if I did the same to you?" I hysterically sobbed.

"Feel free. I hate clutter.

"Well I love clutter!" I bellowed as deep feelings of outrage once more welled up inside. "Remember I was brought up in children's homes so for most of my young life I hardly had anything to call my own. So to do this to me, is way beyond mean, in truth it's the actions of a callous cold hearted monster," I said lowering my voice to a most pitiful sob.

"Look Tricia, I understand you're upset."

"Upset? John I've got steam pouring out my ears!"

"Honey, you really must try to understand that I took this drastic action to help you. It really was for your benefit, trust me. I mean, I only got rid of clothes you never ever wear!"

"Rubbish! Let me tell you that, by doing this behind my back, you have done incalculable damage to our relationship," I cried as I gave myself permission to begin bawling into a ridiculously thick bundle of tissues.

"You've just helped yourself to more than half the box."

"John, I'll take as many tissues as I choose for, this time I'm really mad at you," I cried, reaching down to grab a further handful.

"Really! You're mad at me, I had no idea."

"Funny ha, ha."

"Well, be as mad as you like, for I can't count the number of times I've begged you to have a clear out, and you agree, and it never happens."

"How has any of this become your business?"

"Well, perhaps it's because I no longer have any hanging space for my clothes, or any drawers for my personal belongings, so the only space left is outside on the bloomin' balcony. No wait, even that is now cluttered with your things."

"Oh right, make it personal."

"Well, how more personal can it get?"

"John trust me, you'd be content to live in a dingy basement with just a lumpy horsehair mattress to sleep on, a threadbare rug on the floor, and a hard wooden chair to sit on, you're so jolly monastic, you've surely missed your true vocation."

"Well, Imelda Marcos, perhaps I'm satisfied with much less, but I still need some space in the closet in order to hang just a few of my clothes."

He was right. It had been a slow and silent takeover bid, but, as he cared so little about material things clothes included, I didn't think it mattered if I took it upon myself to remove almost all his clothes from the wardrobe, in order to make way for all my recent very genuine bargains. It had long come to the point where his clothes were causing mine to be so severely crumpled, so that every dress or blouse I pulled from the closet had to be re-ironed and this simply would not do, hence the drastic measures were considered by me to be very necessary. Also, in my defense, I deserved the extra hanging space as I had always been most conscientious in purchasing my clothes during the store sales, otherwise the bargain basement, so no item was ever purchased at its full price, well only very occasionally.

So, at the end of the day, maybe in my dysfunctional mind I needed to hang on tight to the decapitated burner as a momentum, a sort of visual reminder of where our abysmal camping trips had rather sadly taken us. I have to confess that I was equally unprepared to spend yet more money on a shopping addiction counselor when there were loads of gorgeous outfits and shoes still sitting in shop windows that had my name written all over them. Needless to say, after a few weeks of unhealthy grieving over the 'thing', John waited for me to leave the house on a shopping expedition and then he hastily binned it. That same summer saw us lend the trailer to one of my brothers, and this was to be the last we ever saw of it, for when we finally got round to asking him to please return it, he rather sheepishly announced that it had been stolen.

"Well I hope the trailer brings more joy to the next owner than it brought us," were John's final thoughts regarding this latest very painful matter. Of course I had come to an entirely different conclusion!

"Oh honey, this is a sign if ever, that we were born for higher things such as Marriott otherwise the Dorchester," I sniffed.

"Oh really."

"Yes really."

"Well let's see if our friendly bank manager thinks likewise."

"Ho ho ho."

"I've told you many times before, you could be put away for impersonating Santa Claus."

"Yeah right."

CHAPTER SEVENTEEN

We Can Do This Really We Can

With our camping cooker now departed to some council run dumpsite I strongly believed our camping days to be well and truly over. Wrong again! It would be less than nine months later when John was once more begging me to give it one last try.

"Look Tricia, this time I have taken away all the headache, for when we arrive at the campsite, you will be delighted to find the tent is already in situ, and the cooker and a fridge are supplied as it's all part of the whole package."

"Sorry honey, but I'm sticking to my guns, no more camping trips for me."

"Oh please."

"Read my lips honey, no."

"Look Tricia, hear me out, for the campsite is in mid France, and it's June, so the weather will almost certainly be fantastic."

"I don't know John."

"Alright, so are you saying you're willing to risk another potentially wet and miserable summer holiday by staying in England?"

"I'm not saying anything, it's just I now have an understandably natural abhorrence towards anything connected to camping."

"Tricia honey, before you give your final answer please take a good look at this campsite. Come on, don't turn your head away, for it's small and it's set in an idyllic part of France, in the very heart of the tranquil countryside, far away from the crowds and the kids can cycle and swim and play pirate games in the woods. Come on now, be a good sport and take a look."

I have decided that my husband, in his quiet way, must be a master in the art of persuasion, either that or I'm just plain losing the plot, for yet again I found myself caving in to his latest hair brain scheme, despite my gut feeling screaming out no.. no … no!

And so it was that, with four or five children in tow, and an equal number of bikes precariously strapped to the back of the car, we once more set off to catch a ferry to France. I was extremely relieved that our old jalopy had finally been laid to rest a few years back, hence we now had ourselves a fairly modern estate car. As we were traveling through the night, we booked a cabin on board that sleeps six, for we had brought along a young girl in her late teens to help us. Sad to say, when our young guest believed we were all fast asleep she quietly removed John's wallet from his back trouser pocket and disappeared off into the night. When she sneaked back into the cabin a few hours later she had no idea that I was wide awake so, when I suddenly turned on the light, it startled her causing her to drop the open wallet to the floor.

"Kathy how could you?" I cried.

"I'm so sorry," was all she could mumble.

Our upset quickly woke John up and, after telling him what I'd just witnessed, he decided that we should all get some sleep and we would deal with it in the morning as he did not wish to disturb the children who were all fast asleep.

Within minutes of this declaration I heard the familiar sound of snoring that came from the direction of my husband but for me, sleep refused to come as I mulled over what this young lass had done. I also wondered just how much holiday money we had left after her late night binge at the expense of our holiday funds. The next day when we challenged her she was very apologetic and so we found it in our hearts to forgive her, but it still hurt. We decided it would be best to hide what had happened from our children, for not only did they truly love her, but we believed something like this might altogether ruin their holiday. Saying that, with the Franc at an all time high against the pound, we knew there was even less in the kitty to splash out on little treats.

As we continued to make our way down the French autoroute heading towards our piece of French paradise, the dark rolling clouds seemed to mischievously tail us all the way to our destination. We arrived at the campsite around mid afternoon as did the downpour, a downpour that remained in close proximity to us for most of our vacation. As John had promised, the tent was set up and I had little to do other than unpack and begin making something hot for us all to eat, in between the showers.

"See, didn't I tell you that this place would be a peaceful paradise," he said giving my waist a friendly squeeze.

"Yes but you never said it was situated in the middle of the rain forests. Look, it's teeming down and the clouds are still rolling in.

"Honey, let's just agree the sun will come out by tomorrow."

"Okay, but I'm also quite concerned that, as of yet, I haven't seen any other kids here that are in their age bracket."

"Well I'm sure there must be other kids on site, it's just a matter of finding them."

"Well I hope so, for the children's sake."

"Look Tricia, I think we did the right thing by choosing a small campsite, for just listen to all those birds singing," he cried as he gave me a little unexpected kiss on the cheek. "It's exciting. Here we are, hidden away in the heart of French countryside, and I'm feeling good…duh duh duh duh.." he said as he broke into the famous Nina Simone song.

"Oh, you're such a crazy romantic," I murmured as I pretended to brush him off. By early evening the weather began turning into a serious torrential downpour.

"Well, let's all have an early night then, shall we?" John suggested.

"Okay."

"I think the heavy rain is finally stopping," he whispered as he clambered into his sleeping bag.

"That's good."

"What was that?" he suddenly cried.

"What was what?" I hastily replied.

"Didn't you feel it.?"

"Sure, but I don't know what it is I felt."

"Tricia, I don't know what is going on, but the earth was literally shaking beneath me."

"Me too." As we continued to lie awake in the dark we found ourselves listening to loud and continuous rumblings.

"If I didn't know better, I'd say that Godzilla has just turned up for a late night snack," I shouted out.

"Goodness, this is crazy?"

"Perhaps it's an earthquake?" I yelled back.

"What, in mid France?"

"Well, we'd better not stay here just incase it is the first rumblings of a seismic quake. By the way John have you ever seen that recently released science fiction movie about giant burrowing worms? I think Kevin Bacon stars in it."

"What on earth are you going on about?"

"Well terrible things began to happen to the townsfolk as they…"

"Uh!"

"Oh this is bad. Look John, you'd better get up and see what's going on," I ordered.

"No way! I'm staying put."

"Well, didn't you choose this place for it's peace and serenity, and if so, you should be the one to venture out of the tent to find out what's going on."

"Yes well once again the brochure lied. So as usual I probably now need a lawyer, don't I?" he angrily barked.

"Maybe."

"Well let's cut to the chase. Yes let's forget all thoughts of a trial by jury and let's just get on with the sentence. If I were to be hung drawn and quartered at dawn, would that suit you and make up for this latest dreadful mistake?"

"No darling you've got it all wrong. You have to conspire against the king or queen to receive that particular punishment.

"Well I'm sure you'll find some other equally suitable form of punishment to mete out to me."

"Look John I've absolutely no idea what is going on, but the shaking is so bad my head is literally vibrating up and down on the pillow," I whined.

"Oh, this is all so jolly ridiculous," he said huffing and puffing as he struggled out of his sleeping bag to finally venture outside.

It didn't take too much detective work on his part before he discovered that this campsite 'nestled deep in the heart of the French countryside' was in fact situated right next to one of France's main north to south arteries, and all that separated us from being directly under the gargantuan wheels of the monster Artic trucks that thundered up and down all night long, was a tall very thin concrete wall! Funny to think that we'd driven for miles and miles through the heart of the French countryside to get here!

This night would be the first of many sleepless nights that would find us struggling to stay awake during the daytime as we continued to battle sleep deprivation as well as high winds and rain with each and every day that passed. All too soon our joie de vivre gave way to unspoken depression, as with heavy hearts as well as a sorely light wallet, we did our very best to enjoy the wettest week on record, attempting all the while to hide our increasingly sorrowful disposition from our children. It wasn't easy!

On phoning home we were mortified to discover that the whole of England was basking in what would officially become one of the hottest weeks on record.

On the homebound ferry I made myself a promise, put simply, should my spouse ever be crazy enough to book another family camping trip, he would indeed be going it alone. Now I'm not saying I wouldn't happily go along for the ride, but after giving him and the kids the obligatory goodnight kiss and cuddle under the stars, I would then make myself at home in a decent 5-star Marriott hotel. Once there, I would eat my fill of decadently scrumptious food before puffing up my feather pillows and sliding under the crisp Egyptian cotton sheets, as surrounded by every imaginable creature comfort, I fell into a deep comforting sleep, without affording myself even the teeniest modicum of guilt.

Back home, despite his many other commitments, John, being in an unusually highly charged state of mind, saw fit to write a stiffly worded letter to the travel operators. A letter of response was eventually received by us that did contain an apology of sorts, plus a very generous discount should we wish to return the following year. Needless to say we declined.

CHAPTER EIGHTEEN

That 90-Minute Presentation!

There came a day while reading a newspaper, that something caught John's attention and therefore his imagination.

"Tricia, have you ever heard of something new called Timeshare?"

"Can't say I have."

"Well, according to this full page advertisement, if we attend one of their presentations, we could win a car, a gold watch, a thousand pounds or even a holiday in America or..." His eyes lit up like a Christmas tree as he read out the long list of potential breathtaking prizes we might well come away with, simply for attending.

"John, save your breathe, just tell me what's the last prize on the list."

"Why, do you want to know?" he asked flashing me a seriously puzzled look.

"Just answer the question."

"It's a bottle of bubbly."

"Right well, that's the gift we'll be coming home with."

"Oh come on Tricia, you're so unbelievably negative."

"And you my dear, are just as charmingly naïve."

"Look, all we have to do is attend a presentation which they guarantee will be no longer than ninety minutes. So go on, just say yes, who knows, we might just win the car." I raised my eyes to the heavens as if to say 'yes and pigs may fly' but this time I followed it on by giving my humungous belly a couple of gentle pats.

"Honey, I'm almost nine months pregnant, so you must realize that to be traveling any distance is downright uncomfortable."

"Oh come on, where's your sense of adventure? The presentation is taking place in a very nice hotel set in a very romantic park."

"Sounds nice but all the same I don't think I'm up to it. The petrol alone will cost at least forty pounds or more."

"Yes I know, but it will be a nice day out, and if we win the car, then it will definitely be doubly worth it."

"And what if we don't, then that's forty pounds down the drain." Needless to say he wasn't listening.

"Look, if you like, we can break the journey up, for we'll stop at a nice restaurant for lunch, that's a promise. Just say yes."

"A nice classy restaurant?"

"Yes."

"Lunch with dessert?"

"Yes yes, anything you like."

"Chocolate cake, ice cream topped with lashings of whipped cream?" I formally asked, while meaningfully examining his facial expressions just to check if he really intended to honor this latest deal that I was in the final throws of negotiating.

"Yes yes, if that will make you happy," he hurriedly responded.

A few days later and we were on our way to our first ever Timeshare presentation. As I sat in the front of the car, I could hardly fit the seat belt around my hugely expanded waist.

"You know something, that last ultrasound can't possibly have it right, for I'm certain that I'm expecting twin dinosaurs," I moaned.

"Don't worry honey, I've studied the map, so you'll be there and back before you can say Jack Robinson, and just think this could be our lucky day."

"Yeah, dream on," I sighed as I pondered just how trusting and overly optimistic my dear husband could be at times. Many hours later and I mean many, we would discover that we were hopelessly lost.

"Honey, I don't know how to say this, but I must have taken the wrong turning, either that or these directions are wrong."

"I said this would happen, what is it with you and maps?" I moaned.

"I must have just missed the sign."

"John answer me this, how come you always manage to get lost when you work for a living running a moving company?"

Rather than answer my challenging query my dear spouse very wisely chose to remain silent. We were booked in for the 3.00pm presentation and we arrived nearly an hour late, hot and flustered, oh as well as starving hungry.

"I don't believe it, not only have we been on the road for a whole five hours, but I also never got the lunch that you promised me, AND I'm supposed to be eating for two," I angrily hissed in his ear.

"I thought you said it was three."

"What?"

"Twin dinosaurs remember?"

"John, I promise to turn into a rampaging flesh eating mama Tyrannosaurus if I don't get me something to eat and soon!" I fumed.

"Honey, if you can just survive the presentation then we'll leave quickly and go in search of a restaurant on the way home."

Moments later we were directed into a small theatre and shown to our seats.

The presentation started with a film show of some of the most glamorous spots in Europe. I tried to show some interest, really I did, but then without warning I began to feel horribly faint. I staggered to my feet clutching my belly and seconds later I began to sway back and forth. The alarmed staff cut short the movie and raced over to give assistance. I could see that their biggest fear was that I was going to give birth on the spot, which no doubt would severely diminish the number of timeshare sales they would make on that day!

"Madam, do you need a doctor?"

"No I don't think so. I just feel terribly peculiar."

"Please allow us to take you to a room where you can rest," a member of their staff anxiously begged.

"Well, wherever she is going I'm going with her," my now very concerned husband chirped up. Moments later we were escorted down a corridor and bundled into a rather nice bedroom.

"Feel free to get into the bed if that will help," the Timeshare lady kindly suggested as she looked down at her watch. "Look, I've got to get back to the presentation but I promise I will come back and check on you later," she feebly stated. I followed her suggestion by getting under the covers for I still felt terribly weak and poorly. What I didn't bank on was John insisting that he be allowed to get into the bed as well.

"John, what are you thinking, get out right now!"

"Why can't I join you? I'm exhausted after all that driving!" he whimpered.

"Because I'm supposed to be the ill one, so come on get out now before they come back and find us canoodling."

"Don't be silly, I just want to give you a cuddle."

"But I don't want a cuddle or anything else at this moment, thank you very much."

"Don't say that for I want to be near you."

"John stop it, if they come back and find us both in the bed, it's going to look really bad," I anxiously protested.

"What's the worst that could happen?"

"Well, for one they could get real mad and kick us out."

"Sorry but I'm staying put."

Nothing worked as he was determined to remain in the bed lying next to me despite my endless protestations. An hour later and he was fast asleep, when suddenly without warning our hosts returned to the room and I was left with the task of waking him up, worst still he was snoring very loudly. I felt incredibly embarrassed as I keenly observed their shocked faces.

"I'm sorry, it's just that the drive down here took forever, and, as you can see, he's very tired." I mumbled as I gave him a sharp jab in the ribs to wake him up.

"Are you feeling better?" one of them asked cutting me off in mid sentence.

"Yes I'm feeling fine now, thank you for asking." John replied.

"Not you, you idiot!"

With John finally fully awake and in his right mind we were briskly escorted back to the presentation room which was now empty of people.

"Where is everybody?" I asked.

"The film show finished some time ago, and so they are on the next stage of the presentation. So, are you up to seeing the film now?" A lady dared ask as she placed a plate of stale looking pastries in front of us.

"What do you mean? Are you suggesting we go through the whole presentation on our own?"

"Well yes, and if you want some coffee or a glass of water, we will happily get it for you."

"Will we still get our prize if we go home now?" John thought to ask

"I'm sorry but you have to go through the whole presentation to receive your gift."

"Is there a prize for getting through half the presentation," John dared to ask.

"No I'm afraid not."

"Oh John, let's forget it, for it took us five hours to get here and we've been here for over two hours already, and, if we stay for the presentation, that's another ninety minutes, and then we've still got to find our way back home, so let's call it a day shall we?"

"Oh no honey, we've made it this far, so to go home now would be really foolish wouldn't it?" he pleaded.

"Tell me truthfully, have all the best prizes gone or are their still some left?" he asked one of the timeshare reps that was standing nearby. I could only sigh and wonder how at his age in life he could remain so innocent and thoroughly gullible. Back in the days when we were courting, this innocence had seemed so intriguing, if not touching. Now I was not so sure.

"Well no sir, there are still some big prizes that could be won."

"See Tricia I told you, so let's take the offer of coffee, and get started," he once again begged.

"Alright then but, as we've already seen quite a bit of the movie, I don't suppose there's any chance of fast forwarding it to the bit where I almost passed out?" Apparently not. And so it was that once more we were left to endure the entire film from beginning to end, which was then followed up by a viewing of their show apartment, followed by a very hard hitting heavy pressure sales interview. For my part, I was actually incapable of getting my head around any of the facts and figures as I was too far gone, hallucinating about triple layer chocolate cake topped with lashings of thick swirling whipped cream.

The day ended with us declining to buy and, as we went to leave, John risked all by politely asking if he could now have his much anticipated prize. The staff were most reluctant to oblige but eventually a girl was sent into another room and she came back bearing the long awaited gift. Surprise, surprise, she handed him a bottle of pink cheap-looking Spanish bubbly that bore little resemblance to real champagne, as well as some tacky plastic flowers in a cheap glass receptacle, the total value of this prize being in my view less than a pound. My beleaguered husband's face dropped and for a moment the room went embarrassingly silent for his disappointment felt curiously tangible. I promised myself that when the time seemed right I would face him with the true cost of this outing, in terms of mileage and petrol as well as a whole day of our precious time, but for now I could only try to empathize with his profoundly depressed state. As he stood in the small conference room clutching the plastic flowers and bottle to his chest he still had one lingering question on his mind.

"Can you tell me, did anyone win the car?" my strangely naïve husband innocently blurted out.

"Sorry sir, afraid not," came the brutishly quick reply from one of the men as he hastily showed us the door.

"Hmm, much as I suspected," I muttered under my breath as I waddled across the almost empty car park heading back towards our car. Once again he got lost once or twice as he struggled to read the signs in the dark, and I ended the day making myself a cheese sandwich after we finally arrived home in the early hours of the next morning. As we snuggled up in the bed I whispered over.

"John, do me an almighty favor."

"Oh and what's that?"

"Never ever mention timeshare again!"

CHAPTER NINETEEN

The Ups and Downs of Timeshare

A few months later he came racing into the kitchen once more clutching our daily newspaper.

"Tricia, honey trust me when I say this is it!"

"This is what?"

"Look, just stop what you're doing and hear me out." Oh, I listened and some.

"John, forgive me, but are you sure we should be doing this?"

"Oh, absolutely. Look, that other timeshare was going to cost us eighteen thousand pounds for just one week, whereas a week at this one on the Costa del Sol in Spain will only cost us three."

"Yes, but that figure does not apply to high season and, as you can see, it's still only half built."

"Please don't state the obvious, for when it's finished, it's going to be amazing. Listen here, it's going to have a fabulous golf course and…"

"But you've never even held a golf club."

"That's not the point."

"Oh right then, please tell me quite what is the point?"

"Look, please stop interrupting and just hear me out," he impatiently cried. "It will also have a full size gymnasium, a theater complex and restaurants, a children's play area and…"

And so it was that, once again, I let him talk me into it, only this time there was no ninety minute presentation to attend, so no booby prize to get overly excited about, all we had to do was send in a check, oh, and get one big hole in our small savings account at the same time. In all fairness to John, I have to admit that the full page advertisement looked incredibly enticing. We were only halfway through another incredibly miserable British winter that found us choking in our thick scarves as, chilled to the bone, we braced high winds and ferocious sleet and rain. I can well imagine that more than half of Britain was equally seduced by this offer, so we could be forgiven for believing we were about to own a little piece of paradise at an exceptional bargain price. We paid up, and the title deeds arrived in the post and, from that moment on, we began dreaming about our next holiday on the Costa del Sol.

Many months later we boarded a plane bound for Malaga in Spain to stay a whole two weeks in our latest luxurious acquisition. First we were held up for over five hours at the airport. All our children were very young and, due to the many cancellations, there was not an empty seat to be found throughout the entire airport. Finally our plane came up on the board. However, by the time it was announced over the speaker system our children were so filthy and grubby from rolling around and playing on the ground that I refused to follow John until I had taken them all to the bathroom for a clean up.

"Come on Tricia, what does it matter if they're a bit dirty?"

"A bit dirty! John are you kidding? They're black as the ace of spades."

"Well, they're boarding our plane so you don't wish to miss the plane do you?"

"Nope, but I don't want airport security questioning their DNA, otherwise their country of origin either."

"Don't be so overdramatic."

"Well I'm still not boarding until I've cleaned them up."

"Oh go on then," he groaned. "I'll wait outside, but hurry up."

And so it was that the children were forced one by one to strip off and sit naked in a basin of water while I attended to each of them by giving them a hearty scrub. When finished I stood each child under a hand dryer to dry them off before dressing them.

"Psst…Tricia are you in there?"

"Yes, I'm almost finished."

"Well hurry up, for the last call for boarding has just been given out." As I left the bathroom he grabbed hold of my arm.

"Goodness, I thought you were giving them all new haircuts and pedicures you've been that long. Now we need to rush, otherwise we will definitely miss the plane."

Happily we landed at Malaga airport with the nose section as well as both wings of the plane intact and, after going through Customs with reasonably presentable looking children, we picked up our small rental car, and, after only just managing to fit ourselves and our luggage in, we headed off towards Fuengirola and our first ever timeshare holiday. The drive was terrifying, for the traffic was fast and unforgiving, so there was little room for mistakes from novice tourists such as we were. If we slowed down to look for signs we were beeped, threatened and sworn at, and changing lanes was a complete nightmare. Before long my anxiety levels were through the roof.

"John, get off this main road before we're all killed," I anxiously cried.

"I can't, I've got no choice but to keep on going," he shouted back. What should have been little more than an hour's drive turned out to be more like three, as we kept getting hopelessly lost. Worst still, our tiny hire car had no air conditioning and the sun was mercilessly beating down so hard on the roof that it wasn't too long before we all began experiencing life from the perspective of live chickens on a spit roast.

"John, we need some cool air and some cold water or we're likely to pass out," I begged.

"Sorry everybody, but you'll have to wait until we get to our destination," was his unacceptable reply.

"Will that be anytime before Christmas?" one of my boys cheekily chided.

"Look, before you all get mad at me I'm doing my very best, really I am." I was thoroughly relieved when we finally saw a large billboard promoting the complex. It was still an hour or so later before we left the reception with the keys and headed towards our apartment. When we finally arrived at our apartment I was surprised to see we had a few extra bodies waiting to be let in. We tried to encourage the family of stray kittens to go elsewhere, but their hearts were firmly fixed on our apartment. When we refused them access, they went in search of other distant relatives to join their cause. They would then congregate outside our apartment, their wailing meows becoming so loud and pitiful, there was simply no way we could continue to ignore them. Having managed to break down all our resistance, eight or more of cats became partakers of our family summer vacation, enjoying our food, and taking over the sofa as they made themselves thoroughly at home, leisurely stretching themselves out throughout the living area to enjoy their regular afternoon siesta. We fed them like they were our own and gave them sanctuary in the forlorn hope that in return they would hold back on their nightly music sessions that saw a gathering of the clans, their voices blending together as they serenaded their way through each and every night. Some time later I would find out that the builders had left a few cats on site and they in turn had continued to propagate until the family of cats had expanded to something in the region of forty to fifty relatives all looking for a free and relaxing timeshare vacation.

After unpacking we decided to go on a discovery walk around the complex. John had brought along the brochure describing all the activities on site. Sadly we were to become very upset that most of it did not exist. No restaurants had been built, no theatre, no gymnasium, no children's play area, the list went on.

"This is all one big lie from unconscionable people," my disappointed husband cried as he crushed his brochure to a pulp.

"I wouldn't do that if I were you. For you might need it for legal reasons," I quietly stated.

"Uh, you're right," he sighed.

We determined to rest a few days before going in search of some answers, however circumstances dictated otherwise, for another disconcerting problem was the large rubbish tip that lay just outside our ground floor apartment. It looked very much as though it was originally nothing more than a large pile of bricks and rubble left by the inconsiderate builders, but very quickly it had escalated and become a common dumping ground for the locals to relieve themselves of all unwanted rubbish, rotting food included! This unpleasant situation left us unable to enjoy the small patio garden at meal times, for as well as the unbearable smell, as soon as we attempted to eat out on the small patio, the very smell of food became a clear signal to every winged insect to abandon all foraging in the dump to come and gate crash our luncheon party as they swarmed around the table looking for a freebie.

"Reuben, stop what you're eating! Don't put that fork in your mouth for some nasty bug is crawling all over your chicken," I hysterically screeched as I reached over to grab hold of the distraught child's fork before he swallowed the chillingly gruesome bug.

"Mummy, we can't stand these flies and bugs," my distressed children cried as they began furiously waving the winged creatures off their food. There were so many that it was a futile waste of time and energy. Finally we decided it was once again time for action. I took the children down to the unheated pool while John, armed with the brochure, made his way to the reception to speak with someone in authority. An hour or so later he returned. The news was not good.

"Tricia, the staff on reception only speak a smattering of pigeon English, and they seem very unwilling to help or answer any of my pertinent questions."

"Now that doesn't surprise me the least."

"However, there is a meeting with the reps that we are encouraged to attend and then we can voice our concerns."

"So when does this take place?"

"Thursday."

"Thursday! But that's another three whole days away."

"Look, we're not the only unhappy ones, there is a long line of outraged Americans who got there before me, and they are all absolutely furious at being charged an extra fifty pounds per week for electricity."

"Are they faring any better?"

"No, their complaints are also being met with extraordinary indifference."

A few years later this same company offered us a week in their latest brand new resort, however we were expected to shell out a large amount of money for the privilege of staying at their first five star resort. Imagine our disappointment as well as disgust when upon arrival we were shipped off to an entirely different resort, and one that needed to be completely refurbished! Our bleak apartment was crawling with ants and the furniture verged on being ready for the bonfire.

At the welcome meeting we quickly discovered that we were not the only ones who had been deceived, for all the holidaymakers on this virtually abandoned resort had likewise paid handsomely for the opportunity to experience their newest luxury resort. I realized then that this was a scam and just a way for them to fill up the otherwise empty resort and make extra money. The resort was up a steep hill and miles from anywhere. It was scandalous! Needless to say the welcome meeting soon became a very unpleasant affair with many, if not all the families demanding to be moved. It fell on deaf ears.

On this occasion we had brought one of our foster girls with us, she was in her late teens and struggled with depression, so having built this holiday up, she was extremely downcast for the majority of our stay. I became desperate to cheer her up so one night I suggested we take Antonia and head down to a seaside bar and restaurant that was having a family Karaoke night. She brightened up immediately. The walk down to the restaurant was a tougher feat than I first thought it would be, so before long we were all tired and exhausted for, despite it being completely dark, it was still extremely hot. Suddenly I saw an opportunity to cut the remaining distance in half. There was no 'Keep Out' or other signs to warn us of what was to come!

"Come on girls, let's cut through this building site and then we're almost there." Oh boy what a mistake! That small decision nearly costs us our limbs if not our lives. Within minutes we were eyeball to eyeball with the hounds from hell. We were terrified.

"Girls walk backwards, very slowly," I shakily cried as the heavily salivating demonized beasts bared their razor sharp teeth and strained on their long metal chains, for they were desperately eager to attack. My heart was in my mouth and I was trembling from head to toe as great fear crept over me.

"Keep moving backwards," I whispered as the dogs continued to drool great lengths of saliva, their hate filled eyes pinned on us, their fierce growls threatening as they fought to free themselves from the chains that bound them. If we had been just a few feet nearer when they first appeared from out of nowhere, there is little doubt in my mind they would have pounced and thrown us to the ground before mauling us like hungry lions, as they stripped the very flesh from our bones. Only the long iron chains prevented them from roaming free and feasting on our flesh. I felt sick for hours to come especially as earlier that evening I had considered bringing my two younger sons as they loved singing Dolly Parton's 'Jolene' at Karaoke parties. Had they accompanied us that fateful evening, then they would have done what they always did and that was to race ahead of us. I thank God I came to the decision to leave them back at the apartment with John.

Once back home in England and despite a high court ruling in our favor we would quickly discover that accountability was zilch, for all their monies are held in offshore accounts.

Years and many disappointing holiday exchanges later, we would make the decision to use our timeshare for the sole purpose of American exchanges, especially when we heard that America had much tougher laws in place regarding timeshare resorts Although it meant shelling out a lot more money, as well as the exhaustion of taking young children on long haul flights, it was well worth it, for we were always delighted by the extremely high standards of all the resorts we stayed at. But for the time being we still had a number of European destinations to try out.

CHAPTER TWENTY

If at First You Don't Succeed, Cry a Little Harder

And so it was that the following year we found ourselves heading off to Lanzarote a beautiful Island just off the coast of Africa which is unfairly known in certain English circles as Lanzagrotty. This time round I was expecting our third child and, despite being six months gone, I was still struggling to keep anything down, so I wasn't the least enamored at the idea of going abroad. However, as usual, my very persistent husband persuaded me otherwise.

"Look Tricia, while we're gone I will get Dick in to redecorate Antonia's room. This way we'll suffer little to no inconvenience, as it will all be done before we get back from our holiday." On reflection he was very clever to use decorating a room as a bargaining tool, and all too quickly I fell for it.

And so it was that we left our house at some unearthly hour of the night to head to the airport, leaving our decorator with the keys to our house, as well as some simple instructions reminding him of what we were hoping for. I even thought to attach a little note asking if he would be so kind as to put all the furniture back in place for our return, after his work was finished.

While we waited for our flight to come up on the board John disappeared saying he would be back shortly. The minutes ticked by and eventually our flight number came up. It was now time to board the plane, however there was a wee problem. It's called an absentee husband! For the sake of the children I tried not to panic, really I did, but with every moment that passed I became more concerned. Feeling flustered I eventually headed over to a desk and begged the person on duty to call out his name on the speaker system. She happily obliged and not once, not twice but a whopping three times. "Will a Mr. Bennett make his way back to his family at Gate 92 as the flight to Lanzarote is now being boarded."

I waited patiently, confident that on hearing this message he would race back to where I was standing with all our carry on luggage and two small and equally worried children.

"Please try again will you," I anxiously begged the lady. She gave a wry smile and promised she would try again in a few minutes. By now both the children were crying.

"Mummy, where has daddy gone?" they whimpered.

"To be honest, I have absolutely no idea."

"Will we miss the plane?"

"Sweetheart, I can't even answer that at the moment."

"Oh, why does daddy always do this?" they pitifully cried.

"I've no idea but just you wait until I get my hands on him," I muttered under my breath as once more I turned to the lady behind the desk to beg her assistance. Happily this last call seemed to do the trick for minutes later I suddenly caught sight of him racing across the concourse in our direction.

"Where on earth have you been?" I barked. "You've been away so long that you've managed to reduce us all to gibbering wrecks." I glowered, our two tear stained children clinging to me for comfort.

"Sorry honey, I was in the Virgin store listening to music and I simply lost all sense of time. By the way, they've got the Moody Blues Greatest hits on special offer…"

"You'll soon be on special offer if I have to listen to anymore of this! For I can't believe you didn't hear any of the urgent messages?"

"Well er um….that's because I was listening to the music on some amazingly powerful headphones that almost took me to outer space. Just listening to Pink Floyd's "Wish you were here" on those magnificent headphones was beyond awesome."

"Wow how amazing, for guess what, the children as well as myself all had that exact identical wish."

"Uh?"

"Wishing you were here, instead of hiding away in some record store."

"I'm so sorry I never meant to do this to you."

"You never do. So please pick up the rest of the hand luggage and let's get going, otherwise the plane will leave without us," I growled.

"Yes daddy, mummy says it's high time you learnt the true meaning of responsibility," my precocious young daughter primly bleated, her large blue eyes blurred by tears, as following her mother's best 'Prima Donna' mode she raised her eyes to the ceiling, tossed her long blond hair to one side, to resolutely march ahead of us, dragging her personal luggage along in a most determined manner.

"Oh great, I'm really in the dog house now aren't I?" he moaned as he hurriedly followed after us as we raced towards the boarding area. Due to the lateness of the hour we were the very last to board.

"I'm so sorry, but we can't seat you all together, so one of you will have to come with me and I will find you a seat at the back of the plane," the dead cute hostess announced giving a deeply concerned look. (No doubt she believed she was about to come under fire for giving us this latest piece of unacceptably bad news). No sooner had the words tumbled from her perfect pouting pastel pink lips, when my husband all too readily volunteered to be the hero of the hour.

"I'll go," he much too eagerly cried, raising a hand in the air as though he were back in a classroom.

"Of course you will darling, for you've always been the perfect gentleman."

"Well sir, I need to inform you that the only available seats are in the smoking section of the plane."

John's forlorn face appeared to plummet far below his waistline at this latest unpleasant revelation for, if he had known this little but most vital piece of information sooner, then never in a million years would he have volunteered, but now it was too late for him to back down.

"Oh dear, I had no idea, and I do suffer from occasional asthmatic attacks," he announced as he tried to squirm out of it.

"Nonsense darling, once you've popped the headphones on and tuned into Pink Floyd then trust me, you'll be fine," I chipped in flashing him a very smug smirk.

"Thank you sir, now if you'll please follow after me, for the plane is almost ready for take off and we need to get you seated as quickly as possible."

"See you in Lanzarote!" I cried out after him as I watched the young stewardess chaperone my now very reluctant husband towards the rear of the plane. As I sat back in my chair, I was supremely confident that being forced to endure the next four hours in the smoking section would be punishment enough and would thus satisfy any further need I might have for personal revenge. Truth be known I was glad to be given the time to calm down. "Let there be space in your togetherness," some wise sage had once stated. Dead right! I really had need of this unexpected but most welcome space if my good man was going to disembark this plane without being hacked to death or otherwise strangled with a pair of his own shoelaces.

It was quite a while before peace and harmony began once more to flood my otherwise disgruntled soul, however I still continued to meditate on the ten best ways to successfully dispose of a very dead husband who by the end of the trip would no doubt be smelling worse than an old ashtray!

Knowing him as well as I did, I knew that once settled he would sink into his latest book which he would now be able to read without any interruptions. Dream on! Sadly for him the punishment was not yet over, for not only was he now seated in the smoking section but he was also seated besides the most friendly extremely talkative person on the plane other than my good self! This more seasoned and extremely thoughtful working class man saw it as his personal mission to get him up to speed on what he could expect from this forthcoming holiday. I would hear the details much later.

"Ere mate, is this your first time going to Lanzagrotty?" the man asked as through a cloud of his own exhaled smoke he honed in on my now rather distraught husband.

"Yes…yes it is," John wheezed and spluttered.

"Well, let me tell you now that most of the time you'll find the island's bloomin' windy. Yeah them Trade winds that come from North Africa are a bit nippy making it pretty impossible to read yer morning paper," he said puckering his lips like a dazed trout as once more he blew large rings of smoke directly into John's forlorn face.

"Oh really!" John spluttered.

"Do you read the Sun or the Mirror?

"Neither actually."

Before John could say another word he was intercepted by his new friend's wife. "Er, Malcolm leave the poor man alone, he probably just wants some peace and quiet."

"No honestly it's fine," John lied, while recalling the Peanuts cartoon caption that remarked on how he loved mankind, it was just people he couldn't stand.

"Actually, come to think of it, I would take you for a Daily Mail reader, have I got that one right?"

"Actually yes, when I get the time".

"Well, if you do find time to read a paper I'd suggest yer pin all four sides down with the help of an ashtray and a couple of cans of lager, that always does the trick for me. Yeah me and Gloria, me trouble and strife, ave been comin' to Lanzagrotty for several years now. We really like it, don't we babes, as it's got such a nice Mediterranean feel to it."

John smiled and politely thanked the man before pushing back his seat and tentatively closing his eyes, a signal that all small talk was now well and truly over. However, in thanking the gentlemen the man misread his politeness to be some form of approval rating, and this encouraged him to resume his monologue.

"Yeah, and it's hard to believe, but as most of the island is desert or semi desert, the sand on the beaches looks pretty similar to black volcanic ash."

"Hmm really," my hapless husband responded as he opened one eye once more out of general politeness.

"Mind, they haven't seen an eruption for many a year, that's not to say it couldn't happen though as I'm told there's been quite a bit of activity lately."

"I think an eruption is probably quite imminent," my husband half heartedly muttered as he tried to rid his mind of my scowling face.

"Anyway, as I was saying, that bloomin sand, I'm telling yer now, it gets up yer nose and in yer ears as well as up a few other places I could mention…."

"Yes, well thank you," my husband patiently replied as yet again he failed to discourage our would be tour guide.

"Tell yer wot, the food's pretty naff too, a lot of rice and fish, yeah fish, fish… and more fish."

"Yes, well it is an island surrounded on all sides by the Atlantic waters,"

"Yeah, but their fish ain't the same as ours, is it babe?"

"No darlin, it sure ain't," his wife chipped in as she momentarily abandoned her True Love magazine to give his arm a friendly supportive squeeze.

"And it's not served up in batter like wot we're used to. No, it's more sardines and tuna and they stink so bad. The Krauts seem to like the food, mind you I think they'd eat anything. Anyways I can tell you now there are a lot of them on the island. You can't mistake them as they're all togged up in those bright colored shell suits. Hmm, and guess what?" he said blowing large circles of smoke into the air, as though he were sending messages to some far off Red Indian reservation. "You'll be lucky as Larry to find anywhere that'll serve up a nice steak and pigmy pie."

"Oh really."

"Mind I could give you the name of a British pub that does a real nice Sunday roast with crackin' roast spuds and Yorkshire puds, as well as the best chip butty on the island. Here, Gloria me missus has just written down the name on this bit of paper. So keep it safe mate," he said stuffing it in my husband's hand with a nod and a wink.

"Why thank you."

"Here mate, how thoughtless of me. Have one of these," he cheerfully said as he kindly pushed a half empty packet of Marlborough cigarettes in John's direction."

"Thanks all the same, but I don't smoke."

"Shame. I couldn't face getting on a plane without my ciggies, could I Gloria?"

"No darlin, you sure couldn't," she said as once more she squeezed his hairy hand. "Yeah, you'd be murder to live with without your ciggies. But don't worry, we got our fair share of the Duty Free didn't we?" she giggled like a nervous schoolgirl.

"Normally Gloria controls how many I smoke a day, but as Duty Free ciggies are so cheap I'm having a bit of a field day," he cheerfully confessed.

"Yes he's become a bit of a chain smoker since getting on this plane," Gloria hurriedly added as once again she affectionately squeezed his arm.

"I hadn't noticed."

"Calms me nerves right down," he confided as he took another deep drag of his cigarette.

"Oh right."

"Anyways Lanzarote is also a great place if you like bird watching."

"Oh really."

"Yeah and I'm talking about the feathered variety," he joked giving John a friendly dig in the ribs. "For what it's worth there are a few other, much smaller islands like Famara where the sand is as soft as a baby's bum," he sniffed, expelling a further amount of smoke that in seconds had John's eyes watering as he then began coughing and spluttering. This as well as ever other coughing fit would be ignored by our friendly co traveler as his views on the island were ultimately of far more importance than John's rapidly deteriorating health.

"Here mate are you on your own? Coz I don't know if you'll wanna hear this, but you're way off course if you're into clubbing, for there ain't too many decent nightclubs in Lanzarote. Now if clubbing and picking up good looking birds is your thing you'd have better luck heading off to Tenerife."

"Actually I'm not here for the nightlife."

"Oh right, so what brings yer out here then?"

"Well I too have a wife and family plus one more on the way."

"Oh right! So where are they? Had a little marital tiff have we? A little fall out?" he cheekily asked with a grin.

"Well yes we did have a little fall-out at the Airport, but actually there wasn't a spare seat for me to remain with them in non smoking, which is why I was sent to the back of the plane."

"Nice one. Well have a great holiday and do try out the bar I was telling you about. They're Brits too. Yeah I think they're from Merseyside. That's right, ain't it babe?"

"No yer great plonker, they're from Manchester."

The plane finally touched down with the bodywork still intact and minutes later we met up again, only to be bustled down the plane's steep steps and into what felt like the inside of a very hot oven with the extractor fan switched on.

"Goodness John, you reek of cigarettes," I commented as I grabbed hold of the children's hands. We were then herded along the hot tarmac and through some doors into the building. Once inside we were instructed to make ourselves into orderly lines to then go through passport control. Needless to say but we were last in line.

Then for some unfathomable reason our luggage failed to make its way along the conveyor belt until everybody else on our plane had long left the building. We were on the verge of reporting our luggage as missing when our suitcases suddenly decided to appear in splendid isolation on the conveyor belt. Sadly for us this meant we were last in line for the car hire. Once all the documents had been signed and with our luggage crammed into the boot of our as always undersized car, we were now ready to set off in search of our timeshare resort

The complex looked exactly like the photo in the timeshare brochure, with a fabulous sparkling pool shaded by glorious majestic palm trees, but the same could not be said for our apartment for it was urgent need of refurbishment. The furniture in the living area was shabby and outdated and the well worn sofa had seen more than its fair share of spillages. The kitchen equipment needed replacing and the walls were crying out for a fresh coat of paint. That said we were just glad to be in a foreign land away from the dismal English weather. A land where the blazing sun dominated the skyline like a huge golden ball as it rose early to greet all us holiday worshippers. As we drove along the coast, with its crystal clear blue ocean sparkling like a million flecked jewels, it whispered for us to take leave of our senses to once more become like unfettered carefree children as we raced each other into the warm deliciously inviting sea.

We had barely settled in when a piece of paper was slipped under our door inviting us to attend a meeting intended to give us all the information we would need. At that same meeting we found ourselves being pressured to sign up for a timeshare presentation. We signed up for just one of the expensive tours as well as the presentation. The next day I felt confused as we were guided around an apartment that had been carefully designed, sparing no attention to detail. It was so unbelievably luxurious and pristine that it was barely recognizable as being on the same site as ours. If this tour was intended to help us open our check books and buy in they were wrong, for all it achieved was to stir up our discontent as we and other disgruntled guests now wanted an apartment similar to the one we had just viewed.

As we lay by the pool we were intermittently forced to hear the loud sound of a clanging bell followed by a tumultuous roar and thunderous applause. This routine was not some local custom but rather an occasion for all staff on site to stop in their tracks to acknowledge that some dear couple or family had just agreed to purchase a week or two at this timeshare. It was a ritual that took place thirty to forty times a day as the ecstatic timeshare staff jumped up and down no doubt glorying in just how much commission they would now be receiving in their next pay check. There came a point when, not wishing to be left out, we decided to join in the general merriment, so we began to dance and shout from the pool deck as we mischievously joined in their joie de vivre.

As for the tours, there was a large and lively Sunday market at the other end of the island in Costa Teguise. There were also cruises to the smaller island that had the white sandy beach but little else. The excursion that that we decided we couldn't afford to miss was a one day coach trip to Timafaya National Park with its still active volcano. As we sat back on the comfortable air conditioned coach we drove through miles of bleak shrub land. Much to our surprise the driver made an unexpected stop at a ravine with the intention of showing all passengers the remains of a bus that had accidentally fallen down into it. For practical reasons the bus had not been towed away and so had become something of a tourist attraction. As the coach driver excitedly jabbered on about the damaged bus we and others more out of curiosity disembarked the coach to go and peer down the ravine.

"Honey, if this is deemed to be the latest tourist attraction then they definitely need some help," I commented as I cautiously peered down the ravine.

"Yes, perhaps our good Queen might be considerate enough to lend them a castle or two."

"Yeah right."

It would be mid morning when we finally arrived at the National Park. We remained seated in the coach with all eyes firmly fixed on the volcano until we reached the large car park. We were then given the freedom to disembark. At the base of the volcano we passed a long line of pompous looking camels, their haughty heads held high as fallen down on bended knees they paid homage to the unquestionable deity of this most spectacular volcano, only rising from the arid dust when a passing tourist demanded a ride and so paid it's owner most handsomely. In that small moment in time I longed to abandon the usual tour guide, with its bland rhetoric, in preference for a ride on one of these splendid creatures of the desert for they surely beckoned me to come take my chances, but as I was expecting our third child, I quickly came to my senses. Such a ride could be no doubt deleterious to mine or the baby's health. Besides I admit to feeling quite troubled as I observed many heavy set tourists clambering into individual chairs that seemed very precariously balanced on the backs of these high smelling ships of the desert. Once the tourist was seated, and in obedience to their master, the beast would then dutifully arise from the dust, their spindly knees wobbling, their cargo looking even more unstable than ever, as the flea ridden beast then struggled like an infant toddler to take its first tentative steps.

"John, did you know that camel meat is considered quite a delicacy"

"Really honey, I never knew that."

"Yes, they cook the camel whole in a humongous metal vat and then the family all sit round with their friends and relations eating it much like you would an elephant, one spoonful at a time."

"You don't say."

"Yes, I saw it on a documentary."

"Honey, it's amazing how much useful information you manage to store away in that little head of yours."

"Now you're poking fun at me."

The outing went very smoothly thanks to our professional guide so, as I sat back on the coach and closed my eyes, I felt a deep sense of gratitude that we were finally having ourselves a holiday free from the usual nightmares, and with this gratitude came a new fresh expectancy that this holiday would mark the beginning of many trouble free holidays in the years to come.

A few days into the holiday I was still celebrating the fact that we were still all one hundred percent alive, when Reuben aged about four accidentally cut his eye open on a sharp corner of the dining table. The cut was so deep that we struggled to stem the blood flow, so sadly we were forced to abandon our proposed trip to the beach to go in search of a doctor. We sat for many long hours in a stiflingly hot doctors office as, with no air conditioning on offer, we waited for our injured son to be treated. The bill for the good doctors services was as usual so hefty we considered he should use some of his profits to invest in some air conditioning. Hungry and wearied we returned home with anti-biotic cream with the doctor's assurance that, given time, the cut would heal and hopefully there would be no visible scar. This was all good news and so we comforted our young ones by promising them that our beach plans were back on for the next day.

However that same night, as we lay fast asleep in our beds, our young daughter not wishing to be outdone, began her own special drama that had her screaming, whilst pitifully clutching her ears. This fresh crisis dictated that we once more abandon our beach plans to spend yet another four or five hours of the day in the same stifling doctors office while we waited for the doctor to examine her ears.

"Give her these antibiotics, and keep her out of the water for at least ten days," the doctor ordered as he scrawled his name on the bottom of the prescription pad before passing it over accompanied by his latest bill.

"Ten days! Oh surely not, she lives in the swimming pool," I privately moaned.

"Well, we'd better follow the doctors orders or.."

"Or what?" I demanded to know.

"Well she might get worse, or maybe even lose her hearing."

"John, if we obey the doctor the rest of our holiday will be wrecked, for can you even begin to imagine the pure torture we will have to endure if we forbid her to enter the water, especially in this heat?"

"Well no" he replied lamely shrugging his shoulders.

"Precisely!"

"Alright, let's just wait and see, shall we?"

"Now, that's more like it."

As promised, the next few days were extremely challenging, for swimming was our little girls passion and so to a young six year old we seemed like very cruel and unreasonable parents. To get even, she punished us with lengthy sessions of uncontrollable shrieking, yelling, screaming and kicking as she rolled around the apartment floor remaining utterly inconsolable. Only our naïve belief that things would eventually get better prevented us from joining her down on the floor to have our own therapeutic roll around, culminating in a lengthy boo hooing session.

"She'll be needing a whole host of counseling in her adult years, for this crisis is bound to traumatize her for life," I cried as I struggled to pick up her squirming body from the ground. Meanwhile I remained aware of annoyed sunbathers peering disapprovingly over their fake Armani sunglasses, while seriously contemplating whether to turn us over to authorities for child cruelty, that way they could re-establish some well earned peace and tranquility on the pool deck. It seemed that this holiday like every other was now beginning to take its toll.

Finally once the antibiotics had kicked in, we decided to abandon the pool deck and head for the beach, for this would serve as the perfect tonic for our shattered nerves. I was done with ringing bells and happy clappy timeshare salesmen. I threw a picnic together and gathered up the children's buckets and spades, which I placed in a bag alongside the picnic bag, for John to place in the boot of the car while I strapped our excited youngsters into the back seat.

"Right this is it kids, we're finally off to the beach," John enthused as he turned the ignition.

"Hooray!" they jubilantly cried back.

Their joy was very short lived for minutes later we discovered we were stuck in a terrible traffic build up. Once again frustration reared its ugly head as the suffocating heat inside the stuffy little car began to rise to match the searing temperature outside leaving us all feeling like skewered chickens on a revolving rotisserie grill. With no air conditioning to keep tempers at bay, our children became increasingly fractious and in no time at all the chilled drinks intended for our beach were all used up. I'd had enough.

"Honey let's just turn back."

"Oh trust me I would if I could, but the traffic is one way and so far we've had to cope with about three major diversions."

What should have taken twenty minutes would take us over two hours. By the time we found ourselves a parking space we were physically and emotionally depleted. The beach, with its black volcanic sand, did not look too inviting to the eye, but all the same it was a beach and the Atlantic waters did summon for us to abandon all misery and enter in. After helping the children into their costumes I slumped down on the ground, feeling so spent I wished for a quick lie down. As every mother knows, time off is almost out of the question when you have young children to deal with. Oh, and to think I spent our first five years of married life feeling jealous of mums and dads as I observed them helping their offspring build sandcastles.

"Mummy, can we have our buckets and spades?" the children excitedly asked.

"I'm going to build the biggest castle ever," Reuben enthusiastically cried.

"Can daddy and you help us with the sandcastle?" Antonia begged jumping up and down for joy.

"John, help me out, where are their buckets and spades?"

"Don't ask me."

"Well I am asking you. Have you left them in the boot of the car?"

"No idea," he replied.

"Well you'd better go and have a look."

"Okay, well keep your fingers crossed that I find them."

He arrived back huffing and puffing and the look on his face betrayed my worst fears.

"Tricia, they're not in the car."

"Then you must have left them back at the apartment," I strongly suggested.

"Maybe you forgot to pack them," he retaliated.

"Oh I packed them alright and I left them by the apartment door for you to bring to the car along with our picnic."

"Oh dear, now you mention it I do remember another bag leaning against the front door" he grimaced.

"Well, what are we going to do now?" I asked.

"I can't go all the way home, it's totally impractical," he despondently replied.

"Well then sweetie, you'd better go in search of a shop and buy some more."

"Oh no I can't do that."

"Why ever not?"

"Tricia the shops out here are so darned expensive."

"Well go back home then."

"Children, listen up, daddy has accidentally left your bucket and spades behind at the apartment, so it looks like no sandcastles will be built today."

They immediately began to wail. "Please daddy we need our buckets and spades."

"Right then it's either go and buy some more, otherwise an afternoon of verbal castration, so I don't appear to have any other choice."

"Got that in one."

I watched on until he disappeared from sight. Seconds later and my young son Reuben began to scream as he'd somehow managed to get sand into the cut of his injured eye, this in turn upset Antonia, so now they were both crying and begging to go home.

"Look, wait for daddy to get back," I urged as I did my best to console them, but to no avail. I was now in panic mode. Think think... what can I do now? Yes brilliant! Let's stuff ourselves silly because they can't eat and cry at the same time, can they?

"Right kids, let's make ourselves a lunchtime treat while we wait for daddy to return," I hurriedly suggested as I reached over towards the bag that contained the lovingly prepared picnic which I then spread out over a towel. Introducing food seemed to do the trick for they both appeared to calm right done. Then when I least expected it the unthinkable happened. The children were on the verge of reaching over to grab a paper plate when suddenly a large beach ball shot past us at top speed. This was followed by a couple of crazed youths who seemed oblivious to the fact that we were in their direct path. To begin with the slightly older one was winning, but only by a hare's breath, but this quickly changed when he was suddenly rugby tackled to the ground by the competition. As the older one fell with an almighty thud the dark sand around him spewed high into air like a volcanic eruption before raining down on our heads as well as our precious carefully laid out picnic. My jaw dropped as the boys spent the next few seconds of their friendly skirmish rolling around in the sand like a couple of mischievous bear cubs as they fought each other for the ball. And me? Well I felt like a mama grizzly ready to rugby tackle both bear cubs for our picnic was now well and truly ruined.

"Boys, are you crazy! Look what you've just done!" I fumed.

"Oops, we're so sorry," they gasped as, still laughing, they ran away at top speed.

Not surprisingly, the children began to cry once more when I refused to allow them to eat the food that was still laid out in front of them.

"Right, I've had enough of this, come on children, get changed, for as soon as daddy returns, we're leaving."

A very hot and sweaty John arrived back just as I was throwing our unsalvageable picnic back into the bag as there were no trash bins this far down the beach.

"Hi honey, sorry I've been away so long, but I had to search a number of shops before I found some reasonably priced buckets and spades, although my goodness, I still feel ripped off for ….."

"Spare me the details," I hissed.

"Honey what's wrong? Why are you packing up when we've only just got here?"

"Forget it, we're leaving."

"But I've just bought new buckets and spades," he cried in great dismay.

"John, see for yourself, the children are in a terrible state of distress, and to top it all, some teenage boys managed to completely ruin our picnic. So much as I wanted this special day on the beach, I'm now ecstatic at the prospect of heading back to our resort to further endure the constant rejoicings of ringing bells and glorious salutations as yet more timeshare weeks are sold to the unfortunate amongst us."

"Oh honey, I'm so sorry, but can't we stay just a while longer?"

"Nope, I think it's best we pack up our things and leave."

"But what about these?" he pathetically asked as he dangled the buckets in front of me.

"So you want to stay to build your own sandcastle do you?"

"Well not on my own."

"John we've no food or drinks and if Reuben gets any more sand in his cut then I think I'm going to join him in screaming blue murder."

"But what about the buckets and spades."

"Well, we could return them to the shop otherwise just swallow our losses and take them back to the apartment, it's really up to you."

"Okay okay….calm down. We'll take them home with us."

"Right then, let's all head back to the car."

That night, as I showered the children and then myself, I could not believe that, in such a short space of time, how much black sand had traveled up into internal areas that before now I never knew existed! Sadly we thought it best to abandon any further attempts at having a day on the beach.

All too soon and it was time to head home to England. Now I'm not trying to be disrespectful to my dear husband, but for some mighty peculiar reason he always manages to get completely lost on route to the airport. Once lost he would always insist that he'd meticulously followed the correct route but the road and the motorway signs not only maliciously conspired against him, but would you believe it they then thought nothing of lying. And I'm not talking small insy wincy lies, but big blatant whoppers, that saw to it that he headed off in entirely the wrong direction.

"Okay John. I promise that, if you'll calm down, as soon as we get home, I'll write a stiff letter to the top government officials demanding a full explanation, but until then would you try to take a deep breath. Good now I know this may well sound very novel but do you like the idea of actually stopping the car long enough to ask a local, if they know the right way to the airport."

"Tricia, there's no way I can stop on this road, besides I haven't got time to stop, otherwise we'll miss the plane."

"Well that's for sure, but if you carry on driving us further into the desert, missing the plane will become something of a certainty."

"Tricia, you're really not helping me."

"Well if you could find it in your heart to just humble yourself long enough to admit that we're well and truly up a gum tree and then stop the jolly car and go find help!" I bellowed in his ear as my anxiety levels reached fever pitch.

We made it to the airport in the nick of time, but only because I virtually braked the car for him, before forcing him out of his seat to go into a small wayside garage to get help.

"Look John trust me when I say it's not that difficult. You simply open your mouth wide and let the words tumble freely. It's not a lot different than going to the dentist. So go on say… 'Is there anybody here who can help me?' Or even better just shout "Aeroporto?' in a very loud commanding voice. Just try it and, if it works, then hopefully you'll find it a whole heap easier the next time round." I cried out in pure exasperation.

Having returned the hire car we struggled quite a distance with our luggage and our children in tow towards the airport terminal.

"My goodness, this heat is killing me," my husband complained.

"Never mind John, for before too long we will be back in freezing cold England and then I predict you'll have a lot more than the intense heat to complain about."

As we stood in a line that ran the entire length of the airport we were dismayed to discover that our plane home had been cancelled. We now had a nine hour wait in a cramped airport that had no air conditioning. The weather outside was now well over a hundred and ten degrees Fahrenheit..

"Oh great, now what?"

"Don't worry Tricia, for I would estimate that it will be a good five or more hours before we get checked in."

By the time we'd had our passports stamped was not a spare seat to be found in the entire airport, and being pregnant while enduring the stifling heat began to take its toll, so it wasn't long before I began feeling extremely ill. Eventually we found a small space on the ground where we could sit down and rest. And after many hours some men in uniform came round handing out tickets that entitled everyone to a free meal from the small airport cafeteria.

"You'd think the end of the world was nigh, looking at the rush for the cafeteria," John casually commented. "I think it would pay us to wait until the stampede is over."

It turned out to be a bad move. Oh why oh why did I agree? It was over an hour before we rose from the floor and headed towards the cafeteria.

"Sorry, but we're almost out of everything," the girl behind the counter sourly sniffed as she pushed a lone plate containing a very unappetizing piece of dried up chicken with some stone cold French fries in our direction.

"But surely you're preparing some more?"

"Sorry, but we really have run out."

"But my wife is pregnant and we have two young children," John hurriedly pointed out.

"Sorry sir, but it was first come first served, and, like I said, we have completely run out."

"Come on John, we're wasting our time," I ruefully stated as I took the plate and headed out of the cafeteria.

We agreed to go hungry and let the children share the plate, but, as the time marched on, my need for food heightened as my blood sugar dropped. Before long I began feeling terribly ill.

The plane was over nine hours late and, as I dragged my weary body with it's swollen feet up the steep steps of the plane, I accidentally dropped a bag of the children's toys. I watched on helplessly as the toys clunked and clanged as they made their merry way down heading for the tarmac. It was the final straw.

"Oh shit!" I loudly cried, immediately placing a hand over my mouth like some naughty little girl.

"Tricia, the children! I can't believe you just said that. And now everyone is looking at us!" he reprimanded.

"Oh my goodness, it's the gallows for me, but wait, even that's not punishment enough! No I should be paraded round the town then boiled alive for this terribly wicked moment of indiscretion."

"Alright that's enough, everyone's now really staring at us."

"Good, let them, for I can't take much more," I bawled.

On the plane I hurriedly found my seat and placed my sunglasses back on, if only to veil the evidence left behind by my tears.

"It's your turn to take care of the kids," I muttered as, hiding behind my dark sunglasses, I once again allowed my tears to flow freely.

"Honey, it's because you're pregnant that you're feeling this emotional," John tried his very best to reassure. I bit my lip and said nothing.

As the plane hovered over London, it was comforting to know that a good friend would be picking us up from the airport, and this guaranteed there would be no lengthy night time search of the vast airport car parks as my 'Detective Columbo' struggled to remember where he'd parked the car two weeks previously. Yes, this very night we would have no need to call on the London Transport Police otherwise a localized surveillance team to not only help us in our search, but also to avert an impending tragedy by becoming marital mediators as they were forced to physically separate the two of us, for by now I was smoldering.

"Tricia, forgive me if I can't remember where I parked the car this time round."

"So what's new?"

"Try to be a bit more charitable."

"Charitable? John you're asking me to be charitable when it's four in the morning, the kids are virtually dropping to the ground with exhaustion and we've been searching the car parks for well over three quarters of an hour!"

"All the same, a bit of help and understanding would be nice."

"Yes, well trust me when I say that all goodness and mercy is well and truly out the window! Come on, think! You must still have the car park ticket."

"Well I know that, for safety sake, I stashed it in my wallet, but it's not there now."

"Okay John, so you would like me to believe that mice, cockroaches or bed bugs have in your absence either borrowed the car in order to go on a reckless rally drive, either that, or in a fit of hunger they decided to devour the entire ticket. Now is this so or would you like to revise that last statement?"

"Goodness, you sound more like a lawyer than my wife. Anyway, be fair for it was a whole two weeks ago," he would never fail to remind as, chilled to the bone we pitifully dragged our heavy suitcases and zombie-like bodies through one miserable car park after another while remaining reluctant players in the stupendously fun-filled game of 'find the jolly car if you can.'

And when we did have occasion to find it, there were never any thunderous rounds of applause, no prizes to be won, just the knowledge that a deep depression had arrived.

"Well, I'm gob smacked! Yes I'll be darned, for I've never even seen this car park before," he would state as we finally approached our vehicle.

"Honey, as our car isn't a bright yellow Volkswagon, neither does it answer to the name Herbie, it's pretty safe to assume it has been parked in the same spot for the entire two weeks."

We touched down at Gatwick around 2.00 am, and went through customs without being arrested for anything, although there was some high drama concerning a gentleman in front of us being cautioned at great length for smuggling in dozens of cartons of cigarettes. I watched on fascinated as two terrifyingly burly officers emptied the suitcases of his plunder.

"I could do with a few cartons of those after this journey," I muttered as we were held up for another thirty or so minutes behind him.

My friend had her usual bright smile as she greeted us, and in record time we were on the road heading for home.

"Jacqui, forgive us but, after the most harrowingly long airport delay, we are all hopelessly tired and expended."

"No problem, you just rest," she said giving my arm a reassuring friendly squeeze.

An hour later we should have been nearly home, and yet we were still on a motorway. Finally my good friend broke the silence.

"Tricia, there's a problem."

"What ?"

"Well, I don't know how to tell you this, but, not only am I thoroughly lost, but the dial on the fuel gauge is registering on below empty."

"Oh no!"

"Tricia, I've never done anything like this before, but I've been driving in the wrong direction for well over an hour. You probably want to kill me for being this stupid."

"Oh no, I don't," I lied as I now fought to suppress the loud voices within, but I restrained all such wicked thoughts as, deep down, I couldn't help think that, in kindly offering to pick us up from the airport, even in the middle of the night due to the flight delay, she had unwittingly taken a nosedive into our tempestuous whirlwind life.

And so it was at a most unearthly hour of the morning that she dropped us off at our house, the only noise coming from birds in nearby trees as they stoically braved the cold dawn in order to welcome us back home. Sadly I was unable to appreciate their chirpiness as, feeling utterly miserable and jet lagged, I left John to help unload our luggage, while I went ahead to take the children into the house and back to bed. Hopefully I too could retire as I yearned for a few hours of deep sleep.

However, as I walked into my young daughter's room, I was dismayed to discover that my decorator had left all the furniture stacked high in the middle of the room, making her bed completely inaccessible. When I finally managed to make a small pathway to her bed I was further discouraged to see that this too was stacked high with a small bookcase, endless children's story books, pictures, piles of clothes and ornaments. My distress was now complete! I had no other choice other than to expend my last fragments of energy in off loading the piled high bed so she could slip into bed. I would eventually find out that the builder's wife had seen red on seeing my polite instructions to put everything back in place.

"The cheek of her! Dick don't you dare do any of it, for you're a builder not a cleaner. So gather up your tools, for we're out of here."

As I lay in my bed, my pillow placed over my head in a futile attempt to drive away all murderous thoughts, I promised myself yet again that this would truly be the last holiday I ever took.

CHAPTER TWENTY ONE

And It's Back to Lanzarote

Some promises are obviously not meant to be kept for the following year circumstances dictated that we take our annual holiday in the month of January. As a result we agreed to head back to Lanzarote because, as the island lies just off the African coast, the chances of guaranteed warm weather were much higher there than at many other European holiday destinations. We sifted the pages of the timeshare brochure and placed a request for two weeks at a large variety of resorts that looked just perfect for us. At first they could offer us nothing. Then, just when we were about to give up, we were suddenly offered a week at a brand new resort. Of course we readily accepted the exchange.

A few weeks later we were even more delighted when, for the first time ever, a week had become available at one of the timeshare's of our choice. We knew then this was going to be a great two week holiday. James, our youngest, had arrived on the scene and was now able to crawl around and we decided to invite a close friend of ours, a single mum, along with her young son, to join us.

This time came around, Brian, one of my husbands employees, was commandeered to get us to the airport in one piece. And so it was that, on the first day of our holiday, I went ahead to wake the children from their deep sleep.

"Mummy, it's only three in the morning, so why do we always have to get up in the middle of the night?" my bleary-eyed young daughter yawned as I wrestled to get her from the bed, "Don't airplanes fly so well during the day?"

"Honey, I'm sorry but the dawn flights work out a bit cheaper."

"Oh alright mummy, but already I'm feeling horribly sick,' she whispered.

Having assisted the children in getting dressed we congregated in the kitchen to eat a piece of toast accompanied by a glass of milk as we waited for our driver to turn up. Antonia still confessed to feeling unwell.

"Honey put this special wrist band on, and take these travel sickness pills with your glass of milk, you too Reuben."

Suddenly we heard the sound of a car pulling up outside our house so we crept out of the house and went on our way. John sat in the front so he could help with the directions and my three children, and myself sat cramped in the back. We would meet up with our good friend and her young son once we reached the airport. As it was the middle of the night, and therefore still dark outside, I closed my eyes and listened in on the men as they quietly chatted away in the front. The boys instantly went back to sleep, but Antonia persisted to wriggle around and complain of feeling queasy.

"Brian, can you stop the car a minute, so she can just stretch her legs and get some fresh air."

"Okay, there's a lay by coming up." he shouted back. Though chilled to the bone, I walked her around all the while instructing her to take deep breaths.

"I'm feeling much better now mummy," she said giving a sort of half smile.

"That's great, then let's get back in the car."

Antonia appeared to settle down, leaving me free to close my eyes and doze. Suddenly she jumped up from her seat and, without any warning, a large projectile of her stomach contents flew high into the air before raining down on my hair and face.

"Stop the car," I yelled.

"I can't, for we're in the middle of the motorway."

"Antonia is still puking up all over me, and I'm covered from head to toe." I cried as the putrefying mess immediately began cascading down my face and neck.

"There's nothing we can do to help, for we're late enough as it is."

"Please stop the car right now!" I pitifully begged.

"We can't. Besides, we're almost there," John shouted back as he stretched over to pat my hand, in his foolish attempt to commiserate me.

"Good grief John, I can't walk into the airport looking and smelling like this?" I screeched.

"Look we'll rush to find the ladies as soon as we can, and then you can put your head under a running tap or something?"

"Or something? John, I need a proper shower and fresh clothes, for there's no way I'm getting on any plane in this sorry state," I announced in shrill decibels.

"Look honey, the flight attendants will perfectly understand for they deal with this sort of thing all the time."

"Oh, don't you honey me, for it's not you in this terrible mess."

"Mummy, I'm feeling so much better now," Antonia chirped in.

Seconds later Brian swerved into a small vacant space at the drop off section outside the airport. I felt so humiliated as I disembarked and stood aside with the children, hurriedly cleaning myself down as best I could while the two men unloaded our luggage.

"Brian, here's some money to get the car steam cleaned."

"I need a steam clean too, so can't I go with him to the car wash?" I hysterically begged.

"Tricia, you're becoming quite irrational."

"No, you're simply not understanding! I can't go into the airport looking and smelling like this, so please let me go back with him."

"Brian, please get back into the car and drive off before she does something really stupid," John barked

The distance to the ticket desk seemed to take forever as I walked with my head down trying to avoid all eye contact with the public at large.

"This feels as bad as my wedding day," I simpered.

"Honey, you may find this hard to believe but I actually have some fond memories of our wedding day!"

"Yeah right! Anyway can't you check in without me?"

"No, it's not possible, for we're running very late and they need to see you."

"I don't see why. Just tell them I've gone to the bathroom," I snapped as I continued mopping my face.

The queue to get checked in was irritatingly long so, with all eyes on me, I wished for the floor to open up and swallow me whole. Finally, having checked in, John agreed to take my good friend Christine and the children to find some seats at a nearby restaurant, leaving me to find my way to the nearest bathroom. Seconds later saw me dispense with all discretion as I erratically stuffed my whole head under the basin tap to then try to shampoo my hair with soap from the dispenser. No matter how much I applied it refused to work itself into a lather. Women from all walks of life came and went and, while reapplying their lipstick or re arranging their hair, some cared to stop and stare in stupefied silence, while others went further by shaking their head or throwing me a pained look of sympathy. How could I hate them for their acts of snobbery when I was far too busy hating myself?

When I eventually came up from under the tap I happened to catch sight of myself in the mirror. What I saw was even enough to frighten me. What with the long streaks of black mascara running the entire length of my face, my resemblance to Alice Cooper was now quite simply undeniable! I hurriedly began violently scrubbing away believing it to be more than necessary to remove the top layer of my facial epidermis. Sadly for me with no conditioner to ease my bedraggled hair of giant knots I was forced to hack through it with my small purse sized hair brush while remaining doubled over under the wall mounted hand drier, which I had to keep on bashing as it automatically cut out every twenty or so seconds.

I arrived back at the restaurant with my new Jimi Hendrix fuzz, the top layer of facial skin almost removed and feeling emotionally bankrupt.

"Where's Christine and Daniel?" I asked.

"You've just missed them, for they've gone to find the bathroom. Oh and honey, you've been away so long, you've missed out on the cooked breakfast, but not to worry, for I've saved you a small bite of my croissant and a drop of coffee," my thoughtful husband brightly informed me.

"How kind of you dear," I replied giving him a cold calculating glare.

"Right, um ..well honey, other than a paper bag to cover your head, is there anything else I can get you?"

Actually he never said that, but as our eyes beheld each other, I was more than convinced that this was what he was thinking, I just couldn't prove it.

I am delighted to say that the flight to Lanzarote went without a hitch and so happily our plane hit the runway with its nose section and both wings still intact, and, after going through customs and then filling in the endless car hire forms that demand we give our whole life history starting at the year AD, we were finally given the keys to our car. We were now ready to set off in search of our timeshare. Our good friend Christine was in good spirits.

"Tricia, it's hard to imagine that we left the bleak blustery shores of England only a matter of hours ago and now we are about to enjoy hot days and warm balmy evenings. Oh, I wish I was staying for the two weeks instead of just the one."

"Christine, the complex we're staying at has only just been built, so it's bound to be really nice, so when we get there let's drop off our luggage in the apartment, and head straight for the pool," I enthusiastically suggested.

The young lady behind the reception desk dealt with us in a very brusque like manner, her face refusing to break into the smallest of friendly smiles even for the sake of our young ones. After handing over the keys she then directed us to our apartment. I was dismayed to discover that it was on the fourth floor and, as I surveyed the balcony area, it seemed potentially very dangerous as there was a large gap between the concrete floor and the bottom railing.

"John, its a potential death trap, for if any of the children accidentally slip over they would easily plunge to their death, so please could you ask the lady at reception if we can change to an apartment on the ground floor."

He was back in less than five minutes.

"Tricia, she says it's not possible unless we're prepared to pay an extra two hundred pounds."

"Is she joking?"

"Nope."

"Well then we'll have to stay put and keep the children off the balcony at all times."

"Okay, but there's worse to come."

"Oh great, spit it out then."

"Well, this is the first week that the resort has officially been open, and so it appears that, apart from one other guest, a single man I believe, we are the only people on the entire complex!"

"You cannot be serious!"

"Well apart from a couple of staff, oh, and a parrot?"

"Parrot?... now I've heard it all!"

"Yes well, if we wish to make his acquaintance, the parrot that is, we'll find him in the bar which is located underground. Anyway, it's disappointing to hear there are no other families on site. It also makes a mockery of not being allowed to change apartments."

"Come along everybody, let's get into our swimming costumes and go for a quick swim," I brightly announced, for having just arrived I was determined to make the best of things.

Minutes later, with bathing towels tightly wrapped round us, we began making our way down to the poolside, our young and overly excited children racing full steam ahead. As the four story concrete complex was built tightly around the pool area and completely empty, I duly noticed that our voices echoed unnaturally loudly as we continued walking and talking. Suddenly we were stopped in our tracks by the deafening sounds of loud screaming that instantly reverberated throughout the entire complex. It was so loud and distressed I thought I must be about to happen on a shark attack, otherwise my children were surely being eaten alive by a shoal of ravenous piranhas! I raced down the remaining steps and towards the pool area only to discover the reason behind their anguished screams. The pool was over half empty and possibly as freezing cold as the night Titanic went down.

"John, this is disgraceful. It will be at least a day or two until the pool is properly filled and then it will need another few days to begin warming up," I announced as I tried my best to console our brood of very tearful children. I knew in that small depressing moment there was every possibility we would not be using the pool this holiday and, as the pool was to be the main event, I wondered if things could get worse? How stupid of me, of course they would!

John kindly agreed to take the children back to the apartment and find something to entertain them, leaving Christine and myself to enjoy some peace as, alone on this isolated complex, we lay down on a couple of sun beds and allowed the almost warm sun to massage our wearied minds and bodies. As I briefly reveled in this precious moment I had absolutely no idea that the weather was about to make a change for the worst and, by the weekend, there would be few available seats on flights leaving Lanzarote as large numbers of disheartened holidaymakers decided to head home early.

By early morning the wind had whipped itself into such a frenzy it now howled like a pack of ferocious wolves baying for blood as it buffeted against the high concrete walls before shrieking its way across the inconsolably bleak and empty complex. If this had been an 'all adults' vacation we would have taken the opportunity to curl up on the couch with a pile of must read books, but we had four children in tow and they were getting more miserable by the minute at the prospect of being holed up in a tiny apartment for the rest of the day and some. Things were beginning to look very bleak.

At one point they attempted to escape onto the balcony if only to get some fresh air, but due to the danger I had no choice other than to demand they all come back inside. I felt so mean.

"Kids, I'm sorry but you know full well that the balcony is out of bounds."

"Sorry mummy," they tearfully whimpered. It was heartbreaking.

As a result of the rapidly deteriorating weather conditions we were forced to endure endless tears for, with all their toys left back at home, there was little if anything to amuse them. There were no English channels on the television, no satellite channels, no cable TV, no nothing!

After two or more frustrating days of high winds and sheet rain, we were momentarily relieved to discover a gentleman of Hispanic persuasion that went from hotel to hotel accompanied by his own stash of very out of date videos that he willingly hired out for a very princely sum of money. His selection of movies was as abysmal as his greed, so our joy at tracking down this man proved very short lived. Flipping through endless boxes of tatty looking videos we struggled to find anything remotely suitable for the youngsters to view.

"Nope don't think "Friday The Thirteenth." is really appropriate," do you Tricia?"

"Oh dear, please keep looking."

"Well, to tell the truth, there's more unsavory movies than I care to share."

"Come on John, you must be able to find something suitable?"

"Well, he's got fifteen or so copies of the Exorcist, ten or more copies of The Omen, six or seven Alien, seven or more Silence of the Lambs three Straw dogs, a number of steamy Emmanuel x rated movies, oh and five or more copies of Unhinged. So take your pick."

I shook my head in general despair for I too was now beginning to feel seriously unhinged.

239

"Don't be daft, ask him if he has any feel good family movies otherwise children's movies?"

"He says there's very little demand for family movies although he has a few hidden away somewhere back at his apartment."

"Great, so tell me what's available?"

We ended up hiring an old Power Rangers video.

"I don't know how much more of the Power Rangers I can stand," I cried out after watching the same video incessantly over the next two days. "Doesn't the man have anything else we can hire?"

"Afraid not. Although he says he has different episode of 'Power Rangers' due back tomorrow as well as a copy of Joe 90." Sadly these videos were well beyond their shelf life with the sound drifting in and out and white lines continually disrupting the quality of picture, but desperate people do desperate things, and by all accounts we were now verging on suicidal. Many days into our holiday, and a fraught John announced that, despite the horrendous weather conditions, we were going to brave all by going for a long walk.

"John, you are officially loop the loop," I cried.

"I know, but I still believe it will do us all a lot of good, besides we need the fresh air. So come on children grab your coats."

"Honey, I hate to say this, but we didn't bring our winter coats, and neither did we pack any warm clothing, for stupidly we were under the false assumption that it was going to be hot and sunny!"

"Oh well, what now?"

Clutching ourselves in an attempt to keep warm, we searched the shops looking for appropriate outdoor clothing. Everything was so expensive.

"Honey, the reason it's all so expensive is because everything has to be shipped in from the Spanish mainland, otherwise the north African coast".

We arrived back at the apartment with two extremely flamboyant junior sized luminous purple and green shell suits.

"Oh daddy, do we really have to wear these?" both older children bawled, their otherwise sweet faces now distorted by a look of sheer horror.

"Look darlings, this is not a fashion show, so don't make such a fuss. Just put them on, besides, as daddy never fails to remind us all, nobody knows us here."

So, with James my youngest infant strapped securely in his stroller and the others togged up in their new outlandish shell suits, and scarves wrapped tightly round their necks, we summoned up the courage to leave the apartment to bravely head into the strong Sahara winds. Within a matter of minutes all our eyes and noses were streaming as the ice cold wind mercilessly bit into our flesh. It took an age to make any headway as, with heads down we forced our way along rough uneven roads, all the while struggling to remain upright as the wind mischievously played with our minds and emotions.

"Daddy, please can we go home," our eldest two begged, tears streaming down their cheeks, their bodies trembling with emotion.

"Just a bit further," he replied.

It wasn't too long before they were once more complaining and I felt a rush of compassion as I observed their swollen noses now shining like bright red beacons, their trembling lips a deathly blue from the cold. Still their father, having been holed up for days, insisted that we all press on, though to where, I and all others around me had absolutely no idea, for ahead was nothing but empty bleak terrain. Further down the road we passed a number of heavy set German tourists similarly struggling to keep both feet on the ground. The high winds roguishly sought to inflate their flamboyant shell suits which, once airborne, threatened to whisk them high above the earth in order to parade them across the skyline like colorful hot air balloons. I prodded John and encouraged him to observe their plight as I was now concerned for all our safety.

"Honey, surely if these heavy set folk are having this much trouble fighting against this powerful Sahara wind, then we would be wise to head for home." Much to everyone's relief, John finally admitted defeat and agreed to turn and head back to the complex.

It came as no surprise when the next morning our children were running high temperatures so I made my weary way down to the reception to seek advice on finding a good chemist. I was surprised to discover the reception desk was empty and, despite waiting over ten minutes, nobody appeared. Desperate for information, I made my way down to the underground family bar where I made my first contact with the only other guest on site, oh as well as the parrot. The other guest appeared seriously depressed as well as thoroughly intoxicated as, propping up the bar, he washed down a further large glass of whisky. The sociable resort manager, now acting as bar manager, appeared at first to ignore me as he poured the guest as well as himself another drink. Meanwhile the parrot, judging by his language, quickly led me to assume he too must be equally intoxicated. He went into a furry frenzy while repeating every imaginable expletive he had over the years been taught.

"Hi there, what are you drinking?" the manager called out.

"What (beep beep).. are you drinking? What (beep beep).. are you drinking?" the flustered parrot chirped up as it hopped around the cage and rattled its beak between the bars. In that moment I wanted to reach into the cage to break the end of his beak right off, but I had the sense to know it wasn't the poor bird's fault that his language was so offensively vile.

"Nothing thank you. I just need some help in finding a nearby chemist."

"Well, my wife's the one to ask."

"Okay so where is she?"

"At the reception desk of course," he loudly burped as he then took another quick slug of his drink.

"Cheeky boy cheeky boy," the rude and disruptive parrot cawed.

"Well apparently she isn't, for I've just left the reception," I replied as I continued to ignore the foul mouthed bird.

"Oh alright, I'd best go find her," he mumbled as pulling up his trousers in a most undignified manner he reluctantly made his way from behind the bar.

"Alright Tom, stay where you are, and I'll be back in a jiffy."

"Back in a (beep beep).. jiffy. Back in .." the restless and unpredictable parrot repeatedly screeched.

I glanced back at Tom, knowing he'd not be going anywhere, at least not in the near future.

"And this is supposed to be a family bar?" I privately mused as I dutifully followed after the manager to go in search of a missing wife and receptionist.

The next few days were spent once more holed up inside the apartment, spooning medicine into sick runny nosed children, while repeatedly watching Joe 90, alternating with the Power Rangers, until I wanted to rip Joe 90's glasses from his nerdy face as well as blast Mighty Morphin along with Rita Repulsa and Lord Zedd Emperor into another solar system as far from planet earth as possible.

On the last night our good friend offered to baby sit so that John and I could go out to a restaurant to celebrate his birthday. We jumped at the opportunity. We chose an expensive looking restaurant that had pretty pink and white tablecloths and waiters dressed in smart bow ties. It was suddenly warm enough to sit outside, and so we sat and watched the sun go down. The garlic mushrooms, normally one of our favorite starters in England, were not only floating in a sea of oil, but we were horrified to witness a number of winged insects experiencing a slow death by drowning. We called the waiter over expecting the plates to be whisked away from under our noses. We were taken back when, having raised his eyes to the heavens, he then shrugged his shoulders before taking the spoon out of my hand to begin expertly fishing them out one at a time. As we watched on I remained steadfast in my conviction that it would've been far less time consuming to place another order for garlic mushrooms, so I was curious to see that, having rescued the mites what other life saving techniques he now had in mind. With a large number of winged insects taking their last breath on our side plates we still wrongly assumed they would bring us a fresh plate of mushrooms. Not so! The waiter cheerfully suggested that, having made the effort to expel all drowning insects, it was now safe for us to continue on eating. By the end of the meal the only thing worth writing home about was the staggeringly high bill. We paid up and left the restaurant, consoling ourselves that this coming week would surely be better as we couldn't imagine sinking much lower.

Before we could head off to our next timeshare we had one remaining task and this was to drop my friend and her son at the airport, for she had only managed to take a week off from work. As we drove towards the airport the sun suddenly decided to make an impromptu appearance and, with the wind having died down completely, in no time at all we were once again sweltering from the sizzling heat of the sun. I could only shake my head in pure disbelief as I hugged our friends goodbye, all the while profusely apologizing for the appalling weather that had ruined their stay. She was a polite good natured sort and therefore very understanding. Now, with the sun shining in the deeply azure sky, it appeared to be heralding a new and more hopeful week ahead.

CHAPTER TWENTY TWO

Let's Get Physical

The next resort exceeded all expectations for, put simply, it was fabulous. I now felt like bursting into song that would surely have heralded Bambi, Thumper, and all other animals from every Walt Disney movie to run and twitter alongside me as they joined me in a joyful sing-a-long. From this day forward I would have no further need of the constant drip feed of caffeine, or endless squares of caramel filled chocolate that did much to comfort and lessen my general sense of despair. This resort was impeccable in every way possible, the accommodation was spanking clean and luxurious, the crystal blue pools were heated, the staff were cheerful and respectful and the children were smiling from ear to ear. So what more could I possibly wish for?

The next morning we attended a complimentary breakfast brunch where management gave us all the information we would need to make our stay a pleasant affair. Linda was the name of the events organizer officiating the meeting, and she was both friendly and helpful as she dutifully ran through all the expensive trips that were on offer. My ears pricked up when for some reason she stopped her professionally rehearsed monologue and, looking slightly uncomfortable, she took a deep breath.

"Finally, ladies and gentlemen, I regret to inform you that Lydia our fitness instructor has unfortunately been taken sick, therefore sadly we have been forced to cancel the early morning fitness class until she returns." There were loud groans and sighs coming from all quarters of the room from disappointed guests who presumably knew Lydia from previous visits and so had been greatly looking forward to some early morning aerobic exercise.

"Look guys, I know you're disappointed, but I'm so sorry, there's nothing much I can do, that is unless there is someone here who would like to take on the class," she said rather flippantly. Looking back I don't think she intentionally meant to find a volunteer, she was just doing her usual job and that included feeling the guests pain. The room fell silent as all guests hurriedly scanned the room searching for a potential volunteer.

Then without warning John suddenly shot an arm in the air. I was gob smacked!

"Surely not," I thought as I effortlessly went back in time to confront memories of the poor man efforts to jog around our estate that in no time had him clutching his belly with one hand as with the other hand he held onto the door knocker for dear life, huge beads of sweat trickling down his pained face, as he struggled to find his breath.

"Congratulations honey, you're back before I even had time to pop the kettle on," I would exclaim as I then waited for his latest explanation that I knew he felt utterly compelled to give. An ache or pain here, or a strained muscle there, or the first signs of a migraine on its way, so in the light of all this, what was the poor man thinking? Was it feasible that this past very trying week had sapped his mind to the point where he had now lost all sense of reality concerning his physical abilities, or lack of them. With a large smile now alighting Linda's face she immediately walked over towards us.

"Sir, thank you for offering to take the class," she said her whole being now brimming with untold enthusiasm. "So tell me straight, are you a fitness instructor?" I instantly started to crease up with laughter, but that would quickly change.

"Well actually, I don't have any experience."

"No experience!"

"No, none whatsoever," he hurriedly admitted as he began to show worrying signs of being flustered, for all eyes were now bearing down on him.

"Then do be good enough to tell me how you propose to run this class?"

"Well, actually it's not me I'm volunteering, it's my wife."

"What!" I hissed. "Are you mad? John, I've never taken a fitness class in my life," I yelled, almost knocking over my half drunk coffee that sat on our table.

"That's true, but you do go to the gym almost every day, as well as to aqua gym, and then there's that Monday evening fitness class, so if anyone could run this class, it would have to be you!"

"John, it's one thing to attend a class, it's quite another to run it."

"Oh come on, be a good sport for you know you can do it."

Maybe it was the heat. Maybe it was the large group of guests that were now clamoring around me like flies on a sugar bowl, as with eyes as large as dinner plates they desperately clung to the hope that I would say yes. But as we made our way back to the apartment I struggled to believe that I had consented to run the early morning class. I was now the one in need of psychiatric care.

"John, I can't believe you put me in such a position," I raged as we crossed the complex heading back to the apartment.

"But honey, can't you see how happy the guests are now feeling."

"Oh don't honey me, for their new found happiness may well be very short lived."

"Come on Tricia, you'll be great at it, trust me."

"Oh right, and what's worse, it's at some unearthly hour of the morning. When you think I work so hard at home, I needed this break to relax and unwind."

"Oh stop being so crabby! If it doesn't work out it won't matter, for nobody knows us at here."

"Oh, so the fact that it won't hit the national tabloids is supposed to make me feel good, is it?"

John was instructed to take the children down to the pool while the next few hours saw me prancing in front of the wardrobe mirror as I tried my utmost to remember as many exercises as I felt able, for if I was going to take on the challenge, I was going to do my utmost to look a tiny bit professional. Sadly I was disappointed to discover how little I actually remembered, for normally I needed to concentrate all my powers into just remembering to go in the same direction as everybody else. My teacher implied that I was a free spirit, but I don't think it was meant as a compliment. As for my regular gym classes, yes it was true I was down at the gym five days a week, but it wasn't all exercise! For many years John had been secretly very impressed by my fervor and commitment. Then in just a matter of a day things changed.

"Honey, did you know that while I was out today I accidentally bumped into your gym instructor?"

"Uh? Oh really."

"There I was praising all your efforts when…." In that split second I knew what was coming. I had been snitched on! The little weasel! I drew in breath as I waited for what was to come.

"Tricia, I have no idea why I'm paying a hefty monthly gym fee when he tells me that, once through the door, you rarely manage to leave the changing rooms."

"Oh, I think he's exaggerating just a little."

"Well, according to him, you see physical exercise as more of a social event than a time to get fit and healthy."

"Oh really."

"Yes, he also added that the majority of your time there is taken up with drinking endless coffees and diet sodas while you freely socialize."

"Yep, I can't deny it."

"Apparently you're the worst offender, though he did also acknowledge how popular you are."

"Well, I don't know about that!"

"Hmm, well he says the only thing that regularly gets exercised is that overused muscle in your mouth."

"John, I think they call it a tongue, but please allow me to explain for there are mitigating circumstances I promise."

"Well on this occasion I think it's you that needs a lawyer!"

Truth be known he was as usual right. Everyday, after dropping the children at their respective schools, I made my way to the gym always fully determined to spend at least an hour or more actually in the gym itself, but this rarely happened, as, while changing into my exercise attire, I would meet all sorts of nice interesting people. Time would quickly march by and all too soon it would be nearing the time to leave and get to another appointment otherwise go to work. Steeped in guilt I would race to the gym to do five minutes on the treadmill, followed by two or three minutes on any other available machine that wasn't in use before racing to the showers. This done, I would then rush down to the pool area, have myself a five minute swim, followed by another five or so minutes lazing in the Jacuzzi, before rushing back up the stairs to have another five minutes in the sauna, as I was by now thoroughly exhausted. This was shortly followed by yet another quick shower. Then, with no time left, I would empty my locker of clothes and hurriedly force them back onto my half dried body. Once dressed, I would throw my gym bag over my shoulder and, after leaving the building, I would race to the car hoping to dodge the pedantic meter man as I had now gone ten or so minutes over my time. Oh, how I hated that meter man!

I didn't fare much better at the aqua gym class either for, with children in tow, I always arrived late to the class as well as stressed up to the eyeballs. I felt so envious of the young carefree girls who didn't have to organize three or more children into the crèche before attending the session. Luckily the teacher was sympathetic to my condition. The worst time had been when, having made it into the water, I suddenly had an apparition of my towel along with my underwear still rolled up on the bed at home. At the end of the class and still dripping wet I had been forced to head to reception in search of a towel, anything to dry myself down with.

"We're really sorry, but we expect the general public to bring their own and so we don't provide towels," the young chic lady behind the desk loudly declared.

"Please I beg you, could you at least look in the lost property locker and see if there happens to be a spare one that I might use. I promise to return it."

She arrived back at the desk not only pinching the end of a towel but holding it some distance away from her body as though it were some recently filled disposable diaper.

"Are you honestly sure you want to use this?" she squirmed.

"I don't have any choice."

"Rather you than me then," she replied her whole body cringing as she leant over the desk to gingerly hand it over.

She was right, for this thread bare towel stunk to high heavens of sweat and mildew, and I was more than convinced there was even a discernible taint of athletes foot weaved into the very fabric of this forsaken towel. There was no doubt in my mind that the original owner had deliberately left it behind, otherwise it crawled out of the locker room all by itself. With all my relaxed muscles now back to tense I chose to towel dry very limited portions of my body, leaving everything else well alone. Having returned the towel to lost property, I picked the children up from crèche, buckled them all up in the car and headed for home. However I was not out of the woods yet!

As I drove home I felt terribly panicked by the thought that, if for any reason I was routinely stopped by the police, I would look so darned guilty they would immediately believe I was hiding something illegal under the seat, then, to save myself being arrested, I would have to confess to driving home wearing no underwear. This was surely a crime? I was already imagining the curt male officer with the four o'clock shadow standing with a disgusted look pervading his entire face as with radio in hand, he asked me to step out of the car.

"Officer, forgive me but I assure you now that there is a valid reason for my stupid mistake of going round the roundabout the wrong way."

"Madam, I'm all ears."

"Yes well I was in the swimming pool when I suddenly realized I'd left my underwear...."

"Madam, am I correct in my understanding when you state that the reason for your erratic and dangerously haphazard driving can be put down to the fact that you are wearing no bra and knickers?"

"Yes well I became really blurry in the head and I panicked thinking if for some reason I was stopped by the police, well they might wrongly assume that I'm a woman of ill repute, and this fact alone was so distressing it made me put my foot down hard on the gas pedal."

"Come in Charlie One, I'm bringing in some pervert who claims she accidentally left her bra and knickers at home on the bed. Right, I didn't think you'd believe that one either. Seriously though, I'm arresting her for reckless driving as, at one point, her speed topped one hundred miles an hour on the public highway, so we'll be doing her for that, as well as for extreme public lewdness and gross indecency. Have the paperwork and cell ready, for we're on our way. Yep I bet this will put a smile on the Judge's face first thing Monday morning. Your right on that one, for it is our duty to rid the streets of Britain of her sort."

With my active imagination working overtime I had even considered leaving my wet bathing suit on under my clothes in preference to being caught on the hop!

To be perfectly honest, I much preferred the evening aqua gym sessions as here I was free of children, and also the evening sessions happened to be run by two young and very muscle bound hunks. However, I was not on my own here, as it appeared that every bodacious girl in town wished, not only to attend this class, but to get a place on the front line in the hope of getting noticed. So, despite the Olympic sized pool, there was rarely any room left for the likes of me by the time I finally turned up, except right at the back. Due to the extraordinary amount of stress it took just getting to these classes, I eventually came to the decision to stop all classes, opting to stay at home and try out an exercise video or two. Oh, I sorely missed the congenial atmosphere of the public classes but I didn't miss the stress of just trying to make it on time, so in the end it seemed a wise move.

However with no Sergeant Major to drill me and scream abuse in my direction, my personal fitness regime never really took off the way I intended. It appeared that, after spending twenty or more exhausting minutes a day attempting to wriggle into my ridiculously tight Lycra and spandex dance clothing, I then needed a fifteen minute coffee break to get my energy levels back up. Add to this the time taken up with stretching down to put on my knitted leg warmers and adjusting my matching sweat band and I was then ready for another fifteen minute coffee break. Finally I would head to the sitting room for that grueling decision time. Yes was today a Jane Fonda day or an Olivia Newton John day? Once that big decision had finally been made it was back to the kitchen to pop the kettle on again and go in search of a doughnut, the special treat for having finally made up my mind. With traces of confectioners sugar still covering my lips, I would then sit in a stupefied trance as just watching those ladies strut their stuff was exhausting enough without actually dropping to the floor to follow through with their somewhat highly excitable but extremely strenuous workouts.

Some days seemed better than others as, with sweatband intact, I burst into song singing "Let's get physical.. physical....", there it goes again, with only that small muscle in my mouth getting any real workout. Truth was I wasn't overly keen on physical exercise in the first place, but I was prepared to show willing and give it a go, and I loved being dressed from head to toe in pink lycra, with those colorful scrunched down knitted leg warmers, coupled with a classy matching sweatband, and if darling Olivia and Jane could do it, then why couldn't I?

So, as I pranced around the holiday apartment room with as much finesse as Miss Piggy at her first ballet class, I felt nothing more than the deepest consternation as I weighed up the possible shock reaction and forthcoming rejection I would receive if I failed to pull this one off. It was therefore of the utmost importance that the workout feel genuinely authentic and more importantly, look effortless. In this moment of truth I sincerely wished with all my heart that I had used both the gym, the pool, and girly workout videos for what they were originally ordained, that is a good old fashioned workout! The next few hours were then spent rummaging through my belongings as I needed to find a suitable music tape to exercise to.

"Oh I have loads of really good dance tapes but they're all at home," I muttered. "John, the least you can do is help me out, for I need to find something with a bit of bounce."

"Well you're more than welcome to look in my suitcase."

"Hmm.. They'll all be suffering from severe depression and 'pig outs' if they're forced to exercise to any of your Leonard Cohen tapes," I snorted as I threw them to one side. "Nope the Moody Blues won't work either. Hmm…as for Melanie well it's goodbye Ruby Tuesday for I can't see that working, can you? and Joni Mitchell, love her, but will they?" It was a good twenty or more minutes before I found anything I could work with.

"John trust me you will pay dearly for doing this to me, that I swear."

The next morning found me moaning away like crazy as, with a deeply resentful heart I prepared to go down to the poolside area for the 7.30am start time, in the full knowledge that I was about to make an absolute fool of myself.

"I can't believe I stupidly agreed to this," I muttered as feeling tired and miserable I made my way towards the door to leave.

"Sshh… honey or you'll wake the kids up," my deeply caring spouse whispered as he continued to lie in the bed, his pillows carefully propped up behind him as, in peace and comfort, he savored an early morning cup of tea.

"Oh, how I hate you for this," I hissed throwing him an uncharitable stare.

"Go for it girl, you'll do good," he impishly called out after me.

On my way to the pool I prayed there would be no takers, then if after five whole minutes nobody had turned up, well then I was surely free to go back to bed, and have an extra hour or more to catch up on my sleep, and nobody would have the gall to complain.

No sooner had I turned the corner than I was flabbergasted to see a large throng of scrawny as well as oversized pensioners, men and women with their brightly colored towels already laid out on the lawn as they waited in great anticipation for my imminent arrival.

"Have they never heard of a holiday lie in," I muttered to myself as I began to take deep breaths to stall a most peculiar onset of queasiness.

A few ladies helpfully pointed over to where Lydia, the former instructor normally placed her towel down, then with a press of the button on my tape machine it was all systems go.

I can tell you hand on heart that I had absolutely no idea as to what I was doing, but as John kindly thought to shout after me, "Tricia, just fake it until you make it!" As a result I had their tubby little bodies twisted into positions they'd never even heard of. I also had them running to and fro like a brood of headless chickens as we danced and gyrated to the beat of the music. When it came to the much calmer but tough floor exercises many of them expressed great difficulty when it came to removing their foot from behind their necks and I wasn't too sure how to get myself out of certain unorthodox positions either.

All too soon the nearby restaurant and bar staff all dropped what they were doing and cautiously made their way to where this new and inspiring class was taking place. They stood silently smirking or with their jaws dropped as they watched the last ten minutes of this exercise session that, although only half an hour in duration, felt to me like an eternity.

Happily there were no heart attacks or seizures reported. Saying that I still expected that having been given a trial run I would quickly be contacted by the complex manager to say my services were no longer required. I was equally convinced that nobody would think turn up the next day, nobody in their right minds anyway! Wrong again! For the next day saw even more eager guests anxiously waiting on the lawn, their towels methodically laid out, as word had got around concerning my very unusual torture training. And once again, as I went on to further destroy their already ancient creaking bodies, the restaurant staff raced to finish their duties in order to stand and watch the next crazed performance. By the end of session two I was privately very worried as to how much longer I could hold out, as my whole body ached from head to toe. I needn't have worried, for the next day turned out to be my final day, and at the end of the session, I can proudly say every attendee was still alive and thankfully there had been no unexpected hospitalizations as a direct result of my unconventional approach to exercise.

The manager thanked me with a gift of chocolates and champagne, and the guests were equally appreciative in bestowing gracious comments, some even wishing me to write down a portion or two of the exercises we'd attempted these past few days, as they now wished to run through them with their own coach otherwise their family doctor! During the week many a guest quietly sidled up to me to express something of their appreciation. "Yes, trust me dear, Lydia's far less exciting," they disloyally whispered in my ear. That night, as John removed the outer seal from the chocolates, I reached over and grabbed the box.

"Don't even think about it buster."

"What, not even one?"

"Nope, not even one!"

"You mean thing. How stingy can you be?"

"After what you just put me through, your lucky to be alive, so, unless you're prepared to get down on bended knee and beg for mercy, they're all mine."

"Well, if you eat the lot you'll need more than a Jane Fonda workout to help you. Oh and by the way, I don't know what you did to the music machine but it appears to have totally packed up."

"It probably needs new batteries."

"Yes that's what I thought so I plugged it into a wall socket and it still didn't work," he said his voice tinged with great sadness at the thought that neither Melanie or Leonard Cohen would be reverberating around the apartment for the remainder of this holiday.

"We could see if there is an inexpensive one in the local shops if you like."

"We'll see."

The rest of the week seemed disturbingly free of any trauma, no sick children, no beach crisis, no fighting for a free sun bed and not a single moody cloud on the horizon. No… everything seemed perfect, could it last I wondered? The answer wasn't long in coming. A few days later, while out on our customary stroll along the promenade, we were accosted by a friendly young couple who implored us to spend just ninety minutes to attend a timeshare tour.

"Please say yes and sign this form, for then we get paid, and we're pretty broke," they pleaded.

"Are you saying you still get paid even if we don't buy?"

"Yes just for the sending you there. Here, take a look at this gift list for there are loads of nice things to choose from, and you get the gift even if you don't buy any weeks." They were very enthusiastic as well as persuasive. John's eyes immediately lit up when he noticed a music machine was on the list of gifts.

"Look honey, if we go along we won't have to buy one. So go on, say yes."

"I don't know. I mean what will the children do while we watch the presentation?"

"Oh that's sorted, for we have a professionally organized children's camp where they are looked after by a large number of qualified staff. They have such a great time," the young couple enthused. Now that was sweet music to my ears.

"A children's club?"

"Yes and they'll love it."

Our children didn't even shed a tear as, led away by two young and pretty girls, they were taken off to their promised land, a land supposedly filled with bouncy castles and all you can eat ice cream. We on the other hand had to forgo such carnal pleasures as we were commandeered into a room filled with smart suited high pressure salesman who smelt high of aftershave. We listened to all they had to say and we were impressed, however we knew we were in no real position to buy, so rather than waste any more of their precious time we told them so, however our man in the suit wasn't prepared to give up, well not without a fight. He asked us to hold on while he went in search of his manager. Eventually John looked down at his watch to then quietly inform me that we had been at this presentation for well over four hours.

"Goodness is that so? Then we need to go and check on the children," I whispered back.

"You're right, I'll go," he volunteered.

Some five minutes later and I was witness to some real blood curdling, spine chilling screaming resounding across the complex. My ears pricked up for the noise was immediately identifiable as coming from one of my brood. I hurriedly excused myself from the table and went outside to find out the reason behind the commotion and, as I looked across the complex I could see John struggling with one of my young sons.

"You're not going back there to watch that terrible movie, it's pure evil," John shouted as he attempted to pull my son away from the gates of the children's area.

"But I love evil," my young son screamed back.

"No you don't," my husband sharply responded.

"Yes I do," my son loudly wailed.

Minutes later and a seriously flustered John along with our brood was back at my side.

"What on earth is going on?"

"Tricia, you'll find this hard to believe but when I walked into the playroom the lights were off and all the youngsters were watching some Halloween horror movie."

"That's terrible, no way are they going back."

We were so furious that we took the children into the presentation room and walked directly up to the manager to complain. Our man gave something of a half hearted apology and then told us to take a seat while he in turn went to find his manager. He came back with a near relative of King Kong, for this man was over seven foot and had the broadest shoulders I had ever seen.

"My goodness, this guy makes Arnold Schwarzenegger look like Minnie mouse, his shoulders are that broad." John quietly commented.

"Shh honey, keep it to yourself," I whispered back.

His facial muscles appeared frozen as, without the teeniest smile, he pulled up a chair and, without any reference to our complaint, he began to talk figures. We tried to insist that we had already spent hours listening to other members of his team and so to be honest we weren't interested, but he wasn't listening.

Finally, as the interaction soured he leaned across the table to stare meanly into my poor husband's face and, in a menacing voice, he asked.

"Tell me something Mr. Bennett, what made you come to this presentation?" His voice was gruff, his very presence intimidating as he leaned his upper torso across the table until he was almost eyeball to eyeball with my dear spouse. John swallowed hard.

"Um, really just because we were stopped by a young couple who persuaded us to attend, and because we wanted the gift."

"Oh, and what gift was that?"

"Well actually the tape player," my husband squeaked, a look of sheer terror in his eyes.

"So let me get this right. When you came here today you really had no intention whatsoever of buying any timeshare from us, did you?"

"No sir, that's true, we didn't," John stammered. The man then remained halfway across the table as he continued to give John the indomitable evil eye.

"Sir, we came here for a 90 minute presentation and we've been here for almost five hours, so can we have our prize, then please will you consider letting us go, for our children are very hungry and upset," my now very apprehensive husband shakily pleaded. The viperous man said nothing as he quietly rose to his feet to stand towering above us while continuing to look down his nose at us squirming little worms wriggling fearfully in our seats. Finally, without saying another word, he turned and disappeared out of the door.

"Tricia, my heart is hammering away, and not at its normal speed either. What's worse, I don't think they have any intention of letting us go," John announced in a despairing tone of voice.

"Don't be stupid, they aren't about to take us hostage, for we're not worth much."

"Well, I don't know if you've noticed but they aren't taking this too well at all."

"This is all too crazy to believe. It was their employees that enticed us here in the first place, and now they are intimidating us like we're wicked criminals."

"Perhaps we should just forgo the tape player."

"No way Tricia. We've been cooped up in here nearly five hours so I'm not leaving without it!"

Finally the man came back and in an extremely contemptuous manner he informed us that we were free to go.

"Sir, if it's alright with you I would like to have our prize," John very gingerly dared to ask. The man closed his eyes and took in a deep breath, his nostrils flaring as he tried his best to control himself. The atmosphere was such that you could slice a knife through it.

"Give them the darned gift," he growled over to his assistant as he scribbled something on a piece of paper and then dismissed us from his presence.

"Goodness John, that was really scary."

"Hmm, it was, but at least we've got ourselves another music machine. Saying that perhaps we should make this timeshare presentation our very last." he whispered as he tightly hugged the suspiciously small box that contained our brand new silver music machine. Back at the apartment we hurriedly removed the packaging.

"What's the make, for it's a bit tinny looking isn't it?" I remarked.

"Hmm well, it's not exactly Sony, and it's tiny too!"

John then knelt down to rummage through a selection of his favorite Leonard Cohen tapes.

"Well at the end of the day, was it really worth the hassle? For we've lost a whole day out of our holiday, and the kids were subjected to a horror movie and all we got for our troubles is this!"

"I agree, so perhaps we should have said a firm no. Anyway, press the button and let's enjoy some music."

With the cassette securely in place I pressed down hard on the play button. Nothing! I checked the plug and the tape, still nothing.

"Honey I hate to say this but we've been well and truly duped!"

"Well Tricia, before you ask the impossible of me, understand this, there is no way I'm standing in front of that seven foot Herculean General to ask him kindly for an exchange."

"Why ever not?"

"Tricia do me a favor, and put a sock in it, then press the mute button just for good measure, please!"

CHAPTER TWENTY THREE

Why Did I Ever Agree to This?

There came a point when my dear thoughtful man believed he'd found the perfect solution to the problem of getting the sort of resorts we were really after and this was to buy another week of timeshare.

"Look, the more weeks we buy, the more negotiating power we have at our disposal." The words emanating from his lips sounded right, but what of the cost?

"Tricia, what do you think of this lovely timeshare in La Manga in Spain, come on, doesn't it sound wonderful? Look, it says that the whole area is totally un-spoilt and this is the place that most good Spanish people choose to spend their family holiday and they would know best, wouldn't they?"

"Yep, but remember things are not always what they appear to be," I gently reminded him.

"Oh honey, you're becoming such a defeatist."

"No I'm not, I just hate pain." I brusquely retorted.

"Listen up, if we do this, we'll have much more chance of getting into the resorts that we want."

"You think so?"

"Yes well to date we hardly ever get anything we request, and I think that's due to our resorts being at the bottom of the rung, so I think it's worth a try."

And so it came to pass that we, the officially courageous ever expectant Bennetts came to own a second week's timeshare, this time in La Manga, off the Costa Calide in Spain. The summer holidays arrived and as usual I left it in my husbands very capable hands to sort out our two week vacation.

"Okay listen up. Our first week will be in our new timeshare in La Manga, and then it's back to our other timeshare in Fuengirola near Malaga. It's all sorted," he proudly announced. Of course, as usual, I dared to believe him. That is until he dropped quite a big bombshell.

"Oh dear, I'm not sure how to say this but I've accidentally made quite a big boob."

"Go on what now?"

"Well, the first week is fine, but there are problems with our second week."

"Problems, quite what do you mean?"

"Well, put bluntly there is one night in the middle of our vacation where, how do I say this? Well, we have no place to lay our heads."

"So we not only lose a night of our Fuengirola week but now we've got to cough up the money and find somewhere else to stay the night, is that what your saying?"

"Look, I'm sorry, I didn't mean to mess up, it just happened."

Yet again we were going on holiday with a limited budget and so I couldn't even begin to think what we would do concerning this fresh crisis so I just put it on the back burner, yes I stupidly forgot all about it. I am thrilled to report that not only did we make it to the airport on time, but nobody in the car was sick over me. The plane also left Gatwick without a hitch and, when the wheels made contact with the tarmac in Spain, I knew for sure that the plane was still 100% intact, and this must surely have been the moment when I began to rather foolishly believe that this holiday might well be the one that turned things around forever. Oh how wrong could I be!

As usual our luggage failed to turn up until almost every other passenger from the plane had left the building. Having made our way out of the concourse we still had to collect our hire car and in those days there was no standing in line in an air conditioned office, for the different car hire firms simply allowed their employees the luxury of a public bench just outside the airport terminal from which to do their transactions from out of their overloaded briefcases.

"Oh John, can you believe it but, due to our luggage being the last off the conveyor belt, as usual, we are last in line in this exceptionally long queue."

"Well, we've got little choice other than to be patient."

We must have stood in that line for an hour or more with the ferocious sun beating down on us. Finally it was our turn. Having filled in the ridiculously extensive forms placed in front of John, the man handed over some keys before pointing to the vehicle which another employee had brought up to pavement outside the terminal. The loud whirring or was it rattling noise coming from the engine quickly got our full attention.

"You are joking! This surely can't be the rental car you intend to give us?" I loudly queried.

"Yes madam, this is your hire car," he beamed.

"Well it's hardly the pride of the fleet, is it?"

"No madam, but it's all we have left," he announced shuffling his paperwork as he spoke.

"Forgive me, but this car looks as though it's only just survived the Eastern European cold war before landing here, it looks that dodgy," I furiously exclaimed as I gave John a personalized dig in the ribs, my way of indicating that I needed him to get on board and, if nothing else, begin feeling something called concern, perhaps even a little distress, actually any emotion that might help the cause.

"Ouch, that hurt!"

"It'll hurt even more if you don't speak up."

"What? Oh yes."

"Look John, if you want to risk life and limb that's your choice, but I'm not prepared to endanger the children's lives, so please speak up," I hissed in his ear.

"Alright alright. Sir, this car is way too small for our needs, so I need your help in getting it exchanged for a larger car, and if necessary I'll pay the diff......"

"If you ask me, it looks more like a trumped up fiat cut in half, otherwise a miserable mini minor minus its dashboard," I menacingly interjected. The man raised a disturbed eyebrow as he chose to ignore my insulting observations preferring to continue his dealings with my much too compliant spouse.

"Sorry Mr. Bennett, I cannot help, for we have no more cars available."

"What! But this is crazy. How and where are we supposed to stash the luggage as well as the children in such a tiny car," John with a look of amazement asked.

"Don't worry darling, if we tie the children to the back bumper they can then run behind us down the motorway."

"Tricia behave!"

"Sorry, but this man doesn't care a fig about our crisis, do you sir?"

"Your absolutely correct. It's your problem not mine," he abruptly replied, then with a self satisfied smugness he slammed shut his files to then squeeze them into his seriously overloaded briefcase. This done, he stood up to leave.

"You can't just leave us with a car that looks as though it's risen from the very bowels of a Moldavian scrap yard!" I angrily yelled.

"Do I have to repeat myself, it's the only car available for your use, Madam."

"Oh please, there's not even a roof rack for the luggage, so tell us what can we do?" my desperate husband implored.

"Sorry sir, but I'm unable to assist you any further. Come back tomorrow and we will see what, if anything can be done," he dispassionately announced.

"Tomorrow's far too late as we're not staying in Malaga, for we're traveling down to near Marbella." He simply wasn't listening. He picked up his brief case, straightened his crumpled jacket, and then with his nose in the air he began walking towards the terminal doors.

"Come on John, we've wasted well over an hour already and the children are desperately hot and thirsty, so let's just try and see what we can do, shall we?"

"We appear to have no other choice," John muttered under his breath as he struggled towards the piddly little car with our mountain of luggage. Now I don't profess to know anything when it comes to cars and their maintenance. In fact my abilities as a mechanic are limited to getting in and out of a car, plus placing a seat belt over my waist, anything else such as finding the brake pedal, opening the glove compartment, switching the lights to full beam and working the radio is quite beyond my realm of expertise. It is also true that within hours of passing my driving test, on my fourth attempt, I immediately drove my car into three parked cars while trying to work out which button I needed to press to open the sun roof, proving that I'm better off as a passenger. But with that said, as we walked around the battered, beat up, pint sized Skoda, I found myself having grave concerns as to whether this car was in anyway reliable enough for the road.

"Well, if I'd wanted to rent a wreck, I think I would have said so," John muttered as feeling extremely defeated he dropped our luggage to the ground.

"I agree, for this car has definitely been involved in an extraordinary number of accidents," I cried as my eyes perused the battered body work. "Listen up John, we need to take some photographs right now, before we set off, otherwise we might well be charged for some, if not all of this damage."

"I'd do it Tricia, but I've no idea where the camera is packed. It's also way past four in the afternoon and, not only do we still have a long drive ahead of us, but we haven't even begun to load up the car.

The challenge was on. It took us well over half an hour to squeeze ourselves plus our luggage into the car and if this had been a competition I think it safe to say we would have won hands down, for there was not so much as an air pocket left to fill. Trouble was we were going some distance and, apart from John who was in the driving seat, the rest of us were forced to even sit on top of various pieces of luggage.

"Right then is everybody comfortable, if so we'll set off."

"What a daft question, for how could any of us be remotely comfortable with our cramped bodies entombed in what feels like a family mausoleum," I rudely retorted. "What's worse, this car has no seat belts, so you had better drive extra carefully."

"Look Tricia, the children are completely wedged in, so they'll be fine," he announced as he placed the key into the ignition.

"Oh, good grief!"

"What now?"

"The fuel gauge is registering well below zero."

"You are joking, aren't you?"

"I wish I was."

"John, you need to go back and find that uncaring excuse for a human being and get him to do something about this."

"Look Tricia, if I have to head back into the airport, trust me I will be gone a long time, besides the chances of finding him now are pretty slim."

"Oh this is bad! John we have got to find ourselves a petrol station before we run out."

"Honey, why is it you always state the obvious?"

The next ten minutes were anxious ones as we searched the unfamiliar highway desperate for a gas station. We found one in the nick of time.

"Alright everybody, the drama is finally over, so let's get on our way before it begins to get dark."

We had touched down in Malaga around two in the afternoon and it had taken over three hours before we were finally on our way. Unbeknown to me those lost hours were going to prove crucial when it came to attempting to reach our destination.

Cocooned by luggage, and with no air conditioning it wasn't too long before we were feeling like boiled peanuts in a pressure cooker, with the stifling heat slowly cooking us.

"Honey, we can't take much more, the children are complaining that their legs are feeling numb. They are also dying of thirst, so you need to stop the car and get us something cold to drink otherwise we all become seriously dehydrated."

"Alright…alright."

Moments later we pulled off the road as John had seen a nice sandy beach.

I pushed the front seat forward and after removing various bags as well as the lighter luggage I managed to excavate the enshrouded children from their seats.

"Right, how do we find their swimming things without hauling everything else out of the car?" I queried.

"Tricia, now is not the time to stand on good old British tradition."

"Uh?"

"Just strip them down and let them swim in their underpants."

"Underpants? John what are you thinking? For this is a public beach filled with young Spanish families."

"Yes, but they're only kids so nobody is going to take a blind bit of notice."

"I don't think so, anyway what about you, what will you do?"

"The same."

"What are you, bonkers?"

"Yep, I intend to swim with my kids in nothing but my underpants."

"You'll get yourself arrested."

"Oh, don't be so daft."

"Are they decent?"

"Is what decent?"

"Your underpants of course."

"They are a nice Tartan design as it happens."

"Well let me take a good look for we can't have your didgeridoo accidentally poking out, can we?"

"Enough! Let's just get down onto the beach before I get really mad."

Moments later I watched on as stripped down to their undergarments their father headed into the water with our youngest in his arms and the older two close by his side.

"Please keep them safe, as they have no armbands on," I begged.

Minutes passed when suddenly I realized that I could no longer see Reuben for he had disappeared under a wave. I leapt up and raced towards the water.

"John, where's Reuben?" I frantically screamed. John turned full circle and shook his head. My heart was pounding. I then ran fully clothed into the water and began thrashing around as I searched for him. What seemed like minutes but was most likely no more than a couple of seconds I grabbed hold of a bundle that thank goodness turned out to be my small son. I placed him over my shoulder and he immediately spewed up a small amount of sea water before starting to cough and splutter.

"Right that's it, we're leaving." I called out. All eyes were on me as I struggled up the beach with Reuben safely in my arms, the weight of the water in my clothes making my progress all the more challenging. John followed on behind with the other two.

"John, what am I going to do for dry clothing?"

"Don't worry, five minutes in this soaring heat and you'll be dry as a bone."

"Well, if I stay here with the children, can you please go and find us some drinks? For we're all dying of thirst."

"Sure thing but I've no idea where to go."

"Well, this beach is so crowded so there must be some facilities nearby, you'll just have to go and look."

"Okay…just hand me my wallet." He was gone for quite a while so I assumed he must have found some sort of cafeteria. Not so. When he finally reappeared he was fuming.

"You're not going to believe this but?"

"Try me."

"Well for starters, they only have a couple of drink machines, so I put some money in the nearest one and nothing happened. I then tried again and nothing, so I attempted retrieve my coins but it wouldn't give them back. I then went down on the beach in search of someone who could give me the exact change that the machine said it took. With that sorted, I headed back and, as I approached the machine, I saw some youngster bend down and take a chilled can from out the dispenser. So once again I inserted the correct money into the machine and yet again nothing happened. No drink and no money back, despite banging the eject button over and over. I knew if I came back empty handed you'd be furious with me so I was forced to head back down onto the beach to ask someone to change my notes. Finally, with the correct money, I went back to the machines only this time I used the other machine, yet again it failed to dispense a can of soda, so after pressing and thumping the eject button numerous times, I found that once again I had lost my money. Well I was in the first throws of assaulting the jolly machine when...."

"Assaulting a machine, is that possible?" I interrupted.

"Yep I gave it a hard bang and kicked it a couple of times."

"Oh right, so who came off the worst?"

"I did for I've hurt my big toe."

"Oh for goodness sake where is this story going?"

"Anyway, while all this was going on, another spotty youth came up to the other machine and immediately pressed the reject button. I then watched on in horror as he collected up the change. He then walked over to my machine and pointed to a handwritten notice that had been taped to the front of the machine."

"Go on I'm all ears for what did it say?"

"Well it was in Spanish, otherwise I wouldn't have even tried putting money into the machine."

"So how did you translate it?"

"I didn't, the young boy did."

"Well what did it say?"

"It said "This machine is a thief.""

"You don't say!"

"Yes and that's why I've been away so long and why we still have no refreshments. I can only suggest we head back to the car and hopefully we can be on the look out for a shop, otherwise a supermarket."

With heavy hearts and tongues that were now cleaving to the roofs of our mouths we climbed back into our seriously overloaded car and went on our way. Finally when we felt all hope was lost we came upon a small garage that had a bathroom and also sold chilled drinks and bottled water, so what didn't enter by way of our mouths we simply poured over our heads for the heat was slowly killing us. It was time to get back on the road. After many hours I began to question John's map reading skills.

"Honey, forgive me asking, but you swore we would be at our destination by the early evening."

"Yes, but remember we lost a great deal of time at the airport, and then there was the beach and..."

"John watch out!" I screamed as he quickly swerved to miss an on coming truck whose full on headlights were virtually blinding us."

"Goodness, the roads are getting more narrow and dangerous by the minute," he exclaimed as he failed to hide his shock at what might have happened if he hadn't moved over in the nick of time.

A few hours later and we were still driving up steep but extremely narrow mountain roads and, as I looked out of the window it was abundantly clear that should we be forced off the road, then no ambulance would be required, for we would all be well and truly on our way into the next life. I was frightened witless as we careered past huge transcontinental trucks whose gargantuan wheels were not only twice the size of our car but were being driven by crazed or overtired drivers desperate to get home to their woman and a plate of paella. I knew if we really wanted to live to see another day then we must quickly get off these menacingly dangerous roads and find ourselves somewhere to rest for the remainder of the night.

"Honey please listen, this is becoming downright dangerous, so we've got to find a hotel for the night," I begged. He needed no further persuasion.. And so it was that, having come off the main road, we were now driving blindly along dark narrow lanes as we searched for some small hotel or motel to take pity on us. We could find nothing.

"John, please make this the last time we go abroad, as I can't handle anymore of this."

"Look Tricia I'm so sorry, I honestly thought we could make it to La Manga in one hit. Now our only hope lies in finding somewhere that will take us in."

"Well, there you go again with that little word 'thought' that never fails to concern me, especially since you are apparently in the transport business!" Finally we pulled up outside what I considered to be a most dubious residence.

"Tricia, I believe we have our miracle."

"Honey don't count your chickens before they hatch! Are you sure this really is a proper motel?" I questioned as I climbed out of the front seat.

"Well, it says so on the board back there."

"Okay, well, you go and find out what it costs per night, and I'll stay behind in the car with the children." Many minutes passed before he was back.

"Right then, sorry I've been so long, but I had to barter with the man."

"Barter?"

"Oh never mind, anyway it's sorted, so come on everybody out of the car."

We went into the reception and my heart instantly sank. The strong smell of stale beer was overwhelming and the floor beneath my feet was covered in waste litter.

"John, please don't even consider asking if they provide food in this place."

"Don't worry, I won't."

"Also, please ask him where the nearest bathroom is, as I desperately need to spend a penny."

As I opened the bathroom door I was hit by the odiously pungent smell of stale urine, but that was not all, for I was then forced to wade through water that having overflowed a cistern or two now had a variety of floating objects swimming freely, including used toilet tissue. My need for relief was by now a matter of urgency so I forced my way to the nearest available cubicle, dodging the human excrement, soiled nappies, tampons and used male contraception as best as I was able. I then raced back to the reception to alert John for I couldn't conceive of spending one hour, let alone the rest of the night, in this squalid dive.

"John we're leaving," I loudly announced.

"Tricia calm down. It's late at night, and I'm much too tired to drive any further, so we have no choice other than to stay put, besides the man insisted I pay up front."

"Oh goodness, can this get much worse?" I cried.

"Well, not only are his prices ridiculous, but I had to argue with him as he refused to allocate us just one room."

"What? There's no way I'm going to allow any of us to be separated while we are forced to endure this rundown backstreet hovel."

"Tricia, please calm down for you're not helping things. He says we need two rooms as there are five of us."

"But James is just a baby, so I hope you argued that one."

"Of course I did."

When John told me their daily price, I immediately baulked.

"That's scandalous, in fact that's extortion! There's no way any right minded person would even think to fork out what he's asking per night, well nobody except us."

We made our weary way down a dank foul smelling passageway until we came to our room number and, having already familiarized myself with their bathroom facilities, I was already bracing myself for the very worst. It came. The bleak room was only slightly larger than the sweat boxes used to punish war time prisoners and, due to its diminutive proportions, it only had space to harbor a rusty iron bed, the only other stick of furniture being a rickety old and much faded padded chair that was covered in numerous highly suspect stains. The sealed small window in the room had thick bars that prevented us from getting access to any fresh air. I believe the installation of the bars had little to do with providing additional safety for guests and more to do with thwarting disgruntled guests from leaving without paying their bill in full. In the corner of the room stood an old china washbasin that had the brightest dark brown rust stain that ran full length of the basin right down to the plug hole and, just like the mean reception clerk, this tap was also not predisposed towards generosity, as having turned the tap on full it inconsiderately dripped just enough water as to become irritatingly annoying.

To add to our predicament there was no air conditioning machine and so the bare concrete walls had little else to do other than hold up the building and absorb the heat of the day. Before long we would experience life from the vantage point of a loaf of bread on the top shelf of a pre heated oven! By the time we abandoned this sweat box, our frail bodies would be suffering excessive water loss, and our parched throats would feel as though they had been scraped with the fine instruments of a dentist, they were that sore.

"Children, listen to me, you mustn't drink from this tap," I solemnly warned.

"Honey I hate to say this but I think you're scaring the children, so you need to remain calm and positive."

"I'm doing my very best really I am, but there's no way I am going to lay my head down while I'm feeling so vulnerable in this dreadful place. So if nothing else please stuff your wallet down the front of your underpants just incase we are robbed before dawn is upon us."

"Oh come on, is that really necessary?"

"Absolutely."

Throughout the remainder of the night we heard the sound of glass shattering as well as intermittent death defying screaming and yelling coming from neighboring rooms. It was all too much for me for I was sincerely torn between going to the rescue, otherwise bashing them around the head with a large piece of our luggage.

"John, can you hear all that blood curdling screaming for it's making me really scared?"

"Yes I can, but honey, do your best to ignore it, and get some rest."

The one and only thing that I could be thankful for was the fact that the children somehow remained oblivious to all the terrifying night time commotion as they lay flat out on the bed fast asleep. John took the chair while I sat on the side of the bed leaning up against the headboard. The next few hours were spent praying for our continued safety, otherwise the end of the world to take place, and preferably as soon as possible. I must have dozed off for I woke to see my young daughter Antonia attempting to drink water from the tap.

"Antonia honey, stop what your doing or you'll make yourself ill. Don't you remember I warned you not to drink from that tap?"

"I'm so sorry Mummy, but I'm so hot and I'm dying of thirst."

It was a warning that came too late. By 5.00 am we'd both had more then enough! My skin felt uncomfortably clammy and my clothes were soaked through due to excessive perspiration.

"John, help me get the children up because we're leaving this hell-hole right now."

As we crept out the building and headed towards the car Antonia began clutching her stomach. A few miles down the road and she was vomiting. We stopped the car and I searched for the potty as it was the only receptacle large enough to handle this latest volatile situation. All too soon and the contents spilling from her mouth were a most vile green.

"John, she's now vomiting bile with streaks of blood, so I urgently need to get her to a hospital or a doctor," I cried.

"Nowhere will be open at this unearthly hour," he responded.

The next few hours were little short of a living hell as she screamed and sobbed and writhed. I felt so utterly powerless as there was nothing whatsoever I could do to help or comfort her as she continued to reach and gag until nothing more would come.

"John, she's so badly dehydrated that I'm extremely anxious and worried."

"Look Tricia according to the sign back there, we are just approaching Cartagena, and so, if we look at my map, it shows that our timeshare complex is just under half an hour away, so, as soon as we get there, I promise I will find help."

Finally we arrived at the complex. John abandoned the car to race inside, the aim being to get us into our apartment as quickly as possible. Five minutes later and he was racing back towards the car.

"Tricia, I've just been informed that not all the apartments on this complex are owned by timeshare, and the man who oversees the bookings is at present otherwise occupied."

"Occupied? John, as this is neither a toilet nor a country at war, what do you mean by occupied? Where is the man with the keys?" I cried.

"Hmm.. his name is Peter, and he runs a bar some twenty minutes back down the road we just came in on."

"Don't you understand that our little girl is now in a very dire state of need?" I cried.

"Yes, but I don't know what I'm supposed to do now."

"Go back to the reception, get his number, then phone him."

"Right." Five minutes later and my very harassed other half was back on the scene, huffing and puffing and sweating like a stuffed pig.

"Honey, help me for this heat is killing me."

"Here take a gulp of this," I said as I handed him our last drop of water.

"So did you get through to him?"

"He's not answering the phone, but I've got the address," John breathlessly stated as he jumped into the driver seat to begin racing down the road like a deranged man under the influence. Finally we came to an abrupt halt outside the so called bar.

"Stay put!" John ordered as he leapt from the car to race inside. I could not help but observe that he had large salt stains running the entire length of his polo shirt. I knew then that the poor man was beginning to suffer the advance signs of dehydration that in no time would have him foaming at the mouth as he nonsensically prattled on like a babbling brook. Five minutes later and he was back.

"Tricia, he's not there."

"What!"

"Yes, apparently he's gone back to his apartment for an afternoon siesta."

"You've got to be kidding me?"

"If only I was."

"John, this is turning into a most ridiculous game of Monopoly."

"Only this game comes minus the 'Get out of jail free card,'" he muttered.

"What?"

"Although right now jail would seem like a most welcome break," he continued to mutter as he attempted to wipe away the sweat that was visibly streaming down his face and neck

"What do we do now?"

"Hmm... well a member of the bar staff has given me his address, although it's another twenty minutes drive from here," he despairingly stated, as once again he jumped into the driving seat and hit the gas pedal to begin driving down the road like a bat out of hell. I closed my eyes and sunk deeper into my private despair. Finally we arrived at the apartment block and rather stupidly I momentarily began to believe that the worst was now over.

"Stay where you are, and I'll be back in a moment," he ordered as yet again he leapt from the car and raced towards the apartment block. I shook my head as I wondered where he thought I might go when I was sitting holed up in the back of a cramped car, surrounded on all sides by sweaty bodies and piled high luggage, whilst holding a potty to our young daughter's seriously ashen face.

Some fifteen minutes later he raced back towards the car, and yet again it was very apparent that all was not well. How did I know? Well for starters he started banging his fists on the bonnet followed closely by kicking the car tires like some deranged madman just released from the local lunatic asylum, either that or I was failing to fully appreciate his personal and illustriously enigmatic interpretation of River Dance.

"John, stop it, you're scaring the living daylights out of us all!" I yelled out the window. He was not listening. He continued to shout and holler while giving the car another round of quite severe and undeserved kicks, beatings and karate chops while making loud gargling noises and it all seemed pretty painful to me.

"John, tell me what on earth is going on?" I cried as the dear man was now giving me great reason for concern. It took him a few minutes before any recognizable sounds would finally spill forth from his lips and even then his words were hardly the words one would expect from a logically coherent man.

"Huh.. Huh.. Um.. Er.. der...."

"John, do yourself a favor, take a deep breath."

"Uh?"

"Your gabbling and almost foaming at the mouth."

"Uh?"

"Yes well, you're not making any sense whatsoever!"

"Well ...er ...er...he, I mean the man who is supposed to manage the bookings says they have absolutely no record of our booking," he gasped.

"What, you must be kidding me!"

"Would I do such a thing?" he gasped as he held onto the cars window frame for moral support

"Well then, don't just stand there like you've just suffered a sudden brain infarction, go back up to the apartment and refuse to budge an inch until he sorts it out."

"Tricia I can't go back inside, for I feel so weak I'm going to collapse, and I'm seriously at the end of my tether," he stuttered, his knuckles white from clutching the half opened window too tightly.

"Well 'Mr. Negotiator', answer me this, are you a man or a ....? Nope don't answer that. Look honey just get back up to his apartment and tell him that our young daughter is desperately ill and inform him that I'm on my way up. Then tell him he doesn't know what scary is until he's met me, so he needs to sort thing out and pronto!"

I felt both helpless as well as perturbed as I watched the desperate man race back inside the building, for I have to say I was now worried as to what might now occur due to my uncharitable words of chastisement. I mean, for my children's sakes, I needed action, but not at the cost of an accidental death that might well take place, all because my seriously hyperventilating 'man of the moment' had taken the challenge a little too far. He was now so fuelled up and supercharged he was clearly ready and willing to die for this latest cause. Some ten minutes later he was back at the car.

"What's the score?" I enquired, at the same time giving way to feelings of great relief as well as trepidation.

"There's some positive movement," he breathlessly reported back.

"Movement! Are we talking a bowel movement, a moving piano recital, what?"

"Tricia, trust me when I say he didn't want me kicking down his door, so he's now on the case." he sighed as he reached down to grab the end of his shirt for the purpose of wiping away the sweat that was dripping furiously from his deeply furrowed brow.

"Yes, as we speak he's on the phone with the timeshare management company."

Finally the man appeared and, despite being impressively heavy set, he appeared very sheepish as he made his way over towards our car.

"Mr. Bennett, sorry for the delay but I've been in touch with the timeshare operators and it seems they've made a huge mistake by double booking this particular apartment."

"But we own this week!" I quickly interjected.

"Yes I know. So we are going to give you the apartment for six days out of the seven, and then we will have to move you to another apartment for the last night, I hope that's alright by you."

I cared nothing regarding future inconvenience, for I was only concerned for my daughters rapidly deteriorating condition that might well see her hospitalized if we didn't get out of this unbearable heat, so we signed the paperwork, grabbed the keys and left.

Once in the apartment we experienced our first sense of real peace. Having plied Antonia with medicine designed to re hydrate her body with essential salts, all she then needed was a long rest, but it took a little longer to calm and soothe our wearied minds and battered emotions.

The following week actually proved to be the best holiday we had ever experienced. Our apartment was bright and pristine, and the pool deck with its abundance of sun beds clustered around the sparkling pool gave it a very welcoming atmosphere. It didn't take long for us to feel at home. The considerably warm and balmy evenings were such that families were forgiven for hurriedly excusing themselves from the dinner table in order to take a pleasurable stroll along the wide promenades. We watched as parents allowed their excitable offspring to race ahead to play a game of hide and seek, otherwise fill any left over room with an oversized ice cream cone. Here in this sought after paradise the pace of life appeared to crawl down to that of an aging snail reaching the end of a ten year global hike. I observed endless tanned bodies slumped on sun beds, otherwise lazing under brightly colored parasols on the white sandy beach. Others of a more energetic disposition favored a leisurely walk along the cool waters of the lagoon, while others chose to meander down the narrow streets stopping only to congregate outside the odd restaurant to peruse the menu as the smell of fish or garlic pervading the air attempted to fully persuade their empty stomachs that it was indeed time to stop everything and begin feasting.

As I cast an eager eye over the natural lagoon I was met by splashes of every color of the rainbow as small sailing vessels, catamarans and windsurfers politely intermingled as they navigated the sparkling waters. Looking upwards I was met by numerous fearless Para gliders who, in the spirit of freedom having left the water below were now at one with the winds above as they headed into the scorching azure skyline. This was indeed a perfect and most splendid paradise.

The splendid solace of this unforgettable place did much to restore our frayed nerves and equally troubled minds. And as for our children they in turn needed very little additional creature comforts for, in much the same spirit, they too were mesmerized and bewitched by the beguiling golden sands and sparkling sea. Now all that was required of us adults was to ensure they tumbled into bed happy and content, after fulfilling the promise of an evening run along the beach with a kite in one hand and a melting cone in the other. As I observed them all fast asleep, a look of pure contentment written all over their young faces, I believed I could have easily made this place my home.

As promised we were forced to move apartments for the last night which was something of an inconvenience, but we refused to allow even this to trouble and spoil this unexpectedly blissful holiday.

Sadly it was soon time to leave and head back towards Malaga for the second week of our holiday. I felt sorry to be leaving this special haven, however I was grateful to be setting off early in the morning as I did not want a repeat performance of all that had taken place just getting here.

"Honey we'll come back again next year," John cheerfully announced as he tried to bolster me.

"I'd love too, but if we are coming back then we're definitely taking a plane to San Javier airport otherwise Alicante, for there's no way I'm prepared to go through such an ordeal ever again."

With the children and our luggage tightly packed into the car we headed back towards Malaga and our second week of timeshare. As we drove along the main artery, the atmosphere in the car was one of complete peace and contentment.

"Honey, you do remember I've rather stupidly messed up on the booking?"

"Yes John how could I possibly forget." Due to our usual extremely low budget it never actually crossed either of our minds to go in search of a cheap hotel for the night, although saying that we had already coughed up on that awful motel on the way down."

"So this is going to be our next hurdle that we are going to have to overcome." I quietly commented.

"Tricia, don't worry, I have every confidence that the timeshare management will come up with something. Why I didn't question this statement as our experience of the management had always been exceptionally poor, I'll never know, but trust my man I did. As to this particular challenge being the next hurdle we needed to overcome as usual I had spoken way to soon. A few hours into the journey and John turned and asked me to help by opening up a bag of sweets for him. I obliged, only instead of using my hands to open the packet I chose instead to use my teeth. Wrong decision!

"Oh my goodness, I think I've just cracked a tooth," I cried as I quickly spat a hard alien object from my mouth into the palm of my hand. "Oh no John, I have just lost half a tooth?" I cried out in despair.

"Oh great, and the dentists out here aren't exactly cheap as chips," he bleated.

"Yes I know, but until we find one I'm just hoping I won't get toothache. Wrong again! Hours later found me writhing around the front seat in stupefied agony. John was very understanding and so as soon as he was able he stopped the car and raced into a pharmacy to get me some painkillers.

"Here take these," he cried as he handed them over along with a bottle of lukewarm water. We arrived at the next timeshare around four in the afternoon but were unable to book in until four pm the next day, so we dragged our luggage down to the poolside area to then sit on some vacant sun beds, me still nursing my tooth and John nursing a bigger headache and that was where were we going to sleep that night?

Now this may seem strange but it never entered our heads to go in search of a hotel, for all previous experience told us there was no such thing as cheap hotel deals when it came to Europe, and as hotels.com and other such sites had not made their way into the official compartments of our minds we seemed to just accept our misfortune, albeit reluctantly. Looking back, at the very least we should have asked around locally, but I guess driving around unfamiliar territory in a car with no air conditioning, the scorching sun bearing down from above it, made going in search of somewhere to stay a complete impossibility.

As the evening wore on and the painkillers wore off, and with no acceptable solution in sight, I have to admit to a certain sense of resentment beginning to well up inside concerning my dearly beloved's stupid cock up. Yes, if it hadn't been for him, we would be in our warm apartment cosseting our tired weary bodies with nice comforting food, instead of which we were being forced to languish in the dark, our only companions being the vicious and menacing mosquitoes who waited in preparation to have themselves an all night feast on our miserable English blood. I was not a happy bunny! Around eleven o'clock that evening I informed John I had a plan. Needless to say it was a plan he didn't warm towards.

"Honey I think it's a very bad idea."

"You don't say? But listen up John, for the very thought of staying out here all night is downright ridiculous. I'm not too sure if you're fully aware but the children are shivering with cold, the ground is already seriously wet with dew, and the hostile sound of blood sucking mosquitoes grooming themselves for an all out brutal attack seems pretty imminent."

"Oh dear."

"Good, I'm glad you're beginning to understand, for in less than a few hours the temperature will have dropped so much that it'll be freezing out here, so you either need to come up with a better alternative, otherwise have the grace to let me try this."

"Tricia it probably won't work.".

"Well guess what, we'll never know the outcome until we've given it a try, so see ya."

"Goodness, you're bad to the bone girl," he said shaking his head in despair.

With my thoughts fully expressed I leapt off the sun bed and headed towards what would become our apartment sometime the following afternoon. The man who opened the door was large, tall and very American.

"Hi there, I apologize for disturbing you at this late hour but...."

"Come on in," he said as he gestured for me to follow after him into the seating area. His three American friends all appeared from nowhere as they were intrigued to find out who could possibly be knocking on their door at this unearthly hour of the night. Despite feeling really embarrassed, I told them my sad pathetic story. They were all ears.

"Look, if it wasn't for the children I would have endured the night outside on a sun bed, so please understand I would never have dreamed of putting you in this awkward position, but as a mother of three young children I'm feeling pretty desperate."

"Hmm."

"And I promise you, hand on heart, that neither my husband or I have ever been in any trouble with the law, although that's not entirely true for he has had a number of speeding tickets, but in England they don't lock you up for that," I casually babbled on. "So we're really Kosher, we truly are and we're willing to pay for your help."

They umm'd and ahh'd then umm'd some more, causing me to begin fidgeting as I now wished I hadn't taken on the challenge.

"Alright we agree, but you must all leave the apartment by five am, as we wish to have our last breakfast in peace before we hand back the keys to the office and then head for the airport."

"Thank you so much," I replied as I jumped to my feet and handed over the money. I raced back to the pool. "Honey grab the kids, and as much luggage as you can carry, for it's sorted."

"Really?"

"Yes really. Oh, by the way, they want to see your driving license just to make sure you're not really Jack the Ripper, that done they've agreed to let us sleep in the lounge as long as we get up and leave by five am at the latest."

"How much did it cost?"

"Don't ask."

We placed the children down on the large sofa and tucked a warm blanket around them, before sitting down besides them to watch on until they were fast asleep. I was unable to doze off due to my aching tooth and because, like many a night before, my brain simply refused to switch off to the endless 'what if' questions that failed to show me any mercy as they unceasingly weaved their merry way through my grey matter like mutated worms searching out a night time partner. At five am precisely and still feeling rough at the edges we gathered up our belongings and then, as quietly as we were able, we shut the door behind us and headed back down to the pool area.

"We didn't say a proper goodbye," John whispered as we placed our children's limp bodies back on the sun beds before covering them up with towels to keep them warm and allow them to sleep a bit longer.

"No but I did remember to leave a thank you note."

"That's good. Now we've only got another eleven hours to get through until the apartment finally becomes ours?"

Around seven am we noticed lights flickering on in some of the apartments. I soon became aware of a ground floor apartment where the occupants kept staring out of the window at us. Half an hour later and even more holidaymakers were standing with their faces glued to the window as they wondered why and what we were doing stretched out on sun beds at this unearthly hour of the morning. Finally a youngish lady came out of her apartment and walked over to speak with us.

"Hi there would any of you like a nice cuppa tea?" she asked in a warm northern British accent. I was slow to respond simply because I was convinced I was now hallucinating. Had my sympathetic guardian angel just popped down to ask me if I would like some hot tea?

"Oh, we would really love some," I mumbled as I wrapped my swim towel round me in a futile endeavor to keep warm.

"How many teas?"

"Two cups would be nice."

"Milk and two sugars?"

"Oh yes please."

We were so grateful to the kind lady and when she came back she sat down to chat and so it was, during this brief interlude, I explained why we were there and not in an apartment.

"Oh my goodness, if only I'd known I could have helped out," she cried.

"How come?" John asked as he brought the hot tea up to his lips.

"Well our good friends who stayed in the next apartment to us decided to leave for home a day earlier than expected, and they left the keys with me, so if I'd known all this you could have used their apartment."

"Do you still have the keys on you?" I enquired as I began daydreaming about taking a long hot shower.

"No love I took them back to reception around midnight last night."

I could only give a deep sigh as I wished she had never made mention of any of this, as my grey matter began once more to feel most shaky and unstable.

"Oh this is all so unbelievably unfair?" I screamed inside my head.

By eleven am the heat was really beginning to build up as was my temper.

"John, you need to stay here and look after the children, while I go for a long walk to stretch my legs," I fumed.

I returned to find him lying back on a sun bed, the children playing down by his side as, with not a seeming care in the world, he contented himself with his latest thought provoking book. What happened next would defy all belief. I was just about to open my mouth and complain, although about what I'm not exactly sure, when a middle aged guest came over to where he was lying stretched out on a sun bed and asked my dear husband one the strangest questions imaginable. At first I questioned the gentleman's sincerity, followed closely by his seeming state of mind for it all sounded a bit too daft for my liking. I was puzzled for the man did not appear to be anything of a 'basket case' and I observed that he too seemed more than a little embarrassed to even be asking the question.

"Sir, allow me to introduce myself, my name is Kevin."

"Hi there, I'm John and this here is my wife Tricia, so what can we do for you?"

"Well I hope you won't mind me asking, but I have been watching you all morning and you sir have the most amazing aura of peace all over you? Are you always this way? And how and what can I do to get it?"

I was speechless, put more bluntly, utterly gob smacked! For, as the obviously sincere man spoke to John, I immediately had visions of the week prior, when, in a seemingly bi polar paranoid schizophrenic aberration he had freaked out and beaten up our poor undeserving car. Now this man wished to bestow some imaginary honor in recognition of his unquestionably superior inner peace?

I wanted to laugh and cry at the same time, but if I'm honest I was also secretly touched for in that small moment I reminded myself that, before this poor misguided man had become joined at the hip to me, he had been a genuinely gentle peace-loving ex-hippy who attracted butterflies in a manner not to dissimilar to pollen attracting bees. This man also loved fields filled to overflowing with daffodils, tall trees, as well as fluffy week old kittens. Had he really managed to preserve even a modicum of his tranquil former self, I privately pondered.

I watched on in amusement as my humbled spouse stuttered and stumbled over his words as he attempted to give the man a satisfactory answer to his somewhat bizarre question. I wanted to intervene and shout "Three years on a kibbutz will do it for you," but on this occasion wisdom prevailed and so I kept my mouth tightly shut. They talked animatedly for a while leaving me to go and find some food for the children and when I came back he was no more.

"John, was that guy for real? I mean forgive me but I can't stop laughing, I hope you were a bit honest with him?"

"If you mean did I tell him about last week's rather unfortunate misdemeanor, well no I didn't feel the need to."

"Well then, Oh Master of the Universe, oh anointed one, you appear to have a keen follower after all."

Finally four O'clock came round and we were given the long awaited keys to the apartment. Once inside, we quickly unpacked our belongings before collapsing down onto the sofa."

"John, I'm doing fine with these painkillers, but I still need to find myself an emergency dentist."

"Right, well I'll ask at reception."

"Also, do realize it's almost forty eight hours since we last sat down to a proper meal and, until we find a supermarket, we don't have enough provisions left for me to even cook a decent meal."

"Right, well let's grab our things and head out to a restaurant."

As usual our sense of timing was impeccable, for every restaurant we approached was full to overflowing with large families of holidaymakers who were in no rush to leave, preferring instead to bide their time shouting across the table at one another as they downed large volumes of beer and Sangria. It left us wondering whether to entirely abandon our mission and head off in search of a supermarket.

"Tell you what, let's just stay put and, if we don't get a table in the next half hour, then we will head off to the local supermarket."

It was almost an hour before we were finally seated then another half hour went by before a waiter came over to take our order. By this time our three very hungry children were getting restless as well as extremely overtired. Finally much to our delight we saw the waiters carrying large trays that were headed in our direction.

"Who is having the cheese and ham omelets with chips?" Carlos the main waiter asked.

"Oh, the children." I watched on as the children were all presented with a plate of food.

"And the paella?"

"That's my husband's."

"And the pasta topped with a chicken breast ?"

"That's mine," I said breathing a huge sigh of relief that finally we could fill our aching stomachs.

As I reached over to pick up a napkin, James my three year old toddler chose this moment to stand up on his chair. He then began to furiously wobble back and forth and, before any further information warning of impending doom could reach my brain, both he and the chair began to topple over. As he went down he lunged forward and grabbed hold of the tablecloth. We all watched on in horror as the plates of food hurtled past our eyes like a derailed high speed commuter train before crashing down on the stone floor.

"Oh my goodness I'm so sorry," I cried out as I then fell to the ground to manically search the floor for any food I might be able to salvage. The waiters rushed over and with a distinct air of disapproval they too fell on their hands and knees and began picking up the food from amongst the broken crockery. I saw my piece of chicken beckoning to be saved, so I reached over to grab hold of it.

"I'll take that from you madam," one of the waiters curtly announced as he reached over to release me of my piece of chicken. I momentarily faltered before closing my hand over the chicken in order to hide it out of sight.

"Madam, please sit back down and let us clear up the mess," the waiter demanded as he continued to hold out his hand. I still declined to hand over the chicken breast as in my tortured little head I began bartering with the waiters. "Look I'm that starving so I need you guys to be reasonable and let me keep the blooming chicken. Look I know it's been on the floor, but can't we just for once ignore all health and safety laws that would sentence this chicken to be binned, for I can just as easily rinse it under the tap at home, and it definitely belongs to me. I ordered it, I'm paying for it so, for heavens sake, just let me keep my bloomin' piece of chicken!"

By now John had crouched down beside me to give a hand with the clearing up. With the waiters hand still expectantly awaiting the transfer of the chicken breast from my tightly closed hand to his.

"Tricia honey, I understand you're hungry, but do everyone a favor and just release it now."

"But it's mine."

"Don't make such a big deal, just give it to him."

"Do I really have too?"

And so it was with the greatest reluctance that I was forced, against my will, to hand over the slimy sauce covered chicken breast like I was some very naughty little girl.

"Anyone would think you were being forced to hand over all our life savings," John quietly commented as he helped me to my feet.

"John, if you really love me, you'll ask the waiter if I can have my chicken breast back," I whispered as my hunger pangs continued to grow.

"Are you crazy?"

"No, just unbearably hungry," I grumbled. "Look if you get it back for me then I promise to run it under the cold tap as soon as we get back to our apartment."

"Tricia stop it. Let's just pay up and get out of here before anything else untoward happens."

And so it was that, with empty stomachs and heavy hearts, we paid a hefty bill for food that never reached our mouths, oh as well as for the broken china.

"They didn't even let me keep the chicken, so we shouldn't have to pay for it," I whispered in a very agitated tone of voice. "So go back to the counter and say something," I hissed.

"No Tricia let's just accept our losses."

"But...."

"Tricia switch on that 'mute' button, then let's get out of here."

"I hope you didn't leave a tip," I mumbled.

We excused ourselves from the table and restaurant with as much dignity as we could muster and, once outside, I was left to comfort my tearful children who were way beyond any form of consolation.

"Right, it's gone ten so the supermarket will be shut, therefore the most we can hope for is to find a late night ice cream vendor."

The triple mint choc chip cones went some way towards relieving the distress signals coming from our hungry stomachs but did nothing to ease the agony of mind as I tucked my sorrowful children into bed that night.

"Mummy, we got no dinner coz of James," Reuben sobbed.

"I know honey. I'm so sorry. Tell you what, after breakfast, let's go out and buy you a new dinosaur, shall we?"

"Alright," he whimpered his bottom lip trembling as he once more rubbed his tired eyes

"What about me, I didn't get anything to eat either?" my young daughter Antonia chipped in.

"Yes well perhaps amongst the Tyrannosaurus Rex, Velociraptors and Brontosauruses, we can find a Tiny Tears doll for you sweetheart."

Happily the rest of the week passed without any further trials day and, by downing endless painkillers, I managed to save on a hefty dentist bill. All too soon it was time to head back to the airport. Despite the inevitably long line at the check-in, I was pleased to note there were no cancellations or delays expected that day. Having checked in we then went in search of some bottled water.

"Honey, you've definitely put on more than a few pounds over this holiday." John whispered as he mischievously gave my derriere a quick pat.

"Oh, you think so?"

"I know so."

"Well thanks for the compliment."

"No, I really mean it, for, from where I'm standing, they look extraordinarily tight around your butt."

I gave a quick wiggle as if to reassure myself that it was all in his imagination.

"Well, they feel just fine to me."

"I was only trying to be helpful."

"Honey, I think it might be considered a wise move if you were to keep all future thoughts and presumptions strictly to yourself and just concentrate all your efforts on buying us some bottled water," I sighed.

The plane arrived safely on the tarmac and we watched from a large window in the lounge of the boarding area as it was cleaned and new provisions were brought on board. Before long we were informed it was now time for us to board. With all passengers seated and all hand luggage safely stowed away we placed our seatbelts around our waists and waited with baited breath for take off. It never came.

Things came to a boiling point when hot irate passengers demanded an explanation as to why the plane was still on the tarmac. Finally the captain made an announcement.

"Ladies and Gentleman, I apologise for the delay, but we cannot take off as a light in the holding has not gone off. We are waiting for the maintenance crew to come and inspect the problem. Please remain in your seats with your belt buckled, and try and be patient."

Two hours later and still no take off. Provoked on by the fierce heat and with the temperature inside the cabin became hotter than the inside of a potters kiln, tempers soon began boiling over. Before too long with no fresh air and nothing to prevent dehydration passengers began to complain of feeling unwell. The pilot decided it was time to console us further.

"Ladies and gentleman, I apologize most profusely for any inconvenience but please allow me to give you an update. We have been unable to make contact with the Spanish maintenance crew as it is believed they are still on their afternoon siesta, so we are waiting the arrival of some maintenance crew who are being flown in from England."

There were gasps of absolute disbelief from inconsolable passengers who were finding it hard to believe this latest piece of information. It wasn't too long before the cabin began smelling of old unwashed pants and socks.

"Why can't they let us off the plane to head back inside the airport?" many passengers desperately cried out, using various strong expletives to express how enraged they felt. Before long, the tension inside the cabin was at such a fever pitch that a bloody mutiny could not be ruled out, as restless fellow travelers exhausted from the heat began to loudly complain and storm back and forth down the aisles searching for equally disgruntled passengers to join them. A potential fracas was only just avoided when one of the pilots wisely gave orders for the flight attendants to begin serving us liquid refreshments. Apparently pottery is only ready to be removed from the kiln when it begins to sing, and I believed myself well past this state for having been left for over four and a half hours to bake in this small overloaded bunker, I was about to crack, all that was left for me to do was link arms with other passengers as I sang my way through Abba's latest hits album. Of course John stepped in to prevent me from taking this riveting thought any further. It would be almost five hours before the pilot was finally given clearance for take off.

The ping and flashing red light ordering us to 'buckle our seatbelts' came on and seconds later the plane was thundering down the runway filled to capacity with sticky sweaty individuals who were mightily relieved that their ordeal was finally at an end. I thought likewise that is until water from nowhere began to rain down on me. I looked up and was shocked to see that water purely intended to put out a fire on board was raining down on me alone! Passengers that were seated all around me began to chuckle and in a matter of just seconds the sound of hysterical laughter could be heard throughout the entire cabin as word of my demise circulated.

"Honey, they are laughing like heavily intoxicated hyenas, but this is not the least bit funny," I announced through gritted teeth as, having soaked my hair, the water now continued to trickle down my face and blouse.

"I know, but I guess everyone's releasing some of their pent up frustration," he suggested as he too failed to stifle his most infuriating giggles.

"Oh, stop tittering like some schoolboy," I simpered as I continued to wipe the water flowing down my face.

The water didn't stop until I was soaked through to the skin and, when I finally decided I could take no more I released my seatbelt and jumped up from my seat with the full intention of making it to the bathroom. However as I leapt to my feet I heard the distinct sound of material ripping. I gasped as it took less than a few seconds to realize that my trousers had split right down the back so my knickers were now on view to a cabin load of passengers.

"Oh thank goodness I've got clean undies on," was all I felt capable of muttering as I feebly attempted to close up the large gap that had just appeared on my rear end. A flight attendant made her way over towards me and was about to rebuke me, that is until she witnessed first hand my pitiful state. She placed a hand across her mouth to stop herself joining in the general merriment.

"I'm sorry, but I'm soaked to the skin and my trousers have just ripped right across the back, so I need help," I weakly implored.

"Stay put, and I will bring you a towel, oh as well as a sewing kit, and you have my full permission to use the bathroom," she said grinning from ear to ear.

"Can we keep this amongst ourselves?"

"What do you mean?"

"I mean the pilots don't need to know anything regarding my predicament, do they?" I said shooting a forlorn grimace.

"Don't worry, mums the word."

With the towel wrapped around my waist in a desperate bid to preserve my dignity, I headed off to the bathroom. Twenty minutes later and I was heading back down the aisle looking for my seat when without warning the whole section I was seated in broke into rapturous applause. I should have used this momentous occasion to take a bow but I was far too embarrassed to do anything other than slink further down into my seat and place my sunglasses over my eyes as I expressly wished with all my might to remain anonymous for the remainder of the flight.

I guess many of the passengers wrote a stiff letter of complaint concerning their ordeal that particular day, and we were no exception. To my surprise I received a very kind letter back expressing deep concern over my unexpected soaking and the subsequent backlash of my ripped trousers and they thoughtfully enclosed a small check with the hope that this would go some way towards alleviating my embarrassing misfortune.

CHAPTER TWENTY FOUR

Death in Venice

To be perfectly honest I am in part responsible for this unquestionably sad and very doomed affair. On the evening in question, a neighbour had just paid us a visit and over a cup of tea I had decided to show him a 'can't miss offer' in one of the national papers.

"Look Kevin, British Airways are offering two week holidays for just ninety nine pounds. It's cheap as chips!" I enthused.

"Yes pretty amazing," came the voice of my husband John in the background.

"I guess since 9/11 all the airlines are struggling" I continued on. "And Kevin, they are offering many exotic destinations, including two weeks in Mexico, so why don't you take advantage of this offer, your wife will love you even more for this surprise gesture."

"Sadly I'd love too, but, speaking as an accountant, it's the wrong time of year. Anyway, thanks for the tea and I'll catch up with you later." That should have been the end of the story regarding the British Airways bargain basement holidays, but sadly it wasn't.

After Kevin left I had a quick errand that I needed to do.

"Honey, I'm just popping over to Brian and Lillian's, I promise I won't be long and then I'll make you some dinner," I called out as I headed for the front door.

"Okay, but don't stay too long for I've not eaten since breakfast so I'm already starving hungry."

"Sure thing, babe."

I rang the doorbell and Lillian answered. "Come on in dear, it's freezing outside," she said, gesturing with her arms.

"Well, I shouldn't really, as John's only just got home from work, and so I need to cook his dinner," I confessed.

"Well then dear, just stay ten minutes, but do come in before you catch yourself a death of cold."

"Oh alright then, just ten minutes," I sniffed as I obediently followed her down a short corridor into her sitting room.

"Brian, we have a surprise guest," she loudly announced. "Here Tricia, take a comfy seat and, as it's Christmas, you will stay for a nice glass of sherry, won't you?" she enthused. "Now you know I won't take no for an answer." I smiled and nodded.

"Perfect. Brian dear, be a poppet and go put the kettle on will you, oh and while you're at it dear, do get Tricia a nice glass of sherry."

Some two hours, two glasses of sherry and three cups of tea later, or was it the other way round, the doorbell rang once more. Instantly I had visions of a demented man entering my head as, feeling most guilt ridden, I leapt out of the comfy chair, deep in the knowledge that I had not one reasonably lame excuse to give my poor half starved husband.

"Come in John dear, we've got your wife here" I heard Lillian say, (as if he doesn't know that I thought to myself!). Fortunately he did not sound too upset, which was a relief. He sat down next to me and a glass of sherry was immediately thrust in his hand.

"It's Christmas, so drink up," Lillian briskly ordered as she passed the plate of peanuts his way. It was then, at that precise moment, that he chose to announce that he had spent the last hour or so on the phone booking a holiday. I was horrified.

"John are you crazy?" I despairingly cried. There was worse to come.

"I was trying to be spontaneous, I tried to get us two weeks in Mexico but it was too late, sadly all those bargains had gone." I waited with baited breath to hear what was coming next. "But don't worry, I've still managed to get us a brilliant bargain," he said his face beaming with pride. My jaw dropped open, but fortunately no words would come forth. Finally I found my tongue.

"What?"

"Yes, I think you'll be pleased when you here where we're going," he announced, a little too enthusiastically for my liking. However it did not fail to escape my notice that he was now shifting about nervously on the couch. In that briefest of moments I knew all was not well.

"John tell me what and where have you booked?" I demanded to know. He momentarily paused.

"John, don't mess with me, tell me where are we going?" There was another few moments of intense silence.

"Now don't get mad, but I've booked us two weeks in Venice."

"Venice?" I shrieked. "Are you crazy? We can't go for two weeks to Venice."

"Well, you are half Italian, and you've always wanted to go to Italy," he quietly stated, his voice faltering as he hoped and prayed for some form of absolution that both he as well as I knew was never going to come.

"John, quite what were you thinking?" There was a slight unease in the room and then, to break the ice, Lillian decided to break the deafening silence.

"Well would anyone like another top up?" We both ignored her kind offer as we continued to lock horns, for our conversation was nowhere near finished.

"John, I cannot believe you've done this," I said, a slight note of irritation betraying the sense of frustration that was now welling up inside. " Answer me this, how are we going to leave the business for two whole weeks? And question two, who is going to look after the children while we're gone? For there is no way I'm going to leave the kids with friends or neighbors for that amount of time."

"Now then dear, Venice can be so very beautiful at this time of year," Lillian quickly interjected in a futile attempt to restore calm as well as find something positive in the situation. It didn't work. She moved onto plan B, which saw her hurriedly leave the room and, on her return, she held up a rather old looking book on Venice which she briskly thrust onto my lap.

"It's a beautiful city Tricia, really it is." I glanced down at the book and shook my head.

"It's Rome I've always wanted to visit, especially as my favorite movie just happens to be Gladiator. Also, that's where my hairdresser went for her last holiday and she has come back positively raving about the place."

"Oh right dear," Lillian muttered as she moved over towards me to officially close her book, at the same time sending me a clear message that she was giving up on any further persuasive techniques.

"Anyway, setting all this aside, there is no way we can afford to take two weeks off to go anywhere, so you might as well tear up the tickets, for it simply is not going to happen." I then stood up to go.

"Lillian thank you for the refreshments. As usual you've been a very kind hostess." John stood up and heaved a huge sigh before following behind, as I made my way towards the front door.

"Tricia, I'm so sorry," he said pulling an apologetic face that he hoped might be enough to appease me. Of course it wasn't nearly enough!

"I only wanted to do something nice, something out of the box to make you happy," his voice trailed off. I looked at him and he reminded me of a wounded puppy dog having pooped on the carpet as, with head down, tail between his legs, he slowly trailed behind me.

"You could at least have thought to check it out with me first," I continued to scold him.

"I would have but you were nowhere to be found," he quickly retorted.

"Well, I did tell you I was popping over to the neighbors" I said still feeling quite irritated.

"Yes, but that was more than three hours ago," he scolded.

As I flopped onto the sofa in the sitting room and stared at the ceiling, my way of showing I was not the least amused, John made one more final try at appeasing me.

"Tricia I always thought you wanted to go to Venice. Admit it, you watch that movie 'Room with a View' over and over," he said, as he continued to try to reason with me.

"That's Florence, you twerp."

"Oh I'm really thinking of that other movie, what was it called? Ah yes, Wings of a Dove, and if you rightly remember you commented that, upon your death, you thought it would be very romantic to have your ashes scattered across the waters of Venice. Remember?......." his voice now almost as raised as mine,

"John, you're obviously not aware that you're raising your voice to new and I might add very vexatious decibels."

"What?"

"Kindly stop shouting! You're much too loud."

"Well, I'm only trying to get my point over," he angrily muttered.

At that point I knew it would be most unwise to say anything further, unless of course I wished for my ashes to be scattered over the waters in Venice very prematurely!

Over the next few weeks we found ourselves constantly at loggerheads over what to do with the tickets, as there was no possibility of a refund and, as with all air line tickets, they were un-transferable. Finally I agreed to taking an extended weekend trip if he could find us a really cheap homeward bound flight.

"How long are you thinking?" I asked

"Four days at the max. If we go first thing on Friday and come back Monday evening, how about it? That way it won't hurt the business too much, and we can surely find a friend to move in and take care of the kids for just a few days."

"Hmm."

"Alright then, if we can find a friend who is happy to take charge of our brood, as well as someone capable of keeping a watchful eye on the business, then let's do it."

John breathed a very visible sigh of relief before rushing off to try and make things happen. Less than twenty four hours later he brightly declared that everything was now sorted. A lovely lady, who some time previous had offered her services as a surrogate grandma to our children, announced that, as she was free of all outstanding commitments, she was therefore more than delighted to take charge.

"John, I really do think we should only say yes to her when we've exhausted every other possible avenue," I tried to suggest.

"Oh nonsense Tricia, she'll be fun, trust me on this one."

Now I have to concede that I found it hard to trust him on this one for Grandma, despite being something of a sweet old lady, had another side that was how shall I say, charmingly eccentric, so I believed my concerns to be entirely justifiable. For starters, there had been an occasion when I had arrived at her home to discover my two and half year old son James standing on a chair over the cooker. He had one hand holding onto the chair for dear life as he wobbled back and forth, while waving a cooking spatula in his remaining free hand. He was devoid of all clothes other than his diaper, as, with great joy, he tried his hand at being a master chef, cooking himself fried eggs and bacon! When I rather hysterically dared to suggest that what she was doing was thoroughly irresponsible, she looked over at me as if to suggest I was obviously quite, quite mad.

"Please get him down from the chair right now for, if he topples forward into the pan, he will instantly be flash fried!" I cried as I went over to forcibly drag my now screaming son down from the chair.

"Eggy bacon," he sobbed.

"No eggy bacon," I retorted as I placed him on the floor well out of harms way.

"Eggy bacon," he continued to bawl, both hands now rubbing his eyes.

"There dear, see what you've done. He was perfectly happy cooking his breakfast, and he was doing it so beautifully," she said shaking her head in a most disapproving manner as if to say, why do you have to wreck everything.

"Well I'm beginning to think you're the one who is quite bananas," I muttered under my breath. She took no offense, her only response being to inform me that before my unwelcome interference she had everything under perfect control.

"Stuff and nonsense deary, he was just experimenting, that's what children like to do," she nonchalantly informed me as she dismissed my deep concerns as though I were some exceptionally neurotic over protective mother.

Then there was the time I arrived to see my infant James lighting the log fire, and the time I witnessed Reuben fall head first into her pond, and I need to say that these were just a few of many incidents that were to cause loud alarm bells to begin exploding like warning missiles inside my head. But then I would reason that maybe I was overly anxious and she, well she really loved the children and they in turn loved her, so I guess that was all that really mattered.

And so it was that, with Christmas out of the way, we found ourselves heading off to Venice on a mini vacation. As we patiently waited at the B.A. desk to be checked in, the beautiful and smartly groomed hostess took it upon herself to announce that, in the event of spare seats being available in first class, we were to be offered them at no extra cost to ourselves.

"Oh that would be so wonderful," I joyfully cried.

"Yes well, a large party has failed to turn up and their time is fast running out," the immaculately dressed hostess informed us.

This delightful piece of information immediately sent me soaring into realms of ecstasy as this long awaited dream was finally just about to happen. I had always wanted the chance to fly first class ever since I was a child watching the Pan Am, and British Airways advertisements on television and I had previously read somewhere that the more presentable your appearance then the better chance you had of getting that highly desirable and long dreamed of upgrade. However, if you had a couple of kids in tow, then that dramatically lessened if not entirely ruined any such chances. And because on this particular occasion our brood were not accompanying us, I had determined from the out set to ensure we were both dressed for the occasion just in case it happened. I therefore set aside all comfortable clothes that bordered on shabby, mainly my husband's, and replaced them with clothes that might feel a bit stiff and starchy but would have us looking positively respectable.

"Put your best suit on," I yelled out to my husband as he staggered out of the shower.

"You are joking aren't you?" he queried.

"No I mean it."

"No way, for traveling in a suit will be awfully uncomfortable, so why can't I just wear something more casual, like jeans and a jumper, as per usual?" he groaned.

"You my dear man, are going to do all that you can to try and look like the respectable gentleman that you are. Besides you're much more irresistible in a suit."

"Unbelievable!" He muttered, or something to that effect, thrusting his head to one side as with the end of a towel he attempted to shake the water out of his ears.

"Come on spoilsport, you know the score. Say, how about you wearing your white Johnny Travolta suit? That'll get you noticed."

"Oh please… the whiteness alone will blind the other passengers, besides the last time I tried it on…well…"

"Go on, spit it out," I urged.

"Well it's still a perfect fit everywhere else, except my waist which rather sadly appears to have expanded somewhat," he stammered as he turned away to ensure there was absolutely no eye contact between us.

"Oh right too many hamburgers on the road."

"Probably."

"Look, if nothing else, please put that very nice light grey suit on."

"Please no for I don't look that good in it."

"Oh stop being so self effacing. Oh and by the way, time is really marching on, and as of yet I see you have not even started to pack a suitcase."

"Yes I have," he replied much too defensively for my liking.

"Well, where is it?"

"Over by the window," he shouted as he headed back into the bathroom to have a quick shave.

"Honey there's hardly anything in it." I retorted as my eyes scanned the bottom of his suitcase.

"I don't need much."

"Don't be daft, all you've packed is the perfunctory pair of socks, those tatty trainers, a few books, and one change of underpants!"

"Yep, that's all I need."

"Well 'Mr. Hygienic', I beg to differ for, without fresh underwear, you'll soon be smelling like an aging water buffalo on a swelteringly hot day."

"Goodness Tricia you never fail to conjure up such colorful images."

"John, I hope you're not giving serious thought to reading all these books while we're in Venice?" I despairingly cried before confiscating a few of them which I then discreetly hid under the bed. There was a brief silence.

"Your suitcase should contain a selection of clothes, as well as books."

"Oh, does it really matter?"

"Look John, if you won't pack properly then I will do it for you," I threatened as I picked up a pair of smart shoes, a replacement for his abysmally shoddy trainers, which I tossed across the room.

"But that's all I need."

"Wrong again! You cannot be thinking straight, for surely you're not traipsing half way across Europe with just a spare pair of underpants in your luggage. For starters, where are your swim shorts? I mean I'm hoping you've booked a hotel that has a swimming pool"

"Yes yes…of course," he quietly muttered. In that distinct moment I had my first sense of unease as I thought back to our last hotel mini break where I sadly discovered that, unless I intended to wear my bathing suit in the bath or shower, I would have no contact with water whatsoever! He was only forgiven when he promised to make sure it was top of his priority list for all future vacations.

"Tricia, if you need extra space, feel free to use up my share." He didn't have to ask twice!

"I'm going to take you up on that generous offer," I shouted back as I went to my case to offload as much of the heavy stuff I could get away with.

"How typical, this man is more suited to a monastery," I mumbled under my breath, as I removed further reading material, before grabbing hold of a number of extra outfits that I had been forced to lay to one side due to a wearisome lack of packing space. I then generously relieved my suitcase of all burdensome items such as a shampoo and conditioner, travel iron, hairdryer, oh as well as our not so small portable cassette player. After rolling up all the electrical appliances tightly in his pajamas and swim shorts I then carefully placed them at the bottom of his suitcase.

"How can he read such heavy duty stuff?" I muttered as I squashed the few remaining books into a small corner, to make room for my essential and very necessary thick stash of women's homemaking magazines. After all, I reasoned to myself, our house only resembled an Ideal Home due to the many hours I had endured sifting through such magazines to gain practical tips. These magazines would go a long way in keeping me both quiet and content, while I got that enviable tan, now wasn't that worth a lot to him?

"Mrs. Maximal married to Mr. Minimalist is an exceedingly tough job," I mused.

Here at the airport it seemed my hard work had finally paid off, for unbelievably our first ever upgrade to First Class was just about to happen. In my mind I was already relaxing in First Class, enjoying the aromatic smell of walnuts and honey from a glass of full bodied Alfred Gratien Cuvee Paradis champagne, whilst the sensors on my tongue were sent into delirious spasms of ecstasy, as I savored the sumptuous gourmet cuisine served up to me by some exquisitely glamorous flight attendant. I was indeed halfway through the Brochettes Et Fraises which I was happily washing down with a glass of Sauterne dessert wine when the sudden appearance of the absentee passengers brought me back down to earth with a horrible thud.

"Oh no this is not meant to be happening," I moaned as I expelled a deeply harrowing sigh as I watched the group make a desperate dash to the ticket desk. I kept a meticulous eye on them, tutting loudly as I observed them breathe deep sighs of relief as that awfully horrid over smiling stewardess rather sickeningly handed over their belated tickets.

"I can't believe this is happening," I groaned.

John was completely ignoring me, as he contentedly concentrated on his latest book.

"Never mind, next time," he muttered.

"John, nothing seems to phase you, does it? Here I am, feeling utterly heartbroken by this sudden turn of events, while you on the other hand have long left earth for some existential planet that accepts the loss of all things, for everything material in this life is to be considered meaningless," I quietly challenged.

"No darling that's Buddhism" he flippantly replied while turning over a page of his book that already had him deeply engrossed.

"Well, I for one wish that stewardess had never mentioned the upgrade, for it got my hopes up."

"Hmm, yes darling."

"John, have you left your head back at home on the bed? If so, let me say now that they simply won't allow it onboard as carry on luggage."

"Uh?"

"Well, nothing seems to trigger a human reaction, it's as though you're a mechanical robot who feels no pain."

My husband took this to mean I required some sort of comfort so, setting his book to one side, he slid his arm round my waist.

"Honey you provide more than enough emotion for the two of us."

"How rude!:

"Well at least the hostess said we were the sort of people they were happy to upgrade, and as that's the first time we have been accredited in such a manner you should be somewhat happy and encouraged by that!"

I can freely admit that his efforts to comfort and console were entirely lost on me, for all I wanted to do was stuff a triple decker ham and cheese sandwich down his throat in order to shut down his wind pipes permanently!

Despite the absence of vintage champagne the BA flight was great, the food they served was well above average, and the flight attendants were simply delightful, but rather worryingly, just before the descent into Venice one of the flight attendants came over to where we were seated and gently leant over to quietly whisper in my ear.

"Are you feeling alright madam?" she asked flashing me a concerned look.

"Yes thank you," I replied, though I had to admit to feeling somewhat confused by her question as I had not pressed the call button. It was very dark when we finally disembarked the plane and in no time we found ourselves on a large passenger boat heading for the mainland and our hotel. However I was taken back by the extent of the cold.

"Gracious me, this is indeed the weather for underwear," I muttered as the howling wind bit mercilessly into my flesh.

"I'm so sorry Tricia, I honestly thought…"

"There goes that dangerous little word again."

"What word?"

"Thought."

"Yes well I honestly believed Venice would be warm like the Costa del sol in Spain."

"Homework my dear Watson, it's good to do our homework before we book."

Unbelievably ours was the last drop that night and, by the time the boat reached its mooring, I cared nothing whatsoever for Venice as, chilled to the bone, I was more than ready to die and get the scattering of my ashes over with as soon as possible! I was further disturbed to hear that we had at least a mile to walk dragging our heavily overloaded suitcases through the frosty streets until we reached the hotel. The hotel turned out to be not only fairly shabby, but I would also quickly learn that it had no swimming pool and therefore no pool deck! Things were not looking too good!

After check in, we made our way up the creaking wooden staircase and into a small dilapidated room which on inspection we were both horrified to discover had no private bathroom.

"Oh this is grim," I muttered as I surveyed the bleak sparsely furnished room with its turn of the century wall paper now barely clinging to the walls.

"Tricia, this is as good as it gets, unless you wish to spend a small fortune."

"Oh, but this is all so uncivilized for there is only one loo servicing this entire corridor And while we're at it, did you by some chance notice the two grimy-looking showers?"

"I'm so sorry honey but we'll just have to make the best of it."

"Right, but there's no tea and coffee making facilities in the room either, and not even a television."

For the duration of our short stay we declined to use the slimy showers and opted to wash ourselves as best as we were able in the heavily stained and cracked bedroom sink, but, as natures call is impartial to both preference or discernment, we were forced against our wishes to use the small communal toilet that was situated right at the end of a long corridor, far away from our room.

"The hotel sounded alright in the travel section of the newspaper," John mused as unsteadily balanced on one foot he plunged his other large foot into the basin to wash away the day's dirt from between his toes.

"Yeah right."

"Look, we'll manage," he quietly muttered clutching hold of the basin in order to change feet.

"Well, that's alright for you to say, but you're not the one with a bladder the size of a shelled pea! So I'm the one going to spend much of the night blindly stumbling down that freezing cold corridor whenever I feel the urge to spend a penny, and you know from much experience that will mean disturbing you virtually every hour throughout the night," I blurted out as I granted myself the privilege of venting the anguish that my martyrdom spirit was feeling most desperate to release.

"Oh dear," he mumbled under his breath as he pulled the plug and then began to towel dry his feet with one of four small threadbare towels, compliments of the hotel. I watched on in amusement as he struggled away.

"Careful you're wobbling."

With his feet finally dried he wandered back to the bed and picked up his book.

"And to think I stupidly packed my bikini for this trip," I miserably simpered. He wasn't listening. I felt chilled to the bone as, having changed into my pajamas, I rolled under the covers and tried hard to sleep

I awoke early the next morning to discover that my eyes felt unusually heavy. Throwing the blankets to one side I staggered across the cold bleak room heading for the mirror that sat just above the yellowing cracked sink.

"Oh my goodness," I shrieked. "John quick. Look at me, something's gone terribly wrong," I bellowed.

"Good grief!" John exclaimed as he leapt from the bed and rushed over to get a better look.

"Honey you look as though you've been in ten rounds with Mike Tyson."

"And lost," I sobbed.

"That too."

"Oh John I can't step out of the hotel looking like this, for I clearly resemble the Elephant Man," I bitterly cried.

"Stop exaggerating for you don't look half as bad as him. Besides, don't worry, nobody knows you out here."

"Have we bought any sunglasses with us?" I pathetically whimpered.

"Nope I don't think so," he replied while frantically emptying both cases onto the bed.

"Come on, we must have brought some with us, we never go on holiday without them," I forlornly cried.

"Well, if they're here I can't see any."

"Look, if you can't find any, then I'm going to stay a prisoner to this room until you go and buy me some," I loudly wailed.

"Yes yes, but calm down. I'm trying to think what could have happened to make your face and eyes swell up like this. Here, just come and lie down on the bed and allow me to place a cold flannel over your eyes."

As I lay on the bed feeling extremely sorry for myself I had a sudden remarkable epiphany. For my Christmas present John had encouraged me to have my first botox treatment. It would also be my last.

"Trust me honey, there's no surgery involved and so it doesn't really hurt." Not that he had ever tried it. "Look Tricia, you're still a good looking girl but, probably due to your difficult childhood, you have developed severe worry lines on your forehead, and botox would temporarily remove them," he reassured me.

"They say that if you have this procedure a number of times then there's a good chance you might altogether rid yourself of those deep frowns, and guess what, nobody will know you've had it done, you'll just look calmer and um… more relaxed, trust me". I was still skeptical.

"But you know full well I hate needles."

"Yes, but it can't be that painful, as everybody is getting it done these days, so at least think about it."

Despite feeling a little apprehensive I soon found myself agreeing, and so the week before Christmas I underwent the so called painless procedure. Looking back I am convinced the botox started its descent from my forehead about the same time the plane started it's descent down into Venice international airport, hence the flight attendant's unusual concern for my deteriorating appearance. Then the cold and dark long walk to the hotel must have made things worse, and my tired husband had failed to notice anything unusual. Now after a heavy night's sleep, the full impact was plainly visible for all to see. I was now holidaying in Venice looking like a one man freak show!

The hotel manager thought so too, for every time we dared venture downstairs, I could see him surreptitiously trailing us, hiding behind doors and in corners as, over the next couple of days, he kept a constant vigil over all our coming and goings. For my part I was forced into wearing dark shades at all times.

"Anyone would think we were criminals," I bitterly complained as looking behind me I saw Inspector Clueso quickly duck behind an internal pillar.

"Well try and see it from his point of view and understand that you do look a little bit suspect in those ridiculously huge sunglasses. Anyway, think on the bright side, maybe he thinks you're some big movie star trying to stay out of the limelight."

"Oh John this is all so unbearable," I continued to bleat

"Don't worry honey, I'm fairly certain I'm more the reason behind his concerns. It's highly likely he thinks I'm a wife beater, either that or we look like a dodgy Bonnie and Clyde partnership who might creep out of the hotel without settling up the balance of our stay."

"Well as long as he doesn't think to call the police. Oh this is all so ghastly and, worse still, we don't even speak the language," I whimpered.

By day two my upper eyelids were in very close communion with my lower ones as my lashes began to intimately intertwine and large bluish bruises began to blossom under both eyes. Eventually I agreed to a little bit of walking and sight seeing as our room was much too bleak to stay penned in all day, besides we needed some fresh air and exercise.

The weather remained at times sunny but bitterly cold and blustery so we clothed ourselves with as many of our skimpy summer clothes as possible. I had the upper hand here as John had resisted packing much except his precious reading material.

"I look perfectly ridiculous!" I exclaimed as I took one final look in the mirror.

"I don't think I look that great either," John commiserated. "But like I said, nobody knows us here, also the fresh air will be good for, and it will surely help heal your face."

The weather was well below zero and we were most alarmed to see that it was now beginning to snow. Despite my swollen eyes I could clearly see fierce-looking elderly women clad in their thick fur coats as they boldly stood unflinching on the decks of the small vessels and public ferries. Everything looked so strangely surreal that I felt as though I were in the middle of some Woody Allen movie.

By mid morning the wind was really beginning to pick up so John suggested that instead of walking back to the hotel we board a small vessel. I readily consented. Minutes later found us standing at the back of a long line of freezing cold passengers as we waited for the next boat to moor. We were just in the process of boarding the craft which, due to the high winds, was swaying back and forth, when John being a true gentleman did his usual thing of allowing me to go first.

Looking back I don't think there was anyway the accident could have been avoided. With my eyesight poorer than ever, coupled with the dark sunglasses, the thickly padded clothing and a boat that was now violently rocking to and fro I somehow managed to completely miss my footing and, in just a matter of seconds, I found myself hurling through the air at great speed. As I flew though the air like a basketball I distinctly heard John call out to me. I also tried to grab hold of someone in order to break my fall. It was not to be, for all passengers in front of me on hearing my spouse yell out instinctively moved to one side so I landed with an almighty thud. As I lay sprawled out on the open deck like a concussed sea cow, other concerned passengers moved quickly to help me to my feet, while another quick thinking man kindly fished my floating purse out of the canal before it sunk to the bottom of the ocean floor.

"Thank you thank you, I am most grateful," I stuttered as I took charge of my purse that was still draining itself of dirty canal water.

"Tricia are you alright?"

"Just about."

"Oh good, for you landed with such a hard thump I was sure you'd badly injured yourself."

"No no ..no I'm absolutely fine," I lied as I bent over to examine both my knees that were now very bloodied, whilst biting down hard on my lip as I began to experience the first searing pains from a twisted ankle.

"Honey, most people choose to take the Venetian water home in a bottle not their handbag," my husband annoyingly whispered as, back on both feet, he continued to support me.

"Oh great, this is going to put an end to any walking expeditions," I agonized. All this took place before the horrific realization that I was still minus my sunglasses. "Oh no!" was all I could mumble. I instinctively shielded my eyes because I quickly realized all the passengers on the deck were now staring at me. Seconds later, my glasses were kindly handed back to me, but not before all on deck had taken a long hard look at my hideously blown up face and swollen panda eyes.

"Yes I know I look like the Elephant Man but please stop gawking," I was screaming inside my dazed head, but, as I had no wish to become more of an idiot than I had already become, I could only force a sheepish weak smile while repeatedly muttering "Thank you, you've all been so kind to me."

"Don't worry, we'll find a place that sells bandages as soon as we disembark," John whispered in my free ear as he continued to steady me.

"I think I might need much more than just a bandage," I shakily replied as I choked back the tears. "Right now, all I want to do is curl up and die very quickly," I hissed as yet again I began feeling the full force of my humiliation and shame.

As the crowded boat headed down the claustrophobic winding canals there were plenty of sympathetic stares from small groups of deathly pale men with dark overcoats, feverishly smoking their Italian cigarettes, as well as from groups of burly-looking weather beaten women in shaggy fur coats and headscarves, the majority wearing painfully bright red lipstick. As most on board spoke Italian I was never privy to any of their conversations during that humiliatingly painful ride back to the hotel, but perhaps at the end of the day it was best kept that way.

Day three arrived early for me at around five am I leapt from the bed desperate to spend a penny. Shutting the door quietly behind me I hurriedly hobbled down the long and draughty corridor shivering all the way. When I arrived at my destination I was dismayed to discover that, despite the early hour, the one and only communal toilet was already occupied. Having no desire to return to my room I chose to stay put. I waited for a considerable length of time, my teeth chattering loudly as I continued to shiver and urgently hold on. As I continued to wait I became the sole witness to what sounded like the eruption of Vesuvius, otherwise a private orchestra consisting mainly of woodwind instruments having an early morning clandestine band practice.

I thought to make a few loud coughs in my bid to alert the person or persons on the other side of the door that I was inadvertently listening in on this impressively moving bowel recital extravaganza. But it was to no avail, for there was still much more to follow, first a lengthy stretch of short blasts from the trumpets, followed closely by the bassoon. Then came the higher sounds from the oboe before a simply glorious finale from an unspecified number of French horns. I was unable to applaud to show the full extent of my appreciation as, like a petulant child, I continued to clutch my extremities while swapping from one foot to another, willing with all my heart and soul for this this very lively recital to come to an abrupt end, as my need to pee was now getting most dire.

Finally, when on the verge of giving up all hope, there came the joyous heavenly sound of a flushing toilet bowl. I was now on the verge of irrepressible elation for in that momentous moment I believed that I only had to hang on for just a few more seconds to get my relief. Suddenly the bolt unlocked, the door sprung open, and I was now face to face with a close relative of Conan the Barbarian. This cumbersome heavily tattooed man struggled as he tried to squeeze his sumo wrestler proportions through the narrow doorway, and, with his timely release came the most disgracefully powerful offensive fumes that almost knocked me semi conscious, they were so pungent in their delivery. I gasped loudly almost reeling over. The bald barbarian with the oversized belly of an elephant expecting triplets, muttered away in some incomprehensible foreign language, as with no conscience whatsoever, he boldly strolled past me, towel flung casually over his shoulder as he stoically made his way towards the shower room.

I stood in a most perplexed state swaying backwards and forwards as I wondered what to do next. The stench was so unbearable as it most inconsiderately devoured all remaining fresh air, however, as I could ill afford to wait even a second longer for the air to clear, I was left with no alternative but to soldier on. I turned my head to one side, inhaled deeply then, pinching the end of my nose, I turned back round and hobbled as fast as I was able into the small smelly closet.

"I can do this," I privately encouraged myself as I pretended I was back in my teenage years, swimming the whole length of the swimming pool underwater. Standing directly in front of the toilet I peered down the bowl and was aghast to see it was completely blocked but I had no alternative other than to stay put, as my need for relief was now way beyond urgent. So with my one available free hand (the other still pinching my nose) I fumbled around as I attempted to loosen my dressing gown, but try as I may, I was unable to free the gown, or release my pajama bottoms whilst jumping up and down, my lungs considerably near bursting point. This was all so insane.

In that terrible moment, I felt I had little choice open to me other than to abandon my mission. So, after turning round to unbolt the door, I hobbled back down the corridor, doubled over and gasping for fresh air. . I was determined to keep going until I reached a place in the corridor where I believed the air would once more be pure and thus sweet. Back in my room, with the door shut firmly behind me I exhaled loudly before slowly slithering down the back of the door heading for the rough wooden floor.

"Pst…John are you awake?" I cried out.

"I am now," he groaned, his bristly face reluctantly surfacing from under the bedclothes. "Goodness Tricia, it's only five twenty in the morning, so what's the problem?"

"John do me a huge favor, don't ask questions, just toss my can of deodorant over this way."

"What…why?"

"Just do it," I despairingly shrieked, my eyes blazing like a deranged madman. I hurriedly pulled myself up from the floor to continue jumping up and down. He quickly got the picture.

"Okay okay," he replied as he sat bolt upright in the bed. He sensed it would be unwise to question me further.

"It's for fumigation purposes, so just chuck it over will you," I begged.

"Here catch," he shouted before disappearing back under the bedclothes.

Clutching the deodorant can in my hand I staggered back down the corridor as fast as I was able, but, as I neared my destination the unexpected happened, for to my absolute horror another hotel guest zipped past me into the one and only toilet. I was now officially delirious and therefore extremely close to becoming Italy's latest crazed homicidal maniac. I turned on my heels and hobbled back to the bedroom and, after closing the door, I threw the can of deodorant onto the bed and then grabbed the nearest available water glass, chucking the contents, which happened to be a tube of toothpaste and toothbrushes, into the cracked basin.

"Forgive me John, but I've no other choice," I gasped as I crouched down to pee into the glass receptacle. "It's at times like this that I wish I was a man," I groaned.

John, out of morbid curiosity chose that moment to resurface from under the covers, a confused look written all over his face.

"Don't even ask," I mumbled as finally I began to experience wondrous relief.

"I expect you'll be needing more than one glass," he teased, throwing back the bedclothes and grabbing his empty glass from the bedside table. I chose to ignore this latest most unhelpful comment, but he wasn't finished.

"After this I don't think I'll ever want to drink water from a glass tumbler in a hotel room," he mischievously mused.

"Funny ha ha.."

"Well concentrate! And do your utmost to aim into the glass," he sniffed raising a disturbed eyebrow. "Oh and try not to overfill it!" he cautioned as he handed me down his empty glass.

"John, please shut it! For, since having kids, I've done more urine specimens than you've had hot dinners, and I might add into containers a mere tenth of this size," I curtly announced.

"My, aren't you a clever girl."

"Go away, for your trite comments are making me more nervous."

"Well crouching tiger, I have to say you almost look ready for an advanced yoga class," he bent down to teasingly whisper in my ear before heading back to the bed.

Despite my ongoing disturbing facial crisis, I still managed to be captivated by the sheer beauty of Venice, with its narrow waterways, cocooned by high exquisitely colorful but ravaged buildings, that appeared as though they were hand painted on a silk canvass by some famous artist. I also found time to stop and smile as I observed the handsomely beguiling gondoliers in their large hats standing attentively by a large flotilla of Gondolas, as they waited and prayed for the chance to give some pretty female tourist a most private guided tour of the narrow intricate waterways. And I could only marvel as I stood captivated by the magnificent Grand Basilica and tower in St Marks Square, while drinking in the visually stunning Italian architecture, but that said, having already experienced two full days of days Venice in mid winter, it was indeed more than enough for me!

Our eyes may have enjoyed the extravagant feast of color and magnificence, but sadly our stomachs experienced something of a famine when it came to dining out. We certainly had not banked on Venice being so unbelievably expensive. The restaurant prices verged on extortionate, and so we were forced to stick to the 'Tourist Menu,' something that in hindsight we should not have done, for in doing so we never feasted on anything remotely sumptuous. The food on this specialized menu could only be described as bland, if not unpalatable, and the portions, well they were so disgracefully minute in size it left us wishing we had settled for Giovanni's local pizza delivery service!

On day three we met a delightful young couple who gushed about everything, including their extremely palatial hotel situated on the promenade right by the sea, to the wonderful food being served up everyday that came as part of the package deal. Yes it was indeed the usual story, completed only by the inevitable realization that this dear couple had forked out considerably less than us. On hearing this, I once more felt very deflated, for, in taking up an offer that included both flight and hotel that had been advertised in a more up-market newspaper, they truly had found themselves the deal of a lifetime. The upside of this unplanned rendezvous was it made us more determined than ever to abandon all further sight-seeing until we had found ourselves a much nicer hotel.

Later that day we were elated to discover a family hotel that had an unoccupied room with that highly desirable essential that we had been longing for, no not a television or a swimming pool, but rather a bathroom-en-suite, and we were further pleased to discover it cost less per night than where we were presently staying. So, after booking in, we made our way back to our former hotel to hastily pack up our personal belongings, and settle up. Happily our very suspicious Inspector Clueso was off on an lunch break, so was not available to check the validity of our credit card, otherwise scrutinize our new Euro bank notes to ensure that the print did not come off on his hands. He was equally unavailable to snap our photo for some future episode of 'Crime Line', England's equivalent to 'America's Most Wanted'.

CHAPTER TWENTY FIVE

More Death in Venice

On our last night in Venice we walked for an eternity around the San Marco district as we tried to find a restaurant with an romantic ambience that was reasonably priced. Sadly it was not to be, for having thought we had found just such a place, we were yet again to be very disappointed. Once more we were deceived by the blackboard with its Tourist Menu and when at the end of a very small and most unsatisfying meal we were handed an exorbitant bill we were visually shocked. My husband even felt moved to adjust his reading glasses more than once as he scrutinized the hefty bill, and, even with the waiters help, we still had no idea as to why they were asking so much. That night I felt more than ready for a fight, but John was quick to remind me that I already looked as though I had been in one and lost! We therefore decided to just pay up quickly and leave.

"John, I definitely think we should write a stiff letter of complaint to the Tourist Board concerning that unscrupulous restaurant owner," I ranted as with a heavy heart I hobbled down the street alongside him.

"Well, if you decide to do that, you'd better hope he doesn't have any Mafia connections," my husband muttered. I knew this was his way of saying, "Leave it."

The next morning we were up with the larks as it was indeed time to head home. I was chuffed to discover that most of the puffiness as well as the bruising had virtually disappeared, so my face and eyes were almost back to normal. Down at reception we were further pleased to discover that we had just the right the right amount of cash to pay this latest hotel bill, with just enough left Pesos over to pay for the taxi to the Marco Polo airport.

We paid the taxi driver his due, plus a fair tip, and, with happy hearts but empty wallets, we headed into the airport. Remarkably no sooner had we arrived at the airport than the sun and some heat decided it was finally time to make their belated appearance, if only to wave us off.

Once in the airport we had little idea where to head, and so we found ourselves some seats from which we could monitor the board of outward bound flights. Having made ourselves as comfortable we waited and waited some more. Eventually I began to feel the faint stirrings of anxiety welling up inside me.

"John something feels wrong."

"Oh don't be silly, you're such a worrier."

"No something definitely isn't right! Look, we've been here for nearly an hour and there isn't even any mention of our flight on the board!"

"Stay put, and I'll go and find someone who can help us," he calmly suggested. Minutes later saw him racing back towards me, a look of extreme panic written all over his face.

"Tricia, I can hardly believe it, but we're actually at the wrong airport," he cried.

"Don't be daft, for this is where we flew into," I cried as the onset of hysteria began to threaten to take over.

"Yes but remember we're not going home with British Airways, and apparently the budget airlines fly out of an entirely different airport."

"Oh, this is bad," I cried.

"Yes I've just been told that the other airport is some thirty odd miles away. So quick, grab a suitcase and we need to go as fast as we can to the taxi terminal."

By the time we reached the outside of the terminal the sun was now in its full peak of glory as it blazed like a red hot iron on the back of our necks until we both were perspiring profusely. Wiping his dripping forehead John raced over to a taxi driver and requested that he take us to the other airport. The taxi driver didn't move an inch as he asked to see our money. John, knowing we had absolutely none left, produced a credit card. The poker faced taxi driver shook his head and in broken English said "No credeet card sir."

"But this is all I have," he cried.

"No sir, once more I say, no credeet card."

John begged and pleaded but it was useless. He ran to the next driver, but he was equally adamant. "No monee....no taxee." He tried a few more taxi drivers but it proved just as fruitless for their response was always the same. They all wanted cash and we had just emptied our pockets of all cash as we settled up our hotel bill. John gave up and raced back over to me.

"Tricia, I've just been told there's a bank inside the airport. So stay and stand guard over our luggage while I go off to find the bank," he breathlessly insisted.

"John please don't leave me," I wailed.

"Look honey, you need to stay here and guard our luggage."

"But can't I come with you?" I anxiously begged.

"No it will take much longer if we have to drag our luggage back through the airport and we can't leave the baggage unattended for since 9-11 everyone is so nervous that it's highly likely our luggage will fall foul of the Italian bomb squad."

Put that way I realized I had no choice than to stay and dutifully stand guard over our property.

In a short space of time I began experiencing very troubling palpations, and sweat began to run down my back and forehead. Minutes later and I was now struggling to hold back the tears as well as keep all troubling thoughts at bay, for the fear of being stranded in Italy was now beginning to grip me. All too soon my eyes began stinging as my sweat began to mix with my mascara before seeping into my eyes that as of yet hadn't entirely recovered from the previous ordeal. As I stood alone whilst becoming more frantic by the minute, I foolishly began to rub my stinging eyes, remaining blissfully unaware that I was now smudging my mascara all over my face. It wouldn't be too long before I once more had large panda eyes.

When John finally reappeared I could see by his troubled face that we were still in hot water.

"The bank does not open for another fifteen minutes so I have no idea what to do next," he said heaving an almighty sigh. "Also I know this isn't a good time to mention it, but your face is covered in black."

"Oh dear, and I've no time to go to the washroom," I cried out in exasperation.

"Do you have a hand mirror?" he sniffed.

"Yes but, as it's made of glass, I wrapped it round in a pair of your underpants and then stowed it somewhere near the bottom of your suitcase."

"Well that's it then, for you're not going to upend my suitcase to rummage around looking for the jolly mirror."

"Oh, this is all so terrible," I wailed.

"Stay put, for I have another idea!" he ordered.

Leaving me again he raced up to a couple of total strangers to ask for their help. After explaining the crisis, he then offered to write them a check for double the amount we were asking, using our passports to prove that we were genuine, if only they would help us. Of course they only looked fearful and then declined, as did the next couple, and the next.

"There's nothing else for it, I've got to go and stand in line, for the bank is our only hope, and it opens in just over ten minutes. So honey, you need to stay put and I'll be back as soon as I can." Looking down at my wristwatch I shook my head in utter despair. "John this is hopeless, you've got to hurry, for time is really running out," I cried out as I watched him yet again race back into the terminal.

The next ten minutes passed and quite frankly it felt more like ten hours as I struggled to resist the onset of hysteria that was rapidly consuming all traces of any maturity I may have previously achieved. Another fifteen anxious minutes passed before he re-appeared. The distress on his distorted face was apparent.

"Give me the passports," he yelled as he raced up towards me. "I immediately threw a case to the floor to then hastily begin unzipping a small side compartment as I frantically searched through a pile of documentation.

"Quick hand them over," he demanded, a strong sense of urgency betraying something of his anxiety.

"The line is now very long and I've just lost my place, for they refused to assist me without proof of identity."

"Oh crumbs, can this get any worse?" I cried. What a stupid question for of course they could! I watched on as he raced back into the airport. Ten minutes later and still there was no sign of him. By now I was feeling even more emotionally unbalanced. I could no longer just stand there doing nothing so I rushed over to a group of taxi drivers that were aimlessly standing around chatting while drawing on their cigarettes. I don't know quite what I was thinking but I pulled off my gold bracelet and neck chain and, in meticulously slow English tinged by a crazy accent that I hoped might help them understand me better, I tried in vain to solicit their help. Even with my jewelry being thrust into their faces they remained unmoved, albeit a little amused. By now I was once more crying and pleading pitifully as they turned to give each other the sort of looks that roughly translated would suggest they considered me to be quite mad. In sheer desperation I fell to my knees on the tarmac as I continued on with my heart rending supplication, but to no avail.

"Please, you don't understand for, if I miss this plane, my young children will have nobody to take care of them."

Still they remained stoic as with grinning faces they rather nonchalantly stood around as if they had all the time in the world, blowing impressively large smoke rings into the air, while occasionally dropping their heads to look back down at me as though I was some squirming vile insect that needed to be trampled underfoot. Suddenly I heard footsteps behind me and then the familiar sound of my husband's voice.

"Tricia, for goodness sake get up from the ground for you're making an absolute spectacle of yourself," he shouted as he grabbed my arm and forced me to my feet.

"I don't care," I shrieked in his ear as he turned to address the group of taxi drivers.

"Look, I've got the money, so now can we go?" he triumphantly shouted as he waved a fistful of notes in front of the cab driver's noses.

Minutes later and we were finally on our way.

"Please hurry up," he constantly begged the taxi driver.

"Sir, I am doing my veree best," came the response from the concerned taxi driver as he sped full throttle down the motorway.

"Look, you need to go faster, for we're about to miss our plane," John repeated as he lent forward to speak directly into the taxi driver's seemingly deaf ear. "If you will go faster then you can have all the money I have," he promised out of sheer desperation.

Finally we arrived at the little airport. After frantically helping the poor taxi driver with off loading our suitcases to save a few extra seconds, John thrust the bundle of notes into his grubby little outstretched hand and, without turning back, we grabbed hold of the suitcases and raced at full pelt towards the terminal. I was shocked to discover that little ride cost us over a hundred pounds.

"John, there's no way they will allow us to board the plane, for in the wake of 9-11 we have to be checked in at least an hour before take off," I gasped as I struggled to drag our suitcases along.

"Well let's just hope for the best, shall we?"

We charged towards the check out desk like a couple of raging bulls, fuelled up and ready for anything, we were that desperate to be allowed past the Customs men and through to the Boarding Gate. I believe that just turning up looking like Alice Cooper was more than enough to convince all behind the desk that it would be most wise to let us through without any lengthy and official confrontation. With passports and papers checked and stamped we were formally escorted through into the boarding area to then stand impassively at the end of the second long line of the day as everyone waited impatiently to board the delayed plane.

"I hate to say this Tricia but you look like an unhinged Freddie Kruger ready to go on a demonical rampage, so you need to go and tidy yourself up."

"John, thanks a bunch, but I'm not about to risk missing the plane, not after what we've just been through," I hissed back.

"Look, the bathroom is just over there, so go as quickly as you can and I promise I won't let this plane take off without you on board."

"Promise?"

"Would I dare let you down now?" he queried as he gave my hand a tight sympathetic squeeze.

I made a quick dash for the washroom and having caught sight of myself in the mirror I instantly realized just how terrifying I looked. There would be no time for reapplying make up. I just gave my face a thorough scrub and pulled down on my fuzzed and bedraggled hair then, with the greatest sense of relief, I raced back to join my husband at the end of the line.

Now as the airline in question had a policy of 'first come first served', a most undignified scrap then ensued as passengers raced and fought each other in order to get the best seats on the plane. Being the last in the line we were not even able to sit anywhere near one another. Not that it mattered, for as I lay back in my seat and considered the mornings most difficult and intense negotiations I knew the angels had chosen to smile on him and thus spare him the inevitable 'flea in the ear', for I was still pretty upset with him. The only remaining anxiety in the forefront of my intricate little mind was, what would happen if the plane went down? I mean, would the search party or forensic team ever connect the two of us as being joined at the hip when he was sitting the other end of the plane from me. As I sat back in my seat and closed my eyes my sense of despair was only alleviated as I envisaged meeting up with my sorely missed children. In no time at all the flight attendants were bustling their overloaded trolley down the aisle laden with a selection of snacks and overly expensive sandwiches. They stopped every once in a while to loudly announce "Ladies and gentleman, may we have your attention. Please have the exact money for all your transactions as we are unable to give change. Unfortunately at present we are also unable to take credit cards."

The trolley finally came to a halt near to where I was seated. The gentleman sitting next to me looked up and flashed a smile at the pretty flight attendant who was serving our side of the aisle..

"Sir, are you interested in purchasing any refreshments?" the cute hostess asked, managing a perfect pouting smile. The gentleman wasted no time in placing his extensive list of requirements.

"Thank you, I'll have a coffee, and hmm… one of those beef and tomato sandwiches, a bag of salt and vinegar chips, a piece of that cherry cake and a bar of Cadbury's Fruit and Nut….oh no wait, make that two bars. Thank you very much," he said as he reached into his back pocket in search of his wallet.

"That will be twenty three pounds and twenty five pence sir."

"Oh, you'd best keep the change as I've only got twenties and fives on me," he replied, breaking into a warm smile as he handed over the money.

"Oh no ..no … no, don't give her your change…give it to me! She might be more beautiful but this is not a "Beauty and the beast' pageant, this is real life and I need it more. So come on hand it over now!" were the anguished deranged cries thrashing around in my mind as I desperately watched on as he removed the crisp notes from his thick wallet.

I now had to restrain myself from just lashing out to grab myself a fiver or two from his disgustingly loaded wallet.

"Thank you sir," she smiled down at him as she took hold of the notes and then placed the money in a small cash tin. With his tray now loaded up with an assortment of 'bad for your health' goodies she then turned her attention on me.

"And you madam, can I get you anything to eat or drink?" she asked giving me a wide thoroughly rehearsed smile that showed off her perfect teeth.

"No thank you …although is there any chance of a glass of water?

"Certainly madam and that will be one pound and twenty pence."

"Oh well then, never mind" I quietly mumbled as I once again struggled with the realization that in this desperate moment I was little more than a penniless pauper! I was left both famished and wallowing in deep self pity.

"Oh give me British Airways any day of the week," I quietly groaned as I wondered what delightful hot meal I would at this very minute be tucking into if only we had been flying home with them.

Instead here I was enviously watching on as the unassuming stranger sitting beside me quietly ploughed his merry way through his own personal mountain of food, remaining so preoccupied in reading his business notes he had not the slightest inkling that sitting right beside him was a very hungry bi polar paranoid schitzo, who for the present was choosing to implode rather than explode as she had neither eaten nor drunk anything for well over twenty four hours! Oh boy, things could well have turned nasty as I was forced to control the irresistible urge to just go ahead and reach over to grab his sandwich from out his sweaty little hand to quickly devour it before he had any time to react. Failing that maybe I could earnestly entreat him to show me compassion by passing me his leftover crusts, surely he could not refuse such a request, especially if I was to burst into tears and give him a blow by blow account of all I had been forced to endure these past few days. If not the sandwich, then could I just have a teeny bite of his chocolate bar, for if he were to be scrupulously honest with himself, he really was rather glutinous in purchasing not one bar but two. What would his dear mother think if she could see him now? Happily for him I kept all deranged thoughts and urges to myself, but still it left me feeling as mad as a hornet with my other half who wisely remained well out of my reach for the entire journey back to London.

The plane landed intact on the ground at Luton Airport instead of the more familiar Gatwick and I finally met up with my heavily repentant spouse as we disembarked. We then went through all the familiar stuff such as Customs and Baggage Reclaim before deciding to do a quick detour into an Airport shop to get a bite to eat!

"Good grief Tricia, you look as though you're bulk buying for Tesco!" he loudly expressed.

"Well guess what… I'm starving!"

"Yes but this lot will cost a small fortune."

"So ….who's counting?"

"Well I still think you need to put some back, for we'll be home before you know it. Anyway, what have you chosen for me?"

"This," I replied as I dug deep and pulled out a sandwich.

"Only a cheese and pickle sandwich?"

"Well you can have these crisps as well if you like?"

"Oh right so pretty much everything else in the basket is for your consumption alone?"

"Correct.'

"Well, I still think you should put some back then."

"No chance, besides some of these sweets and chocolate are for the kids when we get home."

"Oh right," he sighed as he produced a credit card from his ultra thin leather wallet, to hand to the cashier.

The journey home seemed a little tense to me and if I'm perfectly honest I couldn't put it all down to my back seat binging session as I munched through one bar of chocolate after another. No, this sense of uneasiness had nothing whatsoever to do with food. John had arranged for one of his employees to pick us up from the airport which in some ways was a relief as it spared us the usual 'Spot the car,' crisis. The ride home still managed to take forever as we weaved our way through a number of tight spots and bad traffic jams. After temporarily satisfying my obsessive compulsive eating disorder to the point where I now felt overloaded and distinctly uncomfortable I sat back with my eyes closed as I pretended to take very little interest in their conversation.

"How have things been in my absence?" my husband took it upon himself to ask concerning the business. It was indeed the wrong time for such a question.

"Well you must have under quoted Friday's job for it took us two whole days to pack up the whole house, yeah so we had to finish the rest of the job over the weekend."

"Two days? Weekend? How come?" John dared ask as he came to the quick realization that he would be considerably out of pocket after paying the men's wages.

"Well part of the problem was that we were down to just two men for most of the Friday afternoon."

"What! Did Charlie not turn up to work?"

"Oh no he turned up alright. But he then abandoned the removal to go off to the dentist."

"Oh no I don't believe I'm hearing this!" my husband muttered.

"Yes well when the customer discovered the real reason he'd left the job had nothing to do with tooth ache and more to do with getting his teeth polished he was livid."

"Goodness how perfectly ridiculous!"

"Yeah you're telling me! Anyway the customer wants to talk with you before he settles up, he is that upset."

I continued to keep my eyes firmly closed as our chauffeur happily went on to give a blow by blow account of how each job had panned out without my husband around to supervise. I have to say he kept my full attention right up until he came to a halt outside our house.

"Well, don't even think to blame me coz it's not my fault, the new bloke definitely told us he was an experienced driver so we let him have a go and before we could say 'Bob's your uncle' he accidentally drove the lorry into the side of a large skip. You'll see for yourself there's a lot of damage to one side."

"Good grief."

"Yeah and that's why we've nicknamed the new boy Skippy… get it?" he chuckled giving a big lop sided grin.

Oh we got it alright! I couldn't speak for John but listening to him trivializing this costly accident made me want to choke the very life out of him, especially as the repairs were likely to run into the thousands.

"Cheer up, for at least we've made it home in one piece," I whispered in his ear as we dragged our luggage towards the front door. Once inside we were greeted by our precious children and, in that small moment in time, all felt well. We thanked Grandma and gave her a gift before attempting to send her on her way, but she refused to budge an inch until we had been forced to hear her vast array of events that had taken place in our absence, laboring particularly on the one story about how Reuben had nearly died! I was so astounded I could hardly think what to say next, especially when I heard she had forced a top physician from the local hospital to come out to the house on a home visit. I could bear to hear no more. I would later hear from a concerned friend that he'd only suffered a dose of the flu. Later that same evening with grandma safely deposited back at her own house I went to feed our goldfish only to discover that the bowl was empty of all water and that our one and only pet had vanished into thin air.

Feeling somewhat upset by this newly discovered revelation I marched into the sitting room and switched off the television.

"Right my little cherubs, now that I have your undivided attention, has anybody anything they'd like to get off their chest?"

The room went deadly quiet and one by one they gave me their best completely vacant looks as they shook their little heads in unison.

"Well I'm still waiting?" Still nothing. Suddenly Reuben decided to act as spokesman.

"Mummy we know nothing about anything, so please be nice and switch the television back on."

"Not until I've had an answer to my question."

"But we don't know what you mean?"

"Oh but I think you do."

"No we don't."

"Right then perhaps it would help if I gave you a little clue. It starts with a f and it swims around in a bowl. Now does that help?" It was at that precise moment that my young daughter burst into tears.

"Oh mummy, please don't punish the others, for it's all my fault. It was me who killed the goldfish," she tearfully confessed as she placed a protective arm around Reuben's shoulder. "I wanted to be a help while you were gone, really I did, so when I noticed that the water in his bowl looked very murky I thought I would help out. As I pressed my nose to the glass I could hardly see him swimming around anymore because the water was so blurry, so I decided to clean out his dirty bowl," she cried, enormous tears now racing down her tightly screwed up little face.

"Go on honey."

"Well I must have squirted too much washing up liquid into the glass bowl coz I couldn't get rid of all those stupid soapy bubbles. Like magic they just kept appearing," she woefully explained, her whole body shuddering as she continued to excessively sob her little heart out. "Anyway, when the bubbles wouldn't stop coming I decided to rinse out the bowl with some bleach and it helped an awful lot coz the bubbles all went pop.. pop and then disappeared."

"Here honey, take this tissue and blow your nose."

"Well I carefully refilled the bowl with water before I put him back in, but then I remembered that I must feed him as there was now no food in the bowl. But as I was sprinkling the fish food the top accidentally fell off and in seconds the water was completely covered with millions of tiny specs." By this point in the story she was once more thoroughly inconsolable as yet again she began to bawl her eyes out. I bent down to put a reassuring arm around her shoulder.

"It's alright honey, really it is." But our young daughter was still not quite finished with her highly emotional and very tragic confession.

"Oh mummy, I tried to scoop some out, really I did, and then I just hoped if he wasn't too greedy then everything would be alright. But it wasn't," she continued to sob. "When I came downstairs the next morning the poor little thing was floating on the top of the water. I even took a lemonade straw and began to blow into its tiny fins in case that would do the trick, but it didn't really work coz even though I blew with all my might he was still very, well just very dead," she spluttered.

"Alright sweetie, come on, let me give you a big hug."

"Oh mummy, I'm so sorry," she cried as she instantly wrapped her small arms around me.

"Well Antonia darling, I hope you don't mind me asking, but what has become of our poor goldfish now that he's dead?" Then came a long silence.

"Uh…. I flushed him down the toilet," she gulped.

"What, down the toilet? Oh Antonia, how could you do such a thing! For we never dispose of God's special creatures in such a thoughtless manner."

"I'm so…so…sorry mummy."

"Yes yes dear, but please never think to do such a thing again, for we always give family pets a decent burial," I announced most determinedly, as I thought back to recent events when the children had come home from the beach bearing a large seagull that had suffered a broken wing. Sadly it was well into the weekend so the automated voice informed us that the bird sanctuary would not be reopening its doors until 9.00 am. on Monday morning.

"Mummy the poor thing can't wait until Monday. It needs our help now," the children pitifully cried.

"Right, Reuben go and find me a large box and Antonia you go and get me a saucer of milk."

"Okay mummy, but does he drink milk?"

"I've no idea, but we'll give it a go."

And so it was that that the ailing bird was gently wrapped in a snuggly blanket and placed in a box along with a saucer of milk. I then went in search of an old tape of Jonathan Livingston Seagull. I'd been given this tape years previously so I felt pleased to find it without too much difficulty. I played the tape over and over throughout the night as I cuddled up to the creature to give it extra love and comfort for I felt compelled to let it know that, if these were to be his last precious hours on this earth, he was not going to be spending them alone.

The next morning the children were all up unusually early as they wished to know the fate of poor seagull.

"I don't think he's breathing anymore," Reuben my eldest son solemnly whispered to the other two as standing in their pajamas they stood in a circle peering down at me.

"Children he now has a name. He's called Jonathan, after this music tape."

"Yes mummy, but we're pretty sure he's very dead," Antonia felt brave enough to loudly suggest. I wasn't listening as I continued to sit cross legged on the kitchen floor cuddling the poor darling bird to my chest. The children put their heads together as they truly wondered what to do next.

"We'd better let daddy know that the bird, I mean Jonathan, is dead," Antonia wisely whispered.

"Yes but daddy worked 'til late and so he's still asleep," Reuben interjected.

"I know, but this is serious, so he really needs to know."

"Well, let's all go and wake him up then," Rueben said shrugging his shoulders and raising his eyes to the ceiling as if to say 'and the day has only just started.' Moments later and the children returned to the kitchen only this time they were not alone.

"Tricia honey, let go of the bird," John said in a very gentle but determined tone of voice as he crouched down beside me.

"No I'm staying with it."

"Come on honey, give me the bird."

"Absolutely not, and by the way his name is Jonathan."

"Alright but Jonathan is clearly very dead and it's also extremely evident that Riga Mortis set in some time ago, and that's why his body is now stiffer than a Florida surf board. So, unless you're planning to serve him up for Christmas dinner, you'd best let me take him from you," he suggested as he reached over to gently prize the dead bird out from my maternally grieving arms.

Moments later, after digging a plot in the garden, we laid the seagull to rest, covering him over before placing a little cross made up from twigs. We then stood for a moments silence before saying the obligatory funeral prayer, and yes if I'd had a trumpet at my disposal I would have blown it! So here this day, as my young daughter stood on trial for flushing the family goldfish down the loo, I felt strangely sad that, unlike Jonathan, this unfortunate little 'Nemo' had been completely deprived of a decent and honorable burial service.

Later that night as I lay staring into the darkness, all memories of our tragic holiday were brushed to one side as yet again I gave serious thought to the goldfish incident, and, try as I may, I couldn't rid myself of the deeply distressing image of our defenseless goldfish being unceremoniously dumped into the toilet bowl to tragically be flushed away into the vast ocean.

"What's wrong now?" my husband sympathetically enquired as he climbed in beside me.

"Oh nothing," I sniffed as I pulled the bed sheet up to my chin.

"Oh yes there is. And I know for sure I won't be getting any sleep until I've got to the bottom of it," he said as he rolled over to give me a comforting cuddle.

"Look I know the holiday didn't go as planned but at least we're home safely and all three kids are still alive to live another day," he whispered in my ear. "So come on, what else is bothering you?"

"Alright then, I never want to go on another holiday ever again," I blurted out.

"After all we've been through in Venice, to come home to the news that Reuben almost died."

"Come on Tricia he only had a touch of flu!" John quickly interjected.

"Yes well… and as for Antonia killing our pet goldfish and then flushing it down the loo, just think what else could have taken place if instead of four measly days we had taken the whole two weeks!"

"One cannot even begin to imagine," came John's very depleted response.

"And to die from too much exposure to bleach and soap bubbles. Did you know that washing up liquid is considered to be highly carcinogenic?" I continued to blubber.

"Come on honey, after all he was only a tiddly little two and a half inch squirt."

"John, I am well aware he wasn't Moby Dick but.."

"I've got to stop you. It was just an accident, so don't make her pay for it anymore than she already has," he sharply retorted.

"John I fully understand you're just a man, and so I can just about forgive you for that, but what I find harder to forgive is you attempting to minimize and trivialize the poor thing's untimely death, for to me that is utterly indefensible."

"Look, I'm not trying to trivialize anything. Tell you what, if it will make you happy, we'll get another goldfish as soon as you say so," he said cuddling up to then give me another friendly squeeze. "In fact, let's go the whole hog and get ourselves a large light up aquarium and fill it full of hundreds of little fishys!"

"Now I know you're being facetious."

"Okay. I'm sorry, it's just that it's been an extraordinarily difficult homecoming, and for some inexplicable reason it appears that it's still nowhere near over, even though it's past midnight, and I have to get up for work tomorrow!"

"Well, if you cared to let me finish, this poor defenseless little thing was entrusted to our care and nurture, and I hate to say this, but we failed him terribly."

"Look I'm not prepared to continue on with this disturbingly daft conversation a moment longer," my restless husband huffed and puffed, as he threw even more effort into pumping up his pillow. "Let's just try and get some sleep, for tomorrow there will be far more urgent things to deal with, mainly that of a very damaged van along with a troublesome new employee who now happily answers to the nickname Skippy!"

CHAPTER TWENTY SIX

Mummy, It's Getting Rather Hot in Here.

"**H**oney, I hope you don't mind but I took the liberty of booking us a long weekend in Belgium."

"What?"

"Yes, would you believe it but our daily paper are running a very special offer, that's as cheap as chips, so we can have a three day break in Belgium at a Center Parc for ninety nine pounds for the whole family, including our car on the ferry, oh plus insurance."

"Really? There's got to be some catch," I mused.

"No there isn't. Come on, say yes, for what have you got to lose?"

"Well John, as a rule, these special offers normally attract some pretty rough types, don't they?"

"Well, if you are referring to young lads who take these trips just to get sozzled on cheap foreign beer, then you might be right."

"John, they're not called larger louts for nothing."

"Tricia more and more you're beginning top sound like Mrs... Oh what's her name from 'Keeping up appearances'?"

"You mean Mrs. Bouquet?"

"Yes, Mrs. Bucket."

"I'm nothing like her!"

"Oh you're more like her than you know, so stop being such a ridiculous snob."

"I'm not, it's the truth. Do you really want to be on a ferry overrun by hundreds of bawdy 'sloshed out of their brains' youngsters puking up all around you."

"My Tricia, you do have such a way with words!"

"I'll take that as a compliment. Anyway, you'd do well to remember the Zebrugge ferry disaster."

"What's that got to do with anything?"

"John, you were on that exact Ferry with a truck heading for Belgium just a week before that awful disaster."

"Tricia honey, that tragedy took place many years ago."

"John, it's entirely irrelevant that the terrible tragedy took place over six years ago, for all such incidents deeply affect me."

"Goodness, you're such a sensitive soul."

"Sensitive? John, hundreds of people died that tragic night in Zebrugge when the Herald of Free Enterprise keeled over, and I still think of just how awful it must have been for those stuck inside unable to find an exit and swim to freedom."

"Look I know it was bad."

"So many lost loved ones, and the worst to suffer were your fellow truck drivers, whose sleeping quarters are always in the bowels of the ship. They had little to no chance of getting out alive, and that could so easily have been you."

"Yes well it's possible that if you hadn't insisted on watching every news channel and documentary produced in the weeks and months that followed, then maybe your head wouldn't be so tangled up, then maybe you'd feel no need to even mention it."

"Oh that's ridiculous. I'll have you remember it was so close to home, why even our neighbors lost someone they knew."

"Your point?"

"Well, what if it were to happen again?"

"Look, you've always wanted to take the children to one of these parks and this way we get a three night stay in Belgium."

"Yes John, but may I be so bold as to remind you, it is mid winter, so perhaps that's why it's as cheap as chips."

"Come on Tricia, let's just do it."

And so it was that I found myself bundling my three young children into the back of our car along with baby seat for my youngest two year old to sit in. Then there was all our luggage, bedding and other provisions we required, oh as well as all four bikes that needed to be strapped to the back.

"Tricia, we're only leaving the country for three days so if you can get all this into the car then you deserve some sort of official award, for there's no way we can take all this stuff with us."

"Look John, I've had to pack food as well as clothes, and we also have to bring all our bedding," I responded as I informed my three young ones that, due to lack of space, they would have to ride with their bedding and pillows tucked in all around them as well as on top of them! Finally we were ready to go and after placing my seatbelt around me I turned to smile at my three children feeling slightly alarmed that I could only just see their perky little faces appearing over the duvets.

"Kids, if it gets too hot and uncomfortable, you need to tell me," I called over.

Half way down the motorway and I was already feeling troubled.

"John, I'm not sure I turned off the iron," I anxiously sighed. "And did you remember to remove all the wall plugs from their sockets, as well as double lock the front door?"

"Hmm, I'm pretty sure I did."

"Well, you were the last one out, so you either locked the front door or you didn't."

"Hmm um.. yes, I must have done."

"You don't sound too convinced, so we'd best head back home just incase."

"No, that's not happening," he assertively cried out. "We've driven too far down the motorway, so no way am I heading back, besides we'll miss the boat if we do. Come on trust me, everything will be fine."

"Oh I've heard that one before."

Before too long we arrived at the docks at Dover. I felt strangely nervous as the cumbersome bearded ferry man dressed in his bright orange waterproofs used large hand signals to beckon us forward onto what felt like a very unstable narrow stretch of steel ramp as we made our way onto the ship.

"John please be extra careful," I cried, my anxiety levels reaching new unexpected heights. "By the way did you read that terrible story that was in the paper last week about an elderly couple who accidentally drove their car off the ramp and into the sea when they were driving onto the Ferry?"

"Yes I did. In fact I saw a picture of the car being pulled from the water by a large crane."

"I can't even begin to imagine the terror those poor darlings went through. Perhaps they should make the ramp sufficiently wide so as to prevent anyone else from enduring such an unpleasant ordeal."

"By anybody I presume you're really referring to us."

"Well yes and no, for while I'm concerned for others, all the same I need you to be extra careful for I'm not too sure I'd ever fully recover from something so terrible."

"Will you ever get to trust anybody?"

"What exactly are you implying?"

"Well I'm forever driving huge trucks onto ferries, and as far as I'm aware I've never toppled into the sea below, so you'd have thought that little insignificant fact would go a long way towards reassuring you."

"Well it can still happen to the very best of us, can't it?"

"I think it best we stop this conversation right now," John mumbled.

With our car parked and our children safely extracted from under the thick pile of bedding we weaved our way through a long maize of parked cars trying hard not to breathe in the offensively strong diesel fumes as we searched for the stairs that would take us up into the main area.

The lounge was rapidly filling up with holiday makers therefore we were only able to find a couple of seats, so John suggested that he take the two elder children to the cafeteria for something to eat.

"Tricia, you stay and save these seats and when I return, you can take James and go for something to eat."

"No no no… You're going nowhere," I cried. "We must stay together at all times."

"Streuth! What is your problem?" he cried. My immediate answer was to shrug my shoulders.

"Are you afraid we might get lost in the crowd?"

"John, I don't want us to be separated, in case anything bad should happen."

"Tricia, you seriously need help, for what you're suggesting is downright daft. These ships go back and forth hundreds of times a day without capsizing otherwise anything else untoward happening."

"John, if you'd ever thought to watch the documentaries otherwise heard some of the poor survivors stories, you'd know many lost loved ones simply because they weren't together when the ship rolled over. I can't under any circumstances allow that to happen to us."

"It's not going to."

"How could you possibly know that?"

"So what happens when you need the ladies room, are we all expected to follow you into the closet?"

"No silly."

"Well what then? Would it help if I went back down to the car deck to check that the bow doors are tightly shut and therefore preventing water from seeping in?"

"Would you?"

"Heavens above! This is bordering on ridiculous, worse still you're putting an inordinate amount of fear into the children. Much more of this and they'll be needing a whole lifetime of costly therapy and counseling!"

"Well I can't help it. I wish I didn't feel this way."

"Well remind me never to take you on a proper cruise."

"Honey I won't need to, because trust me I'm never going on one. Oh no not for all the tea in China."

"Oh and why is that?"

"Well as you ask, I have read too many stories about women who've mysteriously disappeared overboard."

"Oh right so you think that's the way I'd choose to dispose of you."

"Well when poor Mrs. Jones remains, otherwise the parts that sharks failed to devour are finally washed up on some Virgin Islands beach nobody is ever interested in investigating what is obviously a potential crime scene. Oh no! Something to do with International waters. Mind you if it was oil then they'd all want their share of the action."

"I'd hate to live inside your head."

"Well let me tell you now that if I ever change my mind I intend to pack a large coil of chain link fencing in my suitcase."

"Whatever for?

"I'm not stupid, for there's no way I'd go for a moonlight stroll on the upper deck without first chaining myself to the handrail. That way if I should 'so called accidentally' fall overboard I'll be able to hang on for dear life until the ship finally docks." Also before the cruise I'd pay a quick visit to the dentist to ensure there are some up to date dental records and get a quick polish at the same time, then I'd check that my life insurance hadn't been secretly upped and finally I'd take myself off to the hospital for a quick mammogram."

"Mammogram! Why the mammogram?"

"Oh no particular reason. It's just I've never had one, that's all."

"There's no answer to that. Anyway, stay put and I promise you hand on heart that we won't be long."

On this occasion John turned out to be right, for the ferry made it safely into the Belgium port, and we also managed to disembark the ramp without tumbling headlong into the sea below. Things were really looking up! But for how long? We had been heading down the motorway for a long while when I turned to John to beg his permission to light a cigarette. (I used to smoke in those days).

"Do you really have too?" he asked pulling a look of pure disdain.

"Yes I desperately need one and it's been almost nine hours since I last had a puff."

"Tricia, it's bad enough that you smoke, but I hate it when you light up in front of the children."

"Come on you know I rarely do that, for most of the time I'm outside the house in the freezing cold at the same time jumping up and down to keep warm."

"Well you'd think that would be enough of a deterrent to make you want to give up.

"John, I've done all I can to kick this habit up, but I started at a very early age."

"Yes you've told me many times. The older kids in the children's home used to give them to the younger children to ensure they would not split on them."

"Yes, so I started smoking around seven or eight years old. It turned out to be my only source of comfort. I even used to pick up dog ends from the roadside and smoke them."

"It's no wonder you didn't contract some terrible disease."

"Look please don't make me feel any worse than I already do about the fact that I smoke."

"I'm not trying to. It's just that we move in circles where this habit is really frowned upon, so for the sake of our friendships, your health, and our children's health, you must still keep trying to quit this disgusting habit."

"John, you're absolutely right, it's a terrible habit, but that's why it's called an addiction, for they are nigh impossible to give up."

At one point John had even refused to marry me unless I gave the habit up. I couldn't and so it was he who relented. It would be many more years plus a part in a TV reality show before I finally kicked the habit.

"John, I may be terrible for having this habit, but may I remind you that I have still managed to do the right thing by our children. I never smoked when I was pregnant, and there's every possibility I would have stayed off them but there always came some terrible crisis that demanded I put a cigarette to my lips to help me get through it. So you see I've tried my best really I have, so please allow me just a few puffs. Look I'll even hang right out of the window so the children don't get as much as a whiff of the fumes."

"Oh alright then, but make it quick, will you please?"

I did as promised and hung as far out of the window as I was able, and there must be no doubt that I would have seemed a sorry sight to all passing cars on the motorway. I only smoked a third of the cigarette, for with John driving at top speed and the freezing wind not only battering my face but ensuring that my hair constantly covered my face it made the task of smoking a cigarette quite arduous if not virtually impossible. Having thrown the remainder of the cigarette out the window I lay back in my seat to allow my face muscles to thaw out.

"Thanks for letting me have a puff."

"Right, but don't wind the window up just yet, as you now smell like an old ashtray!" Seconds later and Antonia called out from the back of the car.

"Yes honey, what is it?"

"Mummy, I'm sorry to complain but I'm getting very hot between my legs."

"What honey? I'm sure it's nothing to worry about!"

"But mummy, I can see smoke." she squealed.

"What! Where?"

"Coming from my legs. Mummy I think my duvet is on fire."

"Oh goodness pull off the road!" I cried.

The car screeched to a halt in a lay by and we both raced to open the passenger doors to pull all three children out to safety. I was freaked out as, while empting out the back seat of all bedding and pillows, I came across the remains of my cigarette. On contact with the fresh air the duvet began billowing smoke. The next ten or so minutes were spent with large artic lorries thundering past us as we stood by the roadside doing a spectacular tribal rain dance which saw us trampling the duvet underfoot until we became convinced the fire was well and truly out. As I sat in stunned silence I quickly realized that, when I threw the cigarette out of my window, the wind had carried it back in through the back window…

"John, please don't say anything, for I'm already beating myself up," I repentantly whimpered.

"Well, if nothing else this should encourage you to quit. We also need to purchase ourselves another duvet."

"Yes yes."

We arrived at the complex and because it was mid winter and with dark overcast skies it unfortunately made the site look very lonely and bleak, not unlike a concentration camp. There were numerous glorified huts, and not a tree or any foliage in sight, with everything centering on a gigantic dome in the middle of the complex. It was so cold we never once used the bikes, or walked the nature trails, so we wiled away our days inside the dome in the large indoor swimming complex with it's large bright fumes. I left John to do the active part of riding down the fumes with the two older children while I amused James our youngest. By day two John's back looked painfully sore as he complained the sharp ridges in the flumes constantly scraped his back.

Soon it was the last night and time for family karaoke. At that time, I had never dared take part in the singing. I was dying to give it a try, but every time I mustered up the courage to go forward I would then find myself panicking and so tearing up the small piece of paper. In my school and college days I had developed a history of messing up on stage, so this was certainly behind my inability to just embrace the moment. Before long the DJ was begging for someone, anyone to come up and sing. Still no one responded. John then turned to me and suggested that we call it a day and head back to the bungalow.

"John, please just hang on for a few more minutes will you, for I'm almost on the verge of getting out my seat," I announced as with renewed fervor I determined to rise from my seat and walk the distance to hand in my song request.

"Honey, either you want to sing or you don't. But you're just spoiling your last evening for yourself and us, sitting there on the edge of your seat, feeling and looking so terribly twitched up. Would it make things easier for you if I simply tossed a coin? Heads you sing, tails you don't."

"Don't be daft."

"Well, if it's tails we can all leave and go back to our bungalow, for the children are really tired and need to get to bed. Anyway, as I've said many times previously, nobody knows you here, so if you make a perfect fool of yourself, well you're going home tomorrow, so who cares?"

"But I care! Just give me ten minutes."

"Alright, but ten minutes is the limit, after that you're on your own."

"I can do this, really I can," I muttered over and over as I stood up to make my way over towards the now very exasperated D.J. Suddenly I heard a earth shattering shriek. It was coming from Reuben. He raced over towards me, the look in his eyes was one of desperation. His mouth was covered in a blackish grey moustache. Antonia raced up besides him and, as Reuben appeared to be in a very distressed state, she offered to be his spokesman.

"Mummy, while you and daddy were talking, Reuben picked up this soda can from that table over there," she said as she then boldly handed me the tin can. I could clearly see that the can had been acting as an ashtray and that my son had just swallowed a mouthful of soda mixed with cigarette ash. For me the evening's entertainment finished at that precise moment as we all raced back to our bungalow to see Reuben throw up everything he had ingested that evening.

The next morning found him back to his usual sunny self, so, with no need of a doctor, we loaded up the car and set off for home. As John placed the key in the ignition he turned to speak with me. His face looked serious.

"No cigarette until we reach home."

"Yes I hear you."

The homeward bound ferry was yet again packed with holidaymakers, many who clearly had been drinking all day long and weren't anywhere near finished. Still we managed to secure a nice spot, well out of harms way. Before long we were driving down the English motorway tired and longing to be back in our own home. As the car pulled up outside our house I was stunned to see that the front door was wide open, and as I entered the house I found myself trampling over a considerable amount of post. We could well have come home to an empty house, literally!

"John, I'm really shocked, for our front door has been left wide open for three whole days," I announced. "Even the postman didn't think to close it! So at the end of the day I had every reason to be anxious, didn't I?"

"Um.. do I need a lawyer?" he mumbled as he threw me a sheepish look that said it all.

"Probably."

"Well I honestly thought I locked it behind me."

"It's that very trying word 'thought' popping up again, isn't it?"

"Yes well, anyone game for a nice refreshing cup of tea?"

CHAPTER TWENTY SEVEN

The Things We Do for Love

Before marrying John I was a college student studying law and English, when Sarah, a college friend, asked me if I would prepare a meal at her house, as she wanted to do something a little special for some of her friends. I readily agreed to her request as long as she paid my fare as she lived in a different town many miles from me. The last guests to arrive were two girls named Sally and Jennifer. From the second I set eyes upon Jennifer I was intrigued. She was slim with pretty facial features. She also had the most beautiful long brown hair and dark eyes, but what made me smile the most was the flashing bow tie that accompanied her immaculate man's trouser suit. As the meal commenced I found myself both fascinated as well as drawn to her. I would discover that Jennifer had been adopted at birth and even that little fact made her more precious than ever to me. She came over as highly intelligent, as well as witty and warm, and I felt strangely sad to say my goodbyes to her when the evening finally drew to a close.

That night, as I lay in bed, I found myself wishing that Jennifer might one day become my sister-in-law. Now I had met many girls over the years who had become personal friends, but never had I given way to such a crazy thought. I had always yearned for a sister, an older one preferably who could have helped and supported me through the endless difficult trials that being a kid in care brings, but sadly it was not to be. I had struggled through the years with three brothers who I failed to understand as much as they failed to understand me. So as I lay in bed visualizing this slightly unusual quirky girl, I dismissed my thoughts as being yet another crazy wish that could never be fulfilled.

A number of years later one of my younger brothers whom I had not seen for years paid me an unexpected visit. I nearly fell over backwards as I opened the door to the girl I had met all those years before! A few weeks later she introduced me for the first time to my two year old nephew. The first thing this incredibly wondrous golden haired little boy did was stand and pee in my brother's open guitar case. I was totally smitten.

In the years that followed I grew to dearly love my new sister in law but as my relationship with my brother was filled with unresolved issues and conflicts it made any sort of close friendship pretty difficult if not nigh impossible. Then tragedy struck. We received a call to say that their house had burnt to the ground. They lost the house as well as every possession in a fire which almost took my brother's life. During his long hospitalization I was given the opportunity to get closer to her.

Jen, as she was called by all who knew her, would go on to have another lovely baby son, followed closely by a beautiful daughter. Then tragedy struck again. Their baby daughter died. We were all heartbroken for their pain and anguish was not only visible but it felt unbearable. In the years to come Jen went on to produce two more children, and if I say it myself, both little girls were incredibly beautiful. For my part I became affectionately known as Aunty T.

Jen lived in a poor neighborhood and, as my brother was often unemployed, money for even the basics was more often than not, scarce, yet I never once heard her complain. Another very touching thing I regularly observed was, despite having very little money, she appeared to feed half the neighborhoods children who seemed to much prefer to play at her home than their own. Often my brother brought strangers home and she thought nothing of sharing what little she had with them. This extremely precious lady seemed straight out of 'Little House on the Prairie', otherwise the 'Waltons', her generous heart was that big. I was not on my own in my thinking for it seemed that everyone who knew Jen appeared to love her, however even this came with it's own set of problems as other girlfriends fought off personal jealousies as they vied for her time.

Whenever I was given the privilege of spending any time with her and the children I found myself loving every precious minute and wishing our time together would never end. There was indeed nothing I wouldn't do for her and I used every opportunity to tell her as much.

There finally came a time when Jennifer inherited a small amount of money. They had never afforded a holiday and so a decision to buy a motor home was made. Their children were very excited as they prepared for their first ever real holiday. On their return my brother chose to park the motor home on a certain piece of land. This was his first mistake, the second was to not immediately insure it. The camper van was stolen only weeks after buying it. When I heard the news it was like a knife going through me as I pondered just how much more this dear family could take.

Then towards the end 1999 my brother and myself became involved in a Government ordered investigation into a London controlled Council and its practices and this meant both my brother and myself becoming potential witnesses to events that had taken place many years ago whilst in care. The investigation took over three years to complete and for a short space of time it brought me and my brother closer, however the downside of this investigation was the toll it took on our immediate families.

I foolishly believed I could handle the extra stress and it soon became equally plain to me that my brother was not faring that well either, the only difference being he was admitting nothing! A few private conversations with Jennifer confirmed this fact, and when the investigative team paid us a visit with the bad news that the Crown Prosecution had made the decision to drop the charges I felt as though my world was crashing in around me. Every day was like trawling through thick mud I felt so miserable and let down. The head of the investigative team paid me a visit to express her sadness that it had gone this way, especially after all the work she had put into making a case. "You also need to know that your former guardians are now taking the police to court," she said giving a deep sigh. "I'm so sorry we didn't get you and the others the justice you deserve."

It was at this point that John decided I needed a break. He knew it was impractical for us both to go away as someone had to stay and look after the business, but he thought it would be nice for me to take Antonia our only daughter and he suggested it would be a wonderful idea to invite Jennifer.

"Tricia, listen up, Jennifer really does bring out the best in you, so I think it's a great idea and let's face it, this whole investigation has been a long ordeal for her as well. Go on, the two of you will have a blast."

My initial response to his suggestion was to shake my head and mutter something along the lines that they could not afford to come away, which wasn't entirely true as for the first time ever both Jen and my brother were finally earning good money, but would my brother allow me to take her and their children on a holiday that would take them to the other side of the world? I very much doubted it.

My brother surprisingly agreed to allow Jen and three of his four children to go as long as he could organize the travel arrangements which included finding a good deal on a flight. I quickly agreed. The accommodation was already taken care of as John and I had our timeshare weeks on which to rely and I knew there was only one place I wanted to take her and that was to my favorite Marriot hotel in Orlando. Still with very little in the way of money I wondered whether it was that good an idea to take them to Orlando and the place where dreams come true when there was no way of enjoying all the wonderful attractions on offer.

"Look Tricia, we've still got some Disney days to use up, and then there are also some Sea World tickets."

"That's true, but we only have five Disney tickets and there are six of us, and those tickets were very expensive."

"Well, take the tickets with you and I'm sure something will work out."

My brother insisted on driving us all to the airport and the goodbyes were indeed a strained affair for I knew he'd found it hard to let them go. Within minutes of stepping into the airport Jen turned and admitted that she had hardly any money with her.

"Jen, it's not as though you have no money in the bank so couldn't you use your card to take a little more cash out?" I dared ask, especially as, including my daughter, we had four fully grown children with us.

At first she faltered and expressed great reluctance at my suggestion. Finally she plucked up courage to go ahead and withdraw an extra hundred pounds. While she was using the machine I was left to privately wonder how we were going to make it through the next two weeks with very little money between us. I was about to get my answer, or so I thought!

As we approached the desk the stewardess behind the counter looked us directly in the eye and asked us if we would consider taking another flight that was scheduled for the following day.

"If you agree, then we will give you all a night at a top London hotel with meal vouchers, plus you will each receive five hundred pounds cash. Oh and tomorrow you will be placed in first class for your trip to the United States." I could not believe my ears. It was an answer to my prayers, yes a dream come true.

"Come on Jennifer, please let's do it," I enthusiastically urged. She needed no further persuasion.

"Alright then ladies, if you would take a seat over there, we will let you know as soon as possible whether you will be on this flight or tomorrows." I sat in silence hoping with all my heart that the news would be good. We could happily occupy ourselves in a hotel for one day and as for the cash, well of all the passengers on our plane we knew we would truly appreciate every single dime! I could hardly breathe I was so desperately anxious for this plan to come to fruition.

Suddenly the stewardess came over only to tell us that the plane was no longer overbooked therefore they no longer required us to be volunteers.

"Mrs. Bennett, the good news is you're all back on today's flight so if you'd like to step this way I'll quickly get you checked in," she cheerfully stated. My heart was now on the Tower of Terror in freefall and not willing to stop until it crashed to a halt in the lowest regions of my bowels, as I was left to grapple with the full realization that our hoped for miracle had literally been snatched from us. I found it hard to hide my disappointment as we passed through the gate heading towards the boarding area. I continued to do all in my power to remain in high spirits, but deep down I felt like an emaciated and wretched donkey just denied his longed for carrot and I wanted to weep.

The flight was not direct so we knew that, upon landing, we still had a five hour wait to endure at Detroit before boarding a smaller plane that would fly directly into Orlando. I began to wonder how I would get through it. In the seats directly behind us were a young couple who had two small children that they seemed unable or unprepared to control. So for the next eight or nine hours we endured having our hair pulled from behind as their toddlers were given free reign to climb over the seats. We were also subjected to additional kicks in the small of our backs as the children threw regular tantrums and screamed blue murder. Many times I had to restrain myself as I wanted to turn round and bitterly complain to both parents but in truth I was still feeling the bitter blow from all that had taken place back at Gatwick airport. Jen more than once leaned over to sympathetically whisper in my ear that she too felt like she'd had enough, but she added that we should try our best to remain charitable as we looked back to a time when our children had been over exuberant toddlers. I marveled at her kindness.

Suddenly the plane began to experience a spate of unexpected turbulence that saw the plane begin to rapidly descend sending food and trays flying, as well as knocking sideways a number of passengers that were waiting to use the bathroom. As for me I just gripped the arms of my seat tightly and breathed in deep.

"Goodness, this has got to be just about the worst turbulence I've ever experienced," I announced as I tried to hide my own personal fear by making light of it. As I made eye contact with my sister in law I became aware that her eyes were filling with tears.

"Oh Jen, are you just as scared?" Her response took me by complete surprise.

"Aunty T, I know this might sound pretty stupid but I feel like the plane is about to crash and we are going to die because I took that money out of the cash machine, without first getting my husbands permission." I looked at her in absolute amazement.

"Jen, stop it! You are the best sister in law anyone could ever wish for, and the last thing God is going to do is punish you for taking a measly one hundred pounds out of your joint account. Besides he's not that vindictive!"

"But what I did was wrong."

"Jen, what you're saying is unbelievably crazy, do you hear me?" I said reaching over to give her a big hug.

We were exceedingly grateful when the turbulence finally came to an end. You could even hear the visible sighs of relief coming from the other passengers on the plane.

The rest of our long Atlantic flight was spent in a similar manner to the first half, as we continued to endure kicks, punches and further hair pulling. By the time we were in American airspace I was ready to ask the couple if their children had been tested for Attention Deficit Disorder, but still I chose to hold my tongue as a sort of act of obedience, though to what I am still unsure! Just before the plane was about to land the lady decided to reach over and tap me on the shoulder. I wondered what was coming next, I mean, had she heard my uncharitable thoughts? I knew I had kept them all safely locked away, so what exactly was her problem? I was ready and willing to deny anything and everything!

"Hi I hope you don't mind me butting in but I heard you say that you're on the connecting flight from Detroit to Orlando, is that right?"

"Yes, that's right."

"Well I can't believe it, but we too are going to Orlando but we still have two internal flights to take because once we land at Detroit we then have to get a plane to Atlanta, and then from Atlanta we will finally get on a plane to Orlando."

"My goodness, that's ridiculous!"

"Yes, and we can't understand why they couldn't just put us on the same flight as yourselves from Detroit to Orlando."

"Perhaps the plane from Detroit was already fully booked?"

"Okay, then tell me when did you lot book your flights?"

"Oh about two weeks ago."

"Then that's even more ridiculous because we booked ours over nine weeks ago, and we were told there were no more seats on the connecting flight to Orlando, that's why we've got to fly from Detroit to Atlanta, before getting to Orlando."

"Sounds like the beginnings of a new song," I muttered.

Not only did I find myself agreeing with her but I also found myself suddenly feeling very sorry for them as they had two young children. I now felt very contrite of heart. The couple now thought to formally introduce themselves,

"Oh by the way my names Doreen and my better half's called Dougie, and you?"

"Oh I'm Tricia and this is my sister in law Jen, and these are some of our kids." We both systematically reached over to politely take hold of her outstretched hand and give it a friendly shake.

"Tricia tell me straight, do you think we should make a complaint as soon as we touch down?" Doreen tentatively asked.

"To be honest I've no idea, but you could go and bang hard on a few desks and see what happens" I replied, knowing full well saying such a thing would have gotten me in deep water if my husband had been sitting next to me.

"Well I only ask as we're already exhausted and we've still two more flights to go."

I stared at her downtrodden face and all hidden anger simply vanished, for I knew from experience just what an ordeal bringing young children across the pond could be without the extra hassle of a further two flights before they reached their final destination.

"Best of luck," I called out as having disembarked the plane we then parted company.

The five hour stop over in Detroit was, as expected, a tremendous ordeal. All Jen's children were very hungry so she gave them the money to go and eat something at one of the many seemingly over priced airport restaurants. Antonia and myself decided to hold on until we got to Orlando. There were moments when I felt so tired and jet lagged that I believed myself to be on the verge of losing it entirely. I chose to confide this to my daughter Antonia who readily admitted to feeling the same way, Jen on the other hand chose to comment that she was still feeling very sorry for the Dougie and Doreen.

"Tricia, if we're feeling this bad, just think how they must be feeling? I mean, they've got two small kids and they've still got to board two different flights. At least our ordeal is almost over."

She was right, but as I glared at the clock on the wall it seemed most reluctant to speed things up for us. Finally we boarded a much smaller plane that would take us all the way to Orlando. We were given the first set of seats just outside the First Class area and I noted there was just a small blue curtain separating us from those in First Class.

As I sat back in the chair I closed my eyes and heaved a sigh of relief when suddenly I thought I heard a voice I recognized. As I pondered on this I knew for sure it was a recent voice. I looked up just in time to see the flight attendant pull back the dividing curtain and, to my absolute amazement, I saw the heads of Dougie and Doreen with chilled wine in their hands as they entered that very defining moment of raising their glasses to toast each other on their amazing good fortune. I was totally gob smacked!

As there were still a number of passengers stuffing their carry on items into the over seat lockers I decided it would not be too improper if I was to get their attention by calling over to them. It was something I would live to regret.

"Dougie! Doreen!" I called out.

Dougie immediately turned his head and a large smile alighted his face as he waved a quick hello. After a few more slurps of wine he abandoned his seat to come and say a more proper hello. He probably needs to get all this excitement off his chest I mused. He raced over to where we were seated and began.

"Guys you'll never guess what?"

"What?"

"Well, we were just about to board the flight to Atlanta when we were told they were overbooked so they had no seats for us. Of course we didn't mind coz we'd never wanted to go to Atlanta in the first place, not that we told them that. So they were falling over themselves to make amends by sending us by cab to a first class hotel. We were all able to take hot showers and have a well earned rest in a lovely king sized bed and then, to cap it all, we had ourselves the most fabulous meal, on the house so to speak. Yes we were told we could order whatever we fancied," he twittered on. "Yes it was fantastic! Me and the missus both ordered a big juicy steak with all the trimmings, and it didn't stop there, oh no, when we got to the deserts well they were to die for."

"You'll be dead soon if you don't shut up," I screamed inside my head.

"Yes there was chocolate lava cake, or Cointreau soaked cheesecake with whipped cream, um crème brulee, oh and ...."

"Move on!" I anxiously interjected as I had no wish to listen any further as he made it his business to describe his gourmet meal in such detail that my mouth had begin to excessively salivate. It was now safe to assume it wouldn't be too long before I began dribbling all down my chin.

"Yes, well not only did they offer us a direct flight to Orlando but guess what?" he said as he rather smugly folded his arms.

"What?" I asked somewhat abruptly.

"As you can see, we're all in First Class!" he squealed with delight.

"Whee Dougie... you're so lucky," I squealed back as I struggled to prevent my hands from finding their way to his neck to rip out his voice box and thus forever terminate all this cruel torment.

"But listen up for it didn't even end there," he continued.

"Really!" I squeaked, my eyes now bulging from their sockets, my heart racing within my breast as I considered whether this might not be the perfect time to jump out of the plane and get it all over with.

"Oh no! For on top of all this, they then gave each of us three hundred dollars to spend as we please!"

"Wow, three hundred dollars!" I spluttered as the fight was now on to keep my facial muscles on the up.

"So altogether we have ourselves a whapping twelve hundred extra dollars to fritter away, now isn't that amazing?" he ecstatically cried out.

"Oh absolutely," I gulped

"Spect we'll do an extra day at Disney, at least that's what the missus's is after, and we've gotta keep her happy haven't we?" he gleefully stated giving a little self satisfied wink."

"Oh yes, of course." I muttered as I tried to rid myself of the murderous plot that was just beginning to take shape inside my head.

"Hey kids look who we've just found. Yes over here… over here. Come on kids, give them a wave," he shouted back at his children who, having settled down in First Class, were far more interested in slurping and burping their way through their divinely thick milkshakes to be bothered waving at us seemingly low level miscreants seated in monkey class.

"Ahh….. bless em, I don't think they heard me," he said as he attempted to excuse them.

Oh I made all the usual polite noises for his benefit, but deep down I was secretly feeling so very distraught that, in good old fashioned English terms, I wanted to 'knock his block off' before storming into First Class to then give my undivided attention to his missus! Of course I left all such evil thoughts in my head where they rightfully belonged under lock and key, leaving only one course of action open and that was to begin furiously biting my nails until I drew blood as I contemplated on just what would it take to shut this man up.

"Look, I'd better get back, coz their about to serve us our hot meal, although I'm not sure how much more I can tuck away after that wonderful meal at the hotel," he said patting his already extended pot belly as he continued grinning from ear to ear.

"Jen did you hear all that?" I grizzled.

"Of course I did."

"I want to squeeze every drop of life out of his podgy little torso, truly I do."

"Me first."

"How could all this happen?" I miserably mused.

"I've no idea."

"Well right now my head is spinning."

"Mine too."

"This really takes the biscuit! I mean, first our amazing offer is withdrawn, we're then forced to endure a nine hour flight while constantly being accosted by their unsupervised ADH children, followed closely by a hideous five hour wait in Detroit airport. Then, as if all this was not enough, we land up getting seats immediately outside First Class with only a flimsy curtain separating us."

"I know it's tough, isn't it."

"Then, to add insult to injury, we are subjected to a lengthy detailed story of how they got to spend those difficult 'in between' hours living it up in a plush hotel, even stumbling down to the restaurant to be served a fine feast of their choice, and now their jubilantly living it up in style in bloomin First Class, while we remain cramped and hungry in monkey class.

"Yes, it's pretty hard to bear," she quietly sympathized.

"Right, and when I believe I can hardly take anymore he then starts bragging about the money. I'm just about ready to throw up, for it's all so intolerable!" I announced feeling very deflated

"Here, take this sick bag."

"Jen, forgive me for this, but life stinks," I murmured under my breath as the internal pillars of my emotional stability were now firmly in the process of collapsing to that of a pile of Greek ruins.

Some time later the flight attendants finally got round to passing out small packets of peanuts, half a limp film wrapped sandwich along with a choice of juice, soda or bitter tasting coffee. As I further discussed this latest excruciating painful and insulting blow with Jen, she immediately came up with an answer.

"Aunty T, we don't know what is going on in their lives, so maybe their need for comfort and a blessing was greater than ours."

"What?" I snorted.

"Well, we'd best keep an open mind, for we have no absolutely no idea how troubled their lives might well be."

"Look Jen I've got a masters degree when it comes to pain and heartache, and so I believe have you, so what you're saying makes no sense at all."

I could only give her a further look of despair as I came to the full realization that this dear woman was surely destined for sainthood! with only the Pope and Mother Theresa standing in front of her in the line of nominees. But as for me I was still teetering on the dark side. I was therefore neither ready nor willing to listen.

"Listen Jen, I'd have to do mental gymnastics to even begin to swallow your charitable explanation of why they more deserved to be treated like kings for if nothing had ever been offered to us back in London, then I doubt very much that we would be sitting here having this conversation, so it all seems so jolly unfair," I stated still feeling wretched and utterly inconsolable.

Having finished my small unsatisfying sandwich I emptied the packet of peanuts on to the tray and began counting them.

"Pathetic isn't it, for there are exactly seventeen peanut halves in this packet, and it's certainly not nearly enough to feed a monkey." Moments later I excused myself and headed down the aisle to the bathroom only to discover there was a long line in front of me. The same applied to the bathroom on the other side of the aisle. I made my way back to my seat only to once again bump into Dougie who, having not been totally satisfied with his first attempts at making us thoroughly jealous and miserable, had come back to try and further deepen our already bottomless depression. This time he was cheerfully reeling off the First Class dinner menu. I'd had more than I could stomach.

"Jen, can you believe it, there's a ridiculously long line of people waiting to use the bathroom," I brusquely interrupted.

"There's no line here, so why not use ours?" Dougie brightly suggested as he assertively pointed towards a door that was just a matter of a few yards away from where we were seated. I was amused by his choice of words. I mean 'ours' normally means it belongs to you, doesn't it?

"So Dougie, they've now added the First Class toilet to your long list of freebies, have they?" I very much wanted to ask, but yet again I curbed my tongue.

"Look Dougie, even though the curtain has been hooked to one side it's still inside the First Class quarters."

"Your point is?"

"Well, do you think it will be alright for me, a mere economy passenger, to use it?" I asked, my tone now reflecting a small note of submission as though I believed it important for 'Lord Dougie' chief administrator to the airways to very considerately grant me the necessary permission to temporarily abandon monkey class in order to plonk my second class derrier down on his superior upper class loo seat.

"Sure, why not?"

I moved quickly towards the door but with my fingers just reaching out to touch the bolt, a very determined stewardess suddenly appeared from nowhere.

"Excuse me Madam, but this bathroom is for First Class passengers only, so please head towards the bathrooms situated at the rear of the plane," She abruptly stated before swiftly pulling the curtain across. I felt like Leonardo aboard Titanic!

"Well, there goes any hope of soft toilet tissue," I muttered under my breath as with my eyes and soul downcast I headed back towards my seat, biting down hard on my tongue. It was no use.

"Dougie, thanks for all the onboard entertainment, but I just need to rest, do you mind," I stated trying my best not to look too sullen.

"Oh, of course not, we'll probably catch up with you guys later."

"Yes, I'm sure you will." I watched on as with an air of jubilation he eagerly made his way back to his large comfortable seat to enjoy further pampering from the slim and sweet smelling flight attendants

"You know something crossing the Atlantic we were all equal, now only a few hours later even Dougie's bodily functions are considered superior to mine."

Having said my little bit, I then despondently flopped back down into my chair, fighting a desperate urge to bypass all further rules by simply peeing in my seat.

The plane landed at Orlando International with it's body still intact and we proceeded through Customs without being manhandled or strip searched, so other than the mandatory quiz to which all foreigners and aliens are subjected, we were now free to go on our merry way.

Just as I imagined, Jen and the girls were mesmerized by both the resort and it's location.

"Wow, this is better than I ever imagined it would be, so thank you Aunty T for bringing us here," Jen announced as wandering around the beautiful complex I happened to observe a lone tear slide down her face.

"Well the truth is that of everyone I've ever known, you really do deserve the best," I said feeling inwardly thrilled to be able to participate in making this small but special event happening. That night, after unpacking our belongings, we quickly changed into our swimming costumes and headed down to the large beautiful pools for a late night swim and Jacuzzi.

"Aunty T, this place is gorgeous," she announced as she entered the pool. The tall gazebos, the beautiful palms that stretch high into the sky, the huge lake with its fountain, my goodness it's all way beyond words."

"Jen, although this resort is rated as a four star, in my mind it deserves ten, really it does, and as for the staff well there's never been a visit where they failed to give us any help we needed."

"That's good to know, anyway the kids are all having such a great time so shall we leave them in the pool, while we head towards the Jacuzzi?

"Sounds like a great idea," I enthused. As we sat in the Jacuzzi we were alone for by now it was late in the evening. The hour was such that I knew that any time soon security would be coming round to politely tell us that our time at the pool was up. As we sat amongst the bubbles Jen pointed out that the floor of the Jacuzzi was scattered with small silver coins.

"Yes I can see them."

"Well, find a penny, pick it up and it's sure to bring you luck," she cried immediately reaching down into the water in an attempt to gather them up. While she was groveling around underwater the security men chose that same moment to arrive and immediately began beaming their torches directly into my face and then into the Jacuzzi. I was immediately startled.

"Sorry to trouble you, but is everything alright ma'am?"

"Yes fine.. thank you."

"Is your good lady friend also alright?" the taller of the two asked as he shone his torch directly in the Jacuzzi as he continued to observe Jen bent over with her head under water as she attempted to pick up the individual coins.

"Yes... yes... my sister in law is just trying to retrieve some loose change from the bottom," I confessed, suddenly feeling like a guilty school child caught in a wrongful act.

"Oh right. Well, unfortunately we have to ask you to gather up your things and leave, for it is time to close up the pool area."

"We're leaving right now."

"Well then, have a nice night."

"You too."

Strangely enough that little incident served to further my despair as I felt angry that anyone should witness my dear sister in law groveling around for a few cents.

The next day at the supermarket I was intrigued to see how long Jen spent examining amounts on the cans and packaging as well as the prices of various food items and I pretty quickly realized that, despite being away from home, she had a natural habit of being very cautious with whatever money she had to play with. Oh if ever I wanted to win the National Lottery it had to be now! I longed with all my heart to really spoil her and, although my need to be careful certainly didn't match hers, I still knew I was in no position to splash out, especially as there would always be six of us to consider.

Finally I decided we must find a way to go to Disney for the day. While driving back from the Mall we noticed a place advertising cheap tickets and so the next time we left the hotel to get food provisions we decided we would stop and find out exactly what an extra ticket might cost. That next night with the boot loaded up with provisions, ice cream included, we decided that it was now or never, so we headed back to the place we had seen advertising the cheap tickets. Before long we found ourselves in a traffic jam that appeared as though it would never let up.

"Jen, a car crash must have taken place for it to be this bad."

"Oh that's okay, don't worry, but I'm not sure how long the ice cream will survive."

"Shall we turn back then?"

"No we've come this far so let's see it through." Finally we arrived at our destination and moments later we were standing at the counter.

"Excuse me, but you are advertising cheap Disney tickets, so we would like to purchase a ticket."

"Just one?"

"Yes, we only need one."

"Oh I'm sorry, but the ticket is only that price if you agree to attend a timeshare presentation."

"What?"

"If you are prepared to attend a ninety minute presentation, then we can offer the ticket at this discount price."

"Oh goodness I should have known better."

"Ninety minutes passes by very quickly," Jen kindly interjected.

"Oh right!"

"Yes Aunty T, what's ninety minutes, when we've got all day on our hands."

"Jen, trust me, they normally turn out to be well over three hours long!"

"Oh let's just do it. In for a penny, in for a pound!"

"I don't believe it," I wailed. "We've come all this way just to discover this."

"Come on Aunty T, all is not lost, let's agree to go to this timeshare thing. Besides we've wasted time, gas and my tub of melted ice cream is now ready to be thrown away, so we may as well get something out of this."

"You think so?"

"Yes. Excuse me ma'am, but we are very interested in attending a presentation," Jen firmly announced to the young lady behind the counter.

"Well, I need to inform you that there is a tiny problem."

"Oh right, and what is that?" Jen immediately quizzed.

"Well, you either have to be married, or in a committed relationship."

"Well we're pretty committed to one another, aren't we Aunty T, she's always telling me how much she loves me, so that should count, shouldn't it?"

"I'm afraid not, you see what I really mean is you have to either be a married couple otherwise ….." She stuttered and stumbled over the next word that refused to come forth from between her richly ruby red lips.

"Go on, spit it out for I think the word you are looking for is gay," Jen loudly challenged. I could only balk and take a step backwards as I watched on, feeling amazed by her sudden very unexpected assertiveness, I mean, up until now she had always been so gentle, so unassuming!

"Well yes I think I meant something like that."

"Something like that? No you really did mean gay."

"Alright, that is what I meant," the poor lady sheepishly confessed. Jen chose this moment to act enraged. She was after all a bit of a feminist, committed to equal rights for women. Her years as a mature student and her first class honors degree had helped her finally find her voice, so she was not going to look back, not this day and not for anybody!

"Well lady, in this day and age, not only is that utterly ridiculous but it's actually has a name that begins with a D, So let me help you out here for it's called discrimination." she announced her eyes blazing with rage.

"I'm so sorry, I didn't mean to offend anyone," the lady behind the desk stuttered, her cheeks burning with embarrassment.

"Sorry isn't good enough for this should be perceived for what it is, utterly scandalous. So it's alright for me to attend a presentation with a man but not another woman unless we are an 'item.' This in itself suggests that all single unattached women are to ugly to be married, otherwise they neither have the means nor the wherewithal to conduct a legal transaction on their own. How jolly primitive!"

"I'm so sorry," the lady stuttered.

"Well answer me this are there any women in the Corporate world?"

"Loads."

"Precisely! Oh and Tricia, do you have your own bank account?"

"Yes I do."

"Right, so do I. So I guess that makes us capable of making sound financial decisions, wouldn't you say?"

"I guess so."

"Well, you guessed right, for this denial could be classed as a violation against our human rights," she announced in such an assertive manner she could easily be mistaken for a trial lawyer.

"Oh dear, I had no idea," the assistant replied as she struggled to keep up her end of the conversation.

"People sue for this you know. I want to speak with your manager."

"I'm so sorry, but he's not available as he's presiding over a meeting," she stuttered as she shrunk back, a look of fear now dominating her entire face.

"What that means is he's out closing some timeshare sale," I hurriedly interjected.

"Well then, what are we waiting for? Put us down as a gay couple." Jen instructed.

"What?" I screeched, my eyes bulging from their sockets.

"You heard! Aunty T we are jolly well going to attend this presentation and, as we have no other options open to us, we will be going as a gay couple."

"Jen stop it! What are you thinking?" I cried.

"Well as you ask, we wasted time, petrol and my ice cream coming here, so, like it or lump it, we are going to attend this presentation and if that means going as a gay couple, then so be it."

"Jen I can't do this, really I can't," I balked.

"Yes you can."

"But I'm not gay."

"So what neither am I."

"I have a husband at home."

"So do I."

"He'll kill me, if he ever finds out."

"Don't exaggerate, for he's far too nice."

"Well all the same Jen I'm not comfortable with it."

"Aunty T, you have always professed that you'd do anything for me, so now's your chance to prove it. Besides, you've always reminded me and many others of Patsy from Absolutely Fabulous."

"What, Joanna Lumley? I always thought I was more like Jennifer Saunders."

"Well either will do, anyway, if anyone can pull this off, then it has to be you."

"Oh, this can't be happening," I forlornly cried as I watched the very resigned lady begin to fill out the necessary form.

"Are you really sure you want to do this?" The young lady queried.

"Oh absolutely!" Jen resolutely replied.

"No not at all," I interjected.

The young lady picked up the phone while shaking her head as though she needed to wake up from some undeniably unpleasant dream

"Steve I've got a couple of ladies here that wish to attend a presentation. Sorry, oh right. Yes um they are on holiday together and yes they say they co habit."

"Jen, please tell her we've changed our minds." I anxiously hissed.

"Nope."

"Is 10.00am tomorrow morning alright with you guys?" she called over.

"Fine by me," Jen shouted back.

Having placed the booking the lady looked over and gave us both one final quizzical look.

"Well it's booked, but I have to say I've never met anyone prepared to go to these lengths just to get themselves a discounted Disney ticket," she sighed, shaking her head in complete disbelief.

"Well desperate people do desperate things, besides we're from England," Jen quickly retorted.

Back at the apartment I continued to express grave doubts about my ability to follow through with this crazy plan.

"Jen, I don't think I'm able to pretend to be something I'm not," I wailed.

"Tricia, trust me you'll do fine. Anyway, for as long as I've known you we've always said you should be on stage, so treat it like an audition."

The next morning found me unable to swallow even a morsel of breakfast cereal for I had completely lost my appetite.

"Oh Jen, I've had no sleep at all and worse still I've got the most terrible butterflies in my stomach."

"For goodness Aunty T, lighten up for anyone would think you were going to your own funeral," she commented as she munched on a slice of toast. "Trust me, in time to come, you'll look back on this day and laugh."

"You think so?" I groaned, as I clutched my stomach feeling hopelessly queasy. "Please, before we leave. Don't be offended but I still need to check something out with you."

"Okay what's that?"

"Well, who's playing the macho part, because if you think It's going to be me, then you can think again for there is no way......."

"Aunty T, calm down. Look, just play yourself and, if you're that freaked out, we could take Ryan with us, I mean he would be extra support."

"Okay," I muttered as I secretly wondered what possible support a tall skinny twenty something could really be in what might easily become a potentially disastrous situation.

And so it was, that an hour or so later, Jen, Ryan and myself headed off to the ninety minute presentation.

"I think I'm going to be sick," I announced.

"I'll open the window, otherwise turn up the air conditioning," Jen replied.

"Take a few deep breaths Aunty T," Ryan helpfully suggested as moving forward from the back seat he placed a concerned hand on my shoulder.

"What if it all goes wrong?" I whimpered.

"Quite what do you mean?"

"Well what if they suspect that something is amiss, for I've never been asked to play gay before! Oh this could be the end of everything."

"Aunty T, get a grip! Who cares what they think? They can hardly challenge us, can they?"

"How do you know that? I mean if they suspect they might well escort us out the building, think how embarrassing that would be."

"Oh right. Excuse me ladies, but we have come to believe that you're not really of the same sexual persuasion, you're just pretending to be gay, ahh ha. And so we've put our little heads together and with a bit of brainstorming we think we've worked out the reason behind this little charade."

"Huh!"

"Yes, you concocted this wickedly evil plan just to get cheap Disney tickets. So ha.. ha it's all over, no discounted Disney tickets will be coming your way, you little cheapskates!"

"Well, they might just do something like that," I murmured.

"Look Aunty T, even if they do suspect, it's highly unlikely they'd risk challenging us, just from the standpoint of a potential backlash."

"Quite what do you mean?"

"I mean, if they did throw us out onto the streets, well then we could go to the papers and the local news media and make such a noise."

"Oh right, like I'd be really keen to go on television with a story such as this."

"I don't see why not."

"Oh, I think I'm going to be sick."

Minutes later and we were being directed into the timeshare resort car park.

"Jen, if I'm going to survive this ordeal then I'm going to have to wear my sunglasses throughout the entire presentation, for there's no way I can look any of them in the eye."

All too soon we were through the doorway and once inside we were quickly directed to a crowded seating area.

"Look Jen, my whole body's trembling," I quietly whispered.

"Just come and sit down right besides me on the love couch," she purred as she playfully took on the voice of Barry White. Moments later I looked up and I could see many of the timeshare reps decked out in their smart suits leaning over the balcony as they surveyed the motley crowd below. A number of them appeared to be pointing down in our direction.

"Jen, convince me it's not my imagination for I feel as though they are boring into the back of my neck with their stares," I hissed.

"No you're right. They are staring down at us, so try to act normal."

"Normal! Are you kidding me?"

"Aunty T calm down for the presentation hasn't even started and you're already getting your knickers in a twist. Look trust me, everything will work out fine," she said as she then made a deliberate show of squeezing my knee.

"Jen, tell me straight we're not going to do any kissing and that sort of thing are we?" I asked, my voice now appearing hoarse from the strain this was putting on me.

"No stupid, just put your arm around me every now and then. By the way, you're sounding rather sexy!"

"Oh stop it" I whimpered. "I'm so crazy to have agreed to this."

"Come on Aunty T, put an arm around me," she ordered as she gave me another affectionate pat on the knee.

We were left until last and I believe this was a deliberate act on their part for I had been keeping a furtive eye on the reps and had witnessed them quietly arguing and deliberating amongst themselves as to which of them would pull the short straw and take us on.

The task was finally given to a young upwardly mobile lady named Suzanne.

"Hi there everybody, sorry for the delay. Please come this way," she instructed in her best professional manner. We were taken into a large room filled with small circular tables and she quickly invited us to help ourselves to something to eat. Jen and Ryan wasted no time as they headed over towards the breakfast bar. I, on the other hand, chose to decline.

"Come on Miss. Bennett, if nothing else you must have yourself a beverage. We've got fresh orange or apple juice, tea, coffee or chocolate. So which is it to be?"

"No thank you, I'm fine as I am," I lied as, sitting down at the table, I adjusted my sunglasses, to ensure they remained securely on the bridge of my nose. Having arrived back at the table with her plate piled high Jen saw it as her duty to come to my immediate rescue.

"Oh don't worry, she's just having one of her usual little pouts," she announced very matter of fact. "Here Aunty T, Ryan thought to bring you a cup of coffee anyway."

"Thanks sweetie," was all I could think to reply.

"She does this a lot you know, especially if she doesn't appear to be getting her own way, for she's always been a little bit of a martyr," Jen prattled on. "It's a Catholic thing, martyrdom." I could only gulp down the coffee as I listened on.

"Back in the U.K. we've all become so used to it that we find it best to try to ignore her until she finally comes round."

Thankfully Suzanne appeared to accept the explanation and so she decided to launch into a bit of idle chit chat as she sought to find some common ground. She did her best really she did, covering every imaginable subject she thought women of our persuasion would be into and therefore would happily discuss. As her confidence grew she began to ask more personal if not slightly impertinent questions, such as how did we find meet and what were the main differences since we had walked out on our husbands to be together? I could only inwardly groan as I left Jen to get us out of this one. I looked over and I could see that Ryan was now beginning to squirm in his seat. Only the night before Jen had suggested that we should rehearse a story, just incase they asked about our relationship.

"We need to keep it really simple," she had cautioned.

"Alright I hear you."

"Especially as you're the one most likely to go into great detail."

"I said I hear you."

"Well it's just that, the more convoluted the story, the more likely it will be for one of us to slip up," she said giving a big grin.

And so I was left to sit back biting my tongue as I allowed her the freedom to divulge our fully rehearsed story. I had to admire her for she certainly wandered as far from the script as possible, nose diving like a kamikaze pilot into a rather lengthy and colorful explanation of how we'd come to find each other and more importantly, in the light of today's poor performance, what could possibly be holding us together! Every now and then she would stop in her tracks to give me a little affectionate pat on the leg. For my part when I thought it safe I gave her a sly kick under the table, a warning from me not to take things too far. I was wasting my time.

"Are we alright there, Aunty T?"

"Yes darling, I'm doing fine," I mumbled before turning away in a most exaggerated manner to express something of my annoyance.

"There you see, she's still playing hard to get."

"Excuse me asking but, as we're indoors, why don't you remove your sunglasses?" the perfectly manicured lady dared ask.

"I actually prefer to keep them on as I suffer from the most dreadful eyestrain, if you don't mind." I hoped that would be the end of it. But alas, Jen was now in full swing!

"Oh, she's such a naughty one, for everybody knows it's got little to do with eye strain and more to do with us still being in the middle of little squabble or tiff! She's such an actress really she is. By the way have you ever seen "Absolutely Fabulous' for if you had you'd quickly realize…."

I could only sit, squirm and gulp down more coffee as I wished with all my being for this ninety minute presentation to come to an abrupt end.

"Has something happened to upset her?" the concerned rep cared to enquire further.

"Not at all, but then it doesn't take that much to upset her, does it Ryan?"

"No mum."

"Oh right." Suzanne mumbled her face looking more and more confused and unsure.

"Look Suzanne, I can call you Suzanne, can I?"

"Feel free." she announced showing more than a hint of exasperation.

"Well, to tell you the truth she wanted to shop for some jewelry this morning, that is until I reminded her that it wasn't possible as we'd already made this arrangement. She was so put out that she ordered me to call and cancel, and naturally I refused, and now she's hopping mad at me, hence she's turned into a real sulky Sue."

"Couldn't you leave the shopping until after this tour, I mean, you'll be free to leave in ninety or so minutes, and that gives you the whole afternoon to shop."

"My sentiments exactly. However if she wants something then she wants it now. Truth be told she can be such a little Mona Lisa what with her tantrums, isn't that so Ryan?"

"Yes mum."

"But don't worry ,she'll soon begin to perk up when we get to view the luxury apartment, otherwise the jewelry counter of some nearby department store."

"Oh dear, well the sooner we get down to business then the quicker you'll be out of here," she said as she tried her very best to keep a positive smile on her beleaguered face.

We did the obligatory tour around the site, and then headed into the exceptionally comfortable apartment that many others were also in the process of viewing. Suzanne still tried to put her best foot forward by finding something to talk about that might just relate to me, but it was obvious she was floundering. We reached the main bedroom with its lavish king sized bed when suddenly, out of the blue, she began talking about the joys of ceiling mirrors. It was at this point that I was ready to break free and make a run for it.

"Psst Jen did you hear her make mention of ceiling mirrors?"

"Yes I did."

"What on earth was she insinuating?"

"Don't ask me."

"Jen, I beg you please keep all conversation to a minimum for I'm finding this really difficult to cope with." Of course she ignored my request, for she was having such a good time. As we passed through the kitchen Jen continued on with her controversial spiel.

"Spoiled rotten all her life," she announced to Suzanne. "Yes trust me, she's used to servants, so no point whatsoever in showing her the microwave or the rotisserie oven for just turning the on/off dial is more than likely to exhaust her to the point where she'll be needing a three hour rest."

By the time we got back to the interview room with its breakfast bar I was ready to throw up, so I hurriedly excused myself to head for the bathroom whereupon I closed the closet door to then jump up and down and hopefully shake off the very intense and overwhelming feelings of stress I was experiencing.

"Aunty T are you in there," Jen called out as she pushed each stall door in her endeavor to track me down.

Yes I'm in here."

Well we can't be too long coz I've left Ryan and Suzanne alone at the table.

"Jen, what do you think you're playing at?" I hissed as I finally opened the stall door.

"Oh come on Aunty T, I'm just having a bit of fun, that's all."

"Fun? Look here Jen I'm feeling so ill that we need to bring this to an end," I begged in hushed tones, just in case there were any staff lurking around. Suddenly we heard someone at the door.

"Psst.....Mum, Aunty T are you still in there?" It was Ryan.

"Yes, we're just washing our hands."

"Well, you need to get back quickly."

"Why, what's the urgency?"

"Well, she asking all sorts of weird questions."

"Such as?"

"Well, what's it really like to have two mums, and what do my friends think of the arrangement? So come on, I need you to come back and take over, for it's like standing in front of a drill sergeant."

"Oh right, we're just on our way."

As we walked back towards our table, two tall very imposing men in expensive suits drew up a chair at our very table. My guts were now in free flow gurgling as loud as Niagara falls.

"Hello there Miss. Bennett, we have come over to relieve Suzanne from her duties and to discuss what we can do to make you ladies happy."

"Getting me out of here would be a good start," I privately thought. I knew in that moment I had to do my best to bring this ridiculous charade to an end and preferably without giving the game away.

"Well Suzanne has been really nice and helpful, and the apartment was more than acceptable, however I don't think it's quite what we're looking for, is it Jen darling?"

"Um no."

"You see Jen here has much different ideas when it comes to holidays." Before I could say anymore Jen thought she'd join in the interaction.

"She's not joking, for I'm at my happiest trekking across the plains of Nepal in open toed sandals with nothing but a walking stick and backpack, whereas Aunty T would never even consider such a thing, would you Aunty T?"

"Heaven forbid I should ever be..."

"No she's much too 'arty farty,' so she's not happy unless she's by a sparkling pool flicking her fingers for a waiter to come along and service her."

"Jen I'm not an old car!" I furiously muttered.

Both men looked at each other somewhat confused.

"Tell us straight, how on earth did you two ever get together?" the taller of the two actually had the temerity to ask.

"Is that a question?" I retorted

"Of sorts."

"Well, it's really none of your business."

"I'm sorry, I was only asking as your interests appear to be so ...so, well so diverse."

"Opposites attract I'll have you know," Jen interjected.

"Yes well, tell us the truth, for we think we've worked out why you've been wearing those sunglasses throughout the entire presentation."

"Oh, and why is that then?" I asked my voice trembling slightly, as I immediately convinced myself that the game was well and truly over.

"We believe you're really that famous English tennis player."

"Are you serious?"

"Yes we are, for while you were down in the reception area we were all talking about it from up on the balcony"

"You are joking, aren't you?"

"No we're not. Now what's that player's name? Hmm Sue something or other.

"Well I must be the other for if you care to hand me a racket I'll prove to you I'm not her, for trust me, when I say I can't even see the ball, let alone wack it hard across the net."

This ridiculous conversation went on for some time before they finally decided to call it a day and, having tried their best to sell us a week, they agreed to release us and send us downstairs to receive our discounted tickets. We had been at this presentation for almost four hours. As we walked across the car park I felt an urgent need to express myself.

"Jennifer, much as I love you, promise right now you'll never ask such a thing of me, ever again."

"Come on Aunty T, it's all over and we've got the extra ticket, so let's agree to enjoy the rest of the day," Jen cheerfully cried as she danced around the car park.

"I can't believe you even told them I was in a foul mood because I wanted to go shopping for jewelry, and as for the kitchen thing, telling them I'd never made myself familiar with an oven, I could have cheerfully throttled you."

"Oh, it was all in the best possible taste."

"I can't wait to tell John about you guys," Ryan announced as he climbed into the back of the car.

"You'll do no such thing!"

"Why ever not?"

"Ryan, promise me now you'll keep your mouth zipped until I've had the opportunity to confess all, for he really needs to hear it from me."

"Alright then Aunty T."

That night the phone rang.

"Aunty T, it's John on the phone," Ryan shouted over to me.

"Hi honey, thanks for ringing. Yes we're all fine. Antonia's doing great and she would love to say hello when I've finished. Yes the resort is absolutely fabulous, as if you need to ask, and yes we're going to Disney tomorrow. Of course we've managed to get ourselves an extra ticket. How much? Well before I tell you, are you sitting down? Because there's something else I badly need to get off my chest... Hmm well no it isn't that bad. I mean I haven't been arrested or anything like that, but I need you to stay calm and hear me out before you think to get mad or say anything. Good, now that I have your full attention I'm honestly not too sure where to start."

Two days later we headed off for our special day at one of Disney's parks. We'd only been in the park a matter of minutes when Antonia suddenly tugged at my sleeve.

"Mum, isn't that the family from the plane," she cried. I followed her pointed finger and I could clearly see them aimlessly wandering along totally focused on chomping their way through some disgracefully large turkey drum sticks.

"Oh my goodness, why am I being punished like this?" I cried as I ducked behind a lamp post.

"Come on mum, if they see us we can just say, fancy that, and then after a quick hello we can walk on by."

"That's never going to happen, for you don't know him like I do, so quick, let's hide," I shouted to the others as I turned on my heels to head down the road in the opposite direction, for mean as it might sound, I couldn't face another game of 'Guess what just happened to us.'

There were a few minor and so very insignificant problems during our Marriot stay but I can tell you now that their staff quickly sorted them out for us.

"My goodness Aunty T, I am so impressed with the service, for I've never experienced anything that matches this."

"Guys I couldn't agree more and that's why Marriott are and always will be my favorite chain.

We were making ourselves comfortable on the homeward bound flight and by some miracle to date there had been no official sightings of Dougie, Doreen and their two little blighters. But just when I believed we were safe, there was a small but all the same disconcerting tap on my shoulder.

"Tricia, I've been up and down this plane more than a dozen times looking for you guys, and now at last I've found you," he squealed with delight.

"Oh, hi there Dougie." I gasped as I tried my very best to look friendly.

"Well, apart from wanting to show you these 'ere photos, I can't wait to tell you what happened when we….."

"I bet you can't," I inwardly groaned as in my head I was voluntarily putting myself forward for some Electro Convulsive Therapy, believing this must be substantially more preferable to having Dougie standing over me like some awkward teenager ready to wet himself if not allowed to expound every minute detail of his ever so fantastic, unbelievably wonderful, beyond mind blowing, positively awesome holiday in good old America, a land flowing with milk and honey where everyone else's dreams really do come true, oh that is with the exception of mine! In that agonizing moment I wished I had a parachute in my carry on luggage for I would cheerfully have given him one final hearty embrace and then jumped.

CHAPTER TWENTY EIGHT

Have You Lost the Children Again?

Strange as this may well sound and, as much as we love our children, we had a rather peculiar habit of losing them, which I shouldn't really so readily admit to as we actually fostered children for well over twenty or more years. It all started when we brought our first child home from the hospital. John decided that we should go into town and purchase our first ever camcorder, that way we could record every dribble, smile and burp our precious baby daughter made in the first weeks of her life. Having parked our car in a local car park we parted company as I needed to get a number of other things such as nappies and cough medicine, also being a woman of limited technical abilities I was more than happy to entrust the whole buying a camcorder bit to him.

"Honey, if it would help in anyway I'll happily take the baby with me, this way you'll have two free hands. We could meet up for coffee later, so how long do you think you'll need?" I quickly agreed and, after stooping down to give my precious bundle a little kiss on her forehead, I then waved him off before setting off in the opposite direction clutching my essential items list of things I needed to purchase.

The hour seemed to go very quickly, so soon it was time to head towards the coffee shop for our agreed rendezvous. I peered inside and there was no sign of him so I found us a vacant table and waited. Five minutes later and he appeared.

"Hi honey, have you ordered the coffee?"

"No not yet."

"Okay, then leave it with me." He must have noticed the confused look on my face.

"Tricia, are you feeling alright?"

"Er.. John darling, where is the baby?"

"Oh, um I thought you had her."

"What, are you mad? You took her with you, remember?" I screeched as I jumped to my feet almost knocking the chair over. My heart was in my mouth. "So where is she?"

"Oh honey at this moment I'm not too sure where I left her for I went into quite a number of shops and …"

"Oh my goodness let's get out of here," I cried as I raced out into the street.

"Come on think …think …What was the last store you went into?"

"Um,, the record store," he said his face flush with guilt.

"I should have known!"

"Yes, well, that's because I still had time on my hands. Oh, and I don't know whether this is the best time to tell you but the new camcorder is in the tray of the buggy."

"Oh what!" We raced to the record store but there was no sign of her or the buggy.

"Right think, where else have you been?"

"Um er….Well I did spend a few minutes in the book section of WH Smiths."

"Right, well let's get going."

We quickly searched the bookstore high and low like two demented and somewhat crazed detectives.

"Okay, I remember I went into the decorating shop, so let's try there."

We raced into the shop and breathed a deep sigh of relief to see our daughter smiling and gurgling away, as she remained oblivious to the crisis.

"Look Tricia, even the camcorder is still where I placed it," he said, the excitement now coming back into his eyes. "Um, now that we've found her I don't suppose there's any chance we can head back to the café for that coffee and ring doughnut, is there?"

"Sorry honey, but you'll have to fill that hole in your head with something other than a doughnut, for, after this scary crisis, we're headed straight for home."

Antonia would live to be a three year old toddler before John would do a repeat performance. Our closest friends Steve and Georgia were paying us a visit and at some point during their stay it was customary for the two men to go for a long walk to discuss whatever it is that men like to talk about, leaving us girls back at the house to make a meal, while keeping a watchful eye on the children.

"Honey, I'm happy to take Antonia along with us and this will give you some time to have some girlie time and perhaps you might find it in your heart to make us all some tea for when we get back."

"That's fine, but it's so cold out there, so make sure Antonia keeps her coat buttoned up and John, please don't even think to take her down onto the beach, as she's only just got over a heavy cold."

"Okay I understand, we'll go to the park instead." I gave my beautiful little girl a big hug and kiss as I wrapped a scarf around her neck.

"Now you be good for daddy, won't you?"

"Yes Mummy, I will," she said her blue eyes widening with delight as she broke into a huge smile. "Daddy take me to the beach?"

"No honey, just the park."

We were in the middle of preparing tea when John and Steve returned from their long walk in the park. I could hear their loud laughter as they walked back into the house.

"We're back," they shouted out.

I rushed into the hallway to greet them.

"Honey, where is Antonia?"

"What! Oh my goodness I forgot we took her with us."

"Oh no no ....I gulped. Please don't say you left her in the park?" I stuttered my heart hammering loudly, my blood draining to my toes. "John how could you do such a thing? The roads by the park are fast and, if she sees the beach, she'll try and cross the road to get to it. Oh my goodness!" I cried as I burst into tears.

"Ok, ok .. Look, don't panic I will race back and look for her."

"I'll come too," Steve announced.

"I'm coming as well," I cried.

"No no, you stay here with Georgia and the kids, for we won't be long."

I was left to fight the most terrible visions that immediately flashed through my head.

"I can't believe this is happening," I wailed as I sat huddled up on the couch

"Tricia, it's going to be alright, really it is," Georgia tried to encourage as she placed a comforting arm around my shoulder. The wait felt like forever. Thankfully Georgia was right, for twenty minutes later they walked back in with my little girl and she still had a beaming smile alighting her entire face. "We go to the beach Daddy," she cried as she came through the front door with her arms wrapped tightly round his neck. At that moment I too wanted to wrap my arms round his neck but for an entirely different objective. John of course, remained very remorseful for the rest of the day, as well as grateful that we had guests as this saved him being on the receiving end of some heavy duty telling off.

Now as our children are the most precious gifts that we have in our lives, you would think two such occasions would be the limit when it comes to losing any of them. Not so! We were taking our three children on vacation to Tenerife, in the Canary Islands, just off the coast of Africa. On this occasion we had split the two weeks and so our first week would be spent at a timeshare resort in Los Cristianos and our second week would be spent at another holiday resort in Playas de America. At the time of this vacation our children's ages ranged from Antonia who was probably ten, Reuben who was almost seven and James our youngest who was nearing four and a half. On this vacation we also had a young troubled girl aged around fourteen with us, and for the sake of the story I will call her Samantha.

When we arrived at the first resort we were immediately concerned to discover that our ground floor apartment was situated just feet away from the busy bar which served it's patrons cheap alcohol until two in the morning. For the entire week we were starved of sleep, as the bar with its endless Karaoke nights was heavily populated by rowdy holidaymakers whose idea of fun was to see just how much cheap alcohol they could consume before they summoned up enough Dutch courage to stumble up to the microphone to give their personal rousing rendition of 'I will survive' before literally passing out on the makeshift stage. Had we been single and carefree I don't suppose it would have mattered quite so much, but we had worked hard all year and were in desperate need of some peace and quiet to restore our weary souls and bodies. We begged and pleaded for a transfer to another apartment but sadly, as this was the height of the season, we were told by management that there was no other apartments available, so we were forced to endure seven long nights of little to no sleep. By the end of that week we looked remarkably like the Adams family, well maybe a little more gray and haunted.

We were therefore very pleased to be spending our second week in a different resort, in an entirely different location., the good news being that this next resort was in a much quieter location so things could only look up, or so we thought! We arrived at the resort around 3 pm but, as with all timeshare resorts our room would not be made available until four, so we left to find some seats on the pool deck with the sweltering sun beating down hard on our backs. As I lay flat out on a sun bed with our suitcases surrounding us I could finally hear birds singing, as well as the comforting sound of crashing waves as they reached the shore nearby, and it all made me feel deeply grateful. Finally we were given the keys to our apartment. As we walked through the door the intense build up of heat inside immediately hit us.

"Good grief, It's like a sauna in here. I can hardly breathe. John, please open all the windows, for there's no air in here." Having unpacked we all agreed to take a small half hour siesta before going back out to the pool for a swim.

"Look guys, if we close all the curtains then hopefully the rooms will start to feel a little cooler."

No sooner had our heads touched the pillow than an almighty racket started up outside our apartment.

"What the dickens is going on?" John yelled as he leapt from the bed and headed towards the window.

"John, please close the window for that awful drilling noise is already grating and the whole room appears to be vibrating."

"Tricia, I can't close the window because the heat inside this apartment is already unbearable."

"But that dreadful noise is killing me."

"I understand but being cooked in a high temperature oven will also kill you."

"Well where exactly is the noise coming from?"

"Tricia, I can see cranes moving back and forth, and unbelievable as this may all sound the whole operation is taking place a mere stone's throw away from us."

"Good grief!"

"Yep and if I stand here long enough, I'll be able to work out the individual contents of the workmen's sandwiches, they're that close."

"How come we never noticed all this before we unpacked everything?"

"That's because the crew have only just arrived back from their afternoon siesta."

"Oh great, this is all very bad news."

"Tricia, try to remain calm, and in the meantime I'll go and have a word with management," he said shooting me a hapless grimace.

"Well, don't get your hopes up too high," I yelled out as he left the apartment.

He was back in less than five minutes.

"Honey, I was right the workman start at seven in the morning, finish around one, go home for lunch and a siesta then wait for it, they come back at five and work on until it gets too dark to carry on, and that according to the girls on reception will be around nine to nine thirty."

"And this happens everyday?"

"Yep except Sundays," he said sounding very disheartened.

"Oh right I suppose Sunday is their day of rest," I sighed as I flopped down onto the bed in a defeated mode.

"Yep, it seems they are removing the entire side of the mountain to make way for another hotel."

"John, as things stand we can't possibly stay here. Let's go to reception together and get something sorted."

We left our children with the young teenage girl and headed for reception.

The top man was called down from his office and after explaining our troubling week at the last resort and our current situation with the building works he appeared sympathetic. We waited with baited breath for his response.

"Okay guys, I'm going to get you moved," he announced.

"Wow, we managed to get through to him without a single harsh word or raised voice. Now isn't that amazing!" I cried as we made our way back to the apartment to begin packing. The move meant we no longer had a small view of the ocean but surviving this holiday without being carted off to some local mental sanatorium was of far more importance. And they put us right next to the lovely pool. Finally we could relax.

As John checked his wallet that night he was taken by surprise.

"Honey, have you removed any money from my wallet?"

"Of course not."

"Well something's not right, because I hate to say this, but we've hardly anything left."

In that small moment I realized that, while staying at the last resort I had imagined I'd heard the sound of the front door clicking long after we had all gone to bed. Some nights even found me creeping out of bed to check on the children and they were always sound asleep, but I knew I had definitely heard the soft padding of feet and the click of the latch on a number of occasions, but, up until now, I had failed to put two and two together.

"John, I think I know what's happened to our money, but for the moment I need you to leave it until there is a better moment to bring the subject up."

Inside I felt devastated for this wasn't the first time we'd taken a teenager away with us, only to discover some of our money gone. Worst still it would be my little girl's birthday in two days time and now we had little money left with which to celebrate.

"There's nothing left to do other than use your credit card."

"But it's already higher than I feel comfortable with."

"John, we have no other choice."

The next morning saw us all attend the welcome meeting where they served refreshments and gave out information about the resort amenities while encouraging guests to sign up for the various tours. I tried to put on a brave face for the sake of the children, but deep down I was feeling sad and defeated. Suddenly they brought out a basket and announced there was a free raffle. Everyone was given a ticket and then the lady grabbed hold of Antonia and asked her to pull a ticket from the basket.

"Okay number ninety five you have just won yourself a meal for two at …… Okay Sweetie just dip your hand back in and pull out another number, Okay we have number eleven number eleven where are you? Oh good you have just won yourself a visit to the … Finally this is the last winner, so Antonia darling pop your little hand into the basket, there's a good girl. Right now number sixty seven. Do we have a sixty seven?"

"Mummy, that's me," she shrieked as unable to contain her excitement a moment longer she began jumping up and down on the spot.

"Yes it's definitely your ticket, so Antonia do you want to know what you've won?"

"Yes please," she squealed.

"Well, you and one other member of your family have won a boat trip to see the dolphins."

"Ooh lovely," she cried, clapping her hands in delight. I was so grateful for that raffle ticket win for she was crazy about dolphins, and now we could use this win to celebrate her birthday after all. It was agreed that we would scrape together enough for another ticket that would allow John to take Reuben on the trip as well.

"I'll stay behind with James and Samantha and you guys go and have yourselves a great time."

"Are you sure?"

"Oh absolutely, you know me I prefer to keep both feet on solid ground."

"Right then, let's book it for two days time."

As this site was much smaller and family orientated it wasn't too long before our children began making friends with other children on site and so naturally we found ourselves becoming friendly with the parents as we all lay by the pool, piling on the sun cream as we attempted to get an even tan. As I lay spread out on a sun bed I produced one of my magazines and began reading.

"Honey, stop reading your book a minute and listen to me for this is a terrible and true story about a small blonde haired boy who was holidaying with his family in Tenerife when he was sadly abducted. The family have spent the last two years doing their utmost to find him. Oh I cannot even begin to imagine the heartache they must be enduring. In fact, did you not notice that there are still posters plastered on a number of lamp posts as well as in shop windows. Do you think this is the same boy?"

"Honey I've no idea, but you're right, it's incredibly sad." Half an hour later and I was once more calling over to him.

"Honey, you really must read this story, it's about a lady who was on a plane and the person sitting beside her was so enormous that he literally spilled over onto the dear lady's lap."

"Hmm, poor woman."

"You can say that again, anyway she tried complaining to the stewardess but it was no use for they could do nothing but apologize and tell her there had been some oversight as the extremely overweight gentleman had in fact booked himself two seats on this flight. Are you still listening?"

"Yes yes," he grunted, his head still buried in his latest book.

"Well, as there were no alternative seats to offer her, the only thing they could suggest was to allow her off the plane and then she could re book a later flight. The distressed lady explained she had an important appointment so their suggestion was not the least bit practical, she was therefore given no choice other than to endure the whole flight with the overweight individual virtually crushing her legs due to the over spill of his flesh onto hers. Oh honey, can you even begin to imagine how that must have felt to the poor darling lady?"

"Hmm.. Yes, most terrible," he grunted back.

"Within hours of arriving at her destination she collapsed and was taken to hospital. She had suffered a deep vein thrombosis that resulted in a stroke. She then endured an eight hour surgery, but wait, for it doesn't end there, for she then developed something called 'Post Phlebitic syndrome.' Honey are you still listening to me?"

"Huh what?"

"Are you still listening to anything I'm saying?"

"Um Yes."

"Well, what was I saying?"

"Uh something about her getting post menopausal syndrome."

"Wrong! Listen, this poor woman's leg was now so chronically swollen and ulcerated that unbelievably she had to lose a leg to the surgeon's knife."

"Good grief, can the menopause really do that to you?"

"Oh my goodness, what a terrible story, promise me now John that if such a thing were to ever happen to you, you would leave the plane rather than risk life and limb. Go on, promise me now."

"Okay okay, I promise, now allow me the pleasure of some peace to read my book."

"Okay, but these things are important."

"Honestly Tricia, I thought these women's magazines were more to do with cake making, health issues and beauty treatments, no wonder you don't sleep at night."

"Oh, you're so back in the dark ages."

We could still hear drilling in the background but between one and five we experienced a sense of precious very welcome solitude. That same evening we took Samantha to one side and challenged her about the missing money, and, after much heated conversation she finally admitted that she had helped herself to some of our money, although she was unable to say exactly how much. We told her that we now had nothing left for extra treats. She in turn was furious at having been found out, so banged the door of her room and went away to have a long hard sulk.

"Honey, leave her be," John wisely advised.

The morning of the boat trip to see the dolphins saw Antonia in a wonderfully excited state.

"Daddy's going to take some video footage of the dolphins so we'll remember this trip forever," she cried clasping her hands tightly together in all the excitement.

"Are you going to be alright staying back here?" John asked as he gave me a kiss goodbye.

"Of course I am, besides it's only for a few hours, so you'll be back before I can say Jack Robinson."

"Well, it's just that Sam is still sulking."

"Hmm I know, but hopefully given time she'll come round. Now give James a quick kiss and then off you go to have a good time. I'll have lunch prepared for when you return. Come here Reuben sweetheart you have a wonderful morning with Daddy and your sister," I said as I bent down to give him his usual quick tickle on his tummy, something which never failed to send him into fits of giggles.

While they were gone I knocked on the Samantha's door, but still she refused to answer.

"Samantha honey, would you like a cup of coffee or a glass of soda?" I waited but there was still no answer so I decided I would leave well alone until lunchtime.

Finally I heard the front door of the apartment open and in walked John with a very excited Antonia clinging to him.

"Oh mummy, we went on the sea in a boat, had some food, and we saw some lovely dolphins." she gleefully cried.

"That's lovely honey, but John tell me quickly, where is Reuben?"

"Oh my goodness, I've absolutely no idea."

"What!" I screeched as my heart plummeted like an elevator downwards towards my ankles and images of the 'Have you seen this child' posters on lamp posts immediately begin flashing through my mind.

"Oh come on John tell me you're messing with me."

"I wish I was. Look I'm sorry, I'll run back to the boat and find him."

"John, he's only six years old, how could you do this to me?" I cried out after him. With the door shut behind me I crumpled to the floor and began sobbing.

"There, there, Mummy, it will be alright," Antonia said ruffling my hair in a most peculiar manner in her attempt to comfort me.

"I hope so Antonia, really I do."

Suddenly there was a knock at the door. It was Reuben. He looked pale and frightened. I reached down and hugged him.

"Mummy, Daddy forgot me and left me at the boat."

"I know, he's just gone back down there to find you. So tell me sweetheart, how on earth did you find your own way home?"

"The cranes and diggers Mummy."

"What, you managed to climb your way up those steep mountain steps all by yourself?"

"Yes mummy".

"But there must be at least a hundred or more steps, so that's pretty amazing."

I could easily have gone over to those cranes and diggers that I had so readily hated and given them a humongous hug, such was my gratitude as I held my young son ever so tightly.

"Mummy, I just found this note in Samantha's room," Antonia suddenly chirped up. "What! So where is she?" Antonia shrugged her shoulders as if to say why ask her, for didn't I remember that she had been out with daddy all morning. I opened the note and began reading.

"Oh goodness, when will it ever end?" I sighed to myself as I attempted to read the scrawled note.

John returned home sometime later and was very relieved to discover that our young son was safe and therefore there was no need to call the police.

"John, unbelievable as this may sound, those dreadful cranes and diggers acted like a sign post, for, without them, he might be lost or worse might have happened."

"You're right."

"Well honey, it's still not time to pop the party poppers, for the bad news is we're now missing another child."

"I don't believe it."

"Well it's true."

"Oh dear so Sam's gone missing, has she?"

"I'm afraid so. We may well have to call in the police, for Antonia just discovered this in her bedroom," I announced as I passed the note over for him.

"Oh goodness, she's met six young lads she fancies and she intends to spend the rest of the week staying at their penthouse suite," he loudly groaned.

"Hmm …Yep, tell you what, I suggest we eat some lunch while we ponder on this one."

Later that day we made contact with Samantha and she refused to come back to the apartment. With only a couple of days left and with no desire for any further drama we decided to leave her be, at least for the time being.

A day or so later and we were packing up the apartment as we prepared to leave for home the following day. Having made friends with a number of the parents as we lazed around the swimming pool, two or three families and ourselves decided it would be a great end to the holiday if we were to all go to eat at a restaurant that did karaoke. John was not so sure but, as I love karaoke, he had little choice other than agree.

At 6.30pm that evening we all met up in the reception area and, as soon as everyone coming was accounted for, we headed down to the seafront and the restaurant.

"Oh no guys, the karaoke doesn't begin until nine, and it's only seven o'clock, so we've got a two whole hours to kill, so what shall we do?"

"Okay, so let's walk along the seafront and get the kids an ice cream?" someone in the group suggested. "It's such an idyllic evening we can sit on a wall and watch while the kids play on the beach." So we strolled along the seafront, brought ice-cream for the kids as well as for a number of adults. We then headed down onto the beach to sit and chat while the children dug trenches with their hands otherwise played racing games with the soap sud tide as they attempted to race up the beach ahead of the tiny waves so as not to get their shoes wet.

The time just flew by and soon it was time to gather everyone together and head back to the restaurant which was some distance away. We continued chatting and laughing as we casually strolled along and before long we were standing outside the restaurant anxious and eager to get tables. It was then that I noticed that our youngest son James who was a little over four years old was missing.

"John, where on earth is James?"

"I thought you had him with you."

"No silly, I took the older two and you were supposed to keep an eye on James. "Oh my goodness, not again, I can't stand it," I shouted, as yet again the blood drained to my toes, my eyes pricked with tears, as in that awful moment my world once again began to crash in. With an ashen face John turned on his heels and began to race back along the promenade, leaving me to collapse into a heap outside the restaurant. All too soon my imagination went into overdrive as I imagined he had either drowned or otherwise been kidnapped. The wait seemed long and agonizing.

John was out of breath when he got back.

"Tricia, I can't find him anywhere."

"Well, he can't have gone far, he's only four years old," I sobbed as I looked out towards the sea imagining the worst.

"Look guys, would it help if we organized a search party?" a concerned member of our group asked.

"Thanks for the offer, you're all terribly kind, but I think our best bet is to head back to the resort and immediately call the police."

I struggled with each and every step I took as I hauled my limp shaking body up the steep steps on the side of the mountain that led up to our resort. How I made it to the top I will never know, for my legs felt like jelly and my heart was pounding so loudly that I wanted to collapse and give up for good. Why oh why hadn't we spent the last night just swimming in the pool and eating pizza I asked myself as feelings of abject depression began to envelop me.

As we walked into the reception area I became aware of a number of people, mainly staff, huddled around something. As I walked towards the circle it opened up and there in the middle stood a little boy, my little boy. "James," I cried out as I raced over to embrace him. "Oh thank God, you're safe. Oh my goodness I've been so scared."

He stood for a moment, just staring at me, his face as white as a sheet, his eyes blurred by tears. He opened his mouth and tried to speak but nothing came out from his trembling lips.

"He's still in a state of shock," someone nearby announced.

"Oh James, we're so very sorry, oh we're so sorry," I cried as I hugged him so close I could actually feel his heart pounding heavily within his tiny breast.

Finally he managed to utter a few words before huge tears began to tumble down his rosy cheeks.

"Mummy, lost Mummy."

Later that evening as I tucked him safely into bed I gently tried to prize out of him how he'd managed to find his way from the promenade back to the resort.

"The big cranes and diggers Mummy. I just followed them."

"You mean, you climbed up all those steep steps all by yourself?"

"Yes Mummy. I was so frightened, but I kept my eyes on the diggers."

"James darling, you're such a clever little boy I want you to know that." I whispered as I hugged him tightly.

"I was so scared mummy, I was so scared."

"Hush now sweetie, I promise it'll never happen again," I announced as I hugged him like I never wanted to let him go all the while appreciating the smell of his sweet young flesh. Now I was further indebted to those diggers and cranes that had annoyed and irritated us on our arrival.

That same night we went in search of our wayward young teenage girl.

"Sorry honey, but you're coming with us right now," I demanded.

"No way!"

"Look, stop this nonsense, we need you to come back to the apartment now."

"I'll come back in the morning," she announced with a show of arrogance.

"Sorry, but it's not open to negotiation, for, if we have to stand here all night long, singing Christmas carols if we have too, for we're not leaving this doorstep without you."

"Okay, I'll come, but on one condition."

"Oh, and what's that?"

"Well, there should be no mention of the missing money or boys and the penthouse apartment when we get home."

"You drive a hard bargain, girl, but okay then, it's a promise."

As I closed my eyes on the homeward flight I made myself a pledge that any future holidays would see all my children kitted out with those personal alarms that emit such a loud piercing noise that we'd never lose any one of our children ever again.

CHAPTER THIRTY

Does It Run in the Family?

Now if further evidence was needed to prove that this propensity for disasters appears to be genetically connected, then allow me to give you a little insight into some of my children's traveling escapades, starting with James, my youngest son who could take first prize when it comes to finding trouble, although he would swear it's the trouble that finds him! Why even recently, we have been called upon to rescue him from the darker suburbs of Budapest, and not once but twice within the space of two weeks!

It seems James fell in love with a young beautiful girl who had been sent to college in England to learn English and as anyone whose anybody knows you're not a real princess until you've learnt Queens English! How they met each other I have no idea for he was and still is, a young penniless almost unknown rap artist, whose songs are all about his pain and his shame, whereas she came from an extremely well to do family who preferred to call her Princess rather than by any other name. It seems that opposites do attract and so in no time at all they were professing dying love for each other. Soon it was time for her to return to Budapest, but, as she left to board a plane home, she promised James she would speak with her father and then hopefully James would be able to pay her a visit and meet the rest of her family. The invite finally came and James set off for Budapest, unaware that he was in way over his head. At a large friends and family gathering the father did not hesitate to express his objection that his socialite daughter deserved much better than a penniless rap artist, so he ordered James to get on a plane, and warned him not to return. James, who from an infant upwards had always had great trouble understanding the word no, ignored the warning and, within days of his departure, he was so lovesick that he decided to throw all caution to the wind by returning.

When I got the crisis call it was from some grubby low grade hostel where James was hiding out, and needless to say I was furious with him. It was during this frantic phone conversation that he decided to reveal that very necessary piece of information that up until now he had 'inadvertently' left out.

"What! Are you telling me that her father is part of the Russian Mafia? James, listen to me, if that's true, you my dear boy are playing with fire."

"Look mum, I'm sorry, I just thought that if I went back and explained everything to her Dad, well things would somehow get sorted."

"How could you possibly think that, when only days ago he ordered you onto a plane and told you never to return. James, what have you got yourself into?"

"Mum, stop worrying for my girlfriend…".

"Ex girlfriend," I hurriedly reminded him.

"Whatever! Anyway if you can stop interrupting me, she reassured me that he left the business some time ago, so there shouldn't be a problem coz he's actually ex-mafia."

"Sweetie, allow me to enlighten you, there's no such thing as ex Mafia! Have you not seen the Godfather Trilogy?"

"Mum, course I have."

"Well then, you must realize that the only way they become ex-mafia, is when they're six foot under pushing up daises, their bloodied corpses riddled with bullets. You know something James, some of the deaths have been done in a most unpleasant manner, yes machine guns, cut throats, a horses head in the bed, that sort of thing."

"Mum, calm down, you're getting hysterical."

"You think this is crazy? Oh son, trust me, I haven't even begun to show you what crazy looks like."

"Mum, please I don't need this from you, for I'm desperate. I've hardly eaten a thing in the last few days and I've run out of money, so I need your help to get me out of here as quickly as possible."

"Well, where are you now?"

"Um, I was dumped in the poor end of Budapest in a run down hostel that's full of flea ridden dogs, pimps, prostitutes, oh and you'll never believe this, but a very nice drugs baron has kindly just brought me a sandwich!"

"What! Son, when you get home you're so dead!" I yelled.

"Well, if that's the case I might as well stay here and take my chances."

Part of me truly wanted to leave him there for at least another week if only to teach him a lesson, but the maternal side of me decided this wasn't the time for recriminations, they could come later; the more urgent need was to get him a plane ticket home and sooner rather than later. I breathed a deep sigh of relief when my daughter finally rang me.

"Mum, he's home but in a bad way but at least he's safe. I've made him up a bed and I'll get him to give you a ring when he's eaten, slept and is generally in much better shape."

There are so many unbelievable stories to tell when it comes to James, most of which took place on his travels over here, so I've decided to put some of them in my next book aptly entitled "Hi America, I've arrived!"

As I bring this book to an end I thought to contact my twenties something daughter Antonia to ask if there had been any terrible holiday dramas that she might care to share.

"Antonia darling, what about your school trip to Russia?.

"Nothing to report. Oh except we all got seriously drunk on Russian Vodka."

"Right, well I think we'll leave that one out, although how come I've never heard about this before now?"

"Mum leave well alone, we were just doing what all students do when they get the opportunity. Anyway Mum, I don't really have any other stories, unless of course you count the Cuban crisis as a worthy story?"

"Cuban crisis?"

"Yes, don't you remember the time Ricky and I took a holiday in Cuba."

"Oh right, now you mention it I do."

"Well, the holiday was great, lots of snorkeling and all that. But when it came time to return home they cancelled all but one plane."

"Why?"

"Heaven only knows! Anyway it was crazy, they opened the doors and it was a race to get onto the plane and find an empty seat. It was a real bun fight. Honest mum, people were tripping others up and hitting one an another with hand luggage as they fought to get a seat. Some chairs had two or more people squashed into the same chair with all parties insisting they got there first. It was like a children's game of musical chairs."

"Antonia darling, if that's all the grief you've suffered, then I have to say you've fared pretty well."

"Sorry mum, I'd like to give you more, really I would, but there really is nothing much else to tell."

"Okay, but while we're speaking, remind me what time your flight gets into Orlando?"

"This Tuesday, mum, around six o'clock."

"Antonia, why Tuesday and not Monday, as you've now lost a day off your holiday."

"I know mum, I was about to book Monday but then for some stupid reason I decided to go for Tuesday, as the fare was twenty pounds cheaper."

"Yes, but you lose a whole day off your stay and as the flight is expensive anyway, it was a bit of a false economy."

"I hear you mum. I should have just paid the extra, stupid old me."

"Well never mind. Anyway I can't wait to give you and Isaac a big hug."

"We're really looking forward to this holiday mum. Isaac keeps on and on about the water park."

On the Monday before she was due we arrived home from our Tea Room to discover a message from her on our answer phone.

"Mum, I have just received an email from Virgin stating that our plane is to be delayed by six whole hours." As I listened to the message I knew she was in an upset state, so I immediately called her.

"Honey, at least they let you know beforehand, we've had some terrible times stuck in airports due to hideous lengthy delays."

"Yes mum I know. It's just that I find it difficult enough doing a transatlantic flight on my own with a robust three year old in tow, and now we won't be arriving until gone midnight."

"I'm so sorry honey. But don't worry we'll be waiting for you Anyway have you thought to find out the reason behind this delay?"

"No mum, I'll see if I can find out what's really going on, and then I will call you back." Ten minutes later her call came through.

"Mum, you'll never believe this, but the Monday departure on Virgin airlines that I originally intended booking."

"Yes ..yes go on."

"Well it was two hours into the flight when there was a fire on board. The plane was forced to return to London. Once the plane had landed a panic ensued as the flight attendants screamed at passengers to jump out. So there have been a large number of injuries ranging from broken bones to burns as passengers toppled onto each other as soon as they hit the ground. All flights were cancelled for the remainder of the day, causing a backlog of passengers, hence the delay. If you get the BBC news you can switch on and see for yourself. Mum, I still can't believe that could so easily have been Isaac and me aboard that very plane."

"Honey, do me a favor, dry your tears and be glad that someone is looking out for you, besides you've just handed me a little story for my book. So see you, late tomorrow night!"

Now my eldest son Reuben has also had his fair share of trials when it comes to traveling. While on a recent trip to Ibiza with some lads from his unit, they had innocently gone through Customs when they were suddenly accosted by Airport Police who, giving no explanation whatsoever, brutally dragged them down some long corridors, and into an interrogation room where they were then ordered to strip completely naked and were grilled for hours. All their bags were hurriedly searched and yes nothing whatsoever was found. Unbelievable as this might seem, there was no apology, nothing! Even though they are tough soldiers from the elite Paras they still found the whole experience very traumatic, especially as this all took place less than forty eight hours after leaving the front-line in Afghanistan!

On another occasion Reuben was halfway through a tour of Afghanistan when his unit were given a weeks R and R, (No idea what that stands for but in layman's terms it means half way through the tour they are flown back to England for a weeks holiday before being shipped back to 'Hell on earth' as Afghanistan is endearingly known as). Being British Paratroopers they are considered the best and therefore they are about as front line as it gets, usually where others fear to tread. They willingly endure tremendous hardships and so suffer a large amount of deaths and casualties as they search out the enemy, so when they get back on British soil the natural thing to do is to let their hair down. So when one of the lads suggested they take a flight from London to Amsterdam and spend a few days clubbing, Reuben and his mates quickly signed up. On day two of the holiday they were at a large nightclub when feeling tired and having had perhaps a few more beers than was wise, Reuben decided to retire early. The frenzied nightclub was so packed out that my son found it impossible to make a pathway through the sweaty bodies to search out his mates so he made the decision to head back to the youth hostel alone. As he was walking through the back streets an Albanian gentleman sidled up to him and began acting friendly. Then without warning Reuben found himself lying flat out on the ground. As he staggered to his feet he realized he now had a gash on his head where he had been clubbed and the Albanian gentleman was nowhere to be found. Reuben felt for his wallet, it was gone. He raced up to a policeman on a motorbike shouting that he had just been robbed. The Police Officer responded by telling my son to hop on the back of his motorbike, and so for the next twenty or so minutes they roared around the beautiful city of Amsterdam like Crockett and Tubbs from Miami Vice! Sadly they were unable to find his attacker. When my son regaled this story I was concerned that such an awful thing should have happen to him, but I was equally amazed by the policeman's actions, for to suggest to Reuben that he hop on the back of his bike was beyond mad, for don't forget he had just been bludgeoned around the head, oh as well as being a little worse for the wear. I mean, what if he'd suffered a concussion and blacked out whilst on the back of his bike that was roaring through the streets of Amsterdam at top speed? Hmm…. it doesn't bear thinking about!

Then at the end of the tour Reuben took on the responsibility of organizing a holiday to Magaluf for some of the lads as well as himself. Once the plane had landed Reuben quickly realized that something was very wrong. Yes he had booked flights to the wrong airport, in fact to the wrong country! He was meant to be five hundred miles away in Magaluf, instead he was in Malaga. The off duty soldiers were forced to spend the night sleeping in the airport terminal and our poor son was left to shoulder the expense of buying new tickets for all the guys. As a direct result of this faux pas he ran out of money and was forced to fly home early. He was also burdened with a large credit card debt that took him a long time to clear.

"Reuben, what can I say except I feel so awful on your behalf," I sighed as I listened to the troubling saga first hand.

"Don't worry mum, for it's taught me one thing, and that's not to volunteer to be the organizer for any more foreign holidays. Next time I'll make sure they all book their own flights."

"Do these painful life lessons ever come to an end?" I dolefully asked my husband as I came to the end of giving John a 'blow by blow' account of all that had just befallen our dear son.

"Apparently not," was all he could mutter as he turned the page of his latest thought provoking book.

Moving on, I feel compelled to tell you the reader this very heartwarming story also involving our eldest son. Back in England Reuben and his fellow Paras were suddenly informed by their superiors that they had to completely clear their rooms of everything in preparation for their next Afghan tour. They were all given two boxes and told that anything they wished to keep on base would need to be stored in these two boxes. Many of the lads had assumed their room would remain theirs even for the duration of the tour. I too felt pretty upset by this latest piece of news as Reuben had spent many months and much of his income buying a nice sound system, television and refrigerator for his room that due to us leaving the country had become his only home. Many of the other soldiers that came from Scotland and as far away as South Africa were in the same predicament having nobody to help with storing their personal possessions. With only a few weeks to go before the tour and without transport these men were forced to struggle down the road to sell their televisions and fridges and so forth at those stores that only give you a fraction of what the goods are really worth. Before Reuben left for Afghanistan he gave us a final call. I felt very anxious for him as I knew something of what he was going back too, but I did my best to remain upbeat, but it felt impossible.

"Reuben, the temperature out there is going to be well below freezing, so how will you cope?"

"Mum, stop worrying that's an order, for believe it or not, I'm trained for this, besides let me tell you I have spent a lot of my own personal money buying extra protective clothing as, due to financial cutbacks, the military is cracking down hard when it comes to handing out additional gear. Oh, I've also treated myself to the latest Apple I phone, and let me tell you now, it's pretty amazing." he said, instantly brightening up.

"That's great son. Anyway, the last time you were in Afghan, not one of our letters and parcels made it to you. Honestly it cost us a small fortune sending them from America only to have them returned six months later having been ripped open and many of the contents missing."

"Listen up Mum, this time round send any parcels to England then Antonia can take them to the Post Office. It won't cost her anything and it is the job of the Post Office to ensure all parcels are gathered up and then sent to military bases so they can be flown out to us."

"Okay Sweetie, I love you sunshine and let me warn you now, don't even think about returning home in a body bag, otherwise you're dead meat! Do you hear me?'

"Yes mum."

He had only been back in Afghanistan just a matter of days when tragedy struck. Lying on his bed in his sleeping bag he was rudely awakened from his slumber to find a rocket propelled illumination with the power of a million candles flying directly towards him. He immediately thought it was an R.P.G. and his life was now over. The noise was beyond terrifying as the missile hit his bed. In just a matter of seconds he was on fire, as was his bedding. He threw himself out of the bed and raced as far away from the bed as his legs would carry him. As he raced outside with his legs on fire his quick acting fellow soldiers rushed over to put him out before racing back inside to tackle the blaze before everything went up in an almighty inferno. In those few but terrifying moments Reuben lost everything he possessed. He now had to face the cruel Afghan winter with nothing, not even a few creature comforts to make life in a war zone just that bit more bearable. It all left me feeling even more devastated on his behalf. When he finally made contact he assured me he was fine and had only suffered minor burns. "Mum, please stop worrying," he ordered. "The angels really are watching over me, for had the rocket hit a little to the left or right of me, I would have been instantaneously incinerated otherwise blown to kingdom come, for I had Kerosene as well as a small stockpile of ammunition and grenades by my bedside."

"Reuben, I'm just so grateful you're in one piece."

"I know mum. If I'm honest I'm most upset at losing my brand new Apple I-Phone, for it's now nothing more than a melted heap of junk."

Many weeks later Reuben was hand picked for a highly dangerous mission, and they were all warned that many of them would not be coming back, so when he phoned he believed it was to say his last goodbyes.

"Reuben, I don't care if you're the last man standing, there's no way you're coming home in a body bag, otherwise you're going to get a good hiding from me."

"Okay mum, I hear you."

"You sunshine are coming back to give me a big hug," I announced my voice wobbling as I struggled to remain positive.

That particular mission was indeed ill fated and many sent on the mission never made it back, but my son did and for that I am deeply grateful. A few months later and much to our relief this latest tour was finally over. At the first opportunity he left his barracks and took a train down to London where he got into a taxi and asked to be taken into Central London. When the cab driver discovered he had only just returned from the front-line in Afghanistan he refused to take his fare.

Reuben then walked into the barbers for a haircut, and yet again, on hearing he had just returned from Afghan, the barber likewise refused all payment, but the day was not yet over! Reuben still had one chore to do before heading back to Colchester barracks, home for some of the British Paratroopers. With his hair now cut he walked into a London Apple Store and brought out the remains of his I-phone from his back pack.

"Excuse me mate, but how much will a replacement phone cost?"

"Goodness gracious Sir, what in the world happened to your phone?" the boggle eyed salesman asked.

"Um, blown up in Afghan, and yes I know the insurance company have no legal obligation as 'Acts of God' and 'Acts of war' are never covered. I also understand you won't be able to retrieve any of my photos but I was wondering if by any chance there was a way of retrieving my contact numbers, as I have no other means of re- establishing links with many of my friends."

"Right, well this one's way out of my league, so I think I'll start by getting the manager, if you don't mind." The well groomed manager quickly appeared on the scene and he too was equally startled by the charred remains of the phone that lay on the countertop. He in turn called for his engineer to come and take a look.

"If this is the state of the phone, then how the heck did you walk out of this alive?" he eagerly wanted to know.

"Um, it's a long story."

"We're all ears." After hearing his story, they all walked off together into a back room. Minutes later they returned and handed him a brand new I-phone.

"We want you to have this on the house," the manager said

"You've no idea how much this means to me," a choked up Reuben replied, while struggling to keep his frayed emotions at bay.

"Oh, and if you would allow my engineer to take a look at the damaged one, we can't promise anything, but we'll see if we can retrieve some of your information."

"Thanks again." The engineer took the phone away and, on his return, he was beaming from ear to ear.

"Sir, not only did we somehow manage to retrieve all your vital contact numbers but, by some unexplainable miracle, we were also able to resurrect all your downloaded photos, so it seems it's your lucky day."

"I've been needing one of those days for a very long time," Reuben quipped as he took it in turn to shake their hands and say a big thank you.

When I heard the story I had myself a good long cry, for it was good for me to be reminded there are still fine and decent men on this earth. So I want to acknowledge and thank the barber, the cab driver and especially the guys at the Apple store for your kind and very touching generosity towards my son.

As I bring this book to a close I cannot finish without regaling a story that in my opinion deserves to be top prize in our catalogue of disasters if we were to ever have such a ceremony, and the top award would definitely go to my husband who clearly continues to live on a very different planet to the rest of us.

At the time of marrying John he may have been an rather shy ex-hippie but still he came over as a calm, level headed guy of immense integrity. I naturally assumed however that he had both feet firmly on the ground which was of the utmost importance, as at least one of us needed to have everything under control. Now all these years on, I'm not so sure he ever did have.

There was the time, when having arrived home from a grueling fourteen day long trip to Portugal, John just dropped his bag at the bedroom door and headed for bed. Now, being the dutiful wife that I am, I decided to help him by emptying his bag of all clothes that now required washing. Imagine my surprise when amongst his sweaty shirts and underpants I suddenly found a mysterious bundle that revealed itself to be a bag of gold jewelry. My imagination went into immediate overdrive as I pulled out a couple of gold watches followed by a bracelet, plus three rings and more. Had my husband just robbed a jewelers shop during his continental travels? Otherwise, did this jewelry belong to the customer? If so, were the police going to turn up at the house and arrest him? I shook my head as if this very act would empty my mind of such irrational thoughts. After all, here was a man who, despite utter physical exhaustion, upon hearing the pitiful meows of the clients cat on board, chose to turn around and head back to Scotland to return the little mite to the bosom of his family. On that occasion he had arrived home looking extremely fatigued as usual, but I would not allow him to head for bed until he explained why he was almost a day later than expected.

"Honey, after discovering the cat had smuggled itself on board, why on earth didn't you just hand him in at the nearest police station?"

"Oh Tricia, I could never do that, for the poor little mite was hundreds of miles from home, and therefore very frightened."

"Oh so now we're after St. Francis of Assisi's Job, are we?

"Look just leave it."

"Only when you're prepared to admit that your little detour cost you virtually all the profit from the job."

"Look it will be a lot less painful if we skip the trial by Jury and move straight to the sentencing."

That day he had no reasonable answers to the multitude of questions that I bombarded him with, for it seemed he lived as always on a much higher plain than my good self. So, while I mulled over the bank statements and asked myself how this month's bills would get paid, he much preferred to comfort himself that, even though the cat was unable to personally thank him, he had done the right thing and if nothing else the Animal Protection Society would be very proud of him. So, as I toyed with the jewelry in front of me, I knew deep down there could not possibly be any criminal intent, but, try as I may, I found it impossible to come up with any remotely plausible explanation for this gleaming golden treasure trove.

Oh, I knew Shell stations had been giving away free glasses with every five gallons of petrol, but surely they've moved on to giving away jewelry? No, there was only one thing for it, and this was to broach the subject when he finally woke up. Many hours later he emerged from the bedroom and came down to the sitting room, announcing that he was starving hungry.

"Oh darling, before I rush off to cook dinner, is there anything you'd like to get off your chest?"

"No, I don't think so."

"Hmm, well there's a little incy wincy issue that I feel a desperate need to bring to your attention."

"Oh and what's that?" he replied giving a wide disinterested yawn.

"Um precisely where has all this gold jewelry come from?" I asked as I deliberately dangled the watches and all in front of his beady eyes.

"Oh those," he mumbled.

"Yes these, and the rest."

"Oh right, well there is an explanation, although I'm not too sure if you'll fully understand."

"Try me."

"Well, having left Portugal and Spain, I was driving through France when I realized I was almost out of diesel. I stopped at a gas station and was half way through filling up my truck when a very distraught and disheveled man raced up to me and began to beg for my help. First, he told me that he had been robbed and he offered me his wedding ring, if I would just fill up his car for him."

"Hmm."

"I told him that I would do it as a kindness for I couldn't possibly take a man's wedding ring from him, for that would seem so heartless, but the distraught man insisted that I take it in exchange."

"Go on."

"Well, he then said he needed money for food as he had a large family to feed and so he pulled out a couple of watches. I gave him one hundred pounds, Then he produced some more jewelry telling me that…"

"Before you go on with this increasingly painful story, could you spare me the prolonged agony and simply tell me how much money you eventually parted with?"

"Um, well, three hundred and fifty pounds."

"What, that much? John, how could you be so jolly naïve?"

"Tricia stop it! He'd been attacked and robbed so the poor man was desperate."

"John, allow me to tell you now, the only one robbed that day was you! Look, a man races up to you saying he's been robbed, so one might wonder how come he still has an excess of jewelry on him. He then wants to swap a watch for money, then another, then another ring followed by a gold bracelet. Tell me now, at what point in this pitiful drama does the penny start to drop?"

"Tricia, whatever you say, I like to think that the man was in genuine need, and that any person with a heart would have done likewise."

"Honey, stop there. It's time to admit you've been fleeced."

"Oh right do I need a lawyer?"

"Maybe! Alright then let's stop all speculation for there's only one thing left to do."

"Oh, and what's that?"

"Well, we do have a friend whose a reliable jeweler. I'll let her examine them and if this bag of gold trinkets turns out to be worthless, are you then prepared to acknowledge you've been duped?"

"Okay, I guess so". Less than twenty fours later and I had the results.

"Honey, I know you're anxious to hear the verdict?"

"Sure thing."

"It's official. They're worthless!"

"What… the whole lot?"

"Yes 'Mr. Sweet and utterly gullible,' the whole jolly lot."

"Oh right, well I still happen to believe the poor man was genuine."

As I looked deep into his soulful eyes, I felt this overwhelming urge to phone the Vatican right there and then to say "Stop everything! Your search for the next Pope is well and truly over, for he's sitting here on the sofa right beside me. Trust me, this amazing ex-hippie will definitely unite all brothers and bring about world peace for he loves and believes all things, so please hurry me an application form so we can get things underway, and thus save our planet from entire ruination."

To this very hour I have kept the treasure trove as a painful reminder that not every blind and legless beggar on the streets is who they really say they are, but still this delightfully stubborn man of mine chooses to believe he did the right and proper thing by loving his neighbor more than himself. I hereby rest my case!

So here we are, bang up to date and at last this book is at an end, so all I have left to do is one more final proof read.

"Tricia, we've been working six days a week for the past six months, so as it's Memorial weekend, I think we should treat ourselves to a weekend getaway."

"Okay honey, that sounds great so I'll leave it in your capable hands to organize. But I will need to take my computer away with me as I want to get this to the publishers straight after the break. Hope that's okay with you?"

On the drive down to Orlando he seemed very excited at the deal he'd managed to find on line.

"Tricia trust me for unlike some of my past cock ups this one looks really great. It's got a large sparkling pool, a decent sized Gym, a spa and nail salon oh and the best thing is I got this hotel at a real discount. So you can thank me now if you like, for WE are going to have ourselves a wonderful break relaxing by the pool, while I catch up with a few of my favorite authors."

"Sounds like just what the doctor ordered."

"Well I think it's true to say, we are seriously in need of this well deserved break in order to fully re- energize ourselves."

As we walked into the hotel lobby my jaw dropped almost as far as my hand luggage that hit the floor with a bang.

"Honey, We've just walked in on a freak show otherwise those miscreants from Dawn of the Dead have just taken over Florida?" I loudly exclaimed as I took in the huge foyer that was swarming with hundreds of flamboyant and over excited adolescents and adults, all of whom were very eccentrically over dressed. One girl in particular had a humongous chainsaw draped around her neck, and I could only hope it wasn't for real. Many had thickly applied theatrical make-up designed to make them look so horrifically gross that I was beginning to feel strangely spooked. Their noise in the lobby was so deafening I could hardly hear myself speak, and no matter which way I turned I was met by screaming hysterical teenagers as they squealed and embraced each other like long lost friends before showing off their latest kooky attire to each other.

"Now I know the end of the world is nigh," I cried as I shook my head in despair.

"Honey I don't know what to say, except I'm flabbergasted."

"John, this is absolute bedlam so you need to find out what exactly is going on, for I feel as though I've just been zoomed onto some intergalactic substation along with a bunch of Alien drifters and, if I can bear to hang around long enough, I'll come face to face with Obi Kenobi and Luke Skywalker!"

John abandoned the line to go in search of answers and when he returned his ashen face said it all.

"Um, do you want the good news first or the bad news?"

"Try the good." I shouted as I placed my hands over my ears in the hope of drowning out some of the noise.

"Well the good news is, this isn't a Star Wars convention but something they call an 'Anime convention.'"

"What on earth is that?"

"Um, well I've never heard of it, but apparently it has a large cult following, and it's got something to do with Japanese cartoons."

"You've got to be kidding me."

"Would I? Apparently Japanese cartoons are becoming increasingly popular over here, so all these weird people are dressed as the different cartoon characters."

"Spare me the details. Just tell me how long these exceptionally rowdy people will be staying?"

"Um, well that's the bad news, for the convention is spread out over the entire weekend."

"Kill me now!"

As we stood for well over an hour in the long line that extended almost out the door of the foyer as overwhelmed staff struggled to cope with check ins and endless guest queries, plus a computer dysfunction, I too felt overwhelmed by the general sense of chaos and I knew with great assurance that I had no wish to become a participant in what would surely be an out of body and mind experience if I stayed here too long, So for the first time in my otherwise tumultuous life I felt like a normal very boring human being and I have to say, it felt good.

"Tricia where do you think you're going?"

"Sorry honey but I'm leaving."

"Get your royal butt back here, for as usual you haven't given me any time to sort things out." I obeyed, but had I known then, how this weekend was going to deteriorate to even lower depths, then I believe I would have left the building to order a taxi cab home.

"John before I think to tear my hair out, please answer me this."

"What?"

"Do you honestly think this is going to be a quiet richly relaxing weekend that will achieve its goal in refreshing our wearied bodies and souls, while re-stabilizing our seriously overstretched minds?"

"Um well when I booked this bargain hotel I thought…"

"There it is, popping up again dearest one, yes that strangely fateful word called thought."

About the author

Tricia Bennett spent her entire very troubled childhood in children's homes back in England, and is the author of a trilogy about a struggling orphan, of which "Polly Brown" and "The Trouble with Polly Brown" have already been published nationally in the USA. She is currently working on "Hi America, I've arrived", and, needless to say, it will be a continuation of her many fateful sagas, and this will also be closely followed by "Why I left home before the kids!" She moved from the UK with her husband John in 2007, and they are currently living in Wildwood, Florida, where they run Polly's Pantry Royal Tearoom, a small but very delightful Tearoom and Gift shop. If you decide to pop by you may well find Tricia donning her crown as she delights her customers with her humorous and colorful tales.

Their Tearoom is located at 819 South Main Street, Wildwood Florida 34785.

You can also contact her on 1-352-330-4002 for speaking engagements, charity events, TV and radio interviews etc, and by e-mail on info@hopeinyourheart.com www.hopeinyourheart.com and also on Facebook.